Population —  History of
+ development

- Reproduction

- Education Eugenics

- Agriculture

- Husbandry   Ed.

- Education

S36 w 132

Amsterda.... + Buz

212 - 865 - 1588

- Suppression of distinction bec. nature + nurture
p. 130

Virtue ?                    p. 185   maternal +
                                            internal

- deformation of custom — p. 132

                    What was your last
   1st Book           favorite chapter to
  — Hypocrisy          write ?

  — How did you get around

  — proven

                  the issues are similar but different
                 cultivating "the self" — hypocrisy
                 is species of "natural" self
 "interaction between           "namural " self
  heredity + environment "

      ↓ "nurture," "cultivation,"
          "climate " — the concept +
          vocabulary of improvement

# BREEDING

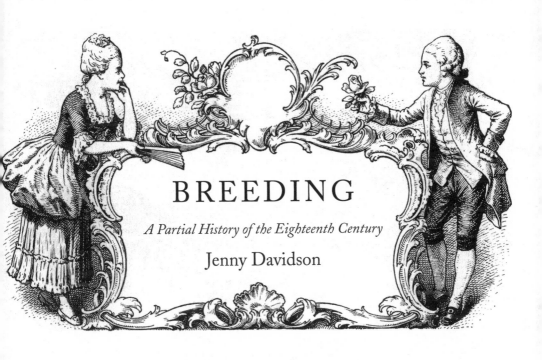

# BREEDING

*A Partial History of the Eighteenth Century*

Jenny Davidson

COLUMBIA UNIVERSITY PRESS

*New York*

Columbia University Press
Publishers Since 1893
New York    Chichester, West Sussex
Copyright © 2009 Columbia University Press
All rights reserved

Library of Congress Cataloging-in-Publication Data

Davidson, Jenny.
Breeding : a partial history of the eighteenth century / Jenny Davidson.
p. cm.
Includes bibliographical references and index.
ISBN 978-0-231-13878-9 (cloth : alk. paper)—
ISBN 978-0-231-51111-7 (ebook)
1. English literature—18th century—History and criticism. 2. Breeding—Great
Britain—Philosophy—History—18th century. 3. Education and heredity—Great
Britain—Philosophy—History—18th century. 4. Nature and nurture—Great
Britain—Philosophy—History—18th century. 5. Breeding in literature. 6. Heredity in
literature. 7. Biology in literature. 8. Eugenics in literature. 9. Eugenics—
History—18th century. 10. Literature and science—Great Britain—History—18th
century. I. Title
PR448.B74D38 2009
809'.93353—dc22
2008024831
∞

Columbia University Press books are printed on permanent and durable acid-free paper.
This book is printed on paper with recycled content.
Printed in the United States of America

c 10 9 8 7 6 5 4 3 2 1

References to Internet Web sites (URLs) were accurate at the time of writing.
Neither the author nor Columbia University Press is responsible for URLs
that may have expired or changed since the manuscript was prepared.

For J.A.D. and M.C.D.

I Wish either my father or my mother, or indeed both of them, as they were in duty both equally bound to it, had minded what they were about when they begot me; had they duly consider'd how much depended upon what they were then doing;—that not only the production of a rational Being was concern'd in it, but that possibly the happy formation and temperature of his body, perhaps his genius and the very cast of his mind;—and, for aught they knew to the contrary, even the fortunes of his whole house might take their turn from the humours and dispositions which were then uppermost:——Had they duly weighed and considered all this, and proceeded accordingly,——I am verily persuaded I should have made a quite different figure in the world, from that, in which the reader is likely to see me.—Believe me, good folks, this is not so inconsiderable a thing as many of you may think it;—you have all, I dare say, heard of the animal spirits, as how they are transfused from father to son, &c. &c.—and a great deal to that purpose:—Well, you may take my word, that nine parts in ten of a man's sense or his nonsense, his successes and miscarriages in this world depend upon their motions and activity, and the different tracks and trains you put them into; so that when they are once set a-going, whether right or wrong, 'tis not a halfpenny matter,—away they go cluttering like hey-go-mad; and by treading the same steps over and over again, they presently make a road of it, as plain and as smooth as a garden-walk, which, when they are once used to, the Devil himself sometimes shall not be able to drive them off it.

—*Laurence Sterne*, The Life and Opinions of Tristram Shandy, Gentleman *(1760), I.i*

# CONTENTS

Acknowledgments  xv

INTRODUCTION. Breeding Before Biology  1
*The language of human nature—the concept of heredity—airs, waters, places—*
*the "Design of Lengthening and Whitening His Posterity"—perfectibility and*
*Enlightenment—looking-glass determinism—the Ghost Structure—*
*archeologies of ashes—a nuance exercise—partial history*

CHAPTER 1  The Rules of Resemblance  14
*The question of scale—theatrical adaptations as cultural indicators—*
*inheriting properties*

WHY CHILDREN LOOK LIKE THEIR FATHERS
The Winter's Tale—*marrying scions and stock—"Art thou my boy?"—*
*"The whole matter / And copy of the father"*

THE RULES OF RESEMBLANCE
*Aristotle's carpenter—the maternal imagination—Jacob and Laban's sheep—*
Aristoteles Master-Piece—*the organs of Adam and Eve—taffeta breeches*

"NATURE'S BASTARDS"
*Perdita's gillyflowers—"The art itself is Nature"—egalitarian eugenics—*
*grafting as metaphor—literary criticism and the science of genetics*

"HER ROYAL IMAGE STAMPT ON THEE"
*Garrick's* Florizel and Perdita—*"This pretty abstract of* Hermione*"*—
*biparental heredity—why girls look like their mothers —Burney's* Evelina—
*Inchbald's* A Simple Story—*Darwin's novel-reading—"To the memory of the
fractured leg of my dear mother"*

CHAPTER 2   Bent   39
*The blank slate—"God has stampt certain Characters upon Mens Minds"—
the two cultures*

THE BLANK SLATE
*Locke's* Essay Concerning Human Understanding—*the mind as white paper—
original tempers and native propensities—"Adam's* Children*"*

SINNERS BY DESCENT
*Augustine's* generatione non imitatione—
*the Pelagian heresy—genetic perfectibility—Timothy Nourse's "Original Curse"*

"A MEER ERRANT CAT"
*"Æsopes Damosell"—blood and kind—"gentlemen born"*

CHAPTER 3   Cultures of Improvement   58
*Habit as second nature—fantasies of improvement, fears of degeneration*

DEUCALION'S KIN
The Georgics—*Dryden's translation—Jethro Tull and*
The New Horse-Houghing Husbandry—*prose georgics and savage nature*

"A LIVING MAGAZINE"
*Defoe's* Robinson Crusoe—*"An education according to nature"—
the work of Providence*

PERFECT WILDNESS
*The Wild Boy of Hamelin—Defoe's* Mere Nature Delineated—
*"A lump of soft Wax"—the Wolf Girls of Midnapore—original sin—
forbidden experiments*

"A PERFECT YAHOO"
*Species thinking—Swift's* Gulliver's Travels—*Locke's parrot—"Teachableness,
Civility and Cleanliness"—"The Females had a natural Propensity to me as one of
their own Species"—prolific mixtures*

# Contents

THE PERFECTIBILITY PROBLEM
Gulliver *redux*—*putting an end to the species*—*Plato's* Republic—
*More's naked women*—A Modest Proposal—*the calculus of breeding*

"PROPERTIES DESCEND!"
*Osmer versus Wall on equine improvement*

"ASCERTAINING WHAT SPECIES CAN PROCREATE TOGETHER"
*Bradley's "cross Couplings"—Bonnet and Spallanzani ponder the mystery of
fecundation—Maupertuis and the* Earthly Venus—*Frederick of Prussia
and the beautification of the nation—hybrids, varieties and human polygenesis—
La Mettrie prunes man like a tree—Vandermonde and Gregory improve
the human species*

DIFFERENCES OF CLIMATE
*Sheep-rearing—"The old hairy Tegument"—climate theory and
Hartley's alterations—bodily organs—man as a domestic animal*

"THE MANAGEMENT OF HUMAN CREATURES"
*Proto-eugenicist arguments—Hume's "Of the Populousness of Ancient Nations"—
multiplying the species—Wallace on the numbers of mankind—
Diderot's* Supplément au Voyage de Bougainville *and global
experiments in breeding*

CRABS AND BRAMBLES
*Smollett's* The Expedition of Humphry Clinker—*Raymond Williams
country—georgic fantasies and filthy realism—the reproductive life—
"The Blackberry is the fruit of the Bramble"—dunghills—"A crab of my own
planting"—fruit of a peculiar flavor*

CHAPTER 4   A Natural History of Inequality   112
*Splitting the culturalist consensus*

THE DIFFERENCE BETWEEN ONE MAN AND ANOTHER
*Rousseau's* Discourse on Inequality—*the idea of perfectibility—the origin of
difference—the savage and the domesticated condition—civilization largely
responsible for misery*

"WE ARE BORN TWICE OVER"
*Rousseau's* Émile—*"Nature's characters"—
"The present confusion between the sexes"*

*Contents*

"NATURE'S OWN PENCIL"
*The elocutionists—"A natural tendency to degeneration"—Thomas Sheridan and the language of Nature—Condillac—Harris's* Hermes—Herries' The Elements of Speech—*human improvement—bound feet and misshapen heads—Hippocratic habit—"Nature framed her self to that Custome"*

THE NATURAL INEQUALITY OF MAN
*Monboddo's savages—acquired habits—custom a second nature—natural inequality*

"A PURITY, HWICH COARTS DOO NOT ALWAYS BESTOW"
*Orthoepy—orthography—waistcoats and cucumbers—"The* onliest *way to rise in the world"—vocabularies unintelligible to eye and ear—Elphinston's* Propriety Ascertained in her Picture—*Priestley on the laws of language and the laws of government—the tacit obligations of language—Noah Webster on the* "ipse dixit *of a Johnson, a Garrick, or a Sheridan"—"I would have all the birds of the air to retain somewhat of their own notes"—the Edgeworths'* Essay on Irish Bulls — *"If an Englishman were born in Ireland"—the logic of shibboleth*

CHAPTER 5    Blots on the Landscape    149
*Promethean thinking on population—"A monster, a blot upon the earth"—sidelining sexual reproduction*

"THIS BLOT IN OUR COUNTRY INCREASES"
*Jefferson's* Notes on the State of Virginia—*"Twenty of the best geniuses will be raked from the rubbish annually"—the varieties of man—"The extermination of the one or the other race"—color mixture—subjects of natural history*

"THE INCESSANT IMPROVEABLENESS OF THE HUMAN SPECIES"
*Godwin's* An Enquiry Concerning Political Justice, and Its Influence on General Virtue and Happiness *and other writings on education—Priestley on man's unbounded improvement—Condorcet on the progress of perfectibility—Gulliver's* Travels *and original sin—mind's tendency to rise—Helvétius on the importance of education—physical influences on man—the perverseness of institutions—differences between human beings—Hercules and his brother—"Human creatures are born into the world with various dispositions"—physiognomy as fatalism*

"ENCUMBERING THE WORLD WITH USELESS AND WRETCHED BEINGS"
*The animal function of sex (Godwin, Condorcet)—Malthus's* Essay on Population—*the restraining bonds of society—Cabanis and others on human improvement*

Contents

CHAPTER 6   Shibboleths   189
*Edwidge Danticat's* The Farming of Bones—*handfuls of parsley*

SHIBBOLETHS
*Walker's* Intermarriage—*Pinker's* The Language Instinct—
*genes and culture—the Ebonics controversy—race and voice*

THE BLACKMAIL OF ENLIGHTENMENT
*Foucault's "What Is Enlightenment?"—gestures of hospitality—accessibility and
difficulty—the problem of disciplines*

CONCLUSION. The Promise of Perfection   199
*"Where is now, the progress of the human Mind?"—Adams versus Jefferson on
the natural equality of mankind —Sandel, Žižek, and Passmore on the allure of
perfectibility—overrating talent —the realm of causation*

Notes   207

Bibliography of Works Cited   253

Index   281

# ACKNOWLEDGMENTS

O ver the course of researching and writing *Breeding*, I received generous help
from more individuals and institutions than I am probably now capable
of recollecting. Columbia University gave me a Chamberlain Fellowship and a
Junior Faculty Development Award, as well as a Lenfest Distinguished Faculty
Award. The Guggenheim Foundation and the American Academy of Arts and
Sciences provided funding for another year of sabbatical, which I spent in the
Academy's Visiting Scholars Program. At the Academy, Patricia Meyer Spacks,
Leslie Berlowitz, Sandy Oleson, and Giffen Maupin deserve particular thanks, as
do the regular members of the Tuesday lunch group and the other scholars visit-
ing in 2003–2004 (especially Beth Lyman). I continue to be immensely grateful
to my dissertation advisors at Yale, Claude Rawson and David Bromwich, and for
the training I received in the English department there.

Many colleagues in the Department of English and Comparative Literature
at Columbia have helped this book come into existence. I will not name every-
body individually, but I would especially single out Joey Slaughter, Rachel Adams,
Sarah Cole, Tricia Dailey, Molly Murray, Ezra Tawil, Nicholas Dames, Eileen
Gillooly, Gauri Viswanathan, Sharon Marcus, Gayatri Spivak, Andrew Delbanco,
Ross Posnock, Edward Mendelson, Michael Seidel, Karl Kroeber, Jim Shapiro,
Bruce Robbins, and Marianne Hirsch. David Kastan and Julie Crawford read my
discussions of seventeenth-century material and saved me from various howlers
(remaining ones are of course entirely my own responsibility). Julie Peters offered
perceptive and elegant suggestions for revision on a full draft of the manuscript. I

am also grateful to the departmental staff members, including Joy Hayton, Maia Bernstein, Virginia Kay, Isabel Thompson, and (especially) Michael Mallick.

Outside the department, Susan Pedersen and Emma Winter kept me in intellectual high spirits, as did Akeel Bilgrami, to whom I am extremely grateful for good conversation over a number of years now. I have also benefited from conversation with David Johnston and the postdoctoral fellows at the Columbia Society of Fellows and from the intellectual generosity of a host of colleagues elsewhere, including Elaine Scarry, Jonathan Arac, Clifford Siskin, Avi Matalon, Robert DeMaria, Annabel Patterson, Gordon Turnbull, Blair Hoxby, Jim Chandler and other members of the University of Chicago English department (especially the eighteenth-century workshop), Peter Holland, Joseph Roach, Harriet Ritvo, Helen Deutsch, Deidre Lynch, Manny Schonhorn, Irwin Primer, Richard Quaintance, Elizabeth Powers, Sophie Gee, Jennifer Thorn, Julie Park, Rebecca Steinitz, Carey McIntosh, and James Griffiths.

Countless students at Columbia have contributed to this project in one way or another over the course of eight years at this university; I owe special thanks to the students who took my seminar on the idea of culture. For research assistance, I am especially indebted to Matthew Zarnowiecki and Adela Ramos; Adela, Alice Boone, and Marina Graham have been among my most generous and thoughtful interlocutors on matters eighteenth-century and otherwise, and I look forward to many years of future conversation with them. My students' enthusiasm for reading, writing, thinking, and talking is one of the great pleasures in my life; though I cannot name anywhere near everyone who matters, I would especially like to thank Abigail Joseph, Christine Varnado, Sara Kile, Atticus Zavaletta, Musa Gurnis, Alicia DeSantis, Jennifer Buckley, Lianne Habinek, Andy Lynn, Judy Stuchiner, Levi Pinsky, Angela Monsam, Sunil Agnani, Dermot Ryan, Craig Beaumont, Judith Goldman, Jeff DeRoche, Jason Kim, Ramsey McGlazer, Patrick Pearsall, Lynn Copes, and Wei Keen Sung.

The reports of the anonymous readers for Columbia University Press helped me a great deal as I revised the manuscript for publication. Ivan Lupić checked quotations for me with Shakespearean wisdom and wit, and in a fashion that led me to trust him more than I trusted myself. The Columbia library system provided most of the wherewithal for *Breeding*, including access to the Eighteenth-Century Collections Online database and the invaluable BorrowDirect, but I also did significant reading, during the project's early days, in the Rare Books and Manuscripts Room at the British Library. I would like to thank the friends and family members who put me up in London while I worked there; Penny Richards and John Pringle, in particular, offered generous hospitality, as did Jane Yeh. I must spare a mention here for my beloved grandmother, Barbara Richards, who died midway through this book's composition but who always thoroughly approved of the economical notion that family visiting could be combined with library work.

I am singularly lucky in the friendship of Amy Davidson, Oscar Tübke-Davidson, and Natasha Shapiro, as well as in a host of other good friends from college and graduate school days; Miguel Sancho, Anna Henchman, Emily Wilson, Emily Steiner, Arielle Saiber, Seeta Chaganti, Marco Roth, and Steve Burt all deserve particular thanks. Ed Park is my much-valued literary co-conspirator and I thank him especially for a stimulating Silver Moon conversation that transformed my notion of the formal possibilities at my disposal for academic writing. Nico Muhly and Liz Gately deserve thanks for cottage pie and other delicacies, for literary conversation and general companionship, and for varied cat-sitting duties. The members of my immediate family have shown themselves to be shockingly tolerant of book-writing's exigencies: Ian Davidson, Caroline Davidson, Jim Kilik, Jon Davidson, Michelle Teague, Michael Davidson, and Jessi Zenquis Davidson. I must especially single out Gene Kilik, my adopted grandfather, for dragging me away from the monastic cell to theaters and restaurants and hosting many a party along the way. I am also grateful to the regular readers and commenters at Light Reading, particularly Maxine Clarke and Colleen Mondor, and to two dear friends I made during the last year of working on this book, Wendy Buckner and Brent Buckner. I thank Wendy especially for her photographs, her e-mails, and her advice about swimming, and Brent for many things—not least for providing a book-revision venue that can fairly and without dispute be described as a romantic tropical island paradise!

Working with Jennifer Crewe at Columbia University Press has been a great pleasure from start to finish, and I thank her and the staff at the press for their wonderful assistance, including Kerri Sullivan for her graceful copyediting. I have presented material from *Breeding* in a wide variety of settings, from which questions and conversation subsequently fed back into the project: these include the Eighteenth- and Nineteenth-Century Colloquium of the Yale English Department; the Eighteenth-Century Workshop at the University of Chicago; the Columbia Faculty Seminar on Eighteenth-Century European Culture; the Clark Library Core Program on "Vital Matters"; a conference on Religion in the English Enlightenment at Princeton; the Sixth Dublin Symposium on Jonathan Swift (held at the Deanery of St. Patrick's Cathedral, where the present dean passed Swift's own snuffbox around the room for each of us to hold); as well as panels at annual meetings of the American Society of Eighteenth-Century Studies, the Western Society for Eighteenth-Century Studies, the Modern Language

Association, and the DeBartolo Conference in Eighteenth-Century Studies. I received thoughtful questions and comments from audiences at the Feminist Interventions series of Columbia's Institute for Research on Women and Gender and at the Friday lunchtime lecture series at the Heyman Center.

A shorter version of the discussion of Garrick's adaptation of *The Winter's Tale* appeared in the volume titled *Shakespeare in the Eighteenth Century,* edited by Peter Sabor and Paul Yachnin and published by Ashgate Press in 2008; I am grateful to Peter and Paul for including me in the spectacular conference they hosted at McGill University on Shakespeare in the age of Enlightenment, and to Ashgate for permission to reprint that material (in somewhat different form) in these pages.

# BREEDING

## Breeding Before Biology

$T$he word *breeding* sets a place for nature at culture's table.

Eighteenth-century British writers often use *breeding* as a synonym for *education,* as in Johnson's *Dictionary* (1755), but the word's connotations include blood as well as upbringing. Breeding folds nature into culture in a way that might save one from having to choose between two competing and (it is possible) largely incompatible accounts of human nature: the first, a hereditarian model in which birth determines one's character and one's place in the world; the second, a model that emphasizes the power of education and other environmental influences to shape essentially malleable human beings into whatever form is deemed best.[1]

Nurture's power to counter or overcome nature became an article of faith in eighteenth-century Britain, and throughout the century, philosophers promoted the uses of education to cultivate the self, novelists experimented with plots of improvement, and writers across a host of technical disciplines explored the hows and whys of nature's betterment. Some authorities even went so far as to argue that culture could change one species of grain into another, or to account for the resemblance between a child and its father by invoking a maternal imagination so powerful "that though a Woman be in unlawful Copulation, yet if fear or any thing else causes her to fix her mind upon her Husband, the Child will resemble him, tho' he never got it."[2] Yet even the most extreme eighteenth-century advocates for culture are aware of nature tugging against nurture, and the word *breeding* itself remains charged with the tension between these two complementary terms.

Writing this book has meant digging up and sorting through a huge mass of what British writers thought about breeding—an umbrella term that can refer to nature or nurture, generation, pregnancy, hereditary resemblance, manners, moral character, social identity, or all of the above—in the several hundred years that preceded the coinage of the modern nouns *biology* (ca. 1802), *heredity* (ca. 1830), and *genetics* (ca. 1906).[3] I have chosen from that mass what seemed to me the most intriguing and suggestive elements and have laid them out in a sort of mosaic that shows unexpected and revealing facets, not just of eighteenth-century discussions but also of the ways in which we continue to explore and explain human nature. Needless to say, human nature represents an unusually challenging subject, given the volume and variety of the source material. Roger Smith puts it well when he observes that "[q]uoting references to human nature in the eighteenth century is a bit like quoting references to God in the Bible."[4] Even the terminology is slippery, impossible. "Nature and the natural are the most porous words in the language; they soak up ideology like a sponge," writes Gillian Beer, and Raymond Williams (after deeming *culture* "one of the two or three most complicated words in the English language") calls *nature* "perhaps the most complex word in the language."[5]

Two historians of science, summing up the results of a recent major conference on the cultural history of heredity, conclude that "no general concept of heredity was underlying the discourse on life (including medicine, anthropology and the moral sciences) in the eighteenth century and that such a concept was only slowly emerging in the first half of the nineteenth century."[6] Given that over the first half of the nineteenth century, British writing about everything from anthropology to horticulture and animal breeding would increasingly come to emphasize hereditary rather than environmental factors, how might this shift be understood? The rise of hereditary explanations can certainly be seen as a rejection of the previous century's cherished environmentalism, a reaction strengthened after the violence that accompanied revolution in France revealed some of the costs associated with the attempt to transcend nature by cultural means. Given that so much eighteenth-century writing about people, plants, and animals already represents nature as a stubborn stowaway on board the vessel of nurture, though, the early nineteenth-century turn to heredity might also be construed not so much as a reversal of earlier arguments about people and their properties but rather as consequent upon them.

In a moment when the cultural and intellectual prestige of genetics has never been greater, this book will bring to bear traditional strengths of scholarship in the humanities (including history and close reading) on breeding's story in the few hundred years before Mendel, before Darwin, and before Galton: a series of impassioned debates about nature and culture, the possibility of improvement, and the price of human perfectibility that clarify and call into question many of our current beliefs about what these things mean and why they matter. Eighteenth-century Britain's growing interest in what we would call selective breeding, the complex and conflicting explanatory schemes people used to account for familial resemblance, the passionate emphasis on the transformative effects of education: *Breeding* will sound the most striking and important conversations around these and related preoccupations in the hope that filling in historical gaps may help us become better prepared for the next stages of decision-making about breeding in all of its manifestations.

---

What does it mean to say that eighteenth-century writers gave environmental causes—everything from nutrition to weather, as in the climate theory associated with Montesquieu—the lion's share of the credit when it came to explaining human nature? Climate theory's origins could be traced back to the Hippocratic "Airs, Waters, Places" (ca. 400 BCE), a medical treatise with a strongly anthropological flavor that enjoyed a great resurgence of popularity in the eighteenth century. Characteristically Hippocratic thinking can be seen in a great deal of eighteenth-century writing, as for instance when the physician John Arbuthnot argues, in his *Essay Concerning the Effects of Air on Human Bodies* (1733), that the "Diversity of National Features and Shapes" cannot be "altogether the Effect of Propagation from the same original Stock; for it is known by Experience, that Transplantation changeth the Stature and outward Shape, both of Plants and Animals."[7] It wasn't that early eighteenth-century British observers couldn't conceive of plants, animals, and people being subject to manipulation of a kind that we would now call genetic. But the language available to them blurred the distinction between environmental and genetic management, as a passage from Addison and Steele's *Tatler* will attest.

The *Tatler* paper for 1 October 1709 opens with Isaac Bickerstaff's declaration that he has been "call'd off from publick Dissertations by a Domestick Affair of great Importance," namely the disposal in marriage of his sister Jenny ("as unspotted a Spinster," he says, "as any in *Great Britain*").[8] Bickerstaff elaborates on this project in a distinctly agricultural vein, invoking an ancestor in the days of King Arthur who "was low of Stature, and of a very swarthy Complexion, not unlike a *Portugueze* Jew" who had the "Design of Lengthening and Whitening his Posterity." After chronicling the vicissitudes of the family's genetic fortunes in subsequent generations, a history of "Defects . . . mended by succeeding Matches," Bickerstaff reflects on the appeal of a set of tactics borrowed from husbandry:

> One might wear any Passion out of a Family by Culture, as skilful Gardiners blot a Colour out of a Tulip that hurts its Beauty. One might produce an affable Temper out of a Shrew, by grafting the Mild upon the Cholerick; or raise a Jackpudding from a Prude, by inoculating Mirth and Melancholy. It is for Want of Care in the disposing of our Children, with Regard to our Bodies and Minds, that we go into an House and see such different Complexions and Humours in the same Race and Family.

Rather than matching his sister with "a Fine Gentleman, who extremely admir'd her Wit, and would have given her a Coach and Six," Bickerstaff finally decides to "cross the Strain" by choosing a businessman who will put his witty sister in her place and ensure that she produces "an Offspring fit for the Habitation of City, Town, or Country; Creatures that are docile and tractable in whatever we put 'em to." All these techniques are strikingly put under the rubric of "Culture": grafting and the related technique of inoculation do not describe coupling so much as manipulation or manuring, and pretty much *all* the words in the constellation around breeding have this property.[9]

Despite Bickerstaff's playful analogy, it was very much up for debate whether the same rules really applied to people and to plants and animals. Shouldn't answers to the question of whether culture or the mysterious quality often just called "blood" contributed more to form the organism be affected by whether that organism had a rational mind—or a soul? How likely was it, as Condorcet speculated in his *Sketch for a Historical Picture of the Progress of the Human Mind* (1795), that not just physical but "intellectual and moral faculties" might be transmitted from parents to children, and that "education, in perfecting these qualities, [might] at the same time influence, modify and perfect the organization itself"?[10] Questions like these—which also touch upon the mechanisms of generation and inheritance, the relative contributions of male and female parents, and the possibility that "acquired" characters might be passed on to offspring—were pursued in many different modes of writing, from novels to popular manuals of practical husbandry to abstruse scientific treatises read by only a tiny subset of the population. Increasingly a consensus developed, though, that the controversial elements of such debates could not easily be confined to animals and vegetables; arguments about husbandry led inevitably to heated speculation about man's origins, the literal truth or otherwise of the account of the creation in Genesis, and indeed the notion of a possible multiplicity of human species, an idea whose consequences were particularly devastating for Europeans and Americans of African descent.

Assuming that properties descended from parents to children—the germ of the idea of heredity, before there was a proper word for it—should the new breeding techniques associated with animal husbandry be extended to people? And if so, how? It made sense, once one thought of man as an animal, to concentrate on bringing the most up-to-date breeding methods to bear on the problem of human sinfulness. Did this, though, commit one to the steady erosion of others' humanity, or even perhaps to programs of eradication? The great question about the eighteenth century's proto-eugenic arguments, if I may call them that, is whether the fact that it is impossible *now* to talk of eugenics without its twentieth-century history coming to mind—everything from the forced sterilization of the mentally retarded in the United States to the Nazis' yoking-together of medicine, racial prejudice, and mass murder—means that violence is intrinsic to the entire family of arguments about breeding and human perfectibility, or whether it's a more contingent and accidental linkage. My anachronistic use of the term "eugenics" (the *OED*'s earliest example is drawn from Francis Galton's 1883 *Inquiries Into the Human Faculty and Its Development*) may seem to predetermine the outcome of this inquiry, but the languages of eugenics and sinfulness are intimately historically intertwined, as Daniel Kevles shows when he cleverly names "the elimination of original sin by getting rid biologically of the original sinner" as eugenics' "chiliastic goal."[11]

Our orientation toward such questions depends in part on our position with regard to a momentous question about Enlightenment thought, one that crops up whether we are talking about empire or literature or science and that was given early and influential articulation by Adorno and Horkheimer. Dorinda Outram's essay "The Enlightenment Our Contemporary" offers a perceptive summary of their iconic work, with its impassioned indictment of the twinned catastrophes of man's sovereignty over nature and rationalism's disenchantment of the world and its deep-seated commitment to a vision of Enlightenment thought, especially scientific thought, as "the precondition for twentieth-century modernity, defined as the domination of technology and science, the restriction of the value sphere, and the consequent facilitation of technological mass murder."[12] What claims do we assent to, Outram asks, when we portray the Enlightenment "as in some sense the origin of modern science"? If we cling to a possessive notion of Enlightenment, she suggests, an Enlightenment that is in important respects one with our own time, "we run the risk of approaching it simply as a mirror to ourselves," a function of "the need to find projections of ourselves in the past"; these "assertions of contemporaneity" ironically limit the possibility of writing a genuinely critical cultural history of the period, because they make it impossible to assemble "external points of reference to validate that critical viewpoint." While I share many of Outram's concerns, including her wariness about quests for origins and her attentiveness to the restrictions of presentism, I confess that I hope to achieve some of the same critical ends by altogether different means: namely, by plunging into a vast sea of eighteenth-century materials and welcoming the sheer disorientation that accompanies such an act of self-immersion. I have especially tried throughout the book to listen closely to the voices of seventeenth- and eighteenth-century writers without letting subsequent developments in the history of the state's interventions in the health of citizens determine the outcome of the investigation. What were the rhetorical and ethical consequences of arguing for the control of human as well as animal propagation? Were doubts about perfectibility mere quibbles or technical caveats, or did the notion of perfectibility itself encompass fundamental ethical dangers?

Perhaps the single most striking fact about the eighteenth-century conversations treated here is that whereas, in our own time, the threat of determinism is perceived to come almost entirely by way of genetics, eighteenth-century writers saw free will seriously eroded by forces like custom and climate and habit—a through-the-looking-glass reversal of our own expectations.[13] Evelyn Fox Keller observes of American science in the years after World War II that "[b]ecause nurture (or culture) had always been seen as a more commodious force than nature, . . . it was nurture, not nature, that was seen as conducive to the kind of unfettered development imagined possible by a victorious and 'free' republic," but her "always" certainly doesn't extend as far back as the eighteenth century, and a longer view shows that the alignment of nurture with freedom and nature with necessity is quite culturally specific.[14] The dimensions of that longer view may be spatial as well as temporal: in the Soviet Union, the influential agronomist Lysenko's ruthless commitment to increasing crop yields by environmental means—in his mechanistic view of plant propagation, a wheat plant might actually be induced to produce rye—contributed to later generations of Soviet progressives holding a degree of admiration for genetic accounts of human nature that would have been altogether antipathetical to (let's say) their liberal American counterparts in the 1970s.[15]

One of the axioms laid out by Eve Kosofky Sedgwick in the introduction to *Epistemologies of the Closet* (1990) speaks directly to the difficulties inhering in these topics. "The immemorial, seemingly ritualized debates on nature versus nurture take place against a very unstable background of tacit assumptions and fantasies about both nurture and nature," she writes, pointing out that though we may be drawn to meditate upon and attempt to adjudicate between mutually exclusive constructivist and essentialist definitions of homosexuality, "any such adjudication is impossible to the degree that a conceptual deadlock between the two opposing views has by now been built into the very structure of every theoretical tool we have for undertaking it."[16] There is no doubt that feelings run high around questions about nature and nurture precisely because of how quickly they carry us into arguments about free will and determinism, but it's worth resisting any easy equation of nurture with liberty in the philosophical sense. "The notion that we 'have a nature,'" Mary Midgley writes in her 1978 book *Beast and Man: The Roots of Human Nature,* "far from threatening the concept of freedom, is absolutely essential to it. If we were genuinely plastic and indeterminate at birth, there could be no reason why society should not stamp us into any shape that might suit it."[17] Many eighteenth-century writers saw custom working so strongly it could actually be written into bodies, an idea often expressed in shorthand by allusion to the Hippocratic discussion of the Macrocephali, or long-headed, tribe:

> The chief cause of the length of their heads was at first found to be in their customs, but nowadays nature collaborates with tradition and they consider those with the longest heads the most nobly born. The custom was to mould the head of the newly-born children with their hands and to force it to increase in length by the application of bandages and other devices which destroy the spherical shape of the head and produce elongation instead. The characteristic was thus acquired at first by artificial means, but, as time passed, it became an inherited characteristic and the practice was no longer necessary.[18]

The notion that acquired characteristics could be inherited was persistent enough that when the biologist August Weismann came to refute it, in a powerful and highly original series of essays on heredity published in the 1880s, he rather belabors the point: "We cannot by excessive feeding make a giant out of the germ destined to form a dwarf," Weismann writes, with an audibly irritable and polemical edge; "we cannot, by means of exercise, transform the muscles of an individual destined to be feeble into those of a Hercules, or the brain of a predestined fool into that of a Leibnitz or a Kant, by means of much thinking."[19]

My goal has been neither to compose a literary-critical account nor to write a history (whether intellectual or cultural or scientific) of the period's changing orientation to the idea of heredity.[20] Instead, I wanted, medium-like, to make these pages a sort of parliament, an auditorium in which the voices of actors in and commentators on the story of heredity in the eighteenth century can be heard, although always with the intention of allowing these long-gone conversations to illuminate aspects of our own thought on heredity and human nature. To separate out the literary from the scientific from the medical from the philosophical, I have come to feel, does a violence to the matters with which all of these disciplines are concerned—disciplines which, by the way, we perceive as being distinct only as a consequence of developments newly underway during exactly this period. In the original preface to his 1963 history of the eighteenth-century life sciences, Jacques Roger called for more studies "to explain what constitutes the unity of an age across the diversity of its forms of art and thought and to justify the interconnections that draw our attention to areas apparently foreign to one another," and went on to suggest that "[l]iterary history is better able than any other discipline to involve itself in an undertaking of this sort."[21]

By virtue of a professional training oriented especially toward language and rhetoric, the literary scholar brings a somewhat different skill set to this sort of investigation than the cultural historian or historian of science. Growing up in Philadelphia, I loved visiting the underground museum below the Ghost Structure, a steel skeleton designed by Robert Venturi to mark the dimensions of Benjamin Franklin's house, razed in 1812. The museum had a sort of phone bank that allowed one to telephone a huge number of different eighteenth-century figures whose names and numbers were posted across a banner like the menu at a fast-food restaurant. Once the call was put through, I would listen to the recording of what Washington or Mozart or whoever I had chosen to dial up that day had to say about Franklin: history as spiritualism-inflected gossip! The metaphor of hearing the dead speak is of course built into our relationship with writing, especially with writing from the deeper past.[22]

The great value of this kind of swerve away from the straight-and-narrow of the historical method—what makes it worth the risk—seems to me to lie in the counterfactual or *path-not-taken* traction it offers on ideas. In "Thick Description: Toward an Interpretive Theory of Culture," an essay whose influence has been even more pronounced in literary studies than in anthropology departments, Clifford Geertz—writing of a passage taken from his own field journal—offers a sardonic and somewhat disingenuous conclusion concerning the interpretive enterprise:

> I do not know how long it would be profitable to meditate on the encounter of Cohen, the sheikh, and "Dumari" (the period has perhaps already been exceeded); but I do know that however long I did so I would not get anywhere

near to the bottom of it. Nor have I ever gotten anywhere near to the bottom of anything I have ever written about, either in the essays below or elsewhere. Cultural analysis is intrinsically incomplete. And, worse than that, the more deeply it goes the less complete it is.[23]

The fact that it may be impossible to "get to the bottom" of breeding seems to me more enabling than inhibiting. (Leave nature some mystery!) And the reporting techniques of cultural anthropologists undoubtedly provide an important precedent for my accumulation of particularities, as do a number of other inquiries whose results have been organized by their authors in a somewhat unorthodox fashion.

Especially attractive to me are rule-based schemes of a fairly stringent nature, which seem to me uniquely capable of expressing what might be called (to coin an oxymoron) irrational arguments, accumulations of words that fulfill a number of evidentiary and persuasive criteria and establish a position or make a case—all within the constraints of formal structures that would seem to be thoroughly at odds with reason. How is it that Georges Perec's "Attempt at an Inventory of the Liquid and the Solid Foodstuffs Ingurgitated by Me in the Course of the Year Nineteen Hundred and Seventy-Four," which is quite literally what the title says—a year's worth of transcribed menu items, sorted out and organized by category ("One milk-fed lamb, three lamb cutlets, two curried lambs, twelve *gigots*, one saddle of lamb")—should be so redolent of meaning?[24] Not simply of an emotional meaning—pathos, poignancy, a certain demented precision—but of a quite clear set of arguments about the history of the Jews in twentieth-century Europe, the burdens of memory, and the nature of humanity? As tempting as I found the prospect of haring off after something of this sort, it seemed to me impossible—or at least highly inappropriate—to contrive a strictly rule-based approach for organizing and presenting my material. Yet other (and less extreme) works than Perec's similarly show how richly a story may emerge from unconventional patterning; I am thinking here especially of Primo Levi's *The Periodic Table* (1975), a remarkable series of autobiographical musings (Levi was a professional chemist) cast into the structure of Mendeleyev's table of the elements.[25] At any rate, the story as it has emerged does follow a roughly chronological sweep whose juxtapositions and necessary shifts of gear allow for the drawing-out of what seemed to me most interesting and valuable about the material.

I gravitated especially, in the end, toward the work of two writers whose imaginative formal and stylistic choices are uniquely well-suited to their intellectual projects. One of these is W. G. Sebald, with his sinuous twentieth-century archeologies of ashes. Though increasingly he abandoned the form of the novel for a kind of documentary prose, Sebald's extended prose pieces are also fictions of a sort, experiments in voice and pastiche (in the literal sense) that touch on very deep questions about memory and the natural history of destruction. Sebald's life work was to chronicle a haunting and highly heterogenous mix of wanderings, literal and literary, and *The Rings of Saturn* (which begins with meditations on Thomas Browne's skull and Rembrandt's painting *The Anatomy Lesson*) offers this description of a meal at the seaside hotel Sebald reaches early in that book's pages:

> That evening I was the sole guest in the huge dining room, and it was the same startled person who took my order and shortly afterwards brought me a fish that had doubtless lain entombed in the deep-freeze for years. The breadcrumb armour-plating of the fish had been partly singed by the grill, and the prongs of my fork bent on it. Indeed it was so difficult to penetrate what eventually proved to be nothing but an empty shell that my plate was a hideous mess once the operation was over. The tartare sauce that I had had to squeeze out of a plastic sachet was turned grey by the sooty breadcrumbs, and the fish itself, or what feigned to be fish, lay a sorry wreck among the grass-green peas and the remains of soggy chips that gleamed with fat.[26]

This gruesome scene of eating—of trying to dig out an almost historical artifact that's simply *not there* ("nothing but an empty shell") or exists only in a sinister ersatz ("what feigned to be fish")—will be echoed later on in a tragic account of the transportation of over ten thousand refugee children, during the Second World War, from Bosnia to Croatia in cattle wagons. At the end of the journey, Sebald—or his narrator—recounts, "Many of those who were still alive were so hungry that they had eaten the cardboard identity tags they wore about their necks and thus in their extreme desperation had eradicated their own names."[27]

My second model is Roland Barthes. At almost every point in his career, Barthes approached the task of criticism in a deeply writerly mode—consider the whimsical alphabetical ordering of the sections of *Le plaisir du texte* (1973), or the literary richness of the work on photography or Michelet or any number of other topics.[28] Like Sebald, Barthes is at once enraptured and troubled by his fleeting encounters with the ever-elusive past; one immediate inspiration has come from a collection of lectures delivered in the late 1970s and published in English as *The Neutral* (2005). Barthes' description of his approach there especially resonates with me: he describes taking "the word 'Neutral' . . . for a series of walks along a certain number of readings," identifying his practice with "the procedure of the topic: a grid over the surface of which one moves a 'subject.'"[29] In an elliptical series of phrases, he goes on to perform arabesques on the metaphor:

> . . . I took the Neutral for a walk not along the grid of words but along a net-
> work of readings, which is to say, of a library. This library, neither analytical
> (I didn't follow a bibliographic program: cf. the intertext that is handed to
> you) nor exhaustive: infinite library: even now, I can read a new book in which
> certain passages will crystallize around the notion of Neutral as a whimsical
> *sourcery:* I read, the water-divining rod rises: there is Neutral underneath, and,
> for this very reason, the notion of the Neutral expands, inflects itself, modifies
> itself: I persist, and I transform myself at the same time.

My own library in this case has been both analytical and as exhaustive as I could make it, and my own grid includes a chronological axis, but the book will indeed take breeding for a walk through the stacks—a walk on a long leash.

Elsewhere in the lectures, Barthes invokes the notion (it exists in the same conceptual universe as Raymond Williams' keyword approach) of a "[n]etwork of closely related words" which one confronts in order to refine "meanings, differences, nuances," the last term spurring a string of phrases in which Barthes reflects on his

> wish for a great "pedagogy" of nuance in the classroom: nuance is one of the
> linguistic tools of nonarrogance, of nonintolerance: civic imperative to teach
> nuances (but I suppose great resistance from kids), to make up nuance exer-
> cises; one of these exercises: inventory of micronetworks of words that are very
> similar but a tiny bit different: → "discourse on the bit of difference": wouldn't
> deny difference but would recognize the price of the "bit." Justness: just be-
> tween being and "bit."[30]

The work I've done here can also be thought of as a "nuance exercise" in this sense, a close consideration of a micronetwork that starts with breeding and fans out very quickly into impossibly huge terms like *nature* and *culture*. Keeping my attention on nuance—on the particularity of each use of each word—is another way of resisting the strong pull of grand narratives of Enlightenment, and of the complementary orbits of self-recognition and self-castigation into which the period always threatens to draw us.

Working on this book has confirmed for me the importance of what might be called the writerly approach, an essayistic or discursive mode that prefers not to participate in all of the disciplinary practices of history or criticism proper. A great part of its value, it seems to me, lies precisely in this sensitivity to the nuance and the particularity of the material. The writers I consider deploy a shared but often contested vocabulary to make their cases, in language frequently studded with metaphors, solecisms, self-contradictions, and a number of other equally suggestive and highly personal rhetorical features. I came to suspect that subordinating individual writers' voices to loosely historicist arguments about dominant tropes and broad sweeps of cultural and linguistic change would in this case be at best ineffectual, at worst actively misleading—certainly far less *interesting* than patterning the material not so much like a monograph as like an oratorio or a grand country dance, so that echoes and responses and recapitulations would emerge from a congeries of voices.

The major social, economic, and political transitions concerning inheritance in eighteenth-century Britain have been amply chronicled elsewhere; the history of science and medicine for this period is equally rich, and many of the literary works I treat have over the years received untold amounts of attention. The principles of selection governing my choice of material differ somewhat from those of a scholar working more straightforwardly in a single established discipline or methodology, and my account is necessarily partial: partial in the sense of selective, of course, as all books must be, but also "partial" in a sense not altogether remote from the practice of the self-described *"partial, prejudiced, and ignorant Historian"* who narrates Jane Austen's "History of England."[31] There's something to be said for the worm's-eye view, and I have more or less deliberately adopted the trope of synecdoche—taking the part for the whole, operating by means of contiguity and association—over the more accepted modes of analogy and argument, though I will pay my courtesies (to borrow an eighteenth-century image) to those interpretive modes.

I have grouped the episodes of my story under six headings, proceeding in roughly chronological order. Though I am most centrally concerned with Britain in the eighteenth century, I visit French discussions when they illuminate aspects of my main story (especially in the case of Rousseau), and I also begin with a number of seventeenth-century discussions that cast light on topics that cannot always be neatly demarcated by a round number like 1700. Because of their interest in generation and their playful experimentation with the notion that "blood will out" (in a familial rather than a homicidal sense), *The Winter's Tale* and its eighteenth-century descendants provide one through-line for my investigation into breeding in seventeenth- and eighteenth-century England.[32] The play, having been almost entirely neglected from 1650 to 1750, was adapted for the stage in the mid-eighteenth century by David Garrick and several others, and it turned out to be a powerful vehicle for later eighteenth-century storytellers trying to work out the nature of the relationship between parents and children—and more especially between fathers and daughters—in an era of immense social transformations. Shakespeare's play thus provides at the outset both a rich language and a stimulating conceptual structure for thinking about generation, inheritance, and the interplay between nature and culture, and I have allowed it to shape the first part of my story about what happened to the concept of "breeding" during this period.

# I

## The Rules
## of Resemblance

In this first foray into breeding's thickets, I want to take advantage of what might be called literary criticism's neutrality with respect to scale. This is a fancy way of saying that, as practitioners in a discipline whose twentieth-century history encompasses both so-called close reading (itself the object of recent consideration by critics as various as John Guillory, Franco Moretti, and Wai-Chee Dimock) and the kind of long view associated with books like Leo Marx's *The Machine in the Garden* (1964) and Raymond Williams' *The Country and the City* (1973), we are allowed or even encouraged to unite the examination of particular detail—often even of usage at the level of a single word—with the consideration of linguistic, literary, intellectual, and cultural elements of considerably larger dimensions.[1] Shakespeare's play *The Winter's Tale* contains thought-provoking languages for and arguments about the mechanisms of inheritance that are worth examining for their own sake, but the play can also serve as an extraordinarily interesting guide to patterns of deployment of related tropes and arguments in the years following its composition, and across all sorts of different kinds of writing.

Just as the practice of literary criticism does not necessarily commit one to a preference for any one particular unit of analysis—it is possible, for example, to look at a word, a metaphor or other trope, a line of verse or a paragraph of argument, a play, a novel, or indeed an entire literary genre or literary period—so it does not necessarily involve an either-or choice between considering an individual literary work as the conscious and determined creation of its author or as a symptom of broader cultural and historical trends. Indeed, the images and arguments of any given work can rarely be considered in isolation; willy-nilly, they help us see things and make connections, with Shakespeare's work especially serving as a kind of common property, the raw material for new literary and cultural fantasies.

*The Winter's Tale* essentially dropped out of the theatrical repertory following Shakespeare's death, and for the first half of the eighteenth century it held relatively little appeal for theatrical companies and audiences.[2] But the play underwent a striking surge in popularity at mid-century, and was acted about a hundred times in several different adaptations between 1750 and 1800.[3] Both the choice of plays to adapt and stage and the nature of those adaptations offer significant indicators of cultural changes since Shakespeare's day, and *The Winter's Tale* clearly offered mid-eighteenth-century adapters an especially valuable opportunity to revise older ideas about breeding, birth, and upbringing. Audiences during this period had largely lost the taste for full-length Shakespearean plays in anything close to their original versions, and while David Garrick and others prided themselves on the faithfulness of their productions, the plays seen by theatergoers usually bore the marks of radical alteration.[4] Because theatrical adapters are charged with tailoring older texts to contemporary tastes, eighteenth-century adaptations are often very revealing about widely held assumptions and attitudes, offering apter evidence of cultural trends than many other kinds of literary work. Taken together with several looser adaptations, in fictional form, these eighteenth-century dramatic borrowings from and reimaginings of *The Winter's Tale* will allow me to sketch out some significant developments in the story of breeding as it concerns children's inheritance of properties from their parents.

## Why Children Look Like Their Fathers

Romance often features a young person whose mysteriously good breeding belies a lowly upbringing, and the working-out of a romance plot mostly reveals breeding to be the result of blood rather than education: it might even be said that part of the *job* of romance is to argue that education doesn't much matter, except insofar as a rustic upbringing happily insulates a young prince or princess from corruption by courtly manners.[5] Even among romances, though, with their structural interest in reuniting families and their celebration of values associated with the natural and the hereditary, *The Winter's Tale* (first performed in 1611 and published in the 1623 Folio) is striking for its obsessiveness about inheritance and

generation. This late play of Shakespeare's explores the transmission of properties from parent to offspring, noting and interpreting the resemblances that mark
familial relationships and regulate patterns of inheritance. The play investigates
inheritance in gardens as well as palaces, with King Polixenes famously defending the art that lets one "marry / A gentler scion to the wildest stock, / And make
conceive a bark of baser kind / By bud of nobler race": a charged topic, given that
the projected marriage between prince and shepherdess (so closely analogous to
the grafting he endorses in the garden) seems to threaten a social order Polixenes
believes to be natural and wants to protect.[6] If the gardener's art allows for the
propagation of new fruits and flowers of mixed lineage, problems may surface
for the stability of human inheritance in Sicilia and Bohemia, and possibly in
seventeenth-century England as well.

All human societies have rules for regulating the passage of property and power
from one generation to the next, and anthropologists take kinship structures and
patterns of inheritance to be two of the most significant and interesting features of
the societies they study. These can be expressed in a wide range of different forms,
from customs, legal instruments, and prescriptions for how to choose a new ruler
to scientific theories about natural relationships and myths, legends, and religious
beliefs about blood and its properties.[7] The kingdom of Sicilia in *The Winter's Tale*
is no exception to this generalization, but one of the most striking facts about kinship and inheritance here is the extent to which Sicilia's king himself understands
them to have been disrupted, most immediately by the threat of female infidelity
and more generally by the frightening, even monstrous aspects of generation.

As well as meaning both upbringing and what's in the blood, the term "breeding" refers to pregnancy, and the metaphor of "issue" (offspring, outcome) dominates a number of the play's conversations.[8] Queen Hermione is right on the
verge of giving birth for most of the play's first three acts, and her visible pregnancy attracts much attention and speculation: she "rounds apace," says one lady-
in-waiting at the beginning of Act Two, another agreeing that "[s]he is spread
of late / Into a goodly bulk" (2.1.16–20). Perhaps because this physical pregnancy
is so conspicuous, metaphors of childbearing come easily to the tongues of the
courtiers of Sicilia: as the faithful Camillo says to his newly hostile master King
Leontes, "Be plainer with me, let me know my trespass / By its own visage. If
I then deny it, / 'Tis none of mine" (1.2.265–267). Camillo plays here on the relationship between ordinary kinds of suspicion and the suspicion of sexual in-
continence, comparing his offense to an illegitimate child whose face must be
seen before the man accused of being its father can accept or deny the charge.
His "trespass"—in one sense nonexistent, for Camillo has not yet betrayed his

master—is implicitly figured as the child, not of Camillo himself but of Leontes' own jealous imagination.

The play's male courtiers mostly express hostility and dislike toward reproduction. As King Polixenes and Camillo try to work out why Leontes is conducting himself so strangely toward his childhood friend, Polixenes asks, "How should this grow?" "I know not," Camillo responds; "but I am sure 'tis safer to/Avoid what's grown than question how 'tis born" (1.2.431–433). Camillo's desire to steer clear of such issue is juxtaposed to his colleague Antigonus' strangely disordered conception of generation. Antigonus is so certain of Hermione's innocence that he threatens to "keep my stables where/I lodge my wife" if the queen prove unfaithful, or to geld his three daughters that they might not "bring false generations": "I had rather glib myself than they/Should not produce fair issue," he concludes (2.1.134–135, 148–150). The excessiveness of his language, surely intended to expose the absurdity of Leontes' suspicions, instead may unpleasantly remind the listener (to borrow the words of Edmund Burke, writing a hundred and fifty years later, about the revolutionary degradation of Marie Antoinette) that "a king is but a man; a queen is but a woman; a woman is but an animal; and an animal not of the highest order."[9]

The barnyard analogy—only domestic livestock are gelded or castrated—calls into question the innocence of the pastoral metaphors invoked by Sicilia's inhabitants, as when Polixenes describes himself and Leontes in the Edenic golden age of their youth as having been like "twinn'd lambs that did frisk i' th' sun,/And bleat the one at th' other" (1.2.67–68), or when Camillo makes the horticultural suggestion that Leontes "cannot show himself overkind" to Polixenes because they "were train'd together in their childhoods; and there rooted betwixt them then such an affection, which cannot choose but branch now" (1.1.21–24). The worlds of barnyard, pasture, and orchard invoked here amalgamate nature and culture rather than expressing unadulterated nature—the language is of agriculture, not wilderness—but cultivation introduces instability rather than security. Leontes' distrust of his "twin" suggests that there is something wrong with reproduction in the natural as well as the social world, just as Camillo's ambiguous word "branch" equally might describe affections flourishing together or splitting apart.

Leontes' greatest anxieties cluster around the question of whether the children of his marriage to Hermione are really his own. "Art thou my boy?" he asks Mamillius, in a scene of radical or even obsessive questioning.[10] Commenting of the boy's "smutch'd" nose that "[t]hey say it is a copy out of mine," Leontes harps disturbingly on a likeness that does not in itself guarantee his wife's fidelity. "How now, you wanton calf," Leontes continues, "Art thou my calf?"

MAMILLIUS
Yes, if you will, my lord.

LEONTES
Thou want'st a rough pash and the shoots that I have,
To be full like me; yet they say we are
Almost as like as eggs; women say so—
That will say any thing. But were they false
As o'er-dy'd blacks, as wind, as waters, false
As dice are to be wish'd by one that fixes
No bourn 'twixt his and mine, yet were it true
To say this boy were like me.

Perplexed as to how to interpret this likeness in a world of falsehood, Leontes overturns the usual order of resemblance, emphasizing the father's likeness to his son rather than the son's to his father:

Looking on the lines
Of my boy's face, methoughts I did recoil
Twenty-three years, and saw myself unbreech'd
In my green velvet coat, my dagger muzzled,
Lest it should bite its master, and so prove
(As [ornament] oft does) too dangerous.
How like (methought) I then was to this kernel,
This squash, this gentleman.               (1.2.153–160)

The kernel is the pip or seed of a fruit, and the squash the unripe pod of the pea.[11] Looking at Mamillius, Leontes sees only himself, and the "recoil" to the days of his youth stimulates something like the rewinding of a time-lapse film in which flowers unblossom into buds as the leaves furl closed around them, the grown man in this case folding himself back up into potential rather than actual being. The king's choice of words makes it hard to imagine that this kernel will undergo the processes of development that lead to maturity: the image of the dagger "muzzled,/ Lest it should bite its master" surely implies some failure of the phallus, and the death of Mamillius in Act Three in this sense only makes real a failure of succession implicit in these figurative distortions of generation and growth.

While Leontes' uncertainty about the parentage of his son is equivocal, he is quite sure that Perdita cannot be his child, and he renounces any claim to the baby after Hermione gives birth:

> This brat is none of mine,
> It is the issue of Polixenes.
> Hence with it, and together with the dam
> Commit them to the fire! (2.3.93–96)

His language is profoundly depersonalizing (Perdita is a "brat," "issue" of Polixenes, and Hermione only "the dam," like a brood-mare), and the outraged waiting-woman Paulina counters it by pointing out the resemblance between the baby and its father. She elaborates the metaphor of "printing off" a child (the same image Leontes himself will use to Florizel in Act Five) in the technical vocabulary of the trade:

> It is yours:
> And might we lay th' old proverb to your charge,
> So like you, 'tis the worse. Behold, my lords,
> Although the print be little, the whole matter
> And copy of the father—eye, nose, lip,
> The trick of 's frown, his forehead, nay, the valley,
> The pretty dimples of his chin and cheek, his smiles,
> The very mould and frame of hand, nail, finger.
>
> (2.3.96–103)

While the image of the mold, stamp, or "imprint" (to borrow Margreta de Grazia's term) is a common one for writers on reproduction, Shakespeare's imaginative updating of the Aristotelian conceit embeds generation in seventeenth-century print culture.[12]

Neither the visual evidence of the baby Perdita's resemblance to Leontes nor the widely felt absurdity of Leontes' suspicion of Hermione prevents Leontes from casting out his daughter, and the play leaves the court of Sicilia in Act Three with the arrival of an oracle from Delphi that tells Leontes that everything he believes is false: "Hermione is chaste, Polixenes blameless, Camillo a true subject, Leontes a jealous tyrant, his innocent babe truly begotten, and the King shall live without an heir, if that which is lost be not found" (3.2.132–136). Shortly thereafter, the death of Mamillius is announced, news which Paulina describes as "mortal to the Queen" (3.2.148). Hermione is carried off in a swoon, her death reported a few minutes later. The burden of the play's last two acts will be to stage a reconciliation between Leontes and his heir, which also means offering an account of how resemblance works that is persuasive enough to counteract the disabling skepticism about reproduction and inheritance that has been expressed by Leontes in the play's first three acts.

## The Rules of Resemblance

What does it mean to say in early seventeenth-century England that a child resembles his or her father? Though there are some interesting conceptual discussions of generation in medieval writing, historians of European medicine generally agree on there not having been any major developments in embryology between the body of Greek writing that includes the Hippocratics, Aristotle, and Galen (roughly from the fifth century BCE to the second century CE) and the late sixteenth century, when Fabricius and others used dissection and experimentation to expand the boundaries of knowledge about the development of the fetus.[13] The terms of debate in the early modern period continued to rely heavily on elements (some of them incompatible) drawn from Galen's model of conception as well as from Aristotle's; Galen argued that both male and female semen contributed to form the body of the child, for instance, while Aristotle emphasized the dominance of the father.

In the *Generation of Animals,* Aristotle says that the mother contributes only the material out of which the child is formed, while the father determines the shape or form it will take: "The male provides the 'form' and the 'principle of the movement,' the female provides the body, in other words, the material."[14] The analogy he offers is that the male semen acts in the female body as fig-juice or rennet works to set milk into cheese, and he suggests later that the child is formed from the male and female "only in the sense in which a bedstead is formed from the carpenter and the wood, or a ball from the wax and the form."[15] The male makes his contribution to generation from outside the female body, and the child develops within the mother's body simply because that's where the material is: "[N]othing passes from the carpenter into the pieces of timber, which are *his* material, and there is no part of the art of carpentry present in the object which is being fashioned: it is the shape and the form which pass from the carpenter, and they come into being by means of the movement in the material."[16]

This does not mean that children always and only resemble their fathers: Aristotle comments more than once on the fact that a child may resemble the father, the mother, or a more remote ancestor.[17] He also remains agnostic on the question of whether acquired traits can be passed on to children, a question crucial to determining whether the semen is drawn from the whole body—in which case traits *would* be passed on—or just from a part of it—meaning that the seed would not be affected by modifications to or mutilations of other parts of the body. But the paramount importance of the father's contribution is clear, and despite being challenged by Galen's theory of the two semens (which emphasized the mother's contribution of form as well as matter to the embryo), Aristotle's discussion of generation continued to set the terms of European investigations into generation well into the seventeenth century.[18] Increasingly, though, investigators turned to a new mechanism for explaining the unpredictable patterns of resemblance between children and their forebears, a theory of resemblance premised on the notion that the mother's imagination could somehow transmit to the fetus whatever sights or thoughts struck her most forcefully: a desire for strawberries might produce a strawberry birthmark, the sight of a mutilated beggar a child with missing limbs.[19]

(It is not only by means of her imagination that the mother was supposed to affect the child. The breastfeeding mother or nurse "was believed to transmit to the child, along with her ideas, beliefs, intelligence, intellect, diet and speech, all her other physical and emotional qualities,"[20] and Leontes invokes this belief when he says to Hermione, "Give me the boy. I am glad you did not nurse him./Though he does bear some signs of me, yet you/Have too much blood in him" [2.1.56–58]. Mamillius was not breastfed by Hermione but by a wet-nurse, in other words, and though attacks on breastfeeding began in England during the Reformation, it would not become fashionable for upper-class women to breastfeed their own children until the eighteenth century. The "blood" Hermione contributed to Mamillius—perhaps an allusion to Galen's argument that the mother's menstrual blood tips the balance of likeness away from the father—cannot efface the "signs" of the father.[21])

The prenatal influence of the imagination on the body and mind of the child was believed to be even more powerful than the effects of breastfeeding, and popular fascination with the potentially monstrous effects of the maternal imagination is explicitly invoked later on in Shakespeare's play, when Autolycus hawks his wares to the naive Mopsa, who says earnestly, "I love a ballet in print, a-life, for then we are sure they are true" (4.4.260–261). Autolycus's pitch is typical of contemporary broadsheet and ballad accounts of monstrous births: "Here's one to a very doleful tune, how a usurer's wife was brought to bed of twenty money-bags at a burthen, and how she long'd to eat adders' heads, and toads carbonado'd," he says (4.4.262–265).[22]

In his treatise on monsters (first published in 1573), the French surgeon Ambroise Paré attributes monstrous births to many different causes, but mainly to the power of the imagination: it should not surprise us when a pregnant woman with a craving for cherries gives birth to a child with a birthmark in the shape of a cherry, he says, "given the force of the imagination being joined with the conformational power, the softness of the embryo, ready like soft wax to receive any form."[23] The story of Jacob and Laban's sheep, cited by Paré and given below in the King James translation, provided key evidence in support of the hypothesis of the maternal imagination: in response to Laban's reluctant donation to his son-in-law of all the spotted or parti-colored sheep to be born in his herd, "Jacob took him rods of greene poplar, and of the hasel and chesnut tree, and pilled white strakes in them, and made the white appeare which was in the rods. And he set the rods which he had pilled, before the flockes in the gutters in the watering troughes when the flocks came to drinke, that they should conceive when they came to drinke. And the flockes conceived before the rods, and brought forth cattell ringstraked, speckled and spotted."[24] "And if Brutes are stigmatized or mark'd by the Force of Imagination," writes one eighteenth-century authority on midwifery, "What then must be the Effects of it in *rational Beings,* whose Memories are more lasting?"[25] The mother's imagination thus has the potential to counter the physical mechanism by which a father transmits properties to his children, leaching the value from resemblance as a test for paternal kinship and threatening to disrupt the patrilineal forms of inheritance on which many societies depend.

The theory of the maternal imagination—a useful complement to theories of reproduction (including "preformationist" theories that postulated the existence from the beginning of time of some germ of every person who would ever be born into existence) that were perplexed by the difficulty of explaining the child's relationship to two parents—directly displaced the father from the task of printing off his children. While literary critics have recently been fascinated with the theory as it pertains to monstrous births, it was also very often invoked to explain ordinary resemblances between a child and its parents or more distant forebears. The maternal imagination comes, for the theory's most passionate advocates, to provide the best explanation not just for the child's resemblance to a particular parent but even for a species remaining constant from one generation to the next. Nicolas Malebranche, the late seventeenth-century French scientist whose name is strongly associated with both preformation and the theory of the maternal imagination, asserted that without the communication between the brains of mother and child, "women and animals could not easily bring forth young of the same species."[26] Indeed, for some seventeenth- and eighteenth-century theorists of generation, a child comes to resemble his or her father primarily because the mother is thinking about the father at the moment of conception, and the significance of resemblance as a proof of legitimacy is thereby eroded: resemblance might be brought about because the mother, lying in her lover's arms, feared discovery by her real husband.[27] In a chapter that addresses the "Reason why Children are often like their Parents," the anonymous author of *Aristoteles Master-Piece* (1684 ed.) suggests that

> in case of the similitude, nothing is more powerful than the imagination of the Mother; for if she conceive in her mind, or do by chance fasten her eyes upon any Object, and imprint it in her Memory, the Child in its outward parts frequently has some representation thereof; so whilst a Man and Woman are in the Act of Copulation, if the Woman earnestly behold his Countenance and fix her mind thereon, without all peradventure, the Child will resemble the Father; nay so powerful is its Operation, that though a Woman be in unlawful Copulation, yet if fear or any thing else causes her to fix her mind upon her Husband, the Child will resemble him, tho' he never got it.[28]

Children are more often like their mothers than their fathers, the book continues, not just because women enjoy sex more than men (axiomatic in this kind of writing) but for other reasons as well:

> Hence it is that the Child more frequently resembles the Mother than the Father, because the Mother confers the most towards its Generation: and further it may be instanced from the great love they bear them, for besides their contributing Seminal matter, they, during the time they are in the Womb, feed and nourish the Child with the purest Fountain of Blood: which Opinion *Galen* confirms, by allowing the Child to participate more of the Mother than the Father, and refers the difference of the Sex to the influence of menstrual Blood; but the reason of the likeness he attributes to the force of the Seed; for as Plants receive more from fruitful ground than from the industry of the Husbandman, so the Infant in more abundance receives from the Mother than the Father.[29]

The history of theories of generation overlaps in a number of places with my story about breeding, as the period I'm concerned with saw many major discoveries in the physiology of reproduction in both the plant and animal worlds.[30] Knowledge of the workings of generation increased in leaps and bounds, thanks to the work of seventeenth-century investigators such as Harvey, De Graaf, Malpighi, Malebranche, Swammerdam, and Leeuwenhoek and a host of eighteenth-century successors.[31] Even the most imaginative and inspired scientists of the day, though, were unable to come up with an account of the mechanics of reproduction that would make sense in modern scientific terms. Generation was thus a topic both of central, indeed obsessive, interest and of telling misprision.

One of the major intellectual controversies of eighteenth-century Europe would concern the question of whether reproduction took place by epigenesis (the fresh development of the embryo) or preformation (the unfolding of preexistent structures). Preformation (also known as "evolution," before Darwin and others claimed the word for a quite different purpose) was also sometimes called *emboîtement,* or encasement, and is summed up well in Swammerdam's statement that "[i]n nature, there is no generation but only propagation, the growth of parts. Thus original sin is explained, for all men were contained in the organs of Adam and Eve. When their stock of eggs is finished, the human race will cease to be."[32] In the ovist version of preformation, the germs that contain all future descendants reside in the egg or ovum; there is also an animalculist version, following Leeuwenhoek's microscopic observation of the sperm (which he terms "animalcules," worms or eels) in the 1670s.

While it is easy to poke fun at features of this theory, the historian of science Clara Pinto-Correia warns readers that the principal historians of early embryology share an unfairly negative orientation toward preformation; she promises instead to tell what she calls "the marvelous story of the losers."[33] Advocates of preformation adopted tactics that may seem undignified to modern readers: Leeuwenhoek assured the editors of *Philosophical Transactions of the Royal Society* (about to publish the letter he had written describing the appearance of animalcules in the male semen) that the human semen he examined "was not obtained by any sinful contrivance on my part, but the observations were made upon the excess with which Nature provided me in my conjugal relations."[34] But the evident appeal for forward-looking eighteenth-century investigators of the idea that all of the essential parts of the fetus are already present in the egg is particularly clear when we consider that even the brilliant experimentalist Lazzaro Spallanzani—who in the 1760s and 1770s pioneered techniques of artificial insemination and dressed male frogs in tiny taffeta breeches to demonstrate that while they continued to have sex with the females, none of the eggs would be fertilized—understood his own experiments, which seem to modern audiences to provide incontrovertible evidence for the major role played by the sperm in reproduction, rather as undeniable proof of the ovist version of preformation.[35]

The prestige and popularity of preformation would undergo rapid changes, decade by decade: sometimes the cutting edge of science, at other times a much-mocked and unwanted legacy of prior investigators. One setback for preformation in the early eighteenth century was that the animalculist version implied immense wastefulness on God's part, given how many germs perished with each emission of semen; also, in the words of one early nineteenth-century translator of Lucretius, acceptance of animalculism meant that "[e]very naturalist, and indeed every man who pretended to the smallest portion of medical science, was convinced that his children were no more related, in point of actual generation, to his own wife, than they were to his neighbours."[36] Ovists had to reckon with the problem that vexed all preformationists, how to explain the resemblance of children to both parents rather than simply to the mother.[37] Yet preformation regained legitimacy in the 1760s on the basis of some important new experimental work and dominated accounts of reproduction through the end of the eighteenth century.[38] Each theory of generation is also associated with a range of political and cultural positions. Pinto-Correia argues that by imagining tiny preformed descendants all encased within the ovary of a progenitor, preformation tended to justify the status quo: "By putting lineages inside each other, preformation could function as a 'politically correct' antidemocratic doctrine, implicitly legitimating the dynastic system."[39] Another way of thinking about it is to say that by reconceiving daughters' relationships to their fathers, scientific investigators would contribute to an increasing tendency in Britain to disinherit daughters at the expense of sons, a disenfranchisement that ironically would only heighten cultural investments in stories about fathers and daughters (one consequence being the imaginative spell *The Winter's Tale* and *King Lear* came to cast over the inhabitants of later eighteenth-century Britain).[40]

## "Nature's bastards"

At the heart of *The Winter's Tale,* as it is now read, is the exchange (during the long scene of festival in Act Four) in which Perdita explains why she has given

Camillo and Polixenes rosemary and rue, "flow'rs of winter," though they are less attractive than those she might otherwise have chosen:

> PERDITA
> Sir, the year growing ancient,
> Not yet on summer's death, nor on the birth
> Of trembling winter, the fairest flow'rs o' th' season
> Are our carnations and streak'd gillyvors
> (Which some call Nature's bastards). Of that kind
> Our rustic garden's barren, and I care not
> To get slips of them.
>
> POLIXENES
> Wherefore, gentle maiden,
> Do you neglect them?
>
> PERDITA
> For I have heard it said,
> There is an art which in their piedness shares
> With great creating Nature.
>
> POLIXENES
> Say there be;
> Yet Nature is made better by no mean
> But Nature makes that mean; so over that art
> Which you say adds to Nature, is an art
> That Nature makes. You see, sweet maid, we marry
> A gentler scion to the wildest stock,
> And make conceive a bark of baser kind
> By bud of nobler race. This is an art
> Which does mend Nature—change it rather; but
> The art itself is Nature.
>
> PERDITA
> So it is.
>
> POLIXENES
> Then make [your] garden rich in gillyvors,
> And do not call them bastards.

PERDITA
I'll not put
The dibble in earth to set one slip of them;
No more than were I painted I would wish
This youth should say 'twere well, and only therefore
Desire to breed by me.               (4.4.79–103)

Perdita rejects carnations and gillyflowers on the grounds that their beauty—the "piedness," or streaky coloring, gardeners prized—is the product not of nature alone but of art in collaboration with nature. By implication, she is usually taken to be justifying a social order based on "natural" distinctions and a commitment to the world of things as they are.[41] In response, Polixenes defends art as another kind of nature ("an art/That Nature makes") and invokes the practice of grafting as an instance where art and nature happily coexist. The irony here is that Polixenes, voicing his approval of a process in which "we marry/A gentler scion to the wildest stock,/And make conceive a bark of baser kind/By bud of nobler race," unknowingly undermines his own later arguments against the projected marriage between prince and shepherdess.

It is important not to make too much of the irony here: the art-nature debate is highly conventional, as Edward Tayler shows in *Nature and Art in Renaissance Literature* (1964), and the threat of what Tayler calls "a program of egalitarian eugenics" of course evaporates at the revelation that Perdita is really the legitimate daughter of Leontes and Hermione.[42] But Perdita declines to accept the account offered by Polixenes by way of a revealing analogy: she won't plant gillyflowers any more than "were I painted I would wish/This youth should say 'twere well, and only therefore/Desire to breed by me."[43] Other writers than Shakespeare bring the art-nature debate down to earth by way of horticultural examples, and the garden manuals of seventeenth-century England provide a particularly productive medium in which to trace the effects of thought about nature and culture on notions of inheritance, including a series of powerful redefinitions of the meaning of breeding.[44] Because it chronicles the restoration of individuals to their proper place in the social order, romance as a genre tends to fall on the side of nature rather than culture. (Romance may of course use nature to expel individuals as well as to restore them to their places, a hereditarian streak marked in Prospero's vicious description of Caliban in *The Tempest* as "[a] devil, a born devil, on whose nature/Nurture can never stick."[45]) The assertion of natural over cultural identity, though, is accompanied in *The Winter's Tale* by arguments about the relationship between nature and culture that tend somewhat to undercut nature's authority, arguments articulated in this important instance in horticultural rather than human terms.

The desire to explore parallels between people and vegetables comes through very strongly in a great deal of seventeenth-century writing. Rebecca Bushnell has outlined the early modern humanist engagement in debates about "how much both a plant's and a person's nature could be altered or improved by cultivation," and such discussions often draw on quite technical material about inheritance in plants and humans.[46] Indeed, the language used to describe plants is often heavily anthropomorphizing, with results that are telling as well as sometimes quite strange, given the widespread confusion about the principles of reproduction in animals and vegetables. Defined by one contemporary of Shakespeare's as "[t]he reforming of the Fruit of one Tree with the fruit of another, by an artificiall transplacing or transposing of a twigge, budde, or leafe,"[47] grafting (or "graffing," as it is often spelled) is necessary to propagate plants that will not breed true from seed. In the words of one recent writer, every seed in every apple "contains the genetic instructions for a completely new and different apple tree, one that, if planted, would bear only the most glancing resemblance to its parents. If not for grafting—the ancient technique of cloning trees—every apple in the world would be its own distinct variety, and it would be impossible to keep a good one going beyond the life span of that particular tree."[48] The rise of the new experimental science in seventeenth-century England would prompt more thoroughgoing inquiries than ever before into the theory and practice of grafting, inquiries conducted both within and alongside an eclectic, often bizarre literature on gardening. Both the more obviously "polite" scientific writing and the garden books reveal how strongly grafting is associated with broad social questions about securing the passage of property from parents to offspring, controlling and limiting mixture between different social classes, and exploring the role of sex in reproduction of all kinds.

The usefulness of grafting as a metaphor for all sorts of highly loaded political and theological topics was well established by this point: both the Old and New Testaments are steeped in horticultural imagery, and Augustine uses the fact that cultivated olive trees produce only wild olive trees, not cultivated ones, as (in the words of Elizabeth A. Clark) his "preferred metaphor to describe the transmission of sin," one which "bolsters the principle that regenerated (i.e., baptized Christian) parents do not transmit to their children the state of their 'rebirth,' but their old 'carnal' natures."[49] (The book's next chapter will take up the question of original sin—of whether man is sinful by *imitation* or by *descent*—as it would be transformed by Locke and others into a scientific conversation about innate qualities whose resolutely secular tone only partly obscures its religious provenance.)

Grafting also raised questions about likenesses between parents and offspring that seemed closely akin to those arising from observations about resemblance and legitimacy in the human world. Published in 1671, Jane Sharp's *The Midwives Book; or, The Whole Art of Midwifry Discovered. Directing Childbearing Women how to behave themselves in their Conception, Breeding, Bearing, and Nursing of Children* explains "the resemblance or likeness of Children and Parents" by an appeal to the idea (supported by the evidence of Jacob's ewes) that "Imagination is powerful in all living creatures."[50] "Plants being grafted, experience shews will bear fruit of the nature of the graft," Sharp goes on to say—so far, so good—then asserts, "but the kernels of that fruit sowed will bring fruit like the stock it was grafted on. Graft an Apricock on a Pear stock you shall have Apricocks, but a stone of those Apricocks set grows a Pear stock. If the forming faculty be free, children will be like their Parents, but if it be overpowred or wrested by imagination, the form will follow the stronger faculty."[51] The mistaken claim that the seeds of the scion will produce fruit like the stock's (a kind of reversion to nature) is made analogous to the operations of resemblance between parents and children, though the analogy is somewhat confusing or contradictory. Sharp seems to imply that grafting and the maternal imagination are alike insofar as they both wrench nature out of her course, overriding the operations of a mysterious "forming faculty" that would otherwise transmit likeness from one generation to the next. Her mistaken assumption that the seeds of the scion will revert to the stock suggests a desire to reassert the power of lineage (albeit through the maternal line) in a world where lines of descent have become increasingly hard to trace.

By the middle of the eighteenth century, the science of the earlier age had come to seem obsolete, even ridiculous. In the 1778 edition of Shakespeare's plays that he co-edited with Samuel Johnson, for instance, George Steevens annotated Perdita's "There is an art" speech with the irritable observation that "[t]his art is pretended to be taught at the ends of some of the old books that treat of cookery, &c. but being utterly impracticable is not worth exemplification."[52] This sense of the scientific allusions being outdated and absurd may account for the Perdita-Polixenes exchange being left out of all the contemporary stage adaptations; the only one of the later eighteenth-century adaptations to retain the art-nature debate in anything like its original form is by Charles Marsh, and was not intended for the stage.[53] John Philip Kemble's important 1802 production of *The Winter's Tale,* though it was famous for restoring much of the text excised from the previous century's versions, nonetheless omitted the art-nature debate, and theater

historians note that the passage is absent from many twentieth-century productions as well.[54]

To the best of my knowledge, the passage is not singled out by any of Shakespeare's major eighteenth- or nineteenth-century commentators, and it was cut
from most if not all of the major stage revivals before the early twentieth century.
Indeed, the now-famous "art-nature" debate seems to have been of virtually no
interest to critics or adapters until Harold Wilson published an essay titled "'Nature and Art' in *Winter's Tale* IV.iv.86ff" in the *Shakespeare Association Bulletin* in
1943, whereupon others scrambled to attend to the passage and its implications.[55]
Important pre–World War II discussions do not mention the passage, even as
they note the relative neglect of *The Winter's Tale* and call for a reappraisal of its
merits,[56] whereas discussions subsequent to the 1943 publication of Wilson's essay
home in on the passage with disconcerting consistency.[57]

What lies behind the long-term lack of interest in what has seemed a crucial
passage to readers over the last sixty or so years? It may be that the debate has always appealed more to readers than to theatergoers, but it is also possible that eigh-
teenth- and nineteenth-century Anglo-American theatrical adapters shared with
their audiences a general conviction that art—in its incarnation as technology—
had *already* triumphed over nature, that Polixenes' defense of art had become redundant and Perdita's reservations outmoded. The social implications of Polixenes' argument seem to some extent to have been naturalized, incorporated in
other ways into the adaptations. It also seems possible that Wilson and other critics of the 1940s were alerted to the force of the passage in part by the new prominence of genetics, the literary-critical development coming ten or fifteen years
after the few first significant histories of plant hybridization and genetics, which
are themselves consequent upon the rediscovery of Mendel's work at the turn of
the century and subsequent rapid expansions in the life sciences.[58] Readers in
the 1940s were accordingly primed, as their eighteenth- and nineteenth-century
predecessors had not been, for a renewed appreciation of the social implications
of horticultural theories of inheritance: for seeing the ways in which *The Winter's
Tale* takes conversations about bastardy, mixing, and inheritance into the garden.

### "Her royal image stampt on thee"

What was it, though, that eighteenth-century audiences took away from this
particular play of Shakespeare's, with its suggestive but contradictory messages
about patterns of likeness and mechanisms of inheritance? *The Winter's Tale* was

seen most frequently in the second half of the eighteenth century in one of three versions: Macnamara Morgan's *The Sheep-Shearing; or, Florizel and Perdita,* first staged in 1754 and published in 1762; David Garrick's *Florizel and Perdita,* first staged in 1756 and published in 1758; and George Colman's *The Sheep-Shearing,* published in 1777.[59] One theater historian has described Morgan's as the main version and Garrick's as the main competitor, and both adapters clearly facilitated the transformation of Shakespeare's account of aristocratic inheritance under threat into an endorsement of a new model of English breeding, one that emphasized middle-class manners and values and asserted that daughters inherit more from their mothers than their fathers.[60]

Rather as readers in the 1940s saw the play's horticultural passages in striking relief, so eighteenth-century readers seem to have been drawn to the germ of the play's argument about domestic life in families. I will say only a few words about Morgan's adaptation of *The Winter's Tale* and its wholesale sentimental celebration of middle-class domesticity. His Perdita wishes that Florizel were "some peasant swain,/Born lowly as [herself]," so that they could "live/Unknown, unenvied in [their] humble state,/Content with love beneath the cottage straw" (6): the trick, of course, is that Perdita is a princess as well as a perfectly modest middle-class young woman. Florizel will find in his bride the best of both worlds, Antigonus states: a princess by blood, "bred, unknowing of her state,/With virtues that may well adorn a throne" (20). This is a way of having one's cake and eating it too: Perdita is a princess by birth, "bred" in a modesty perhaps unavailable to upper-class women, yet equally untainted by baseness since the shepherd who raised her is here really a nobleman in disguise.

Of more pressing interest, especially because of its telling revision to the tropes of familial resemblance but also because of the actor and theatrical impresario's unique status as influential cultural arbiter, is David Garrick's *Florizel and Perdita.* While Garrick retains more of the original play than Morgan, including Leontes' jealous tirades (the part was one of Garrick's showcase roles) and the statue scene at the end, it is in many ways a less intelligent version than Morgan's; Michael Dobson has called it "a priggish, corrective revision of Macnamara Morgan's bawdier adaptation" and points to its "full-scale celebration of the sanctified nuclear family."[61] The sentiments expressed by Garrick's characters are irreproachable to the point of banality, as this sample of Perdita's song (interpolated into the sheep-shearing scene) shows:

> By mode and caprice are the city dames led,
> But we, as the children of nature are bred;

By her hand alone, we are painted and dress'd;
For the roses will bloom, when there's peace in the breast. (23)

This is a familiar opposition between city and country manners. In contrast to
the corrupt and luxurious manners of the town, Perdita identifies those of herself
and her country peers as having only the art that nature makes (the language
obliquely revises the omitted lines of Polixenes): they are "bred" or raised as the
children of nature. When Florizel, under his father's threat to disinherit him,
promises Perdita that they will fly together to a place "[w]here no base views our
purer minds shall move;/And all our wealth be innocence and love" (41), he proposes a retreat from worldly realms of money and power, and at the play's conclusion, when all is happily resolved, he asks Perdita to "[b]e still my queen of *May*,
my shepherdess,/Rule in my heart; my wishes be thy subjects,/And harmless as
thy sheep" (66). Metaphorically, at least, he subjects his own desires to his wife's
governance, rendering them harmless as her flock of sheep, and it is clear that
Perdita's authority within the house and the marriage will have to compensate her
for the loss of the power to rule in her own right that will accompany her marriage
to Florizel.

In Shakespeare's play, both male and female children are described in terms of
their resemblance to the father: Shakespeare's Perdita may also resemble Hermione, but nobody comments as concretely on her resemblance to her mother as
on how much she looks like her father.[62] As I said earlier, Paulina notes the baby
Perdita's resemblance to Leontes when she asks the court to behold in Perdita,
"Although the print be little, the whole matter/And copy of the father" (2.3.99–
100), and for Shakespeare, it is fathers, not mothers, whose form stamps their
offspring, as when Leontes later compliments the grown-up Florizel by telling
him that his mother must have been true to her husband, "For she did print your
royal father off,/Conceiving you" (5.1.124–125). Shakespeare's focus on the child's
resemblance to the male rather than the female parent makes sense within the
conceptual framework of early seventeenth-century theories of generation: it was
not that observers from Aristotle onward had not *noticed* the puzzle that a child
may look like any one of his or her forebears, male or female, but the dominant
theories of generation did not offer a satisfactory account of that fact.

Garrick makes an extraordinary revision to Shakespeare's language, one that
would seem inexplicable without knowledge of the investigations into generation conducted during the intervening years but that has broader social and cultural implications as well. His Leontes observes of Perdita that "whilst I gaze
upon/This pretty abstract of *Hermione*,/So truly printed off, I can't forget/My

blemishes in them" (57). This sentence could scarcely have been written in Shakespeare's time: in the preferred theories of generation, the daughter could not have been printed off the mother, for the father provided the form for both sons and daughters.[63] In other words, Garrick's phrasing echoes Shakespeare's, but he departs radically from the tradition of Aristotelian thought on generation, in which there is no real mechanism for the daughter to be printed off the mother, except insofar as the power of the mother's imagination (jokingly referred to in *The Winter's Tale* when Autolycus invokes the ballad of the usurer's wife who gave birth to moneybags) acts as a wild card, introducing unexpected physical traits in the offspring.[64] Garrick's transformation of the image cannot be careless or accidental, moreover, for he does it *again:* at the unveiling of Hermione's "statue," Garrick's Perdita comments that twenty years would not be too long a time to stand and admire it, and Florizel adds, "So long cou'd I / Admire her royal image stampt on thee, / Heiress of all her qualities" (62). Here Garrick adopts the more conventional word "stampt," as opposed to Shakespeare's very distinctive conflation of physical reproduction with the terminology of the new technology of print, but the revision of Shakespeare's trope is unmistakable.[65]

A hundred and fifty years after the first appearance of *The Winter's Tale*, British writers had come to a very different understanding of the meanings of family. Ruth Perry has recently traced in the novels of later eighteenth-century Britain a significant movement from the earlier period's "axis of kinship based on consanguineal ties or blood lineage to an axis based on conjugal and affinal ties of the married couple. That is, the biologically given family into which one was born was gradually becoming secondary to the chosen family constructed by marriage." Perry sees the popularity of sentimental fiction in this period, full as it is of reunions and reconciliations between lost family members, as "compensatory—evidence of persistent nostalgia for what had been lost in a changing society," suggesting that such fiction glorified and "sentimentalized the consanguineal basis for obligation that was being phased out in the new dispensation."[66] The broad social changes of the intervening century and a half—the enclosure of common lands, the commercialization of agriculture and the growth of industry, migration from country to city, and political transformations at both the national and local levels, as well as changes in the law's regulation of marriage and inheritance—provide an important context for Garrick's striking revision of the mechanisms of genetic inheritance as Shakespeare presented them.[67] Cause and effect are difficult to disentangle here, but common sense suggests a feedback loop in which socioeconomic transformations affect legislation and guide observations of the natural world, also prompting new ideas or interpretations that may in turn augment ongoing social changes. Programs of scientific inquiry are themselves clearly inflected by the sociopolitical issues of the day, but literary and scientific responses to such issues also participate in or even at times instigate further changes.

In spite of a general practical acknowledgment that children might look like either of their parents, a strong theory of biparental heredity really emerged only in the 1740s in France, and would remain highly controversial in the decades following.[68] Ovism saw a resurgence of popularity at mid-century and the ovist version of preformation was not really abandoned until late in the century. The explanatory schemes surrounding resemblance and the relations between parent and offspring, which stayed more or less recognizable between the late classical period and the late sixteenth century, have in other words by this point been radically disrupted by experiments and theories in generation, leaving a free-for-all, a brawl in which no single one out of a number of competing and often incompatible theories decisively dominates, though ovist preformation on the whole prevails over its competitors. In this environment, one in which generation is at once of compelling (almost paramount) intellectual interest and yet still quite enigmatic, people write their desires into theories of generation more clearly than into most other aspects of science and culture.

The plot of *The Winter's Tale*—with its story of a princess lost and found and its complex argument about the meanings of breeding—provides a powerful framework for articulating arguments about personal identity in relation to the social world, particularly as to whether social differences are natural or acquired. Garrick's revision to Shakespeare can in this regard be thought of as generating a kind of "soft" ovism.[69] His imagination—powerful but also highly conventional— would seem not to encompass the idea that his pastoral princess looks more like her father than her mother, if only because the shared fact of femaleness trumps other relations of resemblance.

Indeed, if we jump forward to consider some other popular fictions of later eighteenth-century Britain, there seems to be a new preoccupation (amounting almost to an obsession) with the idea that daughters look like their mothers.[70] Frances Burney's first novel, *Evelina*, published in 1778, tells the history of a young lady's entrance into the world, including her attempt to claim her identity as the legitimate daughter of Sir John Belmont, who has never acknowledged her. It emerges that Evelina has been displaced by an imposter: a wet-nurse substituted her own child for the baby Evelina, a child subsequently raised privately by Sir John as his own daughter. Yet Sir John's conviction that Evelina herself must be the imposter is exploded when they meet face-to-face and he sees her resemblance to her dead mother: "My God! does Caroline Evelyn still live! . . . lift up thy head, thou image of my long-lost Caroline!," he tells Evelina in their third-volume reunion. Here Burney clearly patterns her novel on *The Winter's Tale*, with the economical reformulation that the reconciliation of the father with his cast-off daughter is united with the coming-to-life of the dead mother in the person of the daughter. Now that the truth has emerged, the reader learns that Sir John Belmont "had *always* observed that his daughter bore no resemblance of either of her parents, but, as he had never doubted the veracity of the nurse, this circumstance did not give birth to any suspicion."[71] The novel solves the problem of having two pretenders to the same role by having "both the real and the fictitious daughter married without delay."[72]

Elizabeth Inchbald's *A Simple Story* (1791) is even more clearly indebted than Burney's novel to *The Winter's Tale*, as its title suggests. A story of separation and reconciliation over two generations, the novel is split into two halves, the first following the misfortunes of the mother, and the second those of the daughter. The Catholic priest Dorriforth, appointed guardian of the charming but wayward Miss Milner, inherits the title of Lord Elmwood and is then released from his vows for the sake of the greater good of the Catholic Church in England. The ex-priest's marriage to his ward Miss Milner is doomed from the start. The second part begins with the revelation that after giving birth to their child, Lady Elmwood committed adultery and was cast out, along with their legitimate daughter, Matilda, by Lord Elmwood, who swore to banish Matilda forever from his sight. A deathbed request from her mother to her father finds Matilda living under her father's roof but only on the condition that she literally stay out of his sight. Deprived of any contact in person, Matilda feels an extraordinary affinity for her father's painted portrait:

> In the features of her father she was proud to discern the exact moulds in which her own appeared to have been modelled; yet Matilda's person, shape, and complexion were so extremely like what her mother's once were, that at the first glance she appeared to have a still greater resemblance to her, than of her father—but her mind and manners were all Lord Elmwood's; softened by the delicacy of her sex, the extreme tenderness of her heart, and the melancholy of her situation.[73]

Inchbald seems to be torn here between the general propriety of a daughter resembling her mother more than her father (the Georgian middle-class consensus, underwritten by contemporary theories of generation and by the socioeconomic transformations that nudged Britain away from blood kinship toward a conjugal model) and the need to insist that Matilda looks like her father in order to ensure that Miss Milner's adultery casts no retroactive shadows on Matilda's legitimacy. This leads to some awkward contortions. In an accidental encounter some chapters later, Matilda faints into her father's arms. He catches her and tries to rouse her: "Her name did not however come to his recollection—nor any name but this—'Miss Milner—Dear Miss Milner'" (3.14 [255]). Yet Inchbald also writes that Matilda's features have "the most striking resemblance" to her father's (4.7 [294]). In reality, of course, a child can bear a striking resemblance to both parents, but we expect novels to streamline such facts, to simplify and make sense of them for us. In the end, Inchbald uses the mother-daughter pair to perform a kind of experiment in the interplay of nature and nurture: the adultery and inevitable unhappy death of Miss Milner demonstrate "the pernicious effects of an improper education," in contrast to the happier product of "that school of prudence—though of adversity—in which Matilda was bred" (4.12 [318]).[74]

For writers of the 1790s and beyond, the novel would become the genre most suited to working out systematic arguments about the effects of external influence, and especially of education, on whatever germ might reside within the growing child, a focus on the interactions of nature and culture widespread enough to give rise to the generic subcategory of the *Bildungsroman*, or novel of education. It is hardly an exaggeration to identify novels like *A Simple Story* as one point of origin of the now familiar opposition between nature and nurture that would be articulated and consolidated by Francis Galton and others in the later nineteenth century. Charles Darwin's list of his own reading in 1840 included not just *A Simple Story* but *Sense and Sensibility* (1811) and *Mansfield Park* (1814), surely the two novels of Jane Austen's that most obviously play with the interactions of nature and nurture.[75] One historian of theories of generation observes that "while modern genetics is, logically, the successful heir to the seventeenth and eighteenth century investigations into generation, there is not much historical connection between the two enquiries. The gap during the early nineteenth century was too great."[76] When the old problems resurface late in the nineteenth century, most scientists are ignorant of the earlier theories: Thomas Huxley is an exception, as are a few others, but Darwin knew little or nothing of the seventeenth- and eighteenth-century controversies alluded to here. Literary texts, though, retained a palimpsest of these arguments, providing one means by which Darwin and others could gain access to the knowledge of earlier generations.

A coda: it is worth pointing out that while the early nineteenth-century French scientist Lamarck is ridiculed in science textbooks for believing in the inheritance of acquired characters—as in the familiar illustration of the theory involving a giraffe whose neck becomes longer by reaching up to eat leaves higher on the tree and who then passes that longer neck on to his descendants—the belief that mutilations and other acquired traits were passed on to offspring was shared by most scientists through the end of the nineteenth century and in some cases into the twentieth. Darwin believed in it, and in 1868 explained it (in conjunction with hereditary phenomena such as resemblance) by coining the term "pangenesis" to describe a hypothesis that "implies that every separate part of the whole organisation reproduces itself" by means of "a multitude of germs thrown off from each separate part or unit" of the body.[77] Indeed, L.C. Dunn comments in his history of genetics on the persistence of the theory well into the twentieth century: "Belief in the possibility of the inheritance of acquired characters survived in the face of lack of evidence long after Mendel's principle and the better knowledge of mutation had made such an assumption generally unnecessary."[78]

A rigorous refutation of the belief that acquired characters could be inherited would have to await the pen of August Weismann, whose devastating critique of the theory echoes a host of earlier discussions of the topic while very frequently turning them on their heads. In an essay titled "The Supposed Transmission of Mutilations" (1888), Weismann provides a remarkably elegant refutation of the argument that acquired characters are passed on to offspring.[79] His discussion makes it very clear both that the revival of Lamarckism (supported by Darwin's development of the theory of pangenesis) was a dominant feature of the contemporary scientific landscape and that this theory was very closely linked to a continuing belief in the power of the maternal imagination. Weismann proposes a series of systematic experiments in mice as the initial step necessary for disproving the hypothesis, but he also observes with regard to humans that "the mutilations of certain parts of the human body, as practised by different nations from times immemorial, have, in not a single instance, led to the malformation or reduction of the parts in question. Such hereditary effects have been produced neither by circumcision, nor the removal of the front teeth, nor the boring of holes in the lips or nose, nor the extraordinary artificial crushing and crippling of the feet of Chinese women."[80]

"Not every *post hoc* is also a *propter hoc*," Weismann argues. "Nothing illustrates this better than a comparison between the 'proofs' which are even now brought forward in favour of the transmission of mutilations and the 'proofs' which supported the belief in the efficacy of so-called 'maternal impressions' during pregnancy, a belief which was universally maintained up to the middle of the present century" (443–444). He notes that only one year earlier a respectable scientific journal had reprinted an 1864 story about a pregnant merino sheep who broke her right foreleg and gave birth four months later to a lamb that "'possessed a ring of black wool from two to three inches in breadth round the place at which the mother's leg had been broken, and upon the same leg'":

> Now if we even admitted that a ring of black wool could be looked upon as a character which corresponds to the fracture of the mother's leg, the case could not possibly be interpreted as the transmission of a mutilation, but as an instance of the efficacy of maternal impressions; for the ewe was already pregnant when she fractured her leg. The present state of biological science teaches us that, with the fusion of egg and sperm-cell, potential heredity is determined.... Such tales, when quoted as 'remarkable facts which prove the transmission of mutilations,' thoroughly deserve the contempt with which they have been received by Kant and His. When the above-mentioned instance was told me, I replied, "It is a pity that the black wool was not arranged in the form of the inscription 'To the memory of the fractured leg of my dear mother.'" (446–447)

No theory could survive such an assault—and yet Weismann's radical skepticism is matched by a wry awareness of how attractive such explanations can be: "The readiness with which we may be deceived is shown by the fact that I myself nearly became a victim during the past year (1888)," he confesses, telling the story of a friend whose ear is marked by a scar from a dueling sword and whose daughter has a very similar mark on her ear (442). Only when Weismann looks at the friend's other ear and notices it has the same ridge does he recognize the mark as a hereditary rather than an acquired character, and the ruefulness with which he narrates the episode speaks to the ease with which resemblance gives itself over to certain kinds of wishful thinking. The detail of its being a dueling scar is also wonderfully evocative as an illustration of the values of an aristocratic past crashing up against the forces of scientific modernity, a detail that grounds even the vibrant modern voice of Weismann's essay in a social world still richly in possession of historical fantasies about resemblance as a form of attachment to the past.

## 2

## Bent

Addressing the age-old question of whether it is nature or nurture that has a more profound effect on character, Steven Pinker asserts in *The Blank Slate: The Modern Denial of Human Nature* (2002) that the debate is mostly over: in the face of recent developments in the life sciences, he argues, opponents of sociobiology and evolutionary psychology can fall back only on massively outdated concepts of human nature—the Blank Slate, the Noble Savage—invented by the writers of the European Enlightenment.[1] In retrospect, the seesaw probably tipped in nature's favor (at least in the United States) roughly forty years ago, beginning with the publication of work by Noam Chomsky, Ernst Mayr, and others, and continuing with such controversial publications as Arthur Jensen's 1969 essay "How Much Can We Boost I.Q. and Scholastic Achievement?" in the *Harvard Educational Review* and E. O. Wilson's *Sociobiology: The New Synthesis* in 1975. Roger Shattuck observes in his 1980 book about feral children that "the theory of innate human capacities shaping our grasp of reality and therefore our behavior has made a strong comeback against the theory of the *tabula rasa*," and the trend has gained ever-greater momentum with the ongoing development of new technologies of the gene.[2]

Pinker has consistently presented himself as a voice of moderation in this controversy,[3] but though he implies that his own position on these matters is shared by most other scientists, many of his professional peers are inclined to question the overweening dominance of the gene in such an explanatory scheme.[4] Pinker also seriously misrepresents Locke's notion of the blank slate. In fact, throughout Locke's writing the idea that children should be considered "only as white Paper, or Wax, to be moulded and fashioned as one pleases" is balanced by an acknowledgment that individual children possess "various Tempers, different Inclinations, and particular Defaults": "God has stampt certain Characters upon Mens Minds," Locke writes in *Some Thoughts Concerning Education* (1693), "which, like their Shapes, may perhaps be a little mended; but can hardly be totally alter'd, and transform'd into the contrary."[5] Despite general acceptance of the blank slate as a suggestive metaphor for a child's mind, in other words, the vast majority of eighteenth-century discussions allow for natural differences between individuals, admitting innate qualities in the guise of "Dispositions" or "Inclinations," as when John Lawson writes in his *Lectures Concerning Oratory* (1758) that "[t]he Air and Features of every Individual in the human Species are different: Not less Diversity is observable in their Minds: Their Dispositions, their Likings, their Powers also are altogether different."[6]

It is true that writers of the period tend to emphasize experience over blood. Even Samuel Johnson, no great admirer of Locke's, "allowed very great influence to education," according to his biographer James Boswell: "'I do not deny, Sir, but there is some original difference in minds,'" Boswell quotes Johnson as saying; "'but it is nothing in comparison of what is formed by education.'"[7] But both Locke's own writings and the great preponderance of eighteenth-century discussions (the exceptions would be the extreme associationists like Hartley and Helvétius) balance experience against propensities, inclinations, and the "bent" of a person's mind.[8] My own frustration with Pinker's position, aside from a temperamental dislike for what seems like intellectual bullying, stems in part from my sense that scholars in the humanities have largely failed to provide thoughtful or persuasive answers to Pinker's admittedly infuriating challenge to liberal-humanist conceptions of human nature. The stakes associated with such questions remain exceedingly high: "[A]ny persuasive theory about human nature," as one recent commentator observes, "is bound to become the basis for policies—about child-rearing, social mobility, educational selection, immigration, even war and peace; and such policies may underwrite radical programs of social engineering."[9] And yet answers to contemporary questions about breeding (a rubric that enfolds topics as various as the nature of biological differences between the sexes and the ethics of genetic modification in plants, animals, and people) seem still to be blocked by a set of unproductive deadlocks: between the political right and the political left, between the sciences and the humanities, and most of all between a hard-core sociobiology that automatically turns to genes for explanations of human behavior and a diehard liberalism—often depicted as unscientific, wishy-washy, and naive—that attributes almost everything to nurture.

Part of this mutual incomprehension arises from lack of contact and conversation between the disciplines. Revisiting C. P. Snow's famous 1959 question as to what should be done about the rift between the "two cultures" of science and the arts, Jonah Lehrer regretfully observes that "the third culture of today," rather than referring (as Snow had hoped) "to a dialogue between artists and scientists," instead describes "scientists who communicate directly with the general public." Though Lehrer finds this development in many respects praiseworthy, he also identifies its "serious limitations," including the tendency of many such scientists to "take a one-dimensional view of the scientific enterprise and its relationship to the humanities," to express antagonism toward the nonscientific, and indeed often to "argue that art is a symptom of our biology, and that anything that isn't experimental is just entertainment."[10] (Many humanists are just as dismissive of the sciences, often as an unhappy consequence of battles for scarce resources.)

Story-telling of the kind I do in this book is scarcely a substitute for scientific investigation. The explanations seventeenth- and eighteenth-century observers give for the phenomena associated with breeding in all its definitions have been superseded by better ones, and I am well aware of the objection, as one reader of this book in manuscript wryly phrased it, "that at some point all the false teleologies have to drop away when the train of science comes roaring down the track." But the ways we understand and explain new developments in science are profoundly inflected by older framings of similar questions. One thing that became disconcertingly clear to me over the course of writing this book, for instance, was the extent to which even the most secular eighteenth-century British writers perceive breeding to be in the shadow of explicitly theological arguments about original sin. Locke's "custom" and "experience" are consistently balanced by a language of "bent" or "bias": a vocabulary that, though it seems neutral with respect to religion, takes us fairly directly to the arena where the controversy concerning original sin was staged. As Augustine and his successors framed it, the debate over man's nature centered exactly on the question of whether man's sinfulness was a matter of birth or whether he chose freely to sin (in which case sin could be considered "actual" rather than "original"). Locke retains this crux in important structural respects even as he moves, in his arguments and definitions, further away from such a vocabulary. Not just the long history of the debate but the magnitude of what's at stake suggests that breeding poses questions that cannot be considered exclusively scientific—at the very least, philosophers and theologians have a right to demur at their being left out of the conversation.

One surprising feature, at least for modern readers, of the associationist model of the human mind developed by Locke and his successors is that it should have proved so compatible with a belief in the meaningful nature of social distinctions, or of birth in the sense that separates, say, a gentleman's son from the son of an artisan. In theory, the emphasis on experience over innate ideas is profoundly leveling, and some later writers would draw out the egalitarian strand in Lockean psychology. In practice, although the leveling aspect is there, Locke's writings also include quite explicit discussions both of the kinds of "natural" distinction that might separate an unintelligent person from an intelligent one and of the other kinds of "natural" distinction that underpin property arrangements. As modern egalitarians (at least notionally), we may have to fight a tendency to orient ourselves wishfully to an anachronistic vision of Lockean psychology, for Locke's arguments about intellectual and temperamental differences between individuals find close equivalents in his assertions about which people deserve to gain the privileges of full-fledged membership in civil society, a pragmatic set of arguments about social difference articulated more explicitly in his writings on education than in the relatively disembodied discussions of mind in the *Essay Concerning Human Understanding* (1690).

## The Blank Slate

In the opening book of the *Essay,* Locke is most immediately concerned to refute the common assumption that the human mind contains innate ideas. That is far from being the same thing as suggesting that all minds are the same as each other at life's outset. "I deny not, that there are natural tendencies imprinted on the Minds of Men," he explains; "and that, from the very first instances of Sense and Perception, there are some things, that are grateful, and others unwelcome to them; some things that they incline to, and others that they fly: But this makes  nothing for innate Characters on the Mind, which are to be the Principles of Knowledge, regulating our Practice."[11] His target is the absurdity of the notion that the more specific propositions of contemporary logic should be considered in any sense innate. "Who perceives not," he asks later on, "that a Child certainly knows, that a Stranger is not its Mother; that its Sucking-bottle is not the Rod, long before he knows, that *'tis impossible for the same thing to be, and not to be?*" (4.7.595). Neither can religious belief be a function of "innate *Ideas*" of God bestowed on us by the deity, although this need not pose a profound challenge to religious faith: "[T]hough he has stamped no original Characters on our Minds, wherein we may read his Being: yet having furnished us with those Faculties, our Minds are endowed with, he hath not left himself without witness: since we have Sense, Perception, and Reason, and cannot want a clear proof of him, as long as we carry our selves about us" (4.10.619).

Locke's self-appointed task is to work through the logical consequences of the notion that we have no innate ideas, which among other things involves making the case for the importance of outside or environmental influences:

> Let us then suppose the Mind to be, as we say, white Paper, void of all Characters, without any *Ideas;* How comes it to be furnished? Whence comes it by that vast store, which the busy and boundless Fancy of Man has painted on it, with an almost endless variety? Whence has it all the materials of Reason and Knowledge? To this I answer, in one word, From *Experience:* In that, all our Knowledge is founded; and from that it ultimately derives it self. (2.1.104)[12]

The image of the mind as "white Paper, void of all Characters," to be inscribed by experience, is not man's exclusively. Locke is strongly interested in exploring similarities between people and animals, and perhaps even in thinking of man as an animal, as when he illuminates aspects of man's nature by noting that other animals have the "faculty of laying up, and retaining the *Ideas,* that are brought into the Mind": "Birds learning of Tunes, and the endeavours one may observe in them, to hit the Notes right, put it past doubt with me," he writes, "that they have Perception, and retain *Ideas* in their Memories, and use them for Patterns" (2.10.154). (Birds would also provide evidence, for some of Locke's contemporaries and successors, in support of the existence of significant differences between individual members of a given species: one rather typical handbook asserts that "in all Birds of the same kind, there is as much difference as between skimm'd Milk-Cheese and Cream, both being Cheese," and another that "[s]ome *Canary-Birds* are much more apt to learn than others."[13])

Experience works in the mind by way of custom, and education or custom can be held accountable for many of the things commonly attributed to nature. "Custom settles habits of Thinking in the Understanding, as well as of Determining in the Will, and of Motions in the Body," Locke writes (this passage would be echoed in the famous opening to *Tristram Shandy* that is given as this book's epigraph); "all which seems to be but Trains of Motion in the Animal Spirits, which once set a going continue on in the same steps they have been used to, which by often treading are worn into a smooth path, and the Motion in it becomes easy and as it were Natural" (2.33.396). To the association of ideas made by custom "might be justly attributed most of the Sympathies and Antipathies observable in Men, which work as strongly, and produce as regular Effects as if they were Natural, and are therefore called so, though they at first had no other Original but the accidental Connexion of two *Ideas*" (2.33.396):

> I say most of the Antipathies, I do not say all, for some of them are truly Natural, depend upon our original Constitution, and are born with us; but a great part of those which are counted Natural, would have been known to be from unheeded, though, perhaps, early Impressions, or wanton Phancies at first, which would have been acknowledged the Original of them if they had been warily observed. A grown Person surfeiting with Honey, no sooner hears the Name of it, but his Phancy immediately carries Sickness and Qualms to his Stomach, and he cannot bear the very *Idea* of it; other *Ideas* of Dislike and Sickness, and Vomiting presently accompany it, and he is disturb'd, but he knows from whence to date this Weakness, and can tell how he got this Indisposition: Had this happen'd to him, by an over dose of Honey, when a Child, all the same Effects would have followed, but the Cause would have been mistaken, and the Antipathy counted Natural. (2.33.396–397)

"[A]s it were Natural," "as if they were Natural": Locke is a distinctly reserved and self-aware language-user whose word choices show a keen sense of the problems with conventional invocations of the term *nature*. It is also worth noting the intense pragmatism of his observations about the difficulty of distinguishing natural from acquired elements in someone's constitution: "I mention this not out of any great necessity there is in this present Argument, to distinguish nicely between Natural and Acquired Antipathies," he says, "but I take notice of it for another purpose, (*viz.*) that those who have Children, or the charge of their Education, would think it worth their while diligently to watch, and carefully to prevent the undue Connexion of *Ideas* in the Minds of young People" (2.33.397).

It should be clear from all this that Locke is far from being the doctrinaire asserter of exact equivalence between individuals that Pinker and others who take the metaphor of the blank slate literally want to assert. Elsewhere, Locke quite explicitly (and perhaps with mild satirical animus) takes off the table the question of innate versus acquired characteristics on the grounds that it cannot be answered:

> Now that there is such a difference between Men, in respect of their Understandings, I think no body, who has had any Conversation with his Neighbours,

will question: though he never was at *Westminster-hall,* or the *Exchange* on the one hand; nor at *Alms-Houses,* or *Bedlam* on the other. Which great difference in Men's Intellectuals, whether it rises from any defect in the Organs of the Body, particularly adapted to Thinking; or in the dulness or untractableness of those Faculties, for want of use; or, as some think, in the natural differences of Men's Souls themselves; or some, or all of these together, it matters not here to examine: Only this is evident, that there is a difference of degrees in Men's Understandings, Apprehensions, and Reasonings, to so great a latitude, that one may, without doing injury to Mankind, affirm, that there is a greater distance between some Men, and others, in this respect, than between some Men and some Beasts. But how this comes about, is a Speculation, though of great consequence, yet not necessary to our present purpose. (4.20.709)

Locke's temperamental preference for suspending the moment of decision-making is very much in evidence here.

The philosophical mode in which the *Essay* is composed to some extent limits the appropriateness of any discussion of real embodied people in the world. Elsewhere Locke tackles socially embedded individuals more directly, perhaps nowhere more clearly than in his writings on education. In *Some Thoughts Concerning Education* (1693), dedicated to the friend for whose son's education the work was initially composed, Locke says that he has been "consulted of late by . . . many, who profess themselves at a loss how to breed their Children," and justifies his publication of the book on the grounds that "Errours in Education should be less indulged than any: These, like Faults in the first Concoction, that are never mended in the second or third, carry their afterwards-incorrigible Taint with them, through all the parts and stations of Life" (79–80). His work is directed in particular to the obligations of "training up Youth" in "the Gentleman's Calling," due to the fact that "if those of that Rank are by their Education once set right, they will quickly bring all the rest into Order."

Somewhat at odds with his emphasis on the different callings, Locke clearly asserts that "the difference to be found in the Manners and Abilities of Men, is owing more to their *Education* than to any thing else," whence his insistence "that great care is to be had of the forming Children's *Minds,* and giving them that seasoning early, which shall influence their Lives always after" (103). Another word for that "seasoning" is habit; habits can be "wrought into the Mind" (111), he observes, the earlier the better, and qualities are made "habitual" and "settled" in the mind "by a continued Practice" (125). Which is not to say that differences between individual children aren't important too: the attempted inculcation of habits will teach the educator about the talents of his or her pupils, revealing

> whether what is requir'd of [the child] be adapted to his Capacity, and any way suited to the Child's natural Genius and Constitution; for that too must be consider'd in a right Education. We must not hope wholly to change their Original Tempers, nor make the Gay Pensive and Grave, nor the Melancholy Sportive, without spoiling them. God has stampt certain Characters upon Mens Minds, which, like their Shapes, may perhaps be a little mended; but can hardly be totally alter'd, and transform'd into the contrary. (122)

The educator is bound to consider the child's "*Temper*, and the particular Constitution of his Mind" (162), adapting his or her methods to the individual child (it's the language Locke offers for these inborn traits that especially interests me here):

> These *native Propensities*, these prevalencies of Constitution, are not to be cured by Rules, or a direct Contest; especially those of them that are the humbler and meaner sort, which proceed from fear, and lowness of Spirit; though with Art they may be much mended, and turned to good purposes. But this, be sure, after all is done, the Byass will always hang on that side, that Nature first placed it: And if you carefully observe the Characters of his Mind, now in the first Scenes of his Life, you will ever after be able to judge which way his Thoughts lean, and what he aims at, even hereafter, when, as he grows up, the Plot thickens, and he puts on several Shapes to act it. (163)

Locke draws on a whole host of words to describe inborn qualities: *temper, cast,* and *stamp* are drawn from a vocabulary associated with metal-working and its ilk, while *propensities, bias,* and *bent* conjure leanings horticultural and gravitational, a sapling or a weighted ball diverging from the straight and narrow. The last sentence of the passage quoted here—"the Plot thickens, and he puts on several Shapes to act it"—imports a language of theatricality like some long-lost ancestor of Erving Goffman's "presentation of self in everyday life."[14]

Locke clearly distinguishes between inborn talents and skills acquired by application (the terminology of talents and skills is my own attempt to clarify the distinction further): he speaks of children having "a Genius" to something (215) or of a strong memory "owing to an happy Constitution, and not to any habitual Improvement got by Exercise" (232), on the one hand, whereas in other cases certain abilities—a good example might be an unusual facility in written or spoken English—are inappropriately and unfairly attributed "to Chance, or [the child's] Genius, or any thing, rather than to his Education or any care of his Teacher" (244). One of Locke's strongest recommendations is that children be given free choice in their recreations, "That it will discover their Natural Tempers, shew their Inclinations, and Aptitudes; and thereby direct wise Parents in the choice, both of the course of Life, and Imployment they shall design them for, and of fit Remedies in the mean time to be applied to whatever bent of Nature, they may observe most likely to mislead any of their Children" (168–169). Thus *bent* can be seen to be loaded, as it were, rather than merely neutral (as it might now be used as a neutral synonym for something more like affinity or leaning, the title of Martin Sherman's 1979 play *Bent* notwithstanding).

Of course, different children will be inclined in very different directions. Locke does not aspire to set out "the general Method of Educating a young Gentleman" with "all those particulars, which his growing Years, or peculiar Temper may require" (194), or to "take in the various Tempers, different Inclinations, and particular Defaults, that are to be found in Children; and prescribe proper Remedies":

> The variety is so great, that it would require a Volume; nor would that reach it. Each Man's Mind has some peculiarity, as well as his Face, that distinguishes him from all others; and there are possibly scarce two Children, who can be conducted by exactly the same method. Besides that I think a Prince, a Nobleman, and an ordinary Gentleman's Son, should have different ways of Breeding. But having had here only some general Views, in reference to the main End, and aims in Education, and those designed for a Gentleman's Son, who being then very little, I considered only as white Paper, or Wax, to be moulded and fashioned as one pleases; I have touch'd little more than those Heads, which I judged necessary for the Breeding of a young Gentleman of his Condition in general[.] (265)

The general tendency of Locke's language, though, is to suggest that inborn tendencies or propensities are often best thought of as a "bent" to be straightened out:[15]

> As he grows up, the Tendency of his natural Inclination must be observed; which, as it inclines him, more than is convenient, on one or t'other side, from the right Path of Vertue, ought to have proper Remedies applied. For few of *Adam*'s Children are so happy, as not to be born with some Byass in their natu-

ral Temper, which is the Business of Education either to take off, or counter-balance. (198)

Though the language here is modern and secular rather than theological, Locke's mention of Adam reminds the reader that this superficially neutral language of "natural Inclination" or "Byass" may echo older conversations about man's inborn sinfulness.

## Sinners by Descent

As Locke's rather cunning invocation of the phrase "*Adam*'s Children" may suggest, even the most resolutely secular conversations conducted during this period about why people are the way they are and how they may be transformed by education or climate or custom (by *breeding* in the most inclusive sense) are only very *recently* secular. The hold such questions still have on us surely has to do with the fact of their being only the latest iteration of a many-centuries-old debate about human nature that was conducted, up until the late seventeenth century, primarily in theological terms.

In its most abbreviated form, the discussion conducted in the wake of Locke's writings of the transformative powers of education can be thought of as a late-breaking development in a conversation initiated by Augustine's writings against the Pelagian heresy. Crucial to Augustine's notion of original sin is that sin is actually transmitted in a hereditary fashion. For Augustine, writes Tatha Wiley, men are "sinners by descent, *generatione non imitatione,*" who "inherit original sin through physical conception."[16] A great deal was at stake, doctrinally speaking, in the question of whether sin was transmitted from one generation to the next by nature or by culture, a vexed point the Council of Trent's 1546 "Decree Concerning Original Sin" would attempt (and fail) to clarify. Here is the relevant part of the text of the decree's third canon, as given by S. Trooster: "If anyone asserts that this sin of Adam, which is one in origin and transmitted to all, is in each one as his own by propagation, not by imitation (*quod origine unum est et, propagatione non imitatione transfusum, omnibus inest unicuique proprium*), is taken away either by the forces of human nature, or by any remedy other than the merit of the one mediator . . . let him be anathema."[17] Trooster emphasizes the crucial nature of what he calls the "corrective formula" of "by descent, not by imitation," which "determines, in opposition to the Neo-Pelagian tendencies of the humanists, that original sin is not purely a personal sin consisting only in the personal imitation of

Adam's bad example" (13). The hostility toward sexual reproduction that may lurk behind such a position is often attributed to an Augustinian influence on later theologians, though it is hard to say whether a taste for Augustine's writings more plausibly precipitates anti-sex leanings or simply serves as an indicator that they are already present. Henri Rondet notes that it was only in Augustine's reformulation of arguments about the sin of Adam that generation became so important: the Augustinians found that "in the carnal use of marriage there was a kind of moral disorder which became, as it were, the effective sign of the transmission of sin," he points out, whereas the Pelagians "emphatically stated that carnal concupiscence is natural, willed by God, necessary for the propagation of the race."[18]

Though the term *perfectibility* itself seems only to have come into use during the eighteenth century (it is attributed to Turgot and was widely disseminated by Rousseau's *Discourse on Inequality*, published in 1755 and discussed later on in this book), the concept has a much longer history. In *The Perfectibility of Man* (1970), John Passmore shows very clearly the ways in which eighteenth-century treatments of man's perfectibility carry the traces of hundreds of years of Christian debate about sin and grace. The point of original sin is that it is visited on all of Adam's descendants; the hard-core case for an original sin ameliorated only by God's grace is associated with Augustine, while the unorthodox decoupling of redemption from grace came to be known (after Augustine's opponent) 'as the Pelagian heresy. "Either man could perfect himself, by the exercise of his own free will," Passmore observes in summary of the controversy, "or else he could be perfected only by the infusion of God's grace," but in seventeenth-century Europe a third position would emerge, whereby men were supposed to be perfected neither by grace nor by free will but rather "by the deliberate intervention of their fellowmen."[19] Locke's writings on education and the human mind "opened up, in principle, the possibility of perfecting men by the application of readily intelligible, humanly controllable, mechanisms," Passmore continues, although Locke's truly revolutionary contribution to understandings of human nature was not immediately apparent to his contemporaries. Later readers would increasingly come to believe that Locke had underestimated the importance of innate tendencies and exaggerated the effects of education, Passmore points out, thereby instigating "that controversy between the proponents of 'nature' and the proponents of 'nurture' which was to prove as persistent and as obdurate as the controversy between Pelagians and Augustinians, of which, in important respects, it is the secular echo."[20]

Interviewed in 1952 for the magazine of the school where he taught, Anthony Burgess answered the question "What do you think is the greatest menace at the present time?" with the words "Neo-Pelagianism (refusal to believe in Original

Sin) which produced Russia, America, youth organizations and holiday camps."[21] The fortunes of neo-Pelagianism have since fallen, to the point where it is difficult to imagine even the most hyperbolic Burgessian identifying it as our society's greatest menace. But Burgess's sense of the unresolved complementarity of Augustinian and Pelagian positions would seem to be borne out by aspects of the Locke scholarship. W.M. Spellman has argued that it's a misrepresentation of Locke to suggest that the philosopher repudiated original sin,[22] and in his book-length study *John Locke and the Problem of Depravity,* Spellman states even more clearly his beliefs concerning the compatibility of Locke's *tabula rasa* with a more-or-less Augustinian understanding of original sin: "What I am suggesting here," he writes, "is that Locke's supposedly novel emphasis upon the malleable nature of human personality and the efficacy of systematic education to engender rational behaviour was not unique for its time, and in no respect undermined his deeper belief, widely shared by so many of his contemporaries, that in Adam's fall all men had inherited a penchant for irrational behaviour which constituted the essential feature of human mortality and was in fact the root of all sin."[23] John Marshall has persuasively countered this argument by tracing Locke's shift from a belief, early in his career, "in a strong inherited disposition to sin," by way of a move "away from Calvinist and Arminian accounts of original sin and towards the effective denial of original sin, a denial whose explicit statement was particularly associated with Socinianism," suggesting that "Locke's account of the understanding as a *tabula rasa* at birth and of the will as a power left it unclear how either could have been in any sense damaged by inherited sinful dispositions."[24]

What most interests me here is the way that the partial forgetting or covering-up of the long tradition of thought on original sin becomes an enabling condition for believing in the need for an "either-or" choice when it comes to nature and nurture. The close homology between the two arguments may give pause to those who argue that nature-nurture debates can be resolved straightforwardly on the basis of scientific evidence made accessible by new insights and technologies associated with genetics. The steady erosion of theology's claims to serve as the dominant mode for understanding questions about freedom and necessity, good and evil, may well have contributed to the new intensity, during this period, of interest in what Passmore memorably calls "genetic perfectibility," the improvement of the human race not by grace, free will, or education but rather by the same kinds of selective breeding practiced by cattle farmers or pigeon-fanciers. Victor Hilts has taken up this strand of Passmore's argument, telling the story of the mid-eighteenth-century revival of the idea (present in Renaissance utopian writings as well as in Plato) "that the state should regulate marriages in order to avoid the propagation of hereditary diseases and defects among its citizens": a premise initially driven not so much by the success of animal breeders as by medical speculation on disease and heritable degeneracy, but increasingly supplemented as the century progressed "by a more positive vision of genetic perfectibility that aimed not only at the prevention of physical degeneration but also at the improvement of human intellectual and moral traits."[25]

It's virtually impossible to separate the secular language of depravity from the religious one, though the pattern of definitions in the *OED* suggests that what had been a relatively neutral word become overwritten more strongly with theological connotations when eighteenth-century writers such as Jonathan Edwards and John Wesley came to discuss the problem of original sin. What is clear, though, is that the link between sexual generation and theories of depravity is very strong, even in contemporary texts not obviously Augustinian in their inflections. In the posthumously published *Campania Fœlix; or, A Discourse of the Benefits and Improvements of Husbandry* (1700), Timothy Nourse (a preacher whose conversion to Roman Catholicism in 1673 had deprived him of a university fellowship, and an approximate contemporary of Locke's) sets out to establish the virtues and pleasures of husbandry: "[W]hat can be more suitable to a serious and well dispos'd Mind," he asks, "than to contemplate the Improvements of Nature by the various Methods and Arts of Culture: The same spot of Ground, which some Time since was nothing but Heath and Desart, and under the Original Curse of Thorns and Bryers, after a little Labour and Expence, seems restor'd to its Primitive Beauty in the State of Paradise."[26] But the gentleman's paradise he sees all around him is constantly threatened by common people, "very rough and savage in their Dispositions, being of levelling Principles, and refractory to Government, insolent and tumultuous": "it will be much more easie for [a gentleman] to teach a Hog to play upon the Bagpipes," he writes, "than to soften such *Brutes* by *Courtesie*" (15). One way of circumventing the problem of recalcitrant laborers is for the gentleman farmer to restrict the size of his estate to what he can manage himself: "A numerous Herd of Servants, (tho' they are necessary Helps to one who has a great deal under hand, and serve to fill up the Measures and Figure of a Family, yet) do in reality impoverish the House they belong to, being like Wenns, and the like Excrescencies, which, tho' they seem to be a Part of the Body, and to add to the Bulk, do in Truth suck the best Juice to themselves, whilst the genuine Parts languish and decay" (17).

Nourse describes the people who inhabit the commons (which he identifies as "Seminaries of a lazy, Thieving sort of People") as "lawless Rogues, engendring upon one another as from the beginning, so on to the end of the World, and preserving themselves frequently from starving, by stealing of Wood, Sheep, and Cattle, and by breaking of Houses, to the great Annoyance of all honest Husbandmen who have the misfortune to live near them" (98). It is a monstrous vision of reproduction, a scene of rampant propagation threatening to overrun civilized society, perhaps even to destroy it altogether. Nourse speaks of such people as if they are animals, his language emphasizing the nearness of man and beast as well as the common effects of nature across the boundaries between people and animals:

> [A]s the Men, so are the Cattle, which are bred upon such Commons, being a starv'd, scabby and rascally Race. Their Sheep are poor, tatter'd and poyson'd with the Rot. Their Cattle and Colts dwarft and ragged: For little, beggarly Stone-Colts, running promiscuously amongst the Herd, beget a miserable, shotten and Bastardly Breed; and generally 'tis that Horses nabb upon such wild and desert Places, half famished; by which means the Race of our Horses becomes tainted and base; whereas the *English* Horse when he comes of a good Kind, and being carefully lookt to when a Colt, may be esteem'd the best, perhaps, in the World[.] (98–99)

The commons injure cattle as well as horses, Nourse continues, "[t]he increase of such Places being nothing but a sort of starv'd, Tod-bellied Runts, neither fit for the Dairy nor the Yoke; so that a Common, upon the matter, is nothing but a Naked Theater of Poverty, both as to Men and Beasts, where all things appear horrid and uncultivated, and may be term'd, not improperly, the very abstract of Degenerated Nature" (99). Shortly afterward Nourse blames the depravity of the people on "the Circumstances of these uncultivated Places, which naturally incline Men to Barbarity and Ignorance" (102). (The only bright spot, Nourse observes, is that "in a Defensive or Civil War, such hardy Rogues as are bred usually upon Commons, may prove excellent good Food for Powder.")

Nourse recommends the institution of workhouses on the Dutch model as an agent of social control: this would mean that children's "tender Fingers are taught to work before they can well use their Tongues, and being thus inur'd from their Infancy their Hands are much more ready and nimble, whilst Labour and Industry grows up and augments with their Nature" (228). This cultivation or conversion to productivity would not only prevent infanticide (Nourse is a sincere Christian!), but would also spare us the sight of "such a Number of little Brats carried at the Backs of Beggar-Women from Door to Door, which, when a little grown up, run begging about the World, till coming to Years of Ripeness, or rather of Rottenness, they ingender the like beggarly Spawn or Fry, and so on to the end of the World" (235). Thus one of the obligations of the cultivator is to control, possibly even to suppress, all forms of biological reproduction that do not further the country's prosperity; the language of "ingender[ing] . . . Spawn or Fry" suggests (in a slightly uncanny anticipation of Swift's sly social-science posturing in *A Modest Proposal* [1729]) that even a program of eradication might be acceptable. The inheritance of original sin by propagation is in a sense literalized in such descriptions of the consequences of the human reproductive life.

### "A meer errant Cat"

On the face of things, Locke's arguments about the human mind and its openness to shaping by experience would seem to be at odds with the workings of romance, with its antiprogressive and backward-leaning propensities. Romance as a genre remains centrally committed to a notion of distinction via birth, a distinction that cannot be damped or dimmed by even the most humble upbringing—an assumption incompatible with the underlying premises of Lockean psychology, even if the "breeding" Locke discerns in gentlemen owes much to their birth as well as to their upbringing. Socially speaking, the possibility of improvement threatens the gentle and noble classes by admitting those beneath them to their society, though this recalls the paradox of Polixenes as it is developed in *The Winter's Tale:* how does it come about that the king defends grafting as an art that nature makes, and yet opposes the social grafting that would marry Florizel's scion to a shepherdess's stock and thereby improve the royal line?

In *Campania Fœlix*, despite his enthusiasm for "grafting one Wilding upon another, by which Mixture more new Species would still appear" (151–152), Timothy Nourse's enthusiasm for propagating "new and curious sorts" is matched by an equally strong sense of the need to maintain distinctions. He places particular confidence in the power of "good Sumptuary Laws"—laws that assign specific colors, fabrics, and styles to different social classes and prohibit the inhabitants of the lower tiers from adopting the dress of their betters—to "remedy . . . Disorders" that include rising wages for servants who then "ape their Masters in riotous Living and Excess."[27] Sumptuary laws represent a cultural means of maintaining and enforcing supposedly natural differences in danger of extinction. They work by

confining every Man to live in a modest *Decorum,* according to his Condition and Quality, and, above all, reducing Servants to their primitive Frugal Habit:

For a Clown, certainly, and a draggle-tail'd Kitchen-Wench, when trick'd up like my Master and Lady, cannot choose but have a mighty Opinion of their own Merit and Improvements. The Cat, when she was dres'd out of the Wardrobe of *Venus,* sate at Table with the State and Demureness of a Virgin-Bride; but as soon as a Mouse cross'd the Room, Puss forgets her Majesty, and running eagerly upon the Prey, shew'd her self to be a pure ravenous Animal, and fit only to live on Vermine. A paltry Chambermaid, which came but just now all perfum'd from emptying and cleansing the Vessels of the Chamber, shall appear at Table in her Flower'd Manteau, and her tottering Commode, forsooth; but notwithstanding all, upon every trivial Accident and Turn, will not fail to shew her self to be a meer errant Cat, destin'd by Nature to feed on meaner Fare.[28]

Writing in an age in which the fables of Aesop had become extremely popular, translators contemporary with Nourse treat this important story in dramatically different ways, invoking it to show everything from the irrational nature of romantic love to the notion that wealth need not be accompanied by virtue.[29] More to the point, it may have provided seventeenth-century British writers with their favorite instance of the limits of culture's power to transform nature. Nourse might have recalled an earlier version in Bacon's essay "Of Nature in Men": "*Nature* is Often Hidden; Sometimes Overcome; Seldome Extinguished," writes Bacon. "Force maketh *Nature* more violent in the Returne: Doctrine and Discourse maketh *Nature* lesse Importune: But Custome onely doth alter and subdue *Nature.*"[30] Though he lays out a number of ways in which nature may be amended, Bacon reminds man not to "trust his Victorie over his *Nature* too farre; For *Nature* will lay buried a great Time, and yet revive, upon the Occasion or Temptation. Like as it was with *Æsopes Damosell,* turned from a Catt to a Woman; who sate very demurely, at the Boards End, till a Mouse ranne before her. Therefore let a Man, either avoid the Occasion altogether; Or put Himselfe often to it, that hee may be little moved with it."

The cat-turned-woman who betrays her true nature by chasing after vermin represents a grotesque mirror-image of the fairy-tale or romance heroine, whose true nature also asserts itself over her surroundings, but with happier consequences. "This is the prettiest low-born lass that ever / Ran on the green-sord," says Polixenes of Perdita. "Nothing she does, or seems, / But smacks of something greater than herself, / Too noble for this place" (4.4.156–159). But writers from Shakespeare onward admit the darker strands that twine around such arguments. When he witnesses the vows between Florizel and Perdita, Polixenes renounces his disguise and discovers himself to them in a rage, denouncing his son as one "too base / To be [acknowledg'd]" (4.4.418–419) and threatening, if Florizel continues to think of marrying beneath him, to "bar thee from succession, / Not hold thee of our blood, no, not our kin, / Farre than Deucalion off" (4.4.429–431). A mythical Greek counterpart to Noah, Deucalion constructed an ark to ride out the flood by which Zeus destroyed all humanity and subsequently (with his wife Pyrrha) renewed the human race by following the advice of the gods to cast behind them the "bones of their mother," whereupon the stones thrown by Deucalion became men and those by his wife women. The story (like that of Cadmus sowing the dragon's teeth, famously alluded to by Milton in *Areopagitica* [1644]) involves an alternative to the ordinary process of sexual reproduction, and Polixenes seems so angry here that he wants to disavow generation altogether: Florizel will be more remote to him than the first ancestor of humanity.

Given that the Shepherd responds with equal fury to the young people's intention to marry, Camillo suggests to Florizel that the couple "make for Sicilia, / And there present yourself and your fair princess / (For so I see she must be) 'fore Leontes" (4.4.543–545). There is a nice ambiguity in Camillo's phrasing: is he giving in to *force majeure* and using the word "princess" as the name for the wife of a prince, accepting that Florizel will marry whom he wishes, or is he actually acknowledging something of the princess in Perdita on her own account? Both men continue to see some special virtue in Perdita. Florizel calls her "as forward of her breeding as / She is i' th' rear 'our birth," and Camillo responds, "I cannot say 'tis pity / She lacks instructions, for she seems a mistress / To most that teach" (4.4.580–583). Florizel's word "breeding" here means primarily rearing or upbringing, Camillo offering in response a paradox that echoes Polixenes' argument about art and nature, only in reverse (here, the untaught governs or educates "most that teach"), and the implied transformation of art back into nature will be matched in Act Five of *The Winter's Tale* by the restoration of Hermione from the figure of the statue, in a scene that responds to the earlier conversation about nature and art by showing the queen's rebirth to be a triumph of art and nature both.

It is the Shepherd's fear of reprisals from the enraged King Polixenes that prompts him to disclaim any blood relationship with Perdita, a declaration that in turn promotes the resolution of the romance plot. The Shepherd and Perdita's adopted brother the Clown show no qualms about casting Perdita off, given the cloud she's under. "There is no other way but to tell the King she's a changeling, and none of your flesh and blood," says the Clown to his father. "She being none of your flesh and blood, your flesh and blood has not offended the King, and so your flesh and blood is not to be punish'd by him. Show those things you found about her, those secret things, all but what she has with her." "I will tell the King all, every word, yea, and his son's pranks too," answers the Shepherd; "who, I may say, is no honest man, neither to his father nor to me, to go about to make me the King's brother-in-law" (4.4.687–702). (The Shepherd is at least as horrified at the prospect of being related to the King as the other way around.)

Following the identification of Perdita in Act Five and their own unexpectedly warm welcome into the royal family, the Shepherd and the Clown have another conversation that offers what may be *The Winter's Tale*'s most touching and profound—certainly its funniest—treatment of character, social identity, and resemblance, one which I invoke here to draw out one or two further aspects of Locke's argument about the interactions of education with birth:

SHEPHERD
Come, boy, I am past moe children, but thy sons and daughters will be all gentlemen born.

CLOWN
You are well met, sir. You denied to fight with me this other day, because I was no gentleman born. See you these clothes? Say you see them not and think me still no gentleman born. You were best say these robes are not gentlemen born. Give me the lie, do; and try whether I am not now a gentleman born.

AUTOLYCUS
I know you are now, sir, a gentleman born.

CLOWN
Ay, and have been so any time these four hours.

SHEPHERD
And so have I, boy.

CLOWN
So you have. But I was a gentleman born before my father; for the King's son took me by the hand, and call'd me brother; and then the two kings call'd my father brother; and then the Prince, my brother, and the Princess, my sister, call'd my father father; and so we wept; and there was the first gentleman-like tears that ever we shed.

SHEPHERD
We may live, son, to shed many more.

CLOWN
Ay; or else 'twere hard luck, being in so preposterous estate as we are.

(5.2.126–148)

As the proverb says, "It takes three generations to make a gentleman,"[31] and yet these tears are really gentlemanlike, even if the effect is spoiled when the Clown in one final slip of the tongue substitutes the word "preposterous" for "prosperous." In the lovely idyll of the play's conclusion, with its powerful enactments of reconciliation and restitution, the distinctions between gentlemen and clowns are only *gently* present, as it were, the clown's endearing misunderstanding of what it means to be born a gentleman expressing the strange truthfulness of the paradox that one may *become* a "gentleman born." So must the young pupil of Locke's *Thoughts Concerning Education* be made as well as born a gentleman.

# Cultures of Improvement

T he notion of habit or culture as second nature may seem on the face of things to offer human beings more control over their identities and fortunes than if they adhered instead to a belief in a capacious but largely inflexible inborn nature, whether conceived in eighteenth-century terms like *blood* or *birth* or in the twenty-first-century language of genetic coding. But culture, defined in these terms, is not necessarily any more amenable to human interference than nature; it may end up simply representing a kind of nature by other means. The fantasy of improvement—improvement of children in the form of education, improvement of landscapes by a whole host of techniques of cultivation—was very widely held in eighteenth-century Britain, to the point that the period's orientation toward culture and cultivation is taken to be one of its most striking and distinctive features. But improvement is haunted not just by the ever-present specter of degeneration but also by a lurking suspicion that habit might in the end be as hard to shake off—harder!—as nature itself. (Eve Sedgwick puts it well: "I remember the buoyant enthusiasm with which feminist scholars used to greet the finding that one or another brutal form of oppression was not biological but 'only' cultural! I have often wondered what the basis was for our optimism about the malleability of culture by any one group or program."[1]) The following pages will pursue a number of different fantasies of improvement and fears about its limits through some of the period's most influential and revealing natural histories (fictional and otherwise) of plants, animals, and people.

## Deucalion's Kin

In eighteenth-century British writing, culture especially evokes transformation, cultivation acting on plants and animals and people to change and improve them. The mode of writing especially associated with improvement and cultivation is the georgic, a term—there is no real consensus as to whether it's actually a literary genre or simply an orientation or cast of thought—derived from Virgil's great poem shoring up traditions of cultivation in danger of disappearing during the last years of the Roman Republic, a poem composed against the backdrop of the depopulation of rural Italy and the civil wars that would culminate in the victory of Octavian (later Augustus) at Actium in 31 BCE. In the dedication prefacing his translation of the *Georgics* (1697), Dryden called it "the best Poem of the best Poet," a judgment many of his contemporaries accepted.[2] Eighteenth-century Britain had a well-documented passion for literary works in the georgic mode: Virgil's own *Georgics* in the original Latin and in translation, Pope's *Windsor Forest* (1714), Thomson's *The Seasons* (1726–1730), and then-popular but now neglected poems like Philips' *Cyder* (1708), Dyer's *The Fleece* (1757), and Grainger's *Sugar-Cane* (1764). Early in the century, Addison had defined the georgic as "*some part of the Science of Husbandry put into a pleasing Dress, and set off with all the Beauties and Embellishments of Poetry,*" but the definition soon relaxed to encompass prose as well as poems about husbandry, the phrase "prose georgic" coming to refer to a host of texts in which man transforms the environment by means of hard work: novels like Defoe's *Robinson Crusoe* (1719) and Smollett's *Expedition of Humphry Clinker* (1771), Jethro Tull's *The New Horse-Houghing Husbandry* (1731), and countless manuals on agriculture.[3]

The poem's fantasies of rural retirement proved especially irresistible to the writers of Britain's new Augustan age, writing a generation after Locke but still in the aftermath of civil war and revolution, with a consequent skepticism about war and warlike values as well as about the genre of epic, which was strongly associated with those values. Virgil's poem displays its own worries about culture's part in the struggle between improvement and degeneration, and the *Georgics* is haunted both by the dangers of luxury (a strain that comes through especially strongly in book 2's lines about rural retirement) and by the limits on culture's power to alter the natural world: Kurt Heinzelman has called Virgilian georgic "a story of largely unrelieved degeneracy," and this seems an apt description.[4] I have chosen to read Dryden's translation here both because of its wide currency in eighteenth-century England—the editors of the California edition say that barring the King James Bible and Pope's translations of Homer, "it is far and away the most successful version, judged by continuous reader acceptance in the face of much spirited competition, of any foreign work ever translated into English"— and because Dryden so perceptively responds to the literary and cultural trends of his own day; the Latin is given in the notes (the fit is sometimes awkward).[5]

In the world of the *Georgics,* nature is harsh or astringent rather than miraculously beneficent, and agriculture part of an "Orig'nal Contract" (Dryden's phrase owes something to Milton's depiction of the Fall) whose laws were "Impos'd by Nature, and by Nature's Cause,/On sundry Places, when *Deucalion* hurl'd/His Mother's Entrails on the desart World:/Whence Men, a hard laborious Kind, were born."[6] The success of each year's crops can only be earned by continual effort, without which "all below, whether by Nature's Curse,/Or Fates decree, degen'rate still to worse."[7] Every stage of the agricultural year, including the harvest celebration, reminds the poet that the future contains unremitting work: "Ev'n when they sing at ease in full Content,/Insulting o're the Toils they underwent;/Yet still they find a future Task remain;/To turn the Soil, and break the Clods again."[8]

Parts of the poem describe happier scenes, of course, like Virgil's well-known lines on grafting, where optimism breaks through the gloom:

> Then let the Learned Gard'ner mark with care
> The Kinds of Stocks, and what those Kinds will bear:
> Explore the Nature of each sev'ral Tree;
> And known, improve with artful Industry:
> And let no spot of idle Earth be found,
> But cultivate the Genius of the Ground.[9]

Fruit trees, "receiving Graffs of other Kind,/Or thence transplanted, change their salvage Mind," the poet continues: "Their Wildness lose, and quitting Nature's part,/Obey the Rules and Discipline of Art."[10] Here Dryden indulges a vision of something much like a late seventeenth-century garden: one of the stage directions in Dryden's never-performed musical adaptation of *Paradise Lost, The State of Innocence, and Fall of Man* (1677), offers a startling description of an orderly paradise with "*Trees cut out on each side, with several Fruits upon them: a Fountain in the midst: at the far end, the Prospect terminates in Walks.*"[11]

But it is not long before the poet reminds the reader of the limits of cultivation: "Salt Earth and bitter are not fit to sow,/Nor will be tam'd or mended with the Plough./Sweet Grapes degen'rate there, and Fruits declin'd/From their first flav'rous Taste, renounce their Kind."[12] The descriptions of reproduction in book 3 verge on the monstrous, breeding often going awry: it is important to feed the steed properly, "For if the Sire be faint, or out of case,/He will be copied in his famish'd Race"; mares "Barr'd from the Male" will experience propagation by the wind, a "prolifick air:/With which impregnate, from their Groins they shed,/A slimy Juice, by false Conception bred."[13] Above all there is the constant menace of degeneration—a white ram with a black tongue might "darken all the Flock," disease threatens to "infect the Fold": "Nor do those ills, on single Bodies prey;/But oft'ner bring the Nation to decay;/And sweep the present Stock, and future Hope away."[14]

The poem consistently undercuts or darkens the pleasures it describes. The idyllic passages about the bees in book 4—a prosperous vision of education and stable if unorthodox inheritance—gives way not long after to a vision of their generation from the head of a bullock that emphasizes the violence of origins:

> The tainted Blood, in this close Prison pent,
> Begins to boyl and through the Bones ferment.
> Then, wondrous to behold, new Creatures rise,
> A moving Mass at first, and short of Thighs;
> 'Till shooting out with Legs, and imp'd with Wings,
> The Grubs proceed to Bees with pointed Stings:
> And more and more affecting Air, they try
> Their tender Pinions, and begin to fly[.][15]

Local juxtapositions of culture and degeneracy are mirrored at the level of the poem as a whole by the contrast between rural retirement and political strife, the poet setting his song "of Fields, and Flocks, and Trees,/And of the waxen Work of lab'ring Bees" against the fact that "mighty *Cæsar*, thund'ring from afar,/Seeks on *Euphrates* Banks the Spoils of War."[16] Both the pastoral vision of a "cultivated Land" yielding up "easy Food" for the swain's comfort and the lingering dream of "Fruits, which, of their own accord,/The willing Ground, and laden Trees afford" have a fantastical quality.[17] Dryden's translation augments this longing when he writes that the poet's "next Desire is, void of Care and Strife,/To lead a soft, secure, inglorious Life./A Country Cottage near a Crystal Flood,/A winding Vally, and a lofty Wood."[18] The vision is of withdrawal from war, wealth, and politics to a lifestyle Virgil vindicates by an appeal to Rome's ancient origins—"frugal," "rude," "homely" are the words Dryden chooses to characterize the early Romans.[19] Nostalgia for a long-lost mythic past, including an Edenic fantasy of life without labor (workers are absent from this landscape), complements the poem's relentless attention to the toils of the cultivator attempting to stave off natural degeneracy, but the fantasy's presence in the poem tends to exacerbate rather than relieve such pains.

Much of eighteenth-century Britain's writing on husbandry reveals an uneasy awareness that agriculture as it presently stands renders gentlemen vulnerable to the hostility of their social inferiors, as when one mid-century authority deplores the fact that "the primitive source of wealth and the vital support of no less than the whole human species are both consigned to the management of very mean ignorant people."[20] Jethro Tull, the important innovator in agriculture whose method of drilling the soil was designed to increase crop yields without requiring any additional manure, wrote one of the many influential and popular treatises (often printed by self-described "gentlemen" at their own expense) that developed the theory and practice of the new agriculture. Like most other treatises on husbandry, it has a fantastical or wish-fulfilling element as well as being deeply practical, but the fantasy is accompanied by a social nightmare: in the *New Horse-Houghing Husbandry* (1731), Tull continually breaks off to scourge "Plough-Servants . . . [who] exalt their Dominion over their Masters, so that a Gentleman-Farmer was allow'd to make but little Profit of his Arable Lands" (indeed, his drill is intended to make servants' labor unnecessary).[21] Both verse and prose georgics, then, lay out the limits of culture as well as its powers, and the authors of georgic novels and treatises on husbandry are exceptionally attuned to the pull of a degeneracy that haunts even the most secure cultural works and improvements.

Anthony Low's working definition stipulates that georgic "is a mode that stresses the value of intensive and persistent labor against hardships and difficulties; that it differs from pastoral because it emphasizes work instead of ease; that it differs from epic because it emphasizes planting and building instead of killing and destruction; and that it is preeminently the mode suited to the establishment of civilization and the founding of nations."[22] Georgic is accordingly and by its very constitution linked to a cluster of tropes that had great resonance in a century that would see Britain establishing an extensive empire overseas and transforming the land at home by means of new agricultural techniques, modes of cultivation associated in the first place with seventeenth-century innovators such as Francis Bacon, Walter Hartlib, and John Evelyn and subsequently with a great many eighteenth-century theoretical and practical husbandmen, from Tull in the earlier part of the century to Coke of Norfolk and Arthur Young at the end of it. Rachel Crawford suggests that British imaginative interest moved over the course of the eighteenth century from georgic poetry to prose treatises in part because "prose came to represent science in a way that poetry could not, and agricultural writings incorporated many aspects of the georgic agenda, particularly its rampant nationalisms."[23] The language of georgic was further enriched by the long-standing back-and-forth connection between the cultivation of plants and the cultivation of human beings. The metaphor had been already so thoroughly domesticated by the late seventeenth century that the two kinds of cultivation had become almost literally synonymous, as when Locke suggests that parents deciding how to educate their children "observe what their Native Stock is, how it may be improved, and what it is fit for."[24] The bumping-up against each other of new agricultural theories and techniques, the idea of man-as-plant-to-be-cultivated, and a dominant and morally compelling ethos of rural retirement in this sense produced a kind of feedback loop: man follows his duty to labor to improve the land and improves himself in the process, the vocabulary of improvement permeating barriers between plants, animals, and people and enriching its own meaning with each new border crossing.[25]

This effect is especially pronounced at mid-century and beyond, as Scottish Enlightenment writers' elaborations of the notion of improvement in the context of progress theory and "four-stages" accounts of the history of civil society migrated into more general discourses of cultivation. Walter Harte (tutor to Lord Chesterfield's son Philip Stanhope) eulogizes improvement in his *Essays on Husbandry* (1764)—a book Chesterfield called "the only prose Georgic that I know, as agreeable, and I dare say much more useful, in this climate than Virgil"—in a way that reveals the rhetorical overdetermination of discussions of cultivation.[26] Harte praises Solomon for recommending "industry . . . to all those that cultivate the earth," for God cannot be counted on to rain manna upon "*the slothful*":

> And by the way, according to the all-wise appointment of Providence, it is the same with the *human mind,* as it is with the *earth;* for education and good agriculture make the like improvements upon either. The wild herb derives a savage nature from the soil round it. The man born in ignorant countries is uncivilized and unenlightened. Transplantation into more kindly ground improves a plant, and unwearied culture increases those improvements.[27]

The two processes—human and plant—are not just homologous, they are in a sense *literally* one and the same thing, for agriculture improves men as well as the crops and land on which they toil. The major eighteenth-century British writers on husbandry emphasize its immediate educational, ethical, and political utility to humankind. Edward Lisle calls the study of agriculture "the best school of education, and the fittest to prepare [men] for the service of their country in the two houses of parliament of Great Britain" and Lord Kames deems husbandry "of all occupations the most proper for gentlemen in a private station"; Arthur Young quotes a letter in which the Earl of Bristol proclaims that "I love agriculture because it makes good citizens, good husbands, good fathers, good children," and responds to Frances Burney's teasing question as to why he finds "farming the only thing worth manly attention" by coining the phrase (the metaphor so dense as to be almost a catachresis) "agriculture for farming your heart."[28]

### "A living Magazine"

*The Life and Strange Surprizing Adventures of Robinson Crusoe, Of York, Mariner* is a foundational text for many discourses of modern European literature and culture, including histories of the novel, of individualism, and the modern self, of the protestant ethic, labor, and the development of capitalism, of human rights and of ideas about savages noble or otherwise, race, and colonization (think of Elizabeth Bishop's poem "Crusoe in England" in *Geography III* [1976], or J.M. Coetzee's *Foe* [1986]).[29] *Robinson Crusoe* is also perhaps the greatest English novel of culture, Protestant theology and its cultural ramifications fueling a georgic ethos of labor and nation-building. Its argumentative and imaginative force led Rousseau—in many respects an enemy to culture—to call it "the best treatise on an education according to nature," and in his own treatise on education he ordered that *Robinson Crusoe* should be "the first book Emile will read; for a long time it will form his whole library, and it will always retain an honoured place."[30]

In a manner somewhat at odds with Rousseau's later interpretation, Defoe's Crusoe possesses a matchless need to subordinate nature to his will, shooting wildlife, making his own tools and implements to recreate the complex world of objects he wants, even reshaping the land itself as he goes about establishing his mastery. Defoe's language emphasizes continuities between all of these projects, and Crusoe's countless "Works and Improvements" (132) include not just the acts of cultivation that might have been undertaken by any country gentleman of the period but also Friday himself: as Friday puts it to Crusoe, in his awful pidgin, *"you teach wild Mans be good sober tame Mans"* (163).

Though Crusoe manages to transform the wilderness of the island into "Plantations, *viz.* my Castle, my Country Seat, which I call'd my Bower, and my Enclosure in the Woods" (120–121), he oscillates madly throughout his time in isolation between a view of nature as brutish and degenerate and one in which nature is supremely bountiful. As a cultivator par excellence, moreover, he is confused, even conflicted, as to what he owes to God and what to his own hard work. In one of the novel's most striking scenes of cultivation, Crusoe is smitten with a short-lived providentialism:

> I saw some few Stalks of something green, shooting out of the Ground, which I fancy'd might be some Plant I had not seen, but I was surpriz'd and perfectly astonish'd, when, after a little longer Time, I saw about ten or twelve Ears come out, which were perfect green Barley of the same Kind as our *European,* nay, as our *English* Barley. . . . [A]fter I saw Barley grow there, in a Climate which I know was not proper for Corn, and especially that I knew not how it came there, it startl'd me strangely, and I began to suggest, that God had miraculously caus'd this Grain to grow without any Help of Seed sown, and that it was directed purely for my Sustenance, on that wild miserable Place. (58)

After scouring the island for more such plants and not finding them, however, Crusoe backtracks:

> at last it occur'd to my Thoughts, that I had shook a Bag of Chickens Meat out in that Place, and then the Wonder began to cease; and I must confess, my religious Thankfulness to God's Providence began to abate too upon the Discovering that all this was nothing but what was common; tho' I ought to have been as thankful for so strange and unforseen Providence, as if it had been miraculous; for it was really the Work of Providence as to me, that should order or appoint, that 10 or 12 Grains of Corn should remain unspoil'd, (when the Rats had destroy'd all the rest,) as if it had been dropt from Heaven; as also, that I should throw it out in that particular Place, where it being in the Shade of a high Rock, it sprang up immediately; whereas, if I had thrown it anywhere else, at that Time, it had been burnt up, and destroy'd. (58)

Crusoe cultivates this crop with extraordinary effort (his God helps those who help themselves) and an absurdly elaborate scheme of husbandry that requires him to reinvent every tool and recreate every step of the processes used to harvest and mill grain in the civilized lands he has left behind (76–78, 86–90).

Crusoe domesticates animals as well as plants: he first has "a Thought of breeding up some tame creatures," he says, "that I might have Food when my Powder and Shot was all spent" (56). Finding that kids "are mighty sagacious tractable Creatures where they are well used" (106), Crusoe builds an enclosure to hold them: "I consider'd the keeping up a Breed of tame Creatures thus at my Hand, would be a living Magazine of Flesh, Milk, Butter and Cheese," he writes, the pungency of the phrase "living Magazine" defamiliarizing the otherwise ordinary enough notion of domesticated livestock (111). Indeed, Crusoe's arrangements tend to intensify, almost to parody, relationships in the world he comes from. Just as he applies the language of the old world to the landscape of the new—surveying the countryside, Crusoe experiences "a secret Kind of Pleasure, (tho' mixt with my other afflicting Thoughts) to think that this was all my own, that I was King and Lord of all this Country indefeasibly, and had a Right of Possession; and if I could convey it, I might have it in Inheritance, as compleatly as any Lord of a Mannor in *England*" (73)—so a kind of family life emerges from his acts of building and cultivation.

His animals—parrots, goats—become Crusoe's "Domesticks" (82), and he suggests that "[i]t would have made a Stoick smile to have seen, me and my little Family sit down to Dinner; there was my Majesty the Prince and Lord of the whole Island; I had the Lives of all my Subjects at my absolute Command. I could hang, draw, give Liberty, and take it away, and no Rebels among all my Subjects" (108). Indeed, he exerts violent mastery over them: after Crusoe's domestic cats breed with the wild ones (to his great surprise, seeing as he "thought it was a quite differing Kind from our *European* Cats; yet the young Cats were the same Kind of House breed like the old one; and both my Cats being Females, I thought it very strange" [75]), he ends up killing them "like Vermine, or wild Beasts" when their offspring become too numerous. The language of extirpation migrates back and forth between human and animal worlds: when fowl threaten Crusoe's crop of corn, he shoots them and then serves them "as we serve notorious Thieves in *England, (viz.)* Hang'd them in Chains for a Terror to others" (85). Crusoe's culture of husbandry is brutal, thoroughly in keeping with the harshness of the natural world he seeks to shape to his will.

By late in the century, attitudes toward improvement had become profoundly ambivalent, a muddle of feelings rendered more painful by observers' awareness of the dire human consequences of the enclosure movement. This can produce a nostalgia for the past—the word "improvement" is frequently used ironically, as in *Mansfield Park* (1814)—or a conviction that improvement really represents a kind of degeneration, as when Young reminisces in 1784 about the Suffolk Punch draft-horses of his youth and wishes that "some sensible intelligent farmer, whose business is on a large scale, may give his attention to preserving the true original breed uncontaminated by any modern improvements."[31] Part of this is a Burkean commitment to the values of tradition and the past; Young's comment also echoes the conviction, laid out by Buffon in scientific terms and Rousseau in political ones, that cultivation is as likely to corrupt as to improve any given species, with humans being no exception.

## Perfect Wildness

In December 1725 a teenage boy arrived at George I's Hanover court. He had been found in a wood near Hamelin (the report is from a contemporary newspaper) "walking upon his Hands and Feet, climbing up trees like a squirrel, and feeding upon grass and moss of trees"; he could not speak.[32] The feral child was brought to London as a curiosity and attracted much attention at the English court and beyond.[33] Shortly after the Wild Boy of Hamelin (now called Peter) was transferred into the care of the physician John Arbuthnot, Defoe published an account of the boy's condition called *Mere Nature Delineated* (1726). The book presents the "perfectly wild, uninstructed, unform'd, *that is,* uninform'd" Peter as a kind of conundrum, a riddle to be solved (164). "[T]hat there is such a Person, is visible," Defoe observes, "and he is to be seen every Day, all wild, brutal, and as Soul-less as he was said to be; acting MERE NATURE, and little more than a vegetative Life; dumb, or mute, without the least Appearance of Cultivation, or of having ever had the least Glympse of Conversation among the rational Part of the World" (156). All of Defoe's language emphasizes the impoverishment of Peter's condition. How did the boy come to be thus?

> [H]ow is it that he cannot speak, and is so meer a Part of wild Species as we still find him? uninform'd by Soul, uninhabited by any thing superior to a Beast; nay, not furnish'd with the usual Sagacity of the ordinary Brutes, who all, by that secret Something, which we, for want of a better Word, call Instinct, are ready and apt to every Action needful to themselves? (160)

Reiterating several times the premise that Peter "gives us a View of mere Nature" (192), Defoe goes on to ask whether the boy's wildness is essential or merely contingent, and more specifically whether or not "his Soul being capable of Improvement, differs from us only in the Loss it has sustained under so long a deny'd Education" (192):

> If that be his Case, he is then only to be considered as an Infant, and that he is just now in the mere State of Infancy and Childhood, with this Disadvan-

tage, as above, That the Soul being left unpolished, and not able to shine, and having lost the Seasons in which it should have been taught and enur'd to its proper Functions, the Organs being grown firm and solid, without being put into a Capacity by due Exercise, are not so easily disposed for the necessary Motion and Application; and so the Difficulty will be the greater to bring it to work, and may not, in a long Time, if ever, be overcome.

If this be the Case, it dictates the Necessity of early Education of Children, in whom, not the Soul only, but the organick Powers are, as a Lump of soft Wax, which is always ready to receive any Impression; but if harden'd, grow callous, and stubborn, and, like what we call Sealing-Wax, obstinately refuse the Impression of the Seal, unless melted, and reduced by the Force of Fire; that is to say, Unless moulded and temper'd to Instruction, by Violence, Length of Time, and abundance of Difficulty.

Mere Nature receives the vivifying Influence in Generation, but requires the Help of Art to bring it to Perfection of living: The Soul is plac'd in the Body like a rough Diamond, which requires the Wheel and Knife, and all the other Arts of the Cutter, to shape it, and polish it, and bring it to shew the perfect Water of a true *Brilliant*. If Art be deficient, Nature can do no more; it has plac'd the Capacity in the Jewel; but till the Rough be remov'd, the Diamond never shews itself. Thus the Soul, unpolish'd, remains bury'd under the Rubbish and Roughness of its own Powers; 'tis given to us to work upon ourselves, and if we do not think it worth while to bestow the Trouble, we must not expect the Blessing. (193)

Defoe concludes the discussion by observing that education seems to be "the only specifick Remedy for all the Imperfections of Nature," and furthermore "that all the Difference in Souls, or the greatest Part at least, that is to say, between the Dull and the Bright, the Sensible and Insensible, the Active and the Indolent, the Capable and the Incapable, are owing to, and derive from this one Article: That the Man is a Rational, or a Stupid, just as he is handled by his Teachers" (193). The "plain coarse Piece of Work" of "Man in the meer Condition he is born in, just coming out of Nature's Hand," of course, means that "the Improvement of the Soul by Instruction, which we call Educating, is of the highest Importance" (197).

Making an argument about feral children almost always involves throwing one's lot in with nature or culture. Writing in the early 1940s, Bishop H. Pakenham-Walsh offered this comment, in a preface to the Reverend J.A.L. Singh's narrative about the so-called Wolf Girls of Midnapore, Amala and Kamala:

If one accepts as natural the use of teeth and nails when they felt themselves annoyed, there was no malice, nor was there any fear, as for instance of thunder and lightning, of big animals, of the dark, etc.; nor, so far as I could ascertain, was there any trace of pride or of jealousy. Human vices seem to have been as little inherited as human virtues, and this fact seems to me to have a very pertinent bearing on the consideration of what we mean by "Original Sin." It certainly shows the tremendous importance of the human environment, and of the training of little children.[34]

Elsewhere in the same volume, Robert Zingg (discussing children raised in isolation) displays more wariness about the ends to which the evidence these children constitute might be turned: "One can little doubt but that the radicals of the present day, as those of Rousseau's," he writes, "will grasp at the sort of material in this work, if they hear of it, as proof that man is completely a creature of his own environment, and for their thesis that human nature is a product of it. For that thesis, unfortunately, there is lacking a case of a wolf or other animal being educated into the behavior of a man."[35]

More recent discussions of feral children reveal dramatic shifts of the pendulum between nurture and nature.[36] Developmental psychology, cognitive science, and a cluster of associated disciplines have filled out our picture of the brain's history in childhood and infancy, the importance of developmental windows, and the difficulty of countering deficits at a later stage of life. In his own book about Victor of Aveyron, *The Forbidden Experiment,* Roger Shattuck explains that the experiment of his title is "one that would reveal to us what 'human nature' really is beneath the overlays of society and culture. Or at least an experiment that could tell us if there is any such thing as human nature apart from culture and individual heredity."[37] In this language can be heard some of the wishfulness and wistfulness that permeate many later eighteenth-century inquiries into the same question: though not, surely, Defoe's, for *Mere Nature Delineated* offers a bleak vision of nature as lack and argues that even the violent tempering of a belated education is preferable to nature's roughness.

## "A perfect *Yahoo*"

Long after the widespread acceptance of Darwin's mind-bending insights about men and monkeys, there remains something odd and uncomfortable about thinking of ourselves as members of a species called *Homo sapiens:* about there actually being a term for *us*, in the taxonomic nomenclature, as precise as those reserved for fruit fly (*Drosophila melanogaster*) or nematode (*Caenorhabditis elegans*). But the classificatory enterprise required that man, too, should be given an appropriate label and accustom himself to his species name. When *Gulliver's Travels* appeared in 1726, the use of "species" in this sense was relatively new.[38] Its primary meanings ("appearance, form, kind") were in general use, but many of the seventeenth-century instances given by the *OED* are primarily philosophical, and the word's strongest connotations at this time evoke various popular modifications of Aristotelian logic. A telling example can be found in the *OED*'s citation of a rhetorical manual published in 1657: "*Species,* is a more special title attributed to divers particulars under it: as, Man to William, Thomas, John" (sense II.7). The loose sense of class or kind was applied quite widely, across a number of different discourses, but the sense of species as a concept in natural history would really only come into general use towards the end of the seventeenth century (II.10), and the earliest quotation in support of species meaning "human race" is from Addison in 1711 (II.9.e).[39] Both this citation and a mid-century one from Fielding are playful and lightly ironized, while a considerably more earnest later instance is drawn from Godwin's *Enquirer* (1797); "If individuals were happy, the species would be happy," Godwin writes—a neat philological demonstration in miniature of Godwin's habit of borrowing the terms and techniques of the Augustan satirists (Swift in particular) and stripping them of irony.

Gulliver's own frequent use of the term *species* is distinctly disorienting. He seems to understand intellectually that Yahoos are a kind of animal, he seems to understand that humans and Yahoos form a single species, and yet much about his language shows that awareness fading bizarrely in and out of his consciousness. In a letter prefatory to the *Travels,* Gulliver recalls having often asked his cousin "to consider . . . that the *Yahoos* were a Species of Animals utterly incapable of Amendment by Precepts or Examples" (ii:xxxiv), as though both he and his cousin fall outside the limits of the Yahoo species-definition. The pronouns elsewhere, though, reveal the instability of such divisions. Having suppressed his Yahoo nature and embraced the government of reason, contact with others has led to a certain amount of backsliding on Gulliver's part. "I must freely confess," he allows, "that since my last Return, some corruptions of my *Yahoo* Nature have revived in me by Conversing with a few of your Species, and particularly those of mine own Family, by an unavoidable Necessity; else I should never have attempted so absurd a Project as that of reforming the *Yahoo* Race in this Kingdom; but, I have now done with all such visionary Schemes for ever" (ii:xxxvi).

The phrase "a few of your Species" shows Gulliver's psychologically plausible desire to hold himself separate from his kind, but given that Cousin Sympson is presumably a relation by blood, the phrase "those of mine own Family" places Gulliver in the thick of the species group he names "the *Yahoo* race."[40] The double sense of himself as Yahoo and not-Yahoo is felt most acutely as Gulliver at the end of the *Travels* observes that "when I began to consider, that by copulating with one of the *Yahoo*-Species, I had become a Parent of more; it struck me with the utmost Shame, Confusion and Horror" (4.11/11:273). The Latinate term *copulating* distances Gulliver emotionally from the experience of sex, his very language coming to seem comically and painfully at odds with the truth of his animal identity.

Elements in book 2 have already primed the reader for some of book 4's disturbing emphasis on man's animal nature. In Brobdingnag, Gulliver describes one of that country's enormous inhabitants, before picking him up, "consider[ing] a while with the Caution of one who endeavours to lay hold on a small dangerous Animal in such a Manner that it shall not be able either to scratch or to bite him; as I my self have sometimes done with a *Weasel* in *England*" (2.1/11:71). He also observes a gigantic monkey reaching for him with its paw "as a Cat does when she plays with a Mouse" and then taking Gulliver up "in his right Fore-foot, and [holding Gulliver] as a Nurse doth a Child she is going to suckle": "just as I have seen the same Sort of Creature do with a Kitten in *Europe*," he adds (2.5/11:106). "I have good Reason to believe that he took me for a young one of his own Species," Gulliver concludes, "by his often stroaking my Face very gently with his other Paw."[41]

Being a small person in the land of the very large lets Gulliver see the same kinds of physical flaw (like giant pores) the Lilliputians saw in him, but littleness and bigness have some moral or ethical freight as well, at least in the gargantuan King of Brobdingnag's verdict on Gulliver's accounts of European history: "I cannot but conclude the Bulk of your Natives," he tells Gulliver, "to be the most pernicious Race of little odious Vermin that Nature ever suffered to crawl upon the Surface of the Earth" (2.6/11:116). The term *natives*, often used by Europeans to describe the existing inhabitants of lands they intend to colonize, is slightly disconcerting in its application here. The king's dehumanizing use of the term *vermin*, along with a host of other pestlike adjectives, also opens up the way for violence, insofar as such terms may serve as the precondition for a campaign of extermination.

The ripple effects of this sentiment are to some extent contained by its being put in the mouth of the King of Brobdingnag, who is morally as well as physically greater than Gulliver, and only *reported* by Gulliver. Book 4 in contrast puts

Gulliver in a position to experience a far more destabilizing perspectival shift, and his time among the Houyhnhnms will convert Gulliver from a self-professed lover to a hater of mankind.[42] On first arriving in the land of the Houyhnhnms, Gulliver takes the Yahoos he sees for a kind of cattle:

> Their Heads and Breasts were covered with a thick Hair, some frizzled and others lank; they had Beards like Goats, and a Long Ridge of Hair down their Backs, and the fore Parts of their Legs and Feet; but the rest of their Bodies were bare, so that I might see their Skins, which were of a brown Buff Colour. They had no Tails, nor any Hair at all on their Buttocks, except about the *Anus;* which, I presume Nature had placed there to defend them as they sat on the Ground; for this Posture they used, as well as lying down, and often stood on their hind Feet. They climbed high Trees, as nimbly as a Squirrel, for they had strong extended Claws before and behind, terminating on sharp Points, hooked. They would often spring, and bound, and leap with prodigious Agility. The Females were not so large as the Males; they had long lank Hair on their Heads, and only a Sort of Down on the rest of their Bodies, except about the *Anus,* and *Pudenda.* Their Dugs hung between their fore Feet, and often reached almost to the Ground as they walked. The Hair of both Sexes was of several Colours, brown, red, black and yellow. Upon the whole, I never beheld in all my Travels so disagreeable an Animal, or one against which I naturally conceived so strong an Antipathy. (4.1/11:207–208)

The language here has the moralized quality of the descriptions in eighteenth-century travel narratives or natural histories. Gulliver's word choice is profoundly unflattering, from the comparison to the beards of goats all the way to the use of the depersonalizing Latin anatomical terms *anus* and *pudenda.*[43] His use of terms like "Females" and "Males" to distinguish the two sorts of Yahoo tends to obscure the identity of Yahoos with humans, although the reader will see through Gulliver's misconceptions and self-delusions.

Upon meeting his first Houyhnhnms later in the chapter and watching them seem to converse with one another, Gulliver is "amazed to see such Actions and Behaviour in Brute Beasts"; he concludes, wide-eyed, "that if the Inhabitants of this Country were endued with a proportionable Degree of Reason, they must needs be the wisest People upon Earth" (4.1/11:209) and "that a People who could so far civilize brute Animals, must needs excel in Wisdom all the Nations of the World" (4.2/11:212). One source for Swift's Houyhnhnms may be Locke's famous discussion of personal identity in the *Essay Concerning Human Understanding*

(1690), which includes an extended meditation on how bodily shape and species contribute to our understanding of human rationality and human identity. In the fourth edition (1700), Locke added a long excerpt from Sir William Temple's account of an unusually articulate parrot (Temple was Swift's mentor, the object of his passionate defense in the ancient-versus-moderns controversy of *Battle of the Books* [1704]) before concluding that even if we take parrots "for a race of *rational Animals*," they nonetheless are parrots rather than men: "'tis not the *Idea* of a thinking or rational Being alone, that makes the *Idea* of a *Man* in most Peoples Sense; but of a Body so and so shaped joined to it" (2.37.335).

Swift's horse-shaped "Brute Beasts" or "brute Animals" are of course nothing of the kind. They are the proper inhabitants of this land and exemplify the pinnacle of reason, the word *Houyhnhnm* actually signifying "a *Horse;* and in its Etymology, *the Perfection of Nature*" (4.3/11:219). As supremely rational beings, the Houyhnhnms respond to the problem of how to identify Gulliver's own kind or sort by an act of comparison, bringing him alongside one of those described alternately as "detestable Creatures," "Animals," or "Beast[s]" and deeming him also a Yahoo:

> My Horror and Astonishment are not to be described, when I observed, in this abominable Animal, a perfect human Figure; the Face of it indeed was flat and broad, the Nose depressed, the Lips large, and the Mouth wide: But these Differences are common to all the savage Nations, where the Lineaments of the Countenance are distorted by the Natives suffering their Infants to lie grovelling on the Earth, or by carrying them on their Backs, nuzzling with their Face against the Mother's Shoulders. (4.2/11:213–214)[44]

Gulliver holds an assumption with regard to human identity and human difference that was widely prevalent both in the ancient world and in early modern European writing, namely that custom has great power to modify human bodies. Superficial differences between human and Yahoo bodies can't conceal the underlying species identity, and Gulliver's only hope now is to hang on to his human clothes as a way of differentiating himself from his loathsome unwanted relations among "that cursed Race of *Yahoos*" (4.3/11:220). Yet when his Houyhnhnm master observes him naked except for his shirt, Gulliver reports, "he said, it was plain I must be a perfect *Yahoo;* but that I differed very much from the rest of my Species, in the Whiteness, and Smoothness of my Skin, my want of Hair in several Parts of my Body, the Shape and Shortness of my Claws behind and before, and my Affectation of walking continually on my two hinder Feet" (4.3/11:221). The phrase "a perfect *Yahoo*" is itself a kind of oxymoron, but as Houyhnhnms don't make jokes, the irony in this case may perhaps be apportioned to Swift.

An especially distinctive feature of Swift's technique in these passages derives from the attribution to Gulliver of a kind of twinned or double consciousness. "I EXPRESSED my Uneasiness at his giving me so often the Appellation of *Yahoo*, an odious Animal, for which I had so utter an Hatred and Contempt," says Gulliver, requesting that his master keep his Yahoo identity a secret (4.3/II:221). "Yahoo" names an identity Gulliver has only incompletely internalized, and his reflections on the Yahoos show an intensity of conceptual or category error unprecedented in the earlier sections of the *Travels*. Speaking of his need for edible and nutritious food, Gulliver confesses, "indeed, I now apprehended, that I must absolutely starve, if I did not get to some of my own Species: For as to those filthy *Yahoos*, although there were few greater Lovers of Mankind, at that time, than myself; yet I confess I never saw any sensitive Being so detestable on all Accounts; and the more I came near them, the more hateful they grew, while I stayed in that Country" (4.2/II:214). This sentence demonstrates Gulliver's increasing cognitive dissonance, the admission of his being "at that time" a great lover of mankind implicitly admitting the equivalence of man and Yahoo (otherwise the observation is an irrelevant non sequitur).

The gesture here toward a conversion experience—the invocation of Gulliver's identity "at that time" versus the present time of writing—is taken up and developed further in later chapters. After having provided his Houyhnhnm master with an extremely unflattering account of human political life, Gulliver stops to consider the potential charge of disloyalty to humankind:

> THE Reader may be disposed to wonder how I could prevail on my self to give so free a Representation of my own Species, among a Race of Mortals who were already too apt to conceive the vilest Opinion of Human Kind, from that entire Congruity betwixt me and their *Yahoos*. But I must freely confess, that the many Virtues of those excellent *Quadrupeds* placed in opposite View to human Corruptions, had so far opened mine Eyes, and enlarged my Understanding, that I began to view the Actions and Passions of Man in a very different Light[.] (4.7/II:242)

Is Gulliver simply deluded? It is impossible to slough off all the layers of irony here to uncover a sole core of meaning. The Houyhnhnms are at once idealized avatars of reason and unattractively inhuman creatures (inhuman in a pejorative sense rather than a simply literal one), almost completely unmoved by the affections or the passions. (One's opinion of the Houyhnhnms will clearly be affected by one's position on the desirability or otherwise of the government of reason.[45]) The "grand Maxim" of the Houyhnhnms is "to cultivate *Reason,* and to be wholly governed by it" (4.8/II:251). In contrast, Gulliver's master sums up the Yahoos (Gulliver amongst them) "as a Sort of Animals to whose Share, by what Accident he could not conjecture, some small Pittance of *Reason* had fallen, whereof we made no other Use than by its Assistance to aggravate our *natural* Corruptions, and to acquire new ones which Nature had not given us" (4.7/II:243). The Houyhnhnms consider Gulliver's desire to learn their language "as a Prodigy, that a brute Animal should discover such Marks of a rational Creature," and are astonished by his "Teachableness, Civility and Cleanliness" (4.3/II:218). (Gulliver of course also confesses to his master that "I was as much astonished to see the *Houyhnhnms* act like rational Beings, as he or his Friends could be in finding some Marks of Reason in a Creature he was pleased to call a *Yahoo;* to which I owned my Resemblance in every Part, but could not account for their degenerate and brutal Nature" [4.3/II:222].)

Gulliver's wishful identification with the Houyhnhnms does not stop him from taunting Yahoos in distinctly Yahoo-like mode. (Augustine would not have been surprised.) He bares his naked arms and chest at them—but only when his Houyhnhnm guardian stands nearby to protect him—and makes the interesting admission that "I have Reason to believe, they had some Imagination that I was of their own Species" (4.8/II:249). At such times, he says, "they would approach as near as they durst, and imitate my Actions after the Manner of Monkeys, but ever with great Signs of Hatred; as a tame *Jack Daw* with Cap and Stockings, is always persecuted by the wild ones, when he happens to be got among them." Gulliver's roaming the neighborhood as an observer of human-Yahoo nature concludes with one of the most striking scenes in the entire narrative. A young female Yahoo spots Gulliver bathing naked in the stream and leaps toward him, even as Gulliver roars with terror and the sorrel nag gallops to his rescue:

> THIS was Matter of Diversion to my Master and his Family, as well as of Mortification to my self. For now I could no longer deny, that I was a real *Yahoo,* in every Limb and Feature, since the Females had a natural Propensity to me as one of their own Species: Neither was the Hair of this Brute of a Red Colour, (which might have been some Excuse for an Appetite a little irregular) but black as a Sloe, and her Countenance did not make an Appearance altogether

so hideous as the rest of the Kind; for, I think, she could not be above Eleven Years old. (4.8/II:251)

From the ancient world to the early eighteenth century, copulation and re-production after the same kind had served as a way of defining species.[46] The seventeenth-century British naturalist John Ray, in a small and altogether en-chanting volume titled *The Wisdom of God Manifested in the Works of the Creation* (1691), "reckon[s] all Dogs to be of one *Species* they mingling together in genera-tion, and the breed of such Mixtures being prolifick."[47] In 1674 Ray had laid out to the members of the Royal Society the importance of fertile interbreeding for species definition: "Diversity of colour in the flower, or taste in the fruit, is no bet-ter note of specific difference in plants, than the like varieties of hair or skin, or taste of flesh in animals; so that one may, with as good reason, admit a blackmore and European to be two species of men, or a black cow and a white to be two sorts of kine, as two plants, differing only in colour of flower, to be specifically distinct; such varieties, both in animals and plants, being occasioned either by diversity of climate, and temperature of the air, or of nourishment and manner of living."[48] Increasingly this would come to be taken as a given, and one impor-tant popularizer of the notion was the mid-eighteenth-century French naturalist Buffon, who in his 1749 *History of Animals* "consider[s] as the same species, that which by means of copulation perpetuates itself and conserves the similarities of that species, and as different species, those that through the same means can produce nothing together."[49] We cannot know whether Gulliver and the young female would have had prolific union, but the "natural Propensity" of the females toward him is certainly interpreted by Gulliver as incontrovertible evidence of species identity.

## The Perfectibility Problem

The threat of Yahoo violence is in many respects less terrifying than the threat posed by Yahoo reproductive capabilities. The Houyhnhnms practice a sort of vol-untary eugenics among themselves, and they also contemplate extending eugenic control over the Yahoo population, even to the point of considering the possible extermination of the Yahoos. The debate begins with the invocation of a myth of origins in which the Yahoos are born from mud or "the Ooze and Froth of the Sea," a mildly stomach-turning act of fecundation in whose sequel "these *Yahoos* engendered, and their Brood in a short time grew so numerous as to over-run and infest the whole Nation" (4.9/11:255). A long-ago generation of Houyhnhnms, the story goes on, initiated a cull followed by the enclosure of the herd and subsequent domestication (insofar as Yahoos can be tamed) of the young ones in kennels. This myth provides an enabling precedent for the contemplation, in the present tense, of what might euphemistically be called population control. Gulliver's master is one of only a handful to question the myth and its implications, suggesting instead (on the basis of his observation in Gulliver of "all the Qualities of a *Yahoo*, only a little more civilized by some Tincture of Reason" [4.9/11:256]) that the Yahoos may instead be a degenerate form of humankind, driven over the sea and becoming "in Process of Time, much more savage than those of their own Species in the Country from whence these two Originals came" (4.9/11:256). On the basis of this *slightly* less revolting origin, he will go on to suggest—the idea has been put into his head by Gulliver's description of how men treat horses in Europe—that rather than being killed, the Yahoos might merely be castrated, "which, besides rendering them tractable and fitter for Use, would in an Age put an End to the whole Species without destroying Life" (4.9/11:257).

Contemplating the elimination not merely of an individual or even of an isolated population but of an entire species takes us to the heart of the perfectibility problem. Population control of the kind the Houyhnhnms entertain for the Yahoos (paired here with the Houyhnhnms' own set of proto-eugenic schemes—their internal population control, as it were, as distinct from the kind they wish to level on others) raises an obvious question about whether belief in natural inequality and the need for social regulation of breeding necessarily entails (or not) a willingness to contemplate the extermination of others. However we assess the utopian society of the Houyhnhnms, it is evidently not a democracy. Houyhnhnms are created unequal, nobility inhering in certain kinds of body rather than others, a fact foregrounded in the narrative when Gulliver's master asks him to observe "that among the *Houyhnhnms*, the *White*, the *Sorrel*, and the *Iron-grey*, were not so exactly shaped as the *Bay*, the *Dapple-grey*, and the *Black;* nor born with equal Talents of Mind, or a Capacity to improve them; and therefore continued always in the Condition of Servants, without ever aspiring to match out of their own Race, which in that Country would be reckoned monstrous and unnatural" (4.6/11:240). Swift's own political views are known to have tended toward the patrician. In an *Examiner* paper of 1711, for instance, he had written of his dislike for those who discover "a Contempt for *Birth, Family,* and *ancient Nobility,*" arguing that even if "there be nothing but *Opinion* in the Difference of Blood; every Body knows, that *Authority* is very much founded on *Opinion*" and suggesting moreover that the "Difference is not wholly imaginary."[50] An even pithier summing-up of

Swift's views can be found a paragraph later: "A Pearl holds its Value although it be found in a Dunghill; but however, that is not the most probable Place to search for it."[51]

The Houyhnhnm caste system may have been drawn in part from writings on actual horses, where the notion that the color of a horse's coat affected its quality had a long and persistent life. "The antient Writers tell us that every *Horse* is *colour'd* as he is *complexion'd*, and according to the Complexion *he* is good or evil dispositioned, as he doth participate of *the* Elements so *he* is complexion'd," announces an early eighteenth-century treatise on horses called *The Gentleman's Compleat Jockey.*[52] It reveals more significant affiliations, perhaps, with a distinguished lineage of philosophical speculation about natural inequality, most clearly harking back to the foundational assumption about human nature expressed in Plato's *Republic,* "that one individual is by nature quite unlike another individual, that they differ in their natural aptitudes, and that different people are equipped to perform different tasks."[53] Socrates invents a myth that will be used to explain to the children of the republic why they have been allocated to different spheres:

> You are all brothers, . . . all of you in the city. But when god made you, he used a mixture of gold in the creation of those of you who were fit to be rulers, which is why they are the most valuable. He used silver for those who were to be auxiliaries, and iron and bronze for the farmers and the rest of the skilled workers. Most of the time you will father children of the same type as yourselves, but because you are all related, occasionally a silver child may be born from a golden parent, or a golden child from a silver parent, and likewise any type from any other type. (108)

The city's guardians must discern the nature of children's souls on the most impersonal basis: "If their own child is born with a mixture of bronze or iron in him," Socrates cautions, "they must feel no kind of pity for him, but give him the position in society his nature deserves, driving him out to join the skilled workers or farmers" (108). Education must work hand in hand with birth, however, to produce the guardians: "If you can keep a good system of upbringing and education, they produce naturally good specimens. These in their turn, if they receive a good education, develop into even better specimens than their predecessors. Better in general, and better in particular for reproduction. The same is true in the animal kingdom" (116). This vision will be achieved by relatively broad supervision and management of the reproductive life, a primary responsibility of the guardians. Wives will be held in common and "no parent shall know its own child, no child its own parent" (155); moreover, just as animals must be bred "from the best," so must people (157), and it is the responsibility of the guardians to exclude "the inferior type" by means of ingenious lotteries, ensuring that the "children of good parents" are raised in a special nursing-pen and that the "children of inferior parents" and "any deformed specimen born to the other group" die by exposure or abortion (158).

Houyhnhnm society similarly depends on birth control of a fairly straightforward kind. After a mother has produced one child of each sex, she will no longer couple with her consort unless they lose a child, at which point she is allowed to bear another one or else to adopt one from another couple: "This Caution is necessary to prevent the Country from being overburthened with Numbers," Gulliver solemnly and approvingly observes (4.8/II:252). The servant race is allowed to produce three of each sex, so as to supply a sufficient quantity of menials, but a eugenic principle obtains throughout: "In their Marriages," says Gulliver, "they are exactly careful to chuse such Colours as will not make any disagreeable Mixture in the Breed." And like the imagined inhabitants of Plato's republic, the Houyhnhnms have done away with those irrational things called families:

> They have no Fondness for their Colts or Foles; but the Care they take in educating them proceedeth entirely from the Dictates of *Reason*. And, I observed my Master to shew the same Affection to his Neighbour's Issue that he had for his own. They will have it that *Nature* teaches them to love the whole Species, and it is *Reason* only that maketh a Distinction of Persons, where there is a superior Degree of Virtue. (4.8/II:252)

The thought-experiment of treating human marriages as though they happen in stables had been envisaged by earlier writers, quite often with satirical import. The Greek aphorist Theognis observes that in "horses . . . we seek the thoroughbred, and a man is concerned therein to get him offspring of good stock; yet in marriage a good man thinketh not twice of wedding the bad daughter of a bad sire if the father give him many possessions."[54] A similar analogy between horses and humans is also invoked in Thomas More's description of how the Utopians choose their marriage partners:

> Whether she be widow or virgin, the woman is shown naked to the suitor by a responsible and respectable matron; and similarly, some honourable man presents the suitor naked to the woman. We laughed at this custom, and called it absurd; but they were just as amazed at the folly of all other peoples. When

men go to buy a colt, where they are risking only a little money, they are so cautious that, though the animal is almost bare, they won't close the deal until saddle and blanket have been taken off, lest there be a hidden sore underneath. Yet in the choice of a mate, which may cause either delight or disgust for the rest of their lives, men are so careless that they leave all the rest of the woman's body covered up with clothes and estimate her attractiveness from a mere handsbreadth of her person, the face, which is all they can see.[55]

Such discussions often emphasize not just the private satisfactions of the suitor but also the public good, sometimes highlighting tensions between the needs and aims of the traditional nuclear family and the good of the state. Plutarch's life of Lycurgus was another important source for the argument that marriages and births fell under the legislator's as well as the physician's mandate: it was because he "considered children to belong not privately to their fathers, but jointly to the city" that the Spartan leader "wanted citizens produced not from random partners, but from the best."[56] And in his wonderfully intemperate *Discourse upon the Nature and Faculties of Man* (1686), Timothy Nourse offers a far more extravagant version of More's conceit when he suggests that any man contemplating marriage would be well advised to have his relatives "get a Sight of the naked Body" so that "all Deformities and Sores are expos'd to View," at least "discreetly, and as far as Modesty will allow, since the Deformity or Diseases of the Parents, leave a Blemish and Taint, many times, upon their Issue; so that besides the Content which every Man may propose to his own Fancy, he ought at least to be as careful of his Race, as he is of that of his Horses, where the Fairest and most Beautiful are made Choice of for Breed; which thing, tho it be practis'd amongst the *Utopians,* might be admitted also as useful in a real Government, under some Circumstances."[57]

Gulliver's master assumes that human society must operate along comparable lines; more particularly he imagines that Gulliver—so obviously superior to other Yahoos—must hail from his country's highest caste. This gives Swift another opportunity to expose the absurdities and topsy-turvydom of his own society, as Gulliver disabuses his master of the misconception that physical health and intellectual capacity are associated in England with high birth. The "Productions" of noble marriages "are generally scrophulous, rickety or deformed Children," Gulliver says; "by which Means the Family seldom continues above three Generations, unless the Wife take Care to provide a healthy Father among her Neighbours, or Domesticks, in order to improve and continue the Breed" (4.6/11:240). In this context, the idea of improving the breed is largely satirical, a hint that may have been drawn from the *Tatler* paper discussed early on in which the short and swarthy Isaac Bickerstaff lays out a "Design of Lengthening and Whitening his Posterity."[58] But references to degeneration occur frequently enough in Swift's writing that we can take this as being more than just a peripheral joke at the expense of the British nobility. The members of illustrious families whom Gulliver summons from the dead in book 3 have already afforded him "melancholy Reflections to observe how much the Race of human Kind was degenerate among us, within these Hundred Years past": "How the Pox under all its Consequences and Denominations had altered every Lineament of an *English* Countenance; shortened the Size of Bodies, unbraced the Nerves, relaxed the Sinews and Muscles, introduced a sallow Complexion, and rendered the Flesh loose and *rancid*" (3.8/11:185).[59] Given this context, the systematic breeding projects of the Houyhnhnms look distinctly prudent, or at least we might speculate that Swift himself found them so.

Human sexual coupling as a consequence seems in Swift's writings to be both contingently and essentially sullied: contingently, because of the loathsomeness of Yahoo desire and the prevalence of sexually transmitted disease and so forth, but in its essence due not just to the ordinary physiological and emotional messiness concomitant upon sex but to the idea that reproduction itself mostly just leads to there being too many people of the wrong sort. The logical end-point of this line of thinking can be found in *A Modest Proposal for Preventing the Children of poor People in Ireland, from being a Burden to their Parents or Country; and for making them beneficial to the Publick* (1729), in which Swift perfectly captures the rhetoric of an as-yet-embryonic social science of population control, a clear benefit of the projector's scheme being "that it will prevent those *voluntary Abortions,* and that horrid Practice of *Women murdering their Bastard Children;* alas! too frequent among us; sacrificing the *poor innocent Babes,* I doubt, more to avoid the Expence than the Shame; which would move Tears and Pity in the most Savage and inhuman Breast."[60] The cant of finding maternal child-killing contemptible while vindicating state-sanctioned infanticide is skewered here by Swift; he has an especially sharp ear for the effects of introducing a language of utility to domains of life where it surely has no place. In the paragraph that follows, the modest proposer offers a statistical enumeration of the number of "Breeders" and offspring to be accounted for in his plan:

> I DO therefore humbly offer it to *publick Consideration,* that of the Hundred and Twenty Thousand Children, already computed, Twenty thousand may be reserved for Breed; whereof only one Fourth Part to be Males; which is more

than we allow to *Sheep, black Cattle,* or *Swine;* and my Reason is, that these Children are seldom the Fruits of Marriage, *a Circumstance not much regarded by our Savages;* therefore, *one Male* will be sufficient to serve *four Females.* That the remaining Hundred thousand, may, at a Year old, be offered in Sale to the *Persons of Quality* and *Fortune,* through the Kingdom; always advising the Mother to let them suck plentifully in the last Month, so as to render them plump, and fat for a good Table. (12:111–112)

This gleeful adoption of a language of agricultural improvement into a calculus of breeding most obviously erodes the humanity of the bodies to be regulated. In response to a suggestion that the lack of venison might be more humanely supplied by the bodies of young men and women between twelve and fourteen years of age, the projector balks:

But with due Deference to so excellent a Friend, and so deserving a Patriot, I cannot be altogether in his Sentiments. For as to the Males, my *American* Acquaintance assured me from frequent Experience, that their Flesh was generally tough and lean, like that of our School-boys, by continual Exercise, and their Taste disagreeable; and to fatten them would not answer the Charge. Then, as to the Females, it would, I think, with humble Submission, *be a Loss to the Publick,* because they soon would become Breeders themselves: And besides it is not improbable, that some scrupulous People might be apt to censure such a Practice (although indeed very unjustly) as a little bordering upon Cruelty; which, I confess, hath always been with me the strongest Objection against any Project, how well soever intended. (12:113)

The idea of women as "Breeders" contributing to the public good is very close to the actual ideas of later economists and population theorists concerning national wealth. Swift's own opinions on these matters are almost always hedged about with layers of protective irony, but on a manuscript list of "Maxims Examind," he once noted that "Encouragin [sic] marriage as all wise nations did, is an appendix to the Maxim of people the riches of a Nation; we ought to discourage it. The wretches we see with children" (12:310). Elsewhere, in a miscellaneous collection of thoughts on religion, he set out the basis for considering reason and reproduction as fundamentally at odds: "Although reason were intended by providence to govern our passions, yet it seems that, in two points of the greatest moment to the being and continuance of the world, God hath intended our passions to prevail over reason. The first is, the propagation of our species, since no wise man ever married from the dictates of reason. The other is, the love of life, which, from the dictates of reason, every man would despise, and wish it at an end, or that it never had a beginning" (9:263).

## "Properties descend!"

As with humans, so with horses; and it is hardly surprising, given the horse's high prestige and its close interweaving with every aspect of human life during this period, that debates about human nature should have migrated so easily into popular and technical writing about horses and their breeding. In a recent essay on the thoroughbred horse in eighteenth-century Britain, Richard Nash shows the extent to which these horses became what he calls an "embodied metaphor," in other words "a site for contesting anxieties about maternal influence . . . [and] for reasserting in the face of anxiety patrilineal doctrines of influence and heritability."[61] Writings on horses also rehash the still heated debates about innate qualities initiated by Descartes and Locke. I want to look briefly at contributions to the argument about improvement made by two treatises published within five years of one another at mid-century, William Osmer's *A Dissertation on Horses: Wherein it is Demonstrated, by Matters of Fact, as well as from the Principles of Philosophy, that* INNATE QUALITIES *do not Exist, and that the excellence of this Animal is altogether mechanical and not in the Blood* (1756) and Richard Wall's *A Dissertation on Breeding of Horses, upon Philosophical and Experimental Principles; Being An attempt to promote thereby an Improvement in the present manner of Breeding Racers, And Horses in general* (1760).[62] Almost by definition, such works (dissertations!) claim the prestige of the modern and the scientific, disowning the folk wisdom published in modest volumes with titles like *The Perfect Horseman* that often recycled material more than a century old.

Wall and Osmer share a desire to differentiate their arguments from the received wisdom on horses and "blood." There is an almost comic symmetry, however—and certainly a high degree of aptness for my own inquiry—in the extent to which their respective positions represent the poles of contemporary thought about breeding. Osmer's subtitle makes clear the polemical nature of his intervention. Innate qualities do not exist, he insists, and the horse's excellence derives from mechanical qualities rather than those of "blood," a term that is itself "of no use, but to puzzle and lead us astray," misleadingly evocative "of occult and hidden causes" and better reframed in mechanistic terms.[63] One of the most telling points against the explanatory force of the term *blood*, Osmer argues, can be found in the difference of quality between siblings. "If any man should boast of the blood of his cocks," Osmer writes, "and say that the uncommon virtue of this animal, which we call game, is innate, I answer no, for that all principles, and all ideas arise from sensation and reflection, and are therefore acquired":

*Locke*

> AMONGST men, do we not perceive agility and strength stand forth confessed in the fabric of their bodies? Do not even the passions and pleasures of mankind greatly depend on the organs of their bodies? Amongst dogs, we shall find the fox-hound prevailing over all others in speed and in bottom; but if not in speed, in bottom at least I hope it will be allowed. To what shall we impute this perfection in him? shall we impute it to his blood, or to that elegance of form in which is found no unnecessary weight to oppress the muscles, or detract from his ability of perseverance? if to blood, from whence shall we deduce it? or from what origin is it derived? Surely no man means more, when he talks of the blood of fox-hounds, than to intimate that they are descended from such, whose ancestors have been eminent for their good qualifications, and have shone conspicuous in the front of the pack for many generations.[64]

Though it may seem obvious, perhaps the most interesting thing here is that Osmer (in stark contrast to our own preference for considering organs as functions of hereditary rather than acquired characters) thinks of the properties appertaining to the organs of men's bodies or the foxhound's elegance of form as mechanical and acquired. He asks his readers to "consider a Horse as a piece of animated machinery (for it is in reality no other)," and consistently emphasizes that a horse's quality results from its physical advantages, "not by any innate virtue, or principle of the mind, which must be understood by the word blood, if any thing at all is intended to be understood by it" (32, 49).

His evidence is drawn from the real-world history of British horse-racing, and more particularly from the fact that of the colts borne by mares put to the Godolphin Arabian, some were good racers and some bad. "[S]hall we condemn the blood of these mares which produced the inferior Horses?" Osmer asks. "If so, we shall never know what good blood is, or where it is to be found, or ever act with any certainty in the propagation of this species, and it is this ridiculous opinion alone of blood, that deceives mankind so much in the breed of racers":

> THE question then is, whether this excellence of Horses is in the blood or the mechanism; whoever is for blood, let him take two brothers of any sort or kind, and breed one up in plenty, the other upon a barren heath; I fancy he will find,

that a different mechanism of the body will be acquired to the two brothers by the difference of their living, and that the blood of him brought up on the barren heath, will not be able to contend with the mechanism of the other, brought up in a land of plenty. Now if this difference of shape will make a difference in the performance of the animal, it will be just the same thing in its consequences, whether this imperfection of shape be produced by scarcity of food, or entailed by the laws of nature; if so, does it signify whether the colt be got by Turk, Barb, or Arab, or what kind of blood his dam be of?[65]

It is clear from the subsequent pages, moreover, that Osmer believes (along with virtually everyone who wrote during this period about the passage of properties from parents to offspring) that acquired traits may be inherited: "the true reason why foreign Horses get better colts than their descendants, if they do get better," he writes (a slightly self-defeating mode of argument), "is that (mechanism alike) their descendants from which we breed, are generally such Horses as have been thoroughly tried, consequently much strained, and gone through strong labour and fatigue" (56–57). As proof, he proposes that we "take two sister hound bitches, and ward them both with the same dog; let us suppose one bitch to have run in the pack, and the other by some accident not to have worked at all, it will be found that the offspring of her who has never worked, will be much superior to the offspring of her who has run in the pack" (57).

Equally dismissive of thoughtless invocations of the term *blood,* Osmer's approximate contemporary Richard Wall takes a completely different tack in his consideration of the problem of how to breed better horses. While Osmer retains a more-or-less traditional belief (it dates back to the ancient world) that the choice of mare mattered more than that of sire, since she "not only joins in the production of the fœtus, but in the formation of it also," Wall warns that breeders must be careful in their choice "both of the male and female,"

for from the many observations that have been made upon various species of animals, it is found (at least by all those who have given themselves the trouble of observing) that there is one fundamental maxim which will always hold good (allowing for the little variations of nature) viz. that Properties descend! Therefore it is reasonable to expect that in the breeding of animals in general, the offspring, for the most part, will bear a near resemblance (when at maturity and perfect in the animal system) in size, colour, symmetry, &c. to either the male or female; but more commonly an equal part (or nearly so) of both, from whom it sprung.[66]

The breeder accordingly should procure a superior sire and dam, Wall goes on to say, and "be likewise partial to the merits of their ancestors through as many generations as possible!" (25). (Wall is partial to exclamation points.) And yet though it may be tempting to call Wall prescient, to think of how he anticipates twentieth-century theories of heredity, and to mock poor Osmer for his dogmatic mechanism, it would be distinctly misleading to credit either Osmer or Wall with an understanding of the hereditary transmission of traits anything like what we now possess. In a sense, these works show us an almost science-fictional vision of paths not taken, of alternate intellectual universes whose very strangeness can sensitize us to elements of present-day conversations become so familiar as to be sometimes inaudible.

## "Ascertaining what species can procreate together"

Though the popular agricultural writer Richard Bradley will be invoked later in these pages as a spokesman for the force of "Pasture" on sheep's conformation, he is also strikingly imaginative on matters of heredity, emphasizing breeding (in his discussions of horses in *The Gentleman and Farmer's Guide* of 1732) in something like the sense of what would later be called sexual selection. Bradley believes diseases and imperfections pass from the sire and dam to their offspring, and he even hints at the possibility of eugenic measures of the sort imagined by Plato and Theognis when he calls the horse "the noblest Creature under Mankind that we find in the Animal Kingdom, for its Use and Beauty, . . . the most regarded in Point of Breed, while the Race of Mankind is almost neglected, as far as it concerns the Strength and Beauty of the Body."[67] Although the book pitches itself as a practical manual for husbandmen from various social strata, Bradley has a strongly scientific or experimental temperament, speculating that piedness in horses may be analogous to stripes or variegation in plants and suggesting that one way to determine whether such a trait is accidental or rather a property descending from the parents (this language is not his, but the thought is quite clear) would be to "take care to examine into the Descent of a Horse and Mare that we design to breed from":

> ONE Thing which might come near towards a Resolution of the Question we have in Hand, would be To enquire into those Families where black Men have coupled with white Women, or white Men coupled with black Women, in order to know if the Father was black, whether the Child was of that Colour; or

whether the Child was black if the Mother was of that Colour, with a white Father. And moreover, whether this cross Strain will not produce sometimes white, and sometimes black, Children; or sometimes those of a tawny Colour, or Mulattoes; as also it would be requisite to know, whether the Black Children in three or four Generations, do not produce Children of a tawny, or Olive Colour; or, whether the Offspring of the Blacks with the Whites, instead of the Wool, do not bring long black Hairs on their Heads, or perhaps white Hairs, and a tawny Complexion.[68]

The pages that follow offer further speculations on cross-breeding and color, with Bradley concluding (he excepts insects from his theory, since he has observed that painted butterflies won't mix with white ones) that "one may likely produce Breeds either in Beast, Fowls, Birds, Fish, or Plants, of various Colours, and differing from the Principals, by cross Couplings."[69]

Cross-coupling proved an object of obsession for eighteenth-century investigators in part because of the light it promised to cast on generation. If you were trying to work out whether it was true, as Swammerdam had suggested, that "all men were contained in the organs of Adam and Eve" and that "[w]hen their stock of eggs is finished, the human race will cease to be,"[70] a great deal hung on whether the existence of hybrids would disprove the notion. There is of course something striking about the idea of monsters and hybrids that can't be attributed to specific cultural and intellectual intersections at this moment in European thought, but the *feel* of the discussion during this period is markedly different from the wild imaginative speculations of the early modern "books of secrets" by Della Porta and others. Certain continental theorists of generation—though these writings would not necessarily have been known even to the later eighteenth-century British writers discussed in these pages—write about cross-coupling with appealing and sometimes bizarre excitement about pushing the bounds of possibility. Here, for instance, is the eminent Swiss naturalist Charles Bonnet writing to the Italian physiologist Lazzaro Spallanzani, a letter published in an English translation of Spallanzani's writings in 1784 (both men advocated a preformationist theory of generation that closely resembled Swammerdam's "ovaries of Eve" hypothesis):

You are now in possession of a sure and easy way of ascertaining what species can procreate together; and the experiments you propose attempting next spring, by putting your voluptuous spaniel in the company of cats and rabbits, promise not so fair as those which you will make, by introducing the semen of this spaniel into the uterus of a doe-rabbit and a she-cat, and on the other hand, by introducing the semen of the male rabbit and cat into the uterus of a bitch. You hold in your hand a precious clue, which will guide you to the most important and unexpected discoveries. I know not, whether what you have now discovered, may not one day be applied in the human species to purposes we little think of, and of which the consequences will not be trivial. You conceive my meaning: however that may be, I consider the mystery of fecundation as nearly cleared up. What remains principally to be discovered, is the formation of the mule, and what occasions the different marks of resemblance between children and their parents.[71]

Though he failed to bring about the dog-cat hybrid he hoped for, Spallanzani retained his conviction that the experiments themselves were worthwhile.[72]

Both Bonnet and Spallanzani dance around the question of whether and with what import such experiments might be practiced on humans, but more explicitly eugenic strains of argument can be found in a wide variety of eighteenth-century writings. Cause and effect are impossible to disentangle here, but the convergence of intellectual excitement about the science of generation (and its sequel, the new way of thinking about generation summed up in the term *reproduction*), widely held beliefs in progress and perfectibility, a georgic passion for the sciences of agricultural improvement, and an emerging science that would come to be called physical anthropology enabled fascinating and often quite disturbing speculations about man's genetic perfectibility. Prophets of the hereditary certainly spoke here and there, in other words, though their words sometimes hold more interest for modern readers than they did for contemporaries. Bradley is one of these pioneers, but perhaps most striking among them is the French scientist Maupertuis, whose investigations into generation made less of a mark during his lifetime than the scandals that seemed to trail in his wake.

Maupertuis was a mathematician and astronomer, a prominent member of the Academy of Sciences in Paris and an evangelist for Newtonian gravitation, later president of the Berlin Academy of Sciences, and close ally of Frederick the Great. His reputation today is still marred by a charge of plagiarism—following his development of "the principle of least action," the statement about the conservation of energy for which he is best known, a colleague accused Maupertuis of having stolen from Leibniz—in a controversy memorialized by Voltaire, whose satire has ensured that literary historians have ever since found Maupertuis primarily a figure of fun: not a difficult matter, given his dandyish pretensions, his embarrassing womanizing, and the heroic-absurd trip he took to Lapland to determine the shape of the earth with the newest English astronomical instruments.[73] But his fortunes began rising with the early twentieth-century science of genetics and the emergence of a history of science interested in exploring long-buried intellectual contexts.[74] George W. Stocking Jr. persuasively called Maupertuis "the most original eighteenth-century speculator on problems of heredity,"[75] and for Maupertuis, as for Darwin a century later (as François Jacob comments in his rich history of heredity), "what the breeder obtains by art is a model for grasping how nature produces new species spontaneously."[76]

Historian of science Mary Terrall has described the occasion of Maupertuis' first major publication on generation, a short piece called *Dissertation physique à l'occasion du nègre blanc* (1744) that reflected on the appearance of a recent human prodigy, or "freak," displayed in the salons of Paris, a four- or five-year-old black albino boy; this work was later expanded (with new chapters on racial difference and albinism, hereditary attributes, and so forth) and published under the title *Venus physique* (1745).[77] Maupertuis' thoughts on heredity include an unusually clear account (anomalous among eighteenth-century explanations of how and why children are like their parents), in a chapter titled "Reasons Which Prove That Both the Father and the Mother Participate in the Embryo's Production," of why the possibility of a child resembling either parent and the existence of animal hybrids "quite destroyed" both ovist and animalculist theories of preformation (1.15.51). He also offered prescient speculation (*pace* his older compatriot Réaumur's work on polydactyly) about the odds of human six-fingeredness *not* being hereditary.[78] But Maupertuis did not simply observe hereditary phenomena; he also hoped to manipulate them. In the passage below Maupertuis meditates on genetic perfectibility and human intervention, moving easily from animals to people:

> Nature holds the source of all these varieties, but chance or art sets them going. So that people whose work is to satisfy the tastes of curiosity seekers become practically creators of new species. We find new breeds of dogs, pigeons, canaries appearing on the market, though they did not exist in nature. At first they were individual freaks, but art and repeated generations turned them into new species. The famed Lyonnés creates each year a new variety and destroys the ones no longer in style. He corrects the shapes and varies the colors to the point of inventing species, such as the Harlequin Dane and the *Mopse* [Pug dog].
>
> Why is this art restricted to animals? Why don't the bored Sultans in their seraglios, filled with women of all known races, have them bear new species?

Were I reduced, as they are, to the only pleasure that form and features can give, I would soon have recourse to greater varieties. But, however beautiful the women born for them might be, they would know only the smallest share of love's pleasures as long as they remained ignorant of the pleasures of the mind and the heart.

Although we do not find among ourselves the creation of such new types of beauty, only too often do we see human beings who are of the same category for men of science, namely, the cross-eyed, the lame, the gouty, and the tubercular. Unfortunately, in order to fix their strain there is no need of a long series of generations. But wise Nature, because of the disgust she has inspired for these defects, has not desired that they be continued. Consequently beauty is more apt to be hereditary. The slim waist and the leg that we admire are the achievements of many generations which have applied themselves to form them.

A Northern king was able to elevate and beautify his nation. His taste for men of height and fine faces was excessive and he induced them to come to his kingdom by various means. Fortune came to men whom Nature had made tall. Today we now see a singular example of the power of kings. This nation is distinguished for its tall men and regular features. So it is with a forest whose trees dominate all the neighboring woods, if the attentive eye of the master forester takes care to cultivate only trees that are straight and well chosen.[79]

This long passage shows the cluster of concerns that would dominate most eighteenth-century discussions of genetic perfectibility. The close connection between the commercial world of pigeon- and dog-breeders and more abstract questions about the nature of species (and more particularly, whether the total number of species had been fixed at the Creation or whether instead—as natural philosophers would come to suspect, often with considerable uneasiness—new species continued to emerge); the idea that people might also respond to new breeding techniques (here a characteristic dandyish Maupertian flourish in the seraglio reference); the example of the King of Prussia's early experiment in national beautification; and, most particularly, the sense that illness and deformity provide the most important model for understanding inheritance: these features can be seen scattered widely throughout the writings of many who would not necessarily have known Maupertuis' writings on generation directly.

A particularly pressing question for eighteenth-century commentators concerned whether the human race was indeed a single species—following the account of man's creation in Genesis, a theory known as monogenesis—or whether the races represented different species of men (Henry Home, Lord Kames was a high-profile exponent of the theory of polygenesis, or multiple origins, a theory that obviously and easily sanctioned certain kinds of scientific racism). At mid-century Buffon observed of humans that "amidst all these differences of colour, and dimensions, the *Negro* and the white man, the *Laplander* and the *Patagonian*, the giant and the dwarf, can together produce individuals capable of reproducing themselves; and consequently these men, so different in appearance, are all of one and the same species; this constant reproduction being what constitutes the species."[80] The British surgeon William Lawrence, in the *Lectures on Physiology, Zoology, and the Natural History of Man* (1822), which represent one of the early nineteenth century's most disturbing and extreme arguments for white racial superiority and the significance of racial difference, observing that the term "*hybrid generation*" cannot apply to the offspring of the copulation of two varieties within a single species (and accordingly that "hybrids are never produced in the human species"), alludes to speaking "in the human subject, of such hybrids as proceed from copulation of the different varieties of one and the same species, as of a cart-horse and a racer, the green and white canary-birds, &c. These unions have a great effect in changing the colour, conformation, and other properties of the offspring, and are consequently employed with wonderful advantage in improving the breeds of our domestic animals, particularly the horse, sheep, and cattle."[81] Thus monogenesis engenders a language of "varieties" that can constitute another form of racism, and it can also be seen as an intellectual successor of an associationist psychology that emphasizes the power of impressions or vibrations (the last term is particularly associated with David Hartley) to change physical appearance.

In *The Earthly Venus*, the chapter on "White Negroes" describes the albino boy whose shameful public display—the description Maupertuis gives is extraordinarily offensive to modern eyes, emphasizing the boy's "ugliness" and the fact that his "hands, large and misshapen, resemble more an animal's paws than the hands of a man" (2.4.75)—seems to have initially prompted these thoughts on generation. (It is an important fact about eighteenth-century theories of genetic perfectibility that they were often intimately bound up with theories of racial difference.) Maupertuis concludes that albinism in black people "can only be of an hereditary variety which becomes established or disappears with successive generations" (2.4.76). "Should we feel the need of investigating the realm of plants in order to confirm my statement," he continues, "we would be told by gardeners that all the variegated colors we find in shrubs and flowers, highly prized in our gardens, are due to selections which have become hereditary but which will revert if neglected" (2.4.77). The need to avert that degeneration provides the necessary justification for acts of intervention that might otherwise seem to challenge the natural order. In *Utopia's Garden: French Natural History from Old Regime to Revolution,* Emma Spary argues that the naturalists of the Jardin du Roi were more interested in "the exploitation of the transformative powers of living beings . . . [than] the exploration of the limits to transformation,"[82] and this is a world in which plants and animals and people are all equally subject to the power of human intervention.

Despite the hostility of Voltaire and others, Maupertuis was taken seriously by many of his French contemporaries; Buffon praised his theory of generation, and in his controversial materialist tract *Machine Man* (1748), Julien Offray de la Mettrie endorses Maupertuis's speculations on heredity. La Mettrie's sequel *Man as Plant* (1748, 1750) takes this thought a step further, arguing for the affinity between plants and animals (including man) and asking whether we shouldn't "prune a man like a tree": "A universally learned author said so before me: the forest of splendid men covering Prussia is due to the care and research of the late King."[83] The example of Frederick of Prussia is telling because of what it reveals about medicine's import for national or legislative issues. Physicians were almost certainly the earliest group to explore such questions in detail, and often with immediate practical import. The French doctor Charles-Augustin Vandermonde is quite blunt: "Puisque l'on est parvenu à perfectionner la race des chevaux, des chiens, des chats, des poules, des pigeons, des sereins," he asks in 1756, "pourquoi ne seroit-on aucune tentative sur l'espèce humaine?"[84] Historian Anne Carol has usefully described the difference between Vandermonde's arguments about human improvement and those of his seventeenth- and early eighteenth-century precursors by observing that where those had been directed at private individuals (husbands considering the choice of a wife, say, or potential parents looking to have children to be proud of), Vandermonde's framework concerns the legislator attending to collective rather than personal interests.[85]

Such speculations were not confined to the continent. In *A Comparative View of the State and Faculties of Man with those of the Animal World* (first published in 1765, but quoted here from the expanded sixth edition of 1774), the Scottish physician John Gregory proposed making use "of the observations made on tame Animals in those particulars where Art has in some measure improved upon Nature. Thus by a proper attention we can preserve and improve the breed of Horses, Dogs, Cattle, and indeed of all other Animals. Yet it is amazing that this Observation was never transferred to the Human Species, where it would be equally applicable."[86] His particular concern is disease and its effects on the families of those who are currently neglecting "to improve not only the constitutions, but the characters of our posterity": "we every day see very sensible people, who are anxiously attentive to preserve or improve the breed of their Horses, tainting the blood of their Children, and entailing on them, not only the most loathsome diseases of the Body, but madness, folly, and the most unworthy dispositions" (1:29–30). His language suggests a strong interest in hereditary phenomena, and indeed mid-eighteenth-century medical writers tend to show a stronger sense of the power of the innate or congenital than their scientific counterparts in other fields. Reflecting on what he calls "Family Character," which "like a Family Face, will often be lost in one generation and appear again in the succeeding," Gregory argues that while "Education, Habit, and Emulation, may contribute greatly in many cases to preserve it," the more important fact is that "independent of these, Nature has stamped an original impression on certain Minds, which Education may greatly alter or efface, but seldom so entirely as to prevent its traces from being seen by an accurate observer" (1:27–28). Rather than focusing on nature or nurture exclusively, Gregory and his peers observe the interactions of both and move quickly to consider the imperative of improvement, whether that means manipulating the properties of plants and animals by means that we would call genetic or simply applying the tools of culture, associated equally with plants (the cultivation of plants and crops) and children (the cultivation of the "germ" within a student, for instance, in the metaphor beloved of the sixteenth-century humanists).

## Differences of Climate

In general, it has to be said that the eighteenth century was a period of belief in environmental culture. Heredity—heredity as a *concept*—really came into its own only during the nineteenth century, and even the terminology available to eighteenth-century writers made it difficult to be precise about hereditary elements. The celebrated later eighteenth-century livestock breeder Robert Bakewell would move over the course of his career from a strongly environmental set of beliefs about animals' being "adapted to live in various climates, by the changes which different situations produce in their constitutions and habits" toward an increasing belief (especially as his contemporaries represented his work) in the greater importance of keeping the breed pure.[87] More broadly, the early years of the nineteenth century undoubtedly saw a move toward explaining visible differences in fleece by internal rather than external causes: while soil and food and so on doubtless influence the animal's coat, asserts John Luccock in his 1805 book on wool, "the influence of pasture, climate and temperature are entirely subordinate to that of blood," a downplaying of environmental influence and concomitant emphasis on intrinsic traits that would be strongly characteristic of the later period's orientation toward the properties of people, plants, and animals.[88]

Nicholas Russell's history of heredity and animal breeding in early modern England shows the extent to which the notion of heritability was confined during the eighteenth century to the animals who lived in the closest and most prestigious association with man, namely dogs and horses, in many respects taken to be special cases among the animal kingdom.[89] Their unusually close relationship with humans, the history of tracking the horse's lineage, and the dog's remarkable plasticity with regard to the selection for traits visible to the naked eye: all these things worked to facilitate a certain willingness to consider these two species as having families and lines of descent as worth recording as those of humans. This was not the case for most domestic animals, though that would begin to change toward the end of the eighteenth century as the prestige of breeding cattle and other livestock increased. Throughout the century, animal breeders—their practice largely insulated from scientific investigations into generation and reproduction—tended to believe that environmental conditions affected reproduction as much as or more than the nature and quality of the parents, and sheep in particular were supposed to be relatively unaffected by hereditary factors.

There was a widespread consensus that sheep imported to England differed from those on the continent due primarily to environmental conditions: "the Difference of Stature and other Qualities among those in *England,* proceeds chiefly from the Diversity of Pasture," writes Bradley in *The Gentleman and Farmer's Guide,* "which, by Experience we find, will alter Sheep of any Kind; so that in Process of Time, a large Kind of Sheep may degenerate, and produce those of a smaller Size; and that from a large Strain, the Sheep in three or four Generations may not arrive at more than half the Weight or Bulk of their first Sires; and on the contrary, Sheep of a small Size may be improved and enlarged by a good Dyet, and a Constancy of it when they are Young, and 'till they are arrived at their natural Period of Growth."[90] Such views were also often applied to people. Climate theory assumed human physiology to be acutely responsive to environmental conditions, and writers in all sorts of disciplines made connections between such susceptibilities across the human-animal divide. The Anglican clergyman James Bate, for instance, in support of the assertion (in his 1766 treatise on original sin) "that the different Complexions of the different Sons of *Noah,* may be occasioned by Difference of Climate, Air, Food, Water, or other natural Causes," invoked both ethnographic material on skin color and settlement and the agricultural evidence of a sheep that when it arrived from Ethiopia to England "was covered with a coarse Kind of strait Hair, like that of a Camel," but whose coat was transformed "after a Year's Feed upon *English* Grass," with "very fine large Flocks of Wool, breaking out, in all Parts of its Body, through the old hairy Tegument."[91]

The influence of climate—so strongly present in the Greek Hippocratic writings—was particularly pursued by Montesquieu, who believed that its effects could be mitigated or even counteracted by nonphysical causes.[92] Climate theory is far from synonymous with associationism, with its emphasis on the force of mental experience, but the two ideas are in certain respects intellectually congruent. It is possible to think of climate theory (as advocated by everyone from Hippocrates to Montesquieu) emphasizing man's responsiveness to physical causes, with associationist thinkers such as Hume and Helvétius equally committed to the importance of external influences and impressions. The associationist David Hartley, moreover, could also be considered a climate theorist. In the discussion of Mosaic history that rather surprisingly makes up part of the second volume of *Observations on Man, His Frame, His Duty, and His Expectations* (1749), Hartley dismisses out of hand the notion that "the *Negro* Nations differ so much from the *Europeans*, that they do not seem to have descended from the same Ancestors":

> We cannot presume to say what Alterations Climate, Air, Water, Soil, Customs, *&c.* can or cannot produce. It is no-ways to be imagined, that all the national Differences in Complexion, Features, Make of the Bones, *&c.* require so many different Originals; on the contrary, we have Reason from Experience to assert, that various Changes of this Kind are made by the Incidents of Life, just as was observed, in the last Paragraph, of Plants, and brute Animals. And, with respect to the different Complexions of different Nations, Dr. *Mitchell* has shewn with great Appearance of Truth, *Phil. Trans. Numb.* 474. that these arise from external Influences. It will confirm this, if it be found, that the *Jews*, by residing in any Country for some Generations, approach to the Complexion of the original Natives. At the same time we must observe from the History of Distempers, that acquired Dispositions may be transmitted to the Descendents for some Generations; which is perhaps one of the great Truths intimated in the Account of the Fall. And thus the Children of *Negroes* may be black, tho' born and bred up in a Country where the original Natives are not so.[93]

The effort to distinguish physical from moral causes and comprehend their relative power drove a number of these speculations, which often ventured into the new territory of an emerging scientific racism.[94] In his essay "Of National Characters," first published in 1748 and now notorious for its explicit assertion of African racial inferiority, David Hume distinguishes moral from physical causes, moral causes being "all circumstances, which are fitted to work on the mind as motives or reasons, and which render a peculiar set of manners habitual to us" (the nature of the government, the country's wealth, and its terms with its neighbors), and physical ones "those qualities of the air and climate, which are supposed to work insensibly on the temper, by altering the tone and habit of the body, and giving a particular complexion, which, though reflection and reason may sometimes overcome it, will yet prevail among the generality of mankind, and have an influence on their manners."[95] Hume goes on to say that he is "inclined to doubt altogether of their operation in this particular": while animals may be affected by air, food, or climate, he believes that humans are largely exempt from such influences (200–202). This is primarily the case, though, for Europeans, a distinction that implies whites are less "animal" in their nature than blacks. "[T]here is some reason to think," he suggests, "that all the nations, which live beyond the polar circles or between the tropics, are inferior to the rest of the species, and are incapable of all the higher attainments of the human mind," and at the end of the paragraph he affixes that notorious footnote on race: "I am apt to suspect" (another characteristic hedge) "the negroes to be naturally inferior to the whites," he begins, and concludes with the observation that "[i]n JAMAICA, indeed, they talk of one negroe as a man of parts and learning; but it is likely he is admired for slender accomplishments, like a parrot, who speaks a few words plainly."[96] Supposing a real difference between northern and southern temperaments, however, Hume concludes, "we can only infer, that the climate may affect the grosser and more bodily organs of our frame; not that it can work upon those finer organs, on which the operations of the mind and understanding depend."[97]

The rationale underlying the case for the importance of physical influences concerned the idea of man as an animal. It would be stated very clearly by the immensely influential German physiologist and comparative anatomist Johann Blumenbach as he came to consider the nature and causes of racial difference. His touchstone (part of the argument for species identity or monogenesis, and in clear contrast to Hume's position) was that *the same causes should be assigned to account for natural effects of the same kind. We must therefore assign the same causes for the bodily diversity of the races of mankind to which we assign a similar diversity of body in the other domestic animals which are widely scattered over the world.*[98] Man's special status derived not from some farfetched exemption from physical causes but rather from his control over them (Blumenbach's language here takes on a distinctly georgic cast):

> Man is a domestic animal. But in order that other animals might be made domestic about him, individuals of their species were first of all torn from their wild condition, and made to live under cover, and become tame; whereas he on the contrary was born and appointed by nature the most completely domesticated animal. Other domestic animals were first brought to that state of perfection *through him*. He is the only one who brought *himself* to perfection.[99]

That bringing-to-perfection also surely echoes the Pelagian heresy, a vision of transformation produced wholly by human effort rather than by the catalyst of divine grace.

## "The management of human creatures"

Certain conceptual patterns seem to bind perfectibility to population control. The proto-eugenicist elements seen in the writings of Vandermonde, Maupertuis, and the other eighteenth-century writers quoted here, taken alongside the slow, steady increase during these years of state intervention in private life, found close analogues in a parallel discourse on population.[100] This is not the place for an extended consideration of such arguments, but I want to say a few words about population as national wealth and breeding as social imperative, arguments more strongly associated with early twentieth-century natalist policies but also strikingly interwoven during the eighteenth century with various theories of political life. Implicit in many discussions of this kind of topic is a utilitarian understanding of the relationship between states and populations, a potentially disturbing instrumentalism whose implications are of considerable interest to Hume. Hume's "Of the Populousness of Ancient Nations" (published in the 1754 edition of the *Essays*) includes extensive consideration of the question of slavery and its effects on population, including an attempt to refute the standard argument that the ancient world's presumed greater populousness may have resulted from masters encouraging the "propagation [of slaves] as much as that of [their] cattle":

> The comparison is shocking between the management of human creatures and that of cattle; but being extremely just, when applied to the present subject, it

may be proper to trace the consequences of it. At the capital, near all great cities, in all populous, rich, industrious provinces, few cattle are bred. Provisions, lodging, attendance, labour are there dear; and men find their account better in buying the cattle, after they come to a certain age, from the remoter and cheaper countries. These are consequently the only breeding countries for cattle; and by a parity of reason, for men too, when the latter are put on the same footing with the former. To rear a child in LONDON, till he could be serviceable, would cost much dearer, than to buy one of the same age from SCOTLAND or IRELAND; where he had been bred in a cottage, covered with rags, and fed on oatmeal or potatoes. Those who had slaves, therefore, in all the richer and more populous countries, would discourage the pregnancy of the females, and either prevent or destroy the birth. The human species would perish in those places where it ought to encrease the fastest; and a perpetual recruit be wanted from the poorer and more desert provinces.[101]

Subsequent pages are peppered with the language of breeding: Hume's Roman sources remark "that scarcely any ever purchase slaves with a view of breeding from them"; "Our lackeys and house-maids, I own," he observes with rather dry irony, "do not serve much to multiply their species"; Roman noblemen had households of four hundred slaves or more, "and I believe every one will allow [Hume adds], that this would scarcely be practicable, were we to suppose all the slaves married, and the females to be breeders."[102] It is hard not to be reminded by this language of Swift's modest proposal: of course Hume's style is often lightly inflected with the ironies of the Augustan satirists, but it sometimes feels almost as though Swift produced over the course of his life an atlas for navigating a modern world only just then coming into existence.

In his *Various Prospects of Mankind* (1758), Robert Wallace, Hume's self-appointed interlocutor on questions of population, linked the ideal form of government to the increase of populations while at the same time outlining some of the costs of pronatalism. "Under a perfect government," he wrote, "the inconveniencies of having a family would be so intirely removed, children would be so well taken care of, and every thing become so favourable to populousness, that though some sickly seasons or dreadful plagues in particular climates might cut off multitudes, yet in general, mankind would encrease so prodigiously, that the earth would at last be overstocked, and become unable to support its numerous inhabitants."[103] The need to augment population always bumps up against the threat of overpopulation (with its specters of famine, abortion, and so forth), and the much-needed attempt to counter the "natural passions and appetites . . .

planted in our frame, to answer the best ends for the happiness both of the individuals and of the species" is seen by Wallace to entail violence and war as people find themselves unable to agree about appropriate measures to control population growth; in this sense, he says, "the tranquility and numerous blessings of the Utopian governments" carry the seeds of their own destruction.[104]

Wallace elsewhere makes a passionate case for government intervention in human reproduction, despite the obvious risks. Bemoaning the unlikelihood of a modern increase in population akin to that of the ancient world (the relative populousness of the modern and ancient worlds was a favorite topic of controversy at mid-century), he continues (in his *Dissertation on the Numbers of Mankind, in Ancient and Modern Times*, published four years earlier in 1753) as follows:

> It were however to be wished, that, as the bountiful Author of nature formed this earth chiefly for an habitation to man, and as with right culture it might support a much greater number than actually live upon it, the present scarcity of people in so many countries were more attended to, and that proper schemes were proposed for putting things on a better footing. Indeed it is true, that those who are employed in the administration of public affairs, are alone able to carry such schemes into execution; yet every private citizen may be allowed to employ himself in speculations, about such matters, as may tend to the good of his country.[105]

Perhaps the century's most bizarre scheme of this nature is the plan of cross-breeding Diderot introduces in the Tahitian dialogue of the *Supplément au Voyage de Bougainville*, written in the early 1770s: "On your arrival," Orou tells the chaplain, "we let you have our wives and daughters. . . . We didn't ask you for money; we didn't loot your ships; we cared nothing for your produce; but our wives and daughters drew blood from your veins. . . . While more robust and healthy than you, we saw at once that you surpassed us in intelligence, and we immediately marked out for you some of our most beautiful women and girls to receive the seed of a race superior to ours. We tried an experiment which may still bring us success."[106] Outside the scope of this inquiry is the real-life historical control exerted by slave-owners over slaves of an age to reproduce, but that must surely color our understanding of contemporary philosophical and scientific discussions of such topics; the passage from Diderot makes clear the extent to which European colonial projects might also be thought of as global experiments in breeding, in this particular case with the twist that the originators of the experiment are not the colonists but the indigenous people themselves.

## Crabs and Brambles

Published in 1771, Smollett's final novel, *The Expedition of Humphry Clinker*, develops a distinctive cluster of arguments about culture, language, and the peculiarities that mark the manners of different individuals as a consequence of interactions between heredity and environment (a.k.a. nurture, cultivation, or climate). Historians and literary scholars have discussed the importance of the concept and vocabulary of improvement to eighteenth-century writing, and the term is especially pertinent to the Scottish writers of the period, as Robert Crawford has shown.[107] What is not often mentioned in these accounts is the scatological fact that in agricultural contexts, the word *improvement* can work as a euphemism for dung or manure.[108] The tension between positive and negative meanings of improvement is crucial to Smollett's novel. Seeming to celebrate the glories of improvement, it also contains a significant counterargument about the limits of culture and the social costs of cultivation in all its incarnations. While Smollett is on the whole a progressivist rather than a primitivist, his praise of the middle state associated with husbandry as the epitome of civic virtues is vexed by disruptive processes of propagation and reproduction that can be only partly regulated by culture. If Rousseau would wipe out the bonds of family by imagining a world in which a shared history or bloodline means nothing, Smollett treats connections between lovers or between parents and children as obstacles to the cultural triumph he anticipates, with reproduction hindering or even actively deforming culture's effects.

Smollett's novel displays a powerful comparative ethnographic impulse, a desire to fix the manners of different populations in print. Headed by Matthew Bramble and his peculiar semiliterate sister Tabitha, and also including Matthew's niece and nephew Lydia and Jery Melford, Tabitha's Welsh servant Win Jenkins, and Humphry Clinker himself (a late addition due to a chance encounter on the road), the Bramble family party travels on a circuit from their home in Monmouthshire on the border between England and Wales—Raymond Williams country!—to Bristol, Bath, and London, then north to Edinburgh, Glasgow, and the Scottish Highlands before returning to the countryside near Manchester in the north of England. The form of the epistolary travel narrative allows Smollett to describe and critique the manners of many different urban, provincial, and rural locations: indeed, the novel as a whole constitutes a comparative study of manners, including a broad moralizing argument about the dangers of luxury and the advantages of simplicity, and in this sense it shares the concerns of arguments about progress made by Scottish contemporaries such as Smith, Ferguson, and Robertson.

Throughout the novel, Smollett systematically turns to georgic examples of cultivation and husbandry to critique bad manners and endorse good ones: thus the novel's conclusion lays out schematically the cases of two proprietors of estates, one of whom (Baynard) has succumbed to extravagance and luxury, and the other of whom (Dennison) has practiced thrift and good husbandry as a remedy for the ills associated with excessive breeding and upper-class extravagance.[109]

Smollett also tells the story of an initially peripheral title character whose role comes to seem increasingly—if puzzlingly—central over the course of the novel. Unlike Fielding's *Tom Jones* (1749) and Burney's *Evelina* (1778), whose apparently illegitimate protagonists, distinguished by their breeding (which is to say manners, the result of both blood and upbringing) from the opening pages, are fully integrated into their families at those novels' conclusions, Humphry Clinker is only partly reclaimed following the revelation that his father is Matthew Bramble, the novel's irritable and ambivalent patriarch. Clinker's differences from the Brambles, based on social class as well as on religion, keep him in the position of a servant, foreclosing the possibility of his full admission into the Bramble family. But Smollett's choices in this regard seem to beg a number of important questions. Is Humphry primarily *like* Matthew Bramble because of breeding in the biological sense or *unlike* Bramble because of breeding in the educational sense?[110] Does culture—an impoverished upbringing, let's say—thwart heredity—resemblance to the parent, in this case the father—or is it the other way round? Which characters hold the best claims to breeding, and who is excluded from Smollett's model of good breeding? What do the parallels between cultivation in fields and cultivation in families tell us about social identity and the effects of cultural transformation? Finally, if Humphry is barred from full membership in the Bramble family, as he seems to be at the novel's conclusion, what does that exclusion say about the limits of improvement, despite the georgic celebration of culture in the novel's third volume?

Many of Matt's diatribes en route concern the corruption of urban society in contrast to the purity and simplicity of its rural counterparts. "What kind of taste and organs must those people have," he asks, "who really prefer the adulterate enjoyments of the town to the genuine pleasures of a country retreat?" (117). Matt's question serves as preamble to an extended georgic encomium to life at Brambleton Hall that promotes the joys of self-sufficiency and "plans of improvement":

I drink the virgin lymph, pure and crystalline as it gushes from the rock, or the sparkling beveridge, home-brewed from malt of my own making; or I indulge with cyder, which my own orchard affords; or with claret of the best growth, imported for my own use, by a correspondent on whose integrity I can depend; my bread is sweet and nourishing, made from my own wheat, ground in my own mill, and baked in my own oven; my table is, in a great measure, furnished from my own ground; my five-year old mutton, fed on the fragrant herbage of the mountains, that might vie with venison in juice and flavour; my delicious veal, fattened with nothing but the mother's milk, that fills the dish with gravy; my poultry from the barn-door, that never knew confinement, but when they were at roost; my rabbits panting from the warren; my game fresh from the moors; my trout and salmon struggling from the stream; oysters from their native banks; and herrings, with other sea-fish, I can eat in four hours after they are taken—My sallads, roots, and pot-herbs, my own garden yields in plenty and perfection; the produce of the natural soil, prepared by moderate cultivation. The same soil affords all the different fruits which England may call her own, so that my desert [sic] is every day fresh-gathered from the tree; my dairy flows with nectarious tides of milk and cream, from whence we derive abundance of excellent butter, curds, and cheese; and the refuse fattens my pigs, that are destined for hams and bacon. . . . Without doors, I superintend my farm, and execute plans of improvement, the effects of which I enjoy with unspeakable delight—Nor do I take less pleasure in seeing my tenants thrive under my auspices, and the poor live comfortably by the employment which I provide. (118)

This passage has many of the traits Raymond Williams identified in seventeenth-century country-house poems such as Jonson's "To Penshurst" (1616), down to the preposterous details of "rabbits panting from the warren" and "trout and salmon struggling from the stream."[111] As a character who is aware of but largely unconcerned with his own absurdity, Matt often speaks in a vein of exaggeration amounting almost to self-parody (the elevated diction is the giveaway, especially the use of self-consciously literary terms like "virgin lymph" and "nectarious"). International trade has a place in this world—Matt imports claret with the help of a reliable correspondent—but only a very limited one, and though the prosperity of Matt's domain depends on a relatively large number of hands, those bodies are elided here until the reassuring final line about tenants and the poor.

Though Matt's praise of the country life marks its own membership in a georgic tradition, his language also remains more-or-less within the bounds of the realism associated with the "rise" of the novel, to use Ian Watt's tenacious phrase. Elsewhere Smollett's Lydia takes a far more ludicrous plunge into the language of literary pastoral:

The air is so pure; the Downs are so agreeable; the furze in full blossom; the ground enamelled with daisies, and primroses, and cowslips; all the trees bursting into leaves, and the hedges already clothed with their vernal livery; the mountains covered with flocks of sheep, and tender bleating wanton lambkins playing, frisking and skipping from side to side; the groves resound with the notes of black-bird, thrush, and linnet; and all night long sweet Philomel pours forth her ravishingly delightful song. (27–28)

Her enthusiastic use of long-outmoded pastoral shows her to be less in touch with reality than her uncle. Both the shabbiness of pastoral language and the fantastic aspect of the georgic ethos are highlighted, though, by their juxtaposition to the obscene barnyards conjured up in the excremental opening letters of Tabitha Bramble and Win Jenkins, whose filthy realism makes both Matt and Lydia sound fanciful.

In contrast to the healthy produce of his country estate, Matt Bramble is particularly disgusted by London vegetables:

As they have discharged the natural colour from their bread, their butchers-meat, and poultry, their cutlets, ragouts, fricassees, and sauces of all kinds; so they insist upon having the complexion of their pot-herbs mended, even at the hazard of their lives. Perhaps, you will hardly believe they can be so mad as to boil their greens with brass half-pence, in order to improve their colour; and yet nothing is more true—Indeed, without this improvement in the colour, they have no personal merit. They are produced in an artificial soil, and taste of nothing but the dunghills, from whence they spring. (119–120)

The noun "improvement" here has a cynical, even a satirical charge, and this method of "improving" greens represents a grotesque parody of the culture of improvement Matt applauds in the countryside. Taken in conjunction, these two passages about food—the georgic ideal of healthy self-sufficiency at Brambleton, the paranoid though probably not much exaggerated attack on urban adulteration—show Smollett's focused interest in and attentiveness to the effects of culture on nature. Matt values Brambleton Hall for its well-ordered, highly cultured aspects, not its natural beauties; similarly he condemns London vegetables for what they show about the dangerous extremes of culture in the metropolis. You boil greens with a copper coin to improve their color only if you place an excessive value on the show of culture at the expense of its substance, and Matt ends by noting the monstrous and scatological aspect of urban vegetables.

Smollett's imagination in *Humphry Clinker* is repeatedly stirred by husbandry, by culture, and by cultivation, which he firmly distinguishes from the forms of overcultivation associated with luxury and urban decadence. Late in the novel, Smollett offers in the contrasting characters of Baynard and Dennison a more extended argument about the national need for georgic as a remedy for luxury and the corruptions of upper-class manners. Visiting his old friend Baynard's country estate for the first time in many years, Matt sees massive destruction in the guise of improvement. After an improvident bachelor period, partly redeemed by marriage to an heiress, Baynard decided to retrench and reduce expenses and "to reside always in the country, of which he was fond to a degree of enthusiasm, to cultivate his estate, which was very improvable" (276). But an "improvable" estate offers only the potentiality of culture, not the security of it, and under the influence of his empty-headed and fashionable new wife, Baynard's country estate merely offers opportunities for new forms of extravagance and waste:

> To shew her taste in laying out ground, she seized into her own hand a farm of two hundred acres, about a mile from the house, which she parcelled out into walks and shrubberies, having a great bason in the middle, into which she poured a whole stream that turned two mills, and afforded the best trout in the country. The bottom of the bason, however, was so ill secured, that it would not hold the water which strained through the earth, and made a bog of the whole plantation: in a word, the ground which formerly payed him one hundred and fifty pounds a year, now cost him two hundred pounds a year to keep it in tolerable order, over and above the first expence of trees, shrubs, flowers, turf, and gravel. There was not an inch of garden ground left about the house, nor a tree that produced fruit of any kind; nor did he raise a truss of hay, or a bushel of oats for his horses, nor had he a single cow to afford milk for his tea; far less did he ever dream of feeding his own mutton, pigs, and poultry: every article of house-keeping, even the most inconsiderable, was brought from the next market town, at the distance of five miles, and thither they sent a courier every morning to fetch hot rolls for breakfast. (281)

Crucial here is the misunderstanding of the relationship between forms and functionality revealed in Mrs. Baynard's decision to replace a stream that turns two mills and provides good fishing with a completely unproductive ornamental basin, so that the estate now fails to supply even the most modest requirements of table and livestock. The Baynards between them have laid waste to their own earlier prosperity: the editors of the Georgia edition of *Humphry Clinker* point out that Baynard has gone from having at the time of his marriage an annual income of fifteen hundred pounds a year, on top of his wife's fortune of twenty thousand pounds, to having at the time of his wife's death a debt of twenty thousand pounds and virtually no income. He is lucky in the end to secure an income of three hundred pounds a year: the exact amount with which his counterpart Dennison began, though that income has increased fourfold by means of prudent management.

Smollett's counterexample shows the fairy-tale logic of improvement and the rewards it promises the virtuous practitioner. Dennison, initially much less well off than Baynard, has garnered quite different fruits. When he initially retires to the country, Dennison's wise intentions make up for his lack of experience as a husbandman (this passage is worth quoting partly to show Smollett's heavy-handedness in treating this ideologically loaded material):

> [Dennison] reflected, that if a peasant without education, or any great share of natural sagacity, could maintain a large family, and even become opulent upon a farm, for which he payed an annual rent of two or three hundred pounds to the landlord, surely he himself might hope for some success from his industry, having no rent to pay, but, on the contrary, three or four hundred pounds a-year to receive—He considered, that the earth was an indulgent mother, that yielded her fruits to all her children without distinction. He had studied the theory of agriculture with a degree of eagerness and delight; and he could not conceive there was any mystery in the practice, but what he should be able to disclose by dint of care and application. (308–309)

Dennison's own narrative of his life as an improver reveals a thoughtful balance between theory and practice (overly theoretical improvers were often mocked by eighteenth-century writers, as in Swift's academy of projectors in *Gulliver's Travels* [3.4–5]):

> I reserved in my own hands, some acres of ground adjacent to the house, for making experiments in agriculture, according to the directions of Lyle, Tull, Hart, Duhamel, and others who have written on this subject; and qualified their theory with the practical observations of farmer Bland, who was my great master in the art of husbandry.—In short, I became enamoured of a country life; and my success greatly exceeded my expectation.—I drained bogs, burned

heath, grubbed up furze and fern; I planted copse and willows where nothing else would grow; I gradually inclosed all my farms, and made such improvements, that my estate now yields me clear twelve hundred pounds a year.
(313–314)[112]

The morality tale could hardly be clearer. Ultimately, georgic values and practices
will redeem even Baynard from his life of wasteful extravagance, a reclamation
enabled by the death of his wife (who is beyond redemption, in Smollett's rather
misogynistic vision), by the instructional zeal and deep pockets of Matt Bramble
(who organizes a massive bail-out package), and by the georgic example of Dennison, to whom Baynard pays an extended visit, finding himself "so pleased with
the improvements made on this estate, which is all cultivated like a garden, that
he has entered himself as a pupil in farming to Mr. Dennison, and resolved to at-
tach himself wholly to the practice of husbandry" (329). Husbandry, culture, cultivation: these are the terms in which Matt lodges his confidence.

Cultivation and husbandry always exist in proximity, though, to less happy
practices and tendencies. Smollett's novel includes a large number of agricultural
jokes about the relationship between parent and offspring that suggest a preoccupation with breakdowns of familial inheritance, failures to reproduce, and
disruptions to the smooth collaboration of culture and nature. Just a few textual
examples will suggest the novel's sheer obsessiveness about biological reproduction. Its opening pages depict a world whose characters are preoccupied with the
disruption or obstruction of conventional processes of sexual reproduction, in
people and in animals. In an early letter to the housekeeper at Brambleton Hall,
for instance, Tabitha Bramble asks with regard to one of her farm animals "if
the cobler has cut Dicky, and how the pore anemil bore the operation" (8). This
cutting-short of the male reproductive life is matched in Matthew Bramble's long-
standing reluctance to take on the role of family man in the more conventional
sense. Writing specifically about the troubles caused by the fact that his sister
and his niece share a tendency to seek unsuitable marital partners, he says, "I am
conscious of no sins that ought to entail such family-plagues upon me—why the
devil should not I shake off these torments at once? I an't married to Tabby, thank
Heaven! nor did I beget the other two [i.e., Lydia and Jery]" (13).

Matthew's insistence on his identity as a nonbegetter of children is matched
by a surprising willingness—despite his own decision not to reproduce—to take
on family responsibilities. This fact is emphasized in another casually recounted
episode of the novel's early pages, in which Jery receives a letter from a friend at
Oxford charging that Jery's conjectural—in fact, nonexistent—"correspondence"

(sexual affair) with one "miss Blackerby" has supposedly "produced something which could not be much longer concealed" (28): a child, in other words, though a child whose alleged father has never had sex with its mother. Good-hearted Jery is perfectly willing to pay the costs associated with this charge, if he must, a decision fully endorsed by his uncle Matt: "The old gentleman told me last night, with great good-humour," Jery writes to his friend, "that betwixt the age of twenty and forty, he had been obliged to provide for nine bastards, sworn to him by women whom he never saw" (29). Fortunately, the pregnancy of Jery's female friend turns out to be a false alarm, further contributing to the reader's sense that reproduction has gone awry in the world of *Humphry Clinker*.

More generally, the agricultural and the human seem to infect each other here with sometimes bewildering results. In a high-society scene at St. James's Court, for instance, the Duke of N. mistakes Matt for another man. When Matt clears up the confusion by identifying himself by his proper name (though names themselves are at issue in the novel as a whole), he receives this reply:

> 'Odso! (cried the duke) I remember you perfectly well, my dear Mr. Bramble— You was always a good and loyal subject—a staunch friend to administration—I made your brother an Irish bishop—' 'Pardon me, my lord (said the 'squire) I once had a brother, but he was a captain in the army—' 'Ha! (said his grace) he was so—He was, indeed! But who was the bishop then? Bishop Blackberry— Sure it was bishop Blackberry—Perhaps some relation of yours—' 'Very likely, my lord (replied my uncle); the Blackberry is the fruit of the Bramble—But, I believe, the bishop is not a berry of our bush—' (96–97)

The humor of Matt's joke here lies in his taking literally the duke's inability to tell the difference between a blackberry and a bramble: as the proprietor of a country estate, Matthew is better equipped than a town political patron to make the distinction. Yet this line also emphasizes something important about Smollett's choice to bestow the name Bramble on this brother and sister: a bramble is a "rough prickly shrub" (*OED*) that may or may not bear fruit, and just as the appearance of Tabitha Bramble (despite her embarrassing eagerness to find a husband) suggests that she is past childbearing, so Matthew Bramble seems unlikely to reproduce. (Of course, in common Scottish usage—not recorded in the *OED*—the bramble can refer to the berry as well as the bush, an odd gloss on Matthew's joke.[113])

Smollett uses the novel's title character to draw further conclusions about the natural and cultural aspects of human identity. Clinker is a kind of "natural," not just a natural (i.e., illegitimate) son but expressive in other ways of simple country virtues. He can turn his hand to many different country trades, he saves Matt's life several times over, and yet he is also a figure of ridicule. Poorly dressed, often half-naked, he serves as the butt of countless jokes, his social class allowing him to be depicted as almost a different species from the Brambles and the Melfords (in this he resembles the Scottish lieutenant Lismahago). After their initial encounter, in which he rescues Matt from drowning and is generously rewarded for his pains, Clinker presents himself to Matt as a potential employee, giving a list of his qualifications and his many and motley accomplishments. Jery narrates his uncle's response: "Foregad! thou art a complete fellow, (cried my uncle, still laughing) I have a good mind to take thee into my family" (82). Although Matthew uses the older sense of the word *family*, which includes servants housed under the same roof, Tabitha is still offended by the prospect, in part because of the exposure of Humphry's bare buttocks beneath his shabby clothes. She issues a challenge to her brother: "But now you shall part with that rascal or me, upon the spot, without farther loss of time; and the world shall see whether you have more regard for your own flesh and blood, or for a beggarly foundling, taken from the dunghill" (85). Sprung from a dunghill and without any known antecedents, Humphry (at least according to Tabitha) is rather like the London vegetables of which Matthew Bramble is so contemptuous, "produced in an artificial soil, [which] taste of nothing but the dunghills, from whence they spring" (120).

The narrative explicitly associates Clinker with a set of leveling arguments that Matt rejects. Clinker's is a voice for social equality, at least before the eyes of God, as emerges in this remark about his Methodist ministry:

> 'Begging your honour's pardon, (replied Clinker) may not the new light of God's grace shine upon the poor and the ignorant in their humility, as well as upon the wealthy, and the philosopher in all his pride of human learning?' 'What you imagine to be the new light of grace, (said his master) I take to be a deceitful vapour, glimmering through a crack in your upper story—In a word, Mr. Clinker, I will have no light in my family but what pays the king's taxes, unless it be the light of reason, which you don't pretend to follow.' (135)

Alluding to the window tax (which drove many Britons during this period to board up existing windows to avoid paying it), Matt stigmatizes "the new light of God's grace" as an illegal and insubstantial thing, something outside of civil society and royal governance; the light of reason isn't sanctioned by the king either, he implies, but he allows that the glimmer of Enlightenment may find a place in his family where the other will not. Arguments for and against social mixing between upper and lower classes have previously been staged between Jery and Matt, Matt taking the line (in response to the mixed social life of Bath) that the central problem of modern urban life is that "men of low birth, and no breeding, have found themselves suddenly translated into a state of affluence, unknown to former ages" (36). In the two men's debate on the effects of luxury—more specifically, on whether "the mixture of people in the entertainments of this place was destructive of all order and urbanity"—Jery takes a more liberal position, but he has little at stake in the argument: Clinker is a more earnest (though also a more ludicrous) exponent of social mixture (49).

After Clinker's second rescue of Matt Bramble, again from the risk of drowning after a coach accident late in the novel, Smollett—in the voice of Jery—provides a telling description: "The faithful Clinker, taking [Matt] up in his arms, as if he had been an infant of six months, carried him ashore, howling most piteously all the way, and I followed him in a transport of grief and consternation" (301). Clinker is depicted as a parent—a mother, indeed—holding his infant in his arms, a metaphor that makes the revelation of Clinker's true identity that follows shortly thereafter all the more startling. Humphry Clinker has the physical evidence (a seal, Matthew Bramble's address, and a certificate of baptism) to support his claim to be Matthew's son, and the novel provides a helter-skelter explanation of how the unlucky loss of contact between Clinker's parents initially came about. The revelation of the servant's identity takes place with extraordinary speed once Dennison recognizes Matthew Bramble as his former friend "Matthew Loyd of Glamorgan" (304).

While Jery has no beef with his "new-found cousin" (305), Tabitha's keen sense of her own status makes her unlikely to welcome the newest member of the family, and Matt hopes to forestall her wrath with a tactical introduction: "Sister, (said my uncle) there is a poor relation that recommends himself to your good graces—The quondam Humphry Clinker is metamorphosed into Matthew Loyd; and claims the honour of being your carnal kinsman—in short, the rogue proves to be a crab of my own planting in the days of hot blood and unrestrained libertinism" (306). The novel's editors hear in this line a possible allusion to a traditional English proverb, "Plant a crab-tree where you will, it will never bear pippins" (434 n. 8). Is Matt also a crab, an inedible wild apple? He has certainly not borne pippins, the domesticated eating kind. A crab only bears pippins by way of grafting; indeed, a pippin bears pippins by means of grafting as well, for the apple does not breed true from seed, a fact that theological commentators from late antiquity onward used to explain why baptized Christians do not transmit their state of grace to their children. The quotation can be contextualized with two other lines from the novel, the first of which is in fact quoted in the *OED* under the synonym "crab-apple." Matt comments vis-à-vis Lismahago that "I have often met with a crab-apple in a hedge, which I have been tempted to eat for its flavour, even while I was disgusted by its austerity" (197), an analogy that reveals the peculiar and equivocal appeal of the uncultivated. Referring later on to the prospect of a marriage between Lismahago and Tabitha Bramble, Jery offers a less flattering metaphor: "I make no doubt but that he will postpone his voyage, and prosecute his addresses to a happy consummation; and sure, if it produces any fruit, it must be of a very peculiar flavour" (258).

The metaphor of the crab-apple insists on the difference between the wild and the cultivated: Humphry Clinker—small, sour to the taste—is related to Matthew Bramble as the crab-apple is—to what? To the eating sort, or to another crab? Presumably Matt is a cultivated man rather than a wild one, but part of the point of the metaphor is that it doesn't matter which he is, for his offspring will revert to wildness in any case. The crab is not invoked here as it might be—as the stock, for instance, onto which better apples are grafted in an improvement of the original, another powerful and usually quite optimistic metaphor used by eighteenth-century writers who want to describe the ameliorative effects of culture on nature. A contradiction in this sense inheres in the very idea that there can be such a thing as a "crab of my own planting": the crab is the antithesis of the cultivar, and nobody deliberately plants a crab for its fruit, so that Smollett's use of the image undercuts the very possibility of improvement, reinforcing the novel's fundamental pessimism about culture by emphasizing the reversion of culture to nature in the second generation.

The novel's conclusion holds out an obscene vision of propagation:

> As for Win Jenkins, she has undergone a perfect metamurphysis, and is become a new creeter from the ammunition of Humphrey Clinker, our new footman, a pious young man, who has laboured exceedingly, that she may bring forth fruits of repentance. I make no doubt but he will take the same pains with that pert hussey Mary Jones, and all of you; and that he may have power given to penetrate and instill his goodness, even into your most inward parts, is the fervent prayer of your friend in the spirit, TAB. BRAMBLE. (264)

Clinker's situation at the end of the novel—his persistence in wanting to marry Win Jenkins, now definitely "beneath" him, and the nature of the fruits she is likely to bear—marks him as not a Bramble proper. In this way, the novel averts the possible threat of mixing. Similarly a clear line can be drawn between good husbandry and bad, or between country and city manners. But there remains something odd about the novel's final settlement, a refusal to resolve differences between incompatible arguments—it can also be thought of as a willingness to let plot and metaphor work against each other. The metaphor of the crab disrupts the narrative of improvement, drawing attention instead to the difficulty of maintaining social distinctions against the threat of mixing. And class mixing begins at home: Clinker is another fruit of the Bramble, one that can be welcomed into the household but never domesticated.

4

# A Natural History
# of Inequality

M eanwhile, the consensus in favor of improvement was being split apart by
one of the most explicitly anticulturalist works in the Western tradition. . . .

### The Difference Between One Man and Another

Rousseau's *Discourse on the Origin and the Foundations of Inequality Among Men*,
hereafter referred to as the *Second Discourse,* adopts the tropes and tactics of
georgic even as it rejects that mode's driving assumption that improvement is
man's highest duty.[1] Written in 1753–1754 in response to the Dijon Academy's
question "What is the Origin of Inequality among Men, and is it Authorized
by the Natural Law?," the *Second Discourse* treats "the various contingencies that
can have perfected human reason while deteriorating the species, made a being
wicked by making it sociable" (159). Rousseau is writing reverse georgic, a narrative of cultivation and a history of civil society in which *progress* and *perfectibility*
(a word first documented a few years earlier in the writings of Turgot, though
Rousseau gave it much wider currency) are paradoxically synonymous with *decline*
and *degeneration,* themselves consequent upon rather than countered by culture.[2]
This anti-georgic position—Rousseau displays an almost erotic investment in the
idea of unaccommodated man, Lear's "poor, bare, fork'd animal" (3.4.106–108)—
coexists in Rousseau's writings with more traditional georgic elements, though, as
when the *Discourse on the Sciences and Arts* (1750) asserts that "strength and vigor

of body will be found under the rustic habit of a Husbandman, and not under the gilding of a Courtier."[3] Leo Marx attributes the belief—virtually universal among eighteenth-century writers, whatever their ideological affiliations—in the superiority of life in the country over the crush and chaos of city dwelling to the need to find a compromise in the raging debate between extreme primitivist views of human nature at one end of the spectrum and extreme progressivism at the other.[4] Given the difficulty of maintaining a "hard" primitivist argument, Marx points out, even Rousseau "was compelled to endorse the view that mankind must depart from the state of nature—but not too far."[5]

Agriculture is certainly the villain of the *Second Discourse:* "[A]s soon as it was found to be useful for one to have provisions for two," Rousseau writes, "equality disappeared, property appeared, work became necessary, and the vast forests changed into smiling Fields that had to be watered with the sweat of men, and where slavery and misery were soon seen to sprout and grow together with the harvests" (167). His ironic adaptation of georgic metaphors brings to the surface doubts about culture similar to those that darken the atmosphere of Dryden's translation of Virgil. Rousseau powerfully places the origin of inequality at the moment man began cultivating plants, planting seed, and deciding "to take an initial loss for the sake of great future gain" (169). With its nascent idea of property—since the cultivator assumes a right to the land he works as well as to the products of his labor—agriculture (together with the discovery of metalworking techniques) can be held accountable for the advent of human inequality: "For the Poet it is gold and silver; but for the Philosopher it is iron and wheat that civilized men, and ruined Mankind" (168).

The forms of cultivation that so many of Rousseau's contemporaries celebrate are here singled out for condemnation, cultivation made analogous to Eve's eating the apple:

> What shall we say about agriculture, an art requiring so much labor and foresight: dependent on other arts, which can quite obviously be pursued only in a society that has at least begun, and which we use not so much to draw forth from the Earth foods it would readily yield without agriculture as to force it to [conform to] the predilections that are more to our taste? But let us suppose that men had multiplied so much that natural produce no longer sufficed to feed them; a supposition which, incidentally, would point to one great advantage for the human Species in this way of living; Let us suppose that without forges, and without Workshops, the tools for Farming had dropped from Heaven into the Savages' hands; that these men had overcome the mortal hatred they all

have of sustained work; that they had learned to foresee their needs sufficiently far ahead, that they had guessed how to cultivate the Earth, sow seed, and plant Trees; that they had found the art of grinding Wheat and of fermenting grapes; all of them things which the Gods had to be made to teach them, for want of conceiving how they could have learned them on their own; what man would, after all this, be so senseless as to torment himself with cultivating a Field that will be despoiled by the first passer-by, man or beast, fancying this harvest; and how will everyone resolve to spend his life doing hard work when the more he needs its rewards, the more certain he is not to reap them? (143–144)

Paradoxically, Rousseau's catalogue retains a certain georgic flair, serving as a compendium of the labor on which civilization depends, one that calls to mind *Robinson Crusoe*—enshrined, after all, as the sole volume on Emile's shelf. The litany of sowing and planting falls into a familiar and almost loving pattern, despite the writer's impassioned rejection of the idea that cultivation equals morality.

I am particularly interested in the story Rousseau tells in the *Second Discourse* about man's perfectibility, as well as in a companion argument about man's degeneracy in civil society. Part of Rousseau's task is to discern the difference between natural and acquired qualities, though his assertions about such things are necessarily conjectural, giving the inquiry a quixotic flavor: "[I]t is no light undertaking," he admits, "to disentangle what is original from what is artificial in man's present Nature, and to know accurately a state which no longer exists, which perhaps never did exist, which probably never will exist, and about which it is nevertheless necessary to have exact Notions in order accurately to judge of our present state" (125). An astonishing confession, and one that cunningly preempts objections to the speculative nature of the work: "Let us therefore begin by setting aside all the facts," Rousseau writes a little later, "for they do not affect the question. The Inquiries that may be pursued regarding this Subject ought not be taken for historical truths, but only for hypothetical and conditional reasonings; better suited to elucidate the Nature of things than to show their genuine origin, and comparable to those our Physicists daily make regarding the formation of the World" (132).

Rousseau's objection to previous arguments about the sources of inequality among men is that previous philosophers, "continually speaking of need, greed, oppression, desires, and pride[,] transferred to the state of Nature ideas they had taken from society; They spoke of Savage Man and depicted Civil man" (132). They failed, in other words, to see man "as Nature formed him, through all the changes which the succession of times and of things must have wrought in his original constitution, and to disentangle what he owes to his own stock from what circumstances and his progress have added to or changed in his primitive state" (124). The paradox in Rousseau's thought, as Derrida has shown, is that education should at once be figured as altogether foreign to nature—nature's other—while also being "described or presented as a system of substitution [*suppléance*] destined to reconstitute Nature's edifice in the most natural way possible": "culture or cultivation . . . must supplement a deficient nature," Derrida points out, "a deficiency that cannot by definition be anything but an accident and a deviation from Nature."[6] Terry Eagleton approaches the same paradox in openly theological language. "Left to its own devices, our reprobate nature will not spontaneously rise to the grace of culture," he writes; "but neither can such grace be rudely forced upon it. It must rather cooperate with the innate tendencies of nature itself, in order to induce it to transcend itself. Like grace, culture must already represent a potential within human nature, if it is to stick."[7]

Rousseau sees the responsiveness to culture that distinguishes man from other animals as deeply regrettable. Inequality marks the moment of the fall and is inscribed in human bodies:

> It is easy to see that it is in these successive changes of man's constitution that one must seek the first origin of the differences that distinguish men who, by common consent, are naturally as equal among themselves as were the animals of every species, before various Physical causes introduced in some species the varieties which we observe among them. Indeed, it is not conceivable that these first changes, however they may have come about, altered all the Individuals of the species at once and in the same way; rather, while some were perfected or deteriorated and acquired various good or bad qualities that were not inherent in their Nature, the others remained in their original state for a longer time; and such was, among men, the first source of inequality, which it is easier to establish thus in general, than it is to assign its genuine causes with precision. (124–125)

Even differences "taken to be natural," Rousseau argues, "are exclusively the result of habit and of the different kinds of life men adopt in Society":

> Thus a sturdy or a delicate temperament, together with the strength or the weakness that derive from it, are often due more to a tough or an effeminate upbringing than to the bodies' primitive constitution. The same is true of strengths of Mind, and education not only introduces differences between Minds that are cultivated and those that are not, but it also increases the differ-

ences that obtain between cultivated Minds in proportion to their culture; for when a Giant and a Dwarf travel the same road, every step they take will give the Giant an added advantage. (157–158)

The difficulty of extracting nature from culture is here instanced in the strange analogy of the dwarf and the giant, an extremely counterintuitive—perhaps deliberately so?—illustration of the cultural origins of what seem to be natural differences, with seemingly innate differences of mental constitution rewritten as differences of culture (a perplexing use of the terminology). Unlike "moral, or political inequality" (the tacit conventions that lead to some men becoming wealthier or more powerful than others), natural inequality establishes itself as a matter of physiology, "differences in age, health, strengths of Body, and qualities of Mind, or of Soul" (131): but Rousseau's point is that the so-called natural inequalities are as much the result of culture as their more obviously artificial political counterparts.

Some of the changes man undergoes as a result of his participation in civil society may look like improvements, but in another sense they all represent degeneration from the original natural man, a fact that leads Rousseau to assert that "the history of human diseases could easily be written by following that of civil Societies" (138). This is what makes it so difficult to detect the difference between culture and nature, he warns, in a passage that echoes the naturalist Buffon's arguments about domestication as a form of degeneration:[8]

Let us therefore beware of confusing Savage man with the men we have before our eyes. Nature treats all animals abandoned to its care with a partiality that seems to indicate how jealous it is of this right. The Horse, the Cat, the Bull, even the Ass are, most of them, larger in size, all of them have a sturdier constitution, greater vigor, force, and courage in the forests than in our homes; they lose half of these advantages when they are Domesticated, and it would seem that all our care to treat and to feed these animals well only succeeds in bastardizing them. The same is true of man himself: As he becomes sociable and a Slave, he becomes weak, timorous, groveling, and his soft and effeminate way of life completes the enervation of both his strength and his courage. Let us add that the difference between one man and another in the Savage and in the Domesticated condition must be even greater than that between one beast and another; for since animal and man were treated alike by Nature, all the conveniences which man gives himself above and beyond those he gives the animals he tames are so many particular causes that lead him to degenerate more appreciably. (138–139)

Yet in Rousseau's sketch of the life of savage man (a sketch he presents as a hypothetical or conditional rather than factual account of human origins), nature is immediately supplemented by culture in the guise of habit: "Accustomed from childhood to the inclemencies of the weather, and the rigor of the seasons, hardened to fatigue, and forced to defend naked and unarmed their life and their Prey against the other ferocious Beasts or to escape them by running, Men develop a robust and almost unalterable temperament; The Children, since they come into the world with their Fathers' excellent constitution and strengthen it by the same activities that produced it, thus acquire all the vigor of which the human species is capable" (135). A constitution or temperament may be judiciously strengthened by culture, in other words, so long as the process does not go too far.

Rousseau echoes the eighteenth-century truism that "each species has but its own instinct, while man perhaps having none that belongs to him, appropriates them all" (135). It is not intelligence ("the understanding") that marks the difference in species, but the "property of being a free agent" (141):

> I see in any animal nothing but an ingenious machine to which nature has given senses in order to wind itself up and, to a point, protect itself against everything that tends to destroy or to disturb it. I perceive precisely the same thing in the human machine, with this difference that Nature alone does everything in the operations of the Beast, whereas man contributes to his operations in his capacity as a free agent. The one chooses or rejects by instinct, the other by an act of freedom. (140)

This echoes theological arguments about free will and human responsibility; it also lets Rousseau introduce the other crucial property exclusive to man, "the faculty of perfecting oneself." Rousseau uses the fact that humans but not animals become senile in old age as a way of elucidating the contrast between the two: "whereas the Beast, which has acquired nothing and also has nothing to lose, always keeps its instinct, man again losing through old age or other accidents all that his *perfectibility* had made him acquire, thus relapses lower than the Beast itself" (141). Perfectibility—man's responsiveness to culture—is a poisoned chalice, and in the following sentences Rousseau laments its ill consequences, the paradox being that *perfection* is really synonymous with *decay:* "It would be sad for us to be forced to agree that this distinctive and almost unlimited faculty, is the source of all of man's miseries; that it is the faculty which, by dint of time, draws him out of that original condition in which he would spend tranquil and innocent days; that it is the faculty which, over the centuries, causing his enlightenment and his errors, his vices and his virtues to bloom, eventually makes him his own and Nature's tyrant" (141).

The ambivalence expressed here—this is hardly the straightforward primitivism sometimes carelessly attributed to the *Second Discourse*—finds an even more poignant sequel in Rousseau's portrait of human relationships in the state of nature before the invention of language, language being one of perfectibility's enabling conditions.[9] These passages are among the most shocking in the *Discourse*, partly because they have a strange charge of fantasy or wish-fulfillment in their wild and wistful longing for a time before individuals became trapped in the webs of dependency called families. This is a world without memory, one in which human connections are so weak as to be negligible:

> [I]n this primitive state, without Houses or Huts or property of any kind, everyone bedded down at random and often for one night only; males and females united fortuitously, according to chance encounters, opportunity, and desire, without speech being an especially necessary interpreter of what they had to tell one another; they parted just as readily; The mother at first nursed her Children because of her own need; then, habit having made them dear to her, she went on to feed them because of theirs; as soon as they had the strength to forage on their own, they left even the Mother; And since almost the only way to find one another again was not to lose sight of one another in the first place, they soon were at the point of not even recognizing each other. (145)

Rousseau attributes the mother's affection for her child to habit, not to some physiological impulse to extend the family line or propagate the species. Indeed, Rousseau largely lets the word *habit* do the work of *nature*, eighteenth-century French and British writers often presenting habit as the agent of a determinism at least as inescapable as the all-powerful gene of popular scientific accounts at the turn of the millennium.

The fantasy of sex without obligation is elaborated in a note to the text in which Rousseau asserts that once the sexual appetite has been satisfied, men and women have no need of each other. He even argues that when a child is born nine months after a sexual encounter, it is not likely that . . . [the parents] will remember ever having known each other: For the kind of memory by which an individual gives preference to an individual for the act of procreation requires, as I prove in the text, more progress or corruption of the human understanding than it can be assumed to have in the state of animality that is at issue here. Another woman can, therefore, satisfy a man's new desires as readily as the woman he had previously known, and another man can similarly satisfy the woman, assuming she is goaded by the same appetite during the state of pregnancy, which may reasonably be doubted. . . . There is, therefore, no reason for the man to seek out the same woman, nor for the woman to seek out the same man. (216)

Sex is an end in itself, not a means to an end. Earlier in the main text, Rousseau calls the appetite that prompts man "to perpetuate his species" a "blind inclination, devoid of any sentiment of the heart, [which] produced only a purely animal act. The need satisfied, the two sexes no longer recognized one another, and even the child no longer meant anything to the Mother as soon as it could do without her" (161). This represents a running theme amounting almost to an obsession: with regard to physical love, he says, "any woman suits" savage man, only acquired tastes leading him to prefer one woman to another, and he earlier calls love "a factitious sentiment; born of social practice, and extolled with much skill and care by women in order to establish their rule and to make dominant the sex that should obey" (155). More generally, Rousseau stigmatizes all attachments between humans as unnatural, shucking off what seem to be the unbearable obligations of sociability. "Indeed," he asserts, "it is impossible to imagine why, in that primitive state, a man would need another man any more than a monkey or a Wolf would need his kind, or, assuming this need, to imagine what motives could induce the other to attend to it, or even, if he did, how they might agree on terms" (149).

The point of all this is to say that Rousseau's picture of savage man—despite his allusion to Montaigne's essay—is quite unlike either Montaigne's cannibals or the "noble savage" conventionally associated with Rousseau.[10] It amounts to a negation of almost everything we experience as making us human:

[W]andering in the forests without industry, without speech, without settled abode, without war, and without tie, without any need of others of his kind and without any desire to harm them, perhaps even without ever recognizing any one of them individually, subject to few passions and self-sufficient, Savage man had only the sentiments and the enlightenment suited to this state, . . .

he sensed only his true needs, looked only at what he believed it to be in his interest to see, and . . . his intelligence made no more progress than his vanity. If by chance he made some discovery, he was all the less in a position to communicate it as he did not recognize even his Children. The art perished with the inventor; there was neither education nor progress, generations multiplied uselessly; and as each one of them always started at the same point, Centuries went by in all the crudeness of the first ages, the species had already grown old, and man remained ever a child. (157)

Rousseau places a positive value on this nightmarish utopia, but it is hard not to see the rejection of education and progress in such passages as being highly equivocal, particularly given the fact that language itself—the medium of Rousseau's own arguments and art—does not exist in the world he depicts. Rousseau's discussion would find a famous sequel in Freud's contention "that what we call our civilization is largely responsible for our misery, and that we should be much happier if we gave it up and returned to primitive conditions."[11] But all such arguments hinge on a foundational act of self-deception or self-contradiction in which the writer only pretends to abnegate a culture on which he depends, however much he may deplore it. Even families, in Rousseau's vision, can be considered the result of culture rather than nature, and nature offers the promise of their dissolution rather than the recovery of some idyllic prelapsarian world of happy ties uncorrupted by modern manners.

### "We are born twice over"

Several years after its appearance in 1762, Rousseau would describe *Émile* as being not "a true treatise on education" but "a rather philosophical work on the principle . . . that *man is naturally good.*"[12] *Émile* "lay[s] it down as an incontrovertible rule that the first impulses of nature are always right; there is no original sin in the human heart, the how and why of the entrance of every vice can be traced" (66), and Rousseau's pair of opening paragraphs set out his beliefs about education and the double bind it presents:

God makes all things good; man meddles with them and they become evil. He forces one soil to yield the products of another, one tree to bear another's fruit. He confuses and confounds time, place, and natural conditions. He mutilates his dog, his horse, and his slave. He destroys and defaces all things; he loves all that is deformed and monstrous; he will have nothing as nature made it, not even man himself, who must learn his paces like a saddle-horse, and be shaped to his master's taste like the trees in his garden.

Yet things would be worse without this education, and mankind cannot be made by halves. Under existing conditions a man left to himself from birth would be more of a monster than the rest. Prejudice, authority, necessity, example, all the social conditions into which we are plunged, would stifle nature in him and put nothing in her place. She would be like a sapling chance sown in the midst of the highway, bent hither and thither and soon crushed by the passers-by. (5)

Indeed, these conditions so thoroughly immerse us that we have no real way of gaining access to natural man in his unadulterated state: "We know not what nature allows us to be," Rousseau writes, "none of us has measured the possible difference between man and man" (33).

Like Locke, with whom he is often lumped together (as in Steven Pinker's reductive invocations of the Blank Slate and Noble Savage), Rousseau admits a language of natural difference, especially when he writes about actual educational practice. The suitability of a particular plan of education, he allows, must depend on the nature of the child's "individual bent":

Every mind has its own form, in accordance with which it must be controlled; and the success of the pains taken depends largely on the fact that he is controlled in this way and no other. Oh, wise man, take time to observe nature; watch your scholar well before you say a word to him; first leave the germ of his character free to show itself, do not constrain him in anything, the better to see him as he really is. (68–69)

The horticultural metaphor of the germ recapitulates an older humanist language, though Rousseau very much also emphasizes the "plasticity of brain" that enables the child "to receive every kind of impression," offering the tutor means by which "all the ideas [the child] can understand and use, all that concern his happiness and will some day throw light upon his duties, should be traced at an early age in indelible characters upon his brain" (90). Of course, the "bent" is also something that may be bestowed by nurture rather than nature—"Let us not give him so fixed a bent in any direction that he cannot change it if required without hardship" (138)—and it may be difficult to untangle their effects. Rousseau particularly warns against "the common error which mistakes the effects of environment for the ardour of genius, or imagines there is a decided bent towards any one of the arts, when there is nothing more than that spirit of emulation, common to men and monkeys, which impels them instinctively to do what they see others doing, without knowing why" (193).

One common error involves tailoring education to the social position into which the pupil has been born. "Fit a man's education to his real self, not to what is no part of him," Rousseau writes:

> You reckon on the present order of society, without considering that this order is itself subject to inscrutable changes, and that you can neither foresee nor provide against the revolution which may affect your children. . . . The crisis is approaching, and we are on the edge of a revolution. Who can answer for your fate? What man has made, man may destroy. Nature's characters alone are ineffaceable, and nature makes neither the prince, the rich man, nor the nobleman. (188)

If the words nature writes "alone are ineffaceable," though, what of those "indelible characters" the tutor should hope to trace on the child's brain? Throughout Rousseau's writing runs a vein of self-contradiction and paradox, something that's even more striking in his full unfolding of the argument. "We are born, so to speak, twice over," he writes; "born into existence, and born into life; born a human being, and born a man" (206). This is very clearly a matter of bodies as well as minds, and the theory is implicated in an important argument about sexuality and sexual difference: the bodily differentiation that distinguishes males and females at puberty signals the time at which "man really enters upon life," a life of the passions (207).

His strong commitment to the social differentiation of men and women based on sex leads Rousseau to express considerable antagonism for Plato's vision, in the *Republic*, of a division of labor based strictly on ability, a system that in Rousseau's disapproving view turns women into men.[13] He objects not so much to "the alleged community of wives," in other words, as to "that political promiscuity under which the same occupations are assigned to both sexes alike, a scheme which could only lead to intolerable evils," and argues that devotion to the state can only "thrive . . . in the soil of that miniature father-land, the home":

> When once it is proved that men and women are and ought to be unlike in constitution and in temperament, it follows that their education must be different. Nature teaches us that they should work together, but that each has its own

share of the work; the end is the same, but the means are different, as are also the feelings which direct them. (390–391)

"If you are a sensible mother you will take my advice," Rousseau continues. "Do not try to make your daughter a good man in defiance of nature. Make her a good woman, and be sure it will be better both for her and us" (392). But if nature is itself insufficient to the task of making good women, how can womanhood be thought of as natural? Assuming women to be genuinely born rather than made, why should such a warning even be necessary?

Rousseau's laying-out of the nature of sexual difference accordingly comes to sound at once anxious and wishful:

Here is a little girl busy all day with her doll; she is always changing its clothes, dressing and undressing it, trying new combinations of trimmings well or ill matched; her fingers are clumsy, her taste is crude, but there is no mistaking her bent; in this endless occupation time flies unheeded, the hours slip away unnoticed, even meals are forgotten. She is more eager for adornment than for food. 'But she is dressing her doll, not herself,' you will say. Just so; she sees her doll, she cannot see herself; she cannot do anything for herself, she has neither the training, nor the talent, nor the strength; as yet she herself is nothing, she is engrossed in her doll and all her coquetry is devoted to it. This will not always be so; in due time she will be her own doll.

We have here a very early and clearly-marked bent; you have only to follow it and train it. What the little girl most clearly desires is to dress her doll, to make its bows, its tippets, its sashes, and its tuckers; she is dependent on other people's kindness in all this, and it would be much pleasanter to be able to do it herself. Here is a motive for her earliest lessons, they are not tasks prescribed, but favours bestowed. Little girls always dislike learning to read and write, but they are always ready to learn to sew. They think they are grown up, and in imagination they are using their knowledge for their own adornment. (396)

With regard to Émile and Sophie's fundamental ordinariness—they are not "prodigies," Rousseau reiterates—even Rousseau's most explicit statement of the gender difference resonates with as much anxiety as confidence: "He is a man and she is a woman; this is all they have to boast of. In the present confusion between the sexes it is almost a miracle to belong to one's own sex" (426). That confusion, one suspects, is associated with all the conditions of modern life, including urbanization and the explosive growth of a popular reading culture: speaking of the neurotic symptoms of Sophie's having fallen in love with Fenelon's Telemachus, Rousseau observes that nature neither makes us need to repress desires nor "gives us these immoderate desires" in the first place, and he concludes by stating—implausibly, aphoristically, resoundingly—that "all that is not from nature is contrary to nature" (441).

## "Nature's own pencil"

Rousseau's books, however clearly they may be seen to emerge from eighteenth-century intellectual contexts of one kind and another, have had a prosperous afterlife. They continue to be widely read, and in that sense they spoke effectively to the future, a goal most of Rousseau's literary contemporaries did not achieve (the majority of writers in any period do not!). They also spoke very effectively, of course, to any number of his contemporaries, some of whom elaborated on Rousseau's themes in bodies of writing that are now often considered to have little more than an antiquarian interest. This seems to me a singularly shortsighted way of considering works whose deployment of certain rhetorical tropes and lines of reasoning can let us hear other things more clearly in the conversations in which they participate, in many instances precisely *because* they are less original or less skillfully argued than some others.

During the 1750s Britain saw the birth of an elocution movement that may represent the century's most glaring instance of a discipline that was committed to rescuing nature by cultural intervention. But the writings of the elocutionists show the extent to which even the most explicitly cultural arguments continued to be dogged by words like *nature* and *blood,* terms that can only be very partially assimilated to a transformative scheme involving habit, custom, training, rearing, and the associated variants. (*Breeding,* once again, disconcerts by finding a place on both sides of the fence.) These writers want to maintain a double commitment, to improvement on the one hand and to nature on the other, a version of the double bind that makes them into rhetorical contortionists.

At the beginning of the eighteenth century British writers rarely expressed curiosity as to why English-language speakers did not all talk in exactly the same way. While your speech might tell people where you'd been raised, accent had not yet become the most obvious marker of social class. Nor had linguistic difference within the English-speaking community become a serious field of inquiry.[14] With the century's waxing, though, a number of factors contributed to heighten awareness of linguistic difference, increasing the painful self-consciousness of speakers whose regional accents prevented them from being able to talk the polite and uniform English associated with London's best speakers: these factors include the 1707 Act of Union that incorporated Scotland's parliament into England's (Wales had been officially incorporated several hundred years earlier), drawing the countries together as a single entity called Great Britain; the rapid growth of Britain's empire overseas; and the rise of commerce and politeness as favored values among the country's political and cultural elite.

Given all of the political, social, and cultural pressures contributing to the appeal of a middle-class metropolitan English, differences between speakers—metropolitan and provincial, English and Scottish, middle- and working-class—came "no longer to be regarded merely as attractive and desirable variations from locality to locality," as one historian of the elocution movement puts it, "but as positive hindrances to the cultural, political, commercial, and occupational welfare of a growing and dynamic world empire."[15] Even the words *pronunciation* and *accent* picked up their modern senses only in the early years of the eighteenth century: *pronunciation* had previously been synonymous with what we might call *delivery*,[16] a central category of classical rhetoric, while *accent* more commonly referred to stress or emphasis than to dialect, and John Walker in his 1781 *Elements of Elocution* takes rather defensive notice "of a usage of the word accent, which, though seemingly inaccurate, will be found upon examination, to be a just application of the word," asserting that "[i]t is the custom, not only of England, but of other parts of the world, which are seats of empire, to call those modes of pronunciation used in parts distant from the capital, by the name of *accents*."[17] The clear implication is that regional variations represent a falling-off, the word *accent* chiefly used to mark departures from the standard of the capital.

In response to the desire (particularly widespread among the Scottish) for a more polite accent, entrepreneurial grammarians began selling lessons in elocution and pronunciation as a passport to full membership in the British nation. But the appeal of the premise that you could reinvent yourself by changing how you spoke was not limited to well-educated Scots like David Hume and James Boswell, both obsessed with eradicating Scotticisms from their speech and writing. Once the intangible quality of "breeding" was made accessible by way of self-help books, public lectures, and private lessons, anyone who cared to could attain it, and even ordinary working men and women (from servants and dustmen to the City of London merchants whose manners are disparaged in so many plays and novels of the period) could learn to speak just like the politicians, barristers, and actors associated with the new polite English. As writers began to suspect that rooting out differences in spoken English could have dangerous political consequences—a private fear of social leveling that runs counter to the public goals of elocutionists like Thomas Sheridan and John "Elocution" Walker—anxieties about social mobility began to be expressed in hints that differences in accent owed more to nature than to nurture, and the supremely culturalist enterprise of elocution was in this sense haunted by the return of a repressed nature.

In the *Plan of a Dictionary* (1747), which lays out the scope of the immensely ambitious encyclopedic work he contemplates, Samuel Johnson writes of pronunciation that its "stability . . . is of great importance to the duration of a language, because the first change will naturally begin by corruptions in the living speech," a fact that puts pronunciation at the center of his undertaking "to fix the English language."[18] In the "Preface to the *Dictionary*" (1755), written after the drastic scaling-down of the project required to complete the task of selection and compilation, Johnson is far less sanguine about the possibility of fixing the language at all. "[T]ongues, like governments, have a natural tendency to degeneration," he writes; "we have long preserved our constitution, let us make some struggles for our language."[19] The prominent Anglo-Irish actor-manager and elocutionist Thomas Sheridan (son of the well-known Irish schoolmaster of the same name, who had been a close friend of Jonathan Swift, and father of playwright and politician Richard Brinsley Sheridan) could have seen only the optimistic aspect of Johnson's exhortation. Over the ups and downs of his career as a popular lecturer and best-selling author on elocution, Sheridan would express many different versions of his favorite argument that elocution could effect political and social reform: that only "a perfect use of the powers of speech"—more particularly, the eradication of regional dialects—would support the British population's "rights, privileges, and all the blessings arising from the noblest constitution that ever was formed."[20]

When it came to elocution, Sheridan was a man obsessed: as one friend of his ruefully wrote, "He thought all the evils of Ireland, civil, moral and religious, were owing to this cause, that the bakers, tailors, and shoemakers, were not brought up orators."[21] In 1762 Sheridan's first major national lecture tour drew great crowds, a success that soon translated into book sales; long lists of the names of eminent subscribers preface his books on elocution, and the number of eighteenth-century editions suggests that he succeeded in reaching a wide audience.[22] Sheridan was well aware of the irony that so much of his success should depend on print, a medium he disliked, as opposed to what he called "the language of nature, the living speech,"[23] and he defended his plan of improving pronunciation by means of print on the grounds that it would make "a noble use of the invention of printing."[24] Relatively early on in his career as an elocutionist, Sheridan already describes a projected grammar and dictionary that will be used by schools throughout the country in order to produce "an uniformity of pronunciation": "Thus might the rising generation, born and bred in different countries, and counties, no longer have a variety of dialects, but as subjects of one king, like sons of one father, have one common tongue. All natives of these realms would be restored to their birthright in commonage of language, which has been too long fenced in, and made the property of a few."[25] The metaphor here suggests that Sheridan's linguistic fantasy includes familial elements (a shared language will make the citizens of a newly incorporated Britain into blood siblings) and political ones (Sheridan's rather paternalistic royalism is tempered by a vocabulary of "birthright" and "commonage" that nostalgically invokes Britain's ancient liberties in the time of the Magna Carta).

National distinctions are at the forefront of Sheridan's mind. His desire to erase distinctions between the Irish, the Scottish, and the English is matched by a patriotic need to urge the English to catch up and overtake continental rivals. "Believe me, there is no time to be lost," Sheridan urged audiences at Oxford and Cambridge in an early public appearance as an elocutionist, having temporarily cast aside his role as a Dublin actor-manager: "The Italians, the French, and the Spaniards, are far before you."[26] In the preface to his *Rhetorical Grammar* (1781), Sheridan insists that elocution is an irreproachable field of study, though later eighteenth-century evangelicals were quite distrustful of oratory, especially when it entered the pulpit.[27] Sheridan goes on to pose a series of rhetorical questions designed to show the obvious benefits of his plan, asking his readers "[w]hether it would not greatly contribute to put an end to the odious distinction kept up between the subjects of the same king, if a way were opened, by which the attainment of the English tongue in its purity, both in point of phraseology and pronunciation, might be rendered easy to all inhabitants of his Majesty's dominions, whether of South or North Britain, of Ireland, or the other British dependencies?"[28]

Sheridan is by no means alone in his millennial optimism about the role of elocution in transforming a collection of parts into a national whole. The elocution movement promoted improvement of a kind that immediately attracted the attention of writers eager to take the edge off their accents and eradicate Scotticisms from their private letters and published books, and the scholar Robert Crawford points out how many well-known Scots—including Lord Kames, Hugh Blair, and James Boswell—subscribed to Sheridan's *Course of Lectures on Elocution*.[29] The Scottish elocutionist James Buchanan argues elsewhere that uniting the Scottish and the English so that they are "of one language and of one speech" is a "truly momentous design," "promoting one of the grandest moral ends that can possibly employ the human mind with relation to so great a community."[30] Not surprisingly, the elocution movement appealed most powerfully to exactly those speakers "whose language it set out to eradicate": the Scottish in Britain's cultural provinces, the Irish in Britain's first colony.[31] Indeed, almost all of eighteenth-century Britain's best-known experts on polite language came from the cultural provinces, a fact frequently invoked by English detractors, as when the 1797 preface to an anonymous dictionary of pronunciation catalogues numerous objections to the specific pronunciations given by Sheridan in his own dictionary, despite admitting that "from the best accounts, his brogue was perceptible, only by the ear of prejudice."[32] Sheridan himself boasted of having had his own pronunciation corrected as a child when he read aloud to his godfather Jonathan Swift, who shared with Lord Chesterfield (Sheridan says) the "uniformity of pronunciation [that] had prevailed at the court of Queen Anne," an accent Sheridan would identify in 1781 as "still the customary one among the descendants of all the politer part of the world bred in that reign."[33]

A central problem for Sheridan is that while the elimination of dialects "will necessarily end in the restoration of the true natural mode of speech," he also believes that English—though it is a "language of Nature"—can "by pains and culture alone, . . . be brought to the highest degree of perfection, of which the human speech is capable."[34] Is language more strongly natural or cultural? In having his cake and eating it, Sheridan's claims often come to sound overemphatic, even anxious. By eradicating regional pronunciations and establishing a "uniformity of speech," he says later on in the same discussion, his plan "will necessarily end in the restoration of the true natural mode of speech," yet if speech is so "natural," why on earth should it need to be restored in the first place?[35] "Art is but *nature improved upon* and *refined,*" Sheridan insists elsewhere, thereby leaching much of the meaning out of the word *nature,* at least as far as modern readers are concerned.[36] Yet Sheridan's assertion that art equals nature—that nature's perfection is actually a matter of culture—echoes other contemporary discussions of similar topics, and questions about what aspects of human character derive from nature and what from nurture are especially likely to surface in eighteenth-century conversations about language and its origins.[37]

In his major essay on the origins of knowledge, for instance, Condillac—after noting how difficult it is to teach a deaf adult to speak—observes, "Experience acts on us so early that it is not surprising we often mistake it for nature itself."[38] By foregrounding experience, Condillac tends to identify speech as a cultural rather than a natural phenomenon, a conclusion shared by many of his peers, most of whom also argue that proper cultivation will always trump natural abilities. The philosopher James Harris's investigation of the origins of language offers a particularly eloquent statement of this position. "IN truth, each man's Understanding, when ripened and mature, is a composite of *natural Capacity,* and of *super-induced Habit,*" Harris writes. "Hence the greatest Men will be necessarily those, who possess *the best* Capacities, cultivated with *the best* Habits. Hence also moderate Capacities, when adorned with valuable Science, will far transcend others the most acute by nature, when either neglected, or applied to low and base purposes. And thus for the honour of CULTURE *and* GOOD LEARNING, *they are able to render a man, if he will take the pains, intrinsically more excellent than his natural Superiors.*"[39] The word *intrinsically* draws attention to the oxymoron of a natural excellence attained by hard work.

Despite the blank slate metaphor's prominence in discussions of human nature, pretty much everyone who weighs in on the topic allows for natural differences between individuals in a way that implies a belief in innateness (whether or not that belief is always articulated), as when Hugh Blair attributes inequalities among men "in part, to the different frame of their natures . . . [but] to education and culture still more."[40] This assertion of culture's power is typical. The linguist John Herries allows "that the benevolent BEING, who created man after his own image, who taught the mind to think, the ear to hear, and the blood to circulate, gave him likewise a power and propensity to communicate his ideas and desires," a concession followed by an insistence that the art of speech is primarily "imitative and progressive" rather than innate.[41] Here is the line of reasoning by which Herries shows language to be a cultural phenomenon:

If a Bullfinch, or any imitative bird, was conveyed from the nest, and confined in a cage, before it heard any of its own species sing; and if a person was to frequently to play to it on a small flagelet or reed, suited to the quality and extent of its tone; it then would imitate the musical airs of the pipe, with as much success as it would have done the native warblers on the bough. . . . From the same analogy, do not the children of one family talk Spanish, and those of another English? Why? Because from their infancy, their ears have been habituated to these particular sounds. But if they had been born in Persia or in China, would not they have acquired with equal facility, the pronunciation of these nations? If therefore a man has no opportunity of hearing the language of his own species, if he is brought up among the beasts of the forest, what sounds then will he utter? What but those which he has constantly heard?[42]

Like Condillac, Herries invokes the difficulty experienced by adults who did not learn spoken language as children (he draws specific examples from well-known cases of feral children as well as from the deaf) to show that men are "naturally" speechless.

Sheridan's own debts to Locke are clear, particularly in his earliest published writings on elocution, where he speaks of the damage done to Irish boys who are sent to school in England and whose love for their own country is diminished by the fact that their "waxen Minds receive their first and deepest Impressions in another."[43] He also subscribes to Locke's belief that early impressions are likely to be lasting: "If the Plant be not properly managed in the Nursery," Sheridan writes, "it will hardly ever prove a good Tree."[44] The parallel between agricultural and educational improvement structures much of his discussion:

> If it be useful, by the Encouragement of Agriculture, to improve the insensible Earth; by planting, and the Arts of Gardening, to adorn the Face of God's Creation, shall the Improvement of the Conscious *Owner* of the Land be deemed not worthy of Regard?. . . . If the training of Horses, Dogs, and other Animals for the Use or Sport of Man; if the breeding of singing Birds; if the rearing of curious Flowers, be thought Objects not unworthy the Attention of many Societies, established for those Purposes, shall the Rearing and Training of their own Children, be considered by Parents as a Matter of less Importance?[45]

Though the syntax here makes *breeding* synonymous with *training* or *rearing,* Sheridan's language calls up the more radical discourses of bodily malleability deployed by Maupertuis, Vandermonde, Gregory, and others.

The fuzziness of the distinction between nature and nurture introduces into all these discussions a dynamic of self-contradiction that is perhaps broadly characteristic of eighteenth-century European thought, a dynamic laid out with particular effectiveness in Derrida's account of the figure of the supplement in Rousseau's "Essay on the Origins of Languages." In an imaginative book titled *Declaring Independence: Jefferson, Natural Language, and the Culture of Performance* (1993), Jay Fliegelman alludes to eighteenth-century writers' need to consider individuals on the one hand as the products of nurture or education and on the other as responsible and fully self-determining agents, arguing that the tension between these two views frames a "still-ongoing crisis in liberalism."[46] Daniel Cottom observes in *The Civilized Imagination* (1985) that eighteenth-century writers called on nature and education "to supplement each other even though this need for a supplement violates both the image of nature and the authority of education."[47] Yet while Cottom's argument—which includes the perceptive formulation that the aristocracy is protected from the ramifications of the contradiction between nature and education "because, for its members, education finally has the meaning of nature"—has certainly been reinforced by the work of John Barrell, Olivia Smith, and others, social class is only one of the factors—others include gender and regional and national difference—that provoke these self-contradictory gestures, and the redefinition of nature as culture (which can also be thought of as an act of substitution in which culture stands in for nature) has consequences well beyond the consolidation of class and regional difference.[48]

In the opening pages of the *Course of Lectures on Elocution* (1762), by no means Sheridan's first publication on the subject but the one that recapitulates the content of his successful national tour, Sheridan introduces the parallel of bodily deformity to represent the linguistic aberrations elocution promises to correct. In an extravagantly rhetorical passage, Sheridan lays out the response of a conjectural traveler to apparently "natural" deformities spied in foreign lands:

> IF any stranger in China, observing the uncommon smallness of feet in all the
> women; or, in some savage countries, the uncouth shape of the head in whole
> nations of Barbarians, some formed into a conical figure like that of a sugar-
> loaf, others flattened at the top and rendered square; should not be acquainted
> with the causes of these extraordinary appearances, he would be apt to conclude
> that they were defects and blemishes of nature. But when he should be told,
> that the feet of the former were bound in the tightest manner with bandages
> from childhood, on purpose to prevent their growth; and the skulls of the latter,
> from the hour of the infant's birth, whilst yet they were unclosed, and yielded
> to impression, were industriously moulded into those forms, from a mistaken
> idea of beauty; how would he wonder at the folly of nations, that could perse-
> vere in such absurd customs?[49]

The vehicle of the metaphor is so striking that Sheridan's revelation in the following paragraph as to his tenor comes across as distinctly anticlimactic: "YET much more to be wondered at, would the conduct of a civilized people be, who should persevere in a custom far more fatal; that of binding up and contracting from early childhood, and moulding into unnatural forms, the faculties of speech." In spite of his striking invocation of the practice of foot-binding in China, Sheridan never quite succeeds in making the mangled feet of these distinctly foreign female bodies directly equivalent to a provincial accent.[50]

His second example reveals another oddity. The example of the tribe with artificially shaped skulls has an ancient provenance—drawn, as my introduction suggests, from the Hippocratic "Airs, Waters, Places"—and is more commonly cited to emphasize the persistence of culture's translation into nature than the artifice of the shaping. When the learned and eccentric Scottish scholar James Burnett, Lord Monboddo paraphrases Hippocrates' remarks about the Scythian tribe "who had been in use, for many generations, to make the heads of their children long, by squeezing them betwixt two boards," it is to show culture actually becoming nature as "the children at last came to be born with such heads"; elsewhere, Monboddo comments that custom or habit "is said to be a second nature in man" and concludes that "it may be said to be his first and original nature," observing that "the nature of man is such, that he, by use and custom, acquires many faculties that other animals have from nature," with the result that "*Habit* . . . in man is what *nature* is in other things."[51]

The Hippocratic passage (I will give it here again in a 1658 version—not credited to Hippocrates—found in Della Porta's *Natural Magic,* a popular sixteenth-century "book of secrets") casts further light on the question:

> And surely Custom was the first cause that they had such heads; but afterward Nature framed her self to that Custome; insomuch that they esteemed it an honourable thing to have a very long head. The beginning of that Custome was thus. As soon as the child was new born, whiles his head was yet soft and tender, they would presently crush it in their hands, and so cause it to grow out in length: yea they would bind it up with swathing bands, that it might not grow round, but all in length: and by this custom it came to passe, that their heads afterward grew such by nature. And in process of time, they were born with such heads, so that they needed not to be so framed by handling; . . . But now they are not born with such heads, because that practise is quite out of use; and so nature, which was upheld by that custom, ceaseth together with the custom.[52]

In presenting the custom of shaping heads as a wholly cultural deformation whose physical consequences only *appear* to be "defects and blemishes of nature," in other words, Sheridan seems to ignore the example's history of serving as a strong piece of evidence for culture's tendency to establish itself as nature. This aspect undercuts Sheridan's belief that the deformities of custom can be reversed by cultural means: released from the constraints of bandages and "swathing bands," bound feet and molded skulls will only very imperfectly revert to their "natural" shapes. Elsewhere Sheridan's figures also often work against his general drift, telling readers as much about his fears as his hopes, as when he points out later in the *Lectures* (with regard to the indistinct pronunciation of the letter R in certain parts of England) that "it would be strange to suppose, that all those people, should be so unfortunately distinguished, from the rest of the natives of this island, as to be born with any peculiar defect in their organs."[53] He tries here for a light irony meant to show that the pronunciation is "plainly to be accounted for, upon the principle of imitation, and habit." But the quasi-medical language of organs and their defects raises a specter of disease not easily laid to rest.

A passage in the early polemical tract *British Education* (1756) shows even more clearly the ways that cultural and natural deformity intertwine in Sheridan's imagination. Sheridan writes here not simply of pronunciation but of manners more generally, in words that suggest both his fear of deformity and his ambivalence about culture and improvement:

> Too long have the beauties of the British muse, like those of our ladies, been concealed, or spoiled, by foreign modes and false ornaments. The paint and patches of the French, the fantastical head-dress, the squeezing stays, and enormous hoop, only spoil the bloom of her complexion, the flowing ringlets of her hair, her easy shape, and graceful mein [sic]. Should a polished Athenian arise, and behold her thus decked out, he would be astonished to see, in a country enlightened by their rules, and example, deformity made a science, and barbarism reduced to rule. Thus adorned like an harlot, she inflames the youth with wanton desires, and spreads infection thro' the land. What hopes can there be of a robust and healthy offspring from such impure embraces? Let us endeavour to recover her from the tyrannical sway of fashion and prejudice, and restore her to her native rights. Let us leave to the sallow French their rouge and white paint, but let the British red and white appear in it's [sic] genuine lustre, as laid on by nature's own pencil. Let them torture the body into a fantastick shape, or conceal crookedness under an armour of steel; let them cover puny limbs, and a mincing gait, under the wide circumference of an hoop; but let the easy mein, the comely stature, the fine proportioned limbs decently revealed, and the unrestrained majesty of motion in the British muse, be displayed to sight in their native charms.[54]

The tenor and vehicle of this metaphor are blurred, the "British muse" oscillating between a real and a figurative body in ways that anticipate the all-too-physically-present bound feet of the Chinese women in the earlier example; it is impossible to say that either the literal or the figurative meaning predominates, as the personification of the muse (standing in for language as well as manners) shares all the traits of the fashionable British ladies whose adornments Sheridan condemns. Furthermore, what initially seems to be superficial damage actually turns out to be an "infection" that can be passed on to offspring, a sexual disease (like syphilis) that becomes congenital. Finally, Sheridan is caught short by the ubiquity of defects that, while they are attributed in the first place to artifice, run so deep now in nature that it is hard to see how culture will alleviate them. Even as the cultural aids associated with French manners (aids that prevail in England as well) take women too far from nature, in ways that are sexually corrupt and potentially damaging to the species, the restoration of "native rights" to the British will itself require the application of art, "the British red and white" achieving "*genuine* lustre, as laid on by nature's own pencil" (emphasis added). Like Derrida's *pharmakon*, Sheridan's culture is a poison as well as a remedy, and the space of the contradiction lets nature jump up and pull the rug out from under elocution's feet.[55] Elocution as eraser of difference turns out to be more a drawer of distinctions between individuals and groups, an agent whose contradictory functions Sheridan either does not understand or prefers not to articulate.

## The Natural Inequality of Man

Thanks in part to Johnson's dismissive remarks in Boswell's *Life*, Lord Monboddo is known today, if he is known at all, mainly as an obscure crank.[56] His notoriety—such as it is—rests on two six-volume works, each issued piece by piece over a twenty-year period, a singularly self-defeating way of disseminating one's views: *Of the Origin and Progress of Language*, published between 1773 and 1792, and *Antient Metaphysics*, published between 1779 and 1799.[57] There is no doubt that Monboddo's writing is peculiar and repetitive as well as voluminous. His most strongly held beliefs include any number of bizarre notions: that the "Orang Outang" (probably a chimpanzee, in modern terminology) is a kind of human, and he tells a story about one who breaks a china bowl and is beaten by his master, "which the animal laid so much to heart, that he abstained from food, and died" (*AM* 2:125); that some humans have tails; that the closest animal analogue to human society can be found among the beavers; that all exercise should be taken naked; that Egypt's early rulers were not human beings but "daimons" or minor gods; and—perhaps hardest of all to swallow—that the Aristotelian syllogism is more powerful than anything in Locke, Newton, or Descartes.

Monboddo's belief that ancient Egypt exemplified a higher degree of perfection than eighteenth-century Europe derived in part from that country's adoption of a caste system. Invoking Cook's experience in the South Seas, where the traveler claimed to have been instantly able to detect the rank of everyone he saw, Monboddo argues that distinction both is and should be (the difference is sometimes blurred) visible at first glance, claiming for contemporary Brahmins as well as for the ancient Egyptian priests just such distinction, and speculating that "in Britain, and in every other part of Europe, a man of rank and family was, some hundred years ago, as readily known at first sight, as a horse of blood is now" (*AM* 4:207). A source of confusion around these matters, Monboddo suggests, is the difficulty of discerning acquired from natural powers. "[I]f we rightly consider the matter," he writes,

> we shall find, that our nature is chiefly constituted of acquired habits, and that we are much more creatures of custom and art than of nature. It is a common saying, that habit (meaning custom) is a second nature. I add, that it is more powerful than the first, and in a great measure destroys and absorbs the original nature: for it is the capital and distinguishing characteristic of our species, that we can *make* ourselves, as it were, over again, so that the *original* nature in us can hardly be seen; and it is with the greatest difficulty that we can distinguish it from the *acquired.* (*OPL* 1:25)

Another difficulty—this thought is prompted by his consideration of the feral Peter of Hanover—concerns the limits of culture's power over savage men:

> It is a common observation, that custom is a second nature; and it is true of civilized men, so true, that, among us, it often happens that the second nature is more powerful than the first. But it is not so among wild men; for Nature is so strong in them, that it is not to be overcome by any custom or education, at least not in the first generation: And, accordingly Kolben the Dutchman, in the account he has given us of the Hottentots, relates that many of the children of the Hottentots have been taken very young by the Dutch, and bred up among them, and even taught arts and professions, but who, nevertheless, whenever they found a proper opportunity, stripped themselves, and ran away to their countrymen in the woods; of which he gives a remarkable instance, and which I see is related by M. Rousseau, in his treatise upon the inequality of Men.—This evidently shows that inclinations, dispositions, and other qualities of the Mind, go to the race, as well as the qualities of the Body. (*AM* 3:222)

The central claim of the final sentence—though it also assumes (as Wall might have said) that "Properties descend!"—is that moral or mental as well as physical qualities can be passed on to one's children, a contention that would become one of the central topics of dispute for practitioners of the new science of man in the final years of the eighteenth century and the early years of the nineteenth.

Though he admires Rousseau greatly, Monboddo departs radically from the author of the *Second Discourse* and *Émile* by making a passionate argument for distinction rather than parity between individuals in the natural state, opposing the idea that "the distinction of birth and family . . . [is] merely a political distinction, without any foundation in Nature" (*AM* 3:233). "That men are different by nature, as well as by education, I think it is impossible to deny," he writes (*AM* 4:177). Differences between individuals are more clearly visible among the civilized, as for instance in Europe:

> I hold the natural difference of Minds, in the civilized state, to be a matter of fact, as clear and indisputable as the difference of Bodies. It is observable in children, in their earliest years, and when they are grown up, the difference of propensities and inclinations is so well marked, that I am persuaded there is no man that is not born with a genius more for one thing than another. . . . [W]e are all born with a capacity of excelling, more or less, in one thing rather than in another; and one of the greatest excellencies of any political constitution is to class men according to their several talents and dispositions, and to make them serve the public in that way. (*AM* 3:234–235)

But difference also applies in the company of "natural" men, a fact Monboddo believes is supported by "the analogy of other animals": "Nobody will deny, who knows any thing of horses, that the spirit of a horse of blood is very different from that of a common horse," he observes (*AM* 3:237). "But I think it cannot be doubted," he adds, "that there is a very great difference of individuals in all specieses, and not only in the different races of the several specieses, but in the same race" (*AM* 3:238).

The inevitable conclusion, as Monboddo sees it, is that certain men are fitted by nature for governing others. Aptness for government is "as easily to be discerned in the features of a man, his look, his voice, and the movements of his body, as blood is in a horse, by his look and movements," he asserts, associating this kind of distinction with birth in the sense of lineage or status (*AM* 4:179). Great men in Greek times, he observes, were always "descended of noble parents": "Among us at this day, no horse is esteemed that is not of a good race; and no reason can be given why there should not be *blood* in men as well as in horses and other animals; for if it were otherwise, it would be a singularity in our species, such as cannot be presumed" (*AM* 4:184). Monboddo's commitment to aristocratic forms of distinction would be strongly compounded by the onset of revolution in France, a historical development that set him off on diatribes about the badness of democracy, whether in ancient Athens or modern France. One chapter summary puts his feelings especially well, and in comically abbreviated form: "No other example necessary to prove how bad a government democracy is, than the example of France before our eyes;—more folly, madness, and crimes, committed under that government by the French, than there is any example of in any other nation in the same short space of time.—Monarchy the best form of government" (*AM* 4:189). The term *blood* works as an evocative shorthand for such arguments.[58]

## "A purity, hwich Coarts doo not always bestow"

The second half of the eighteenth century featured both widespread consensus in Britain about the need for linguistic reform and deep disagreement as to what kinds of improvement were really wanted. Sheridan, Walker, and the other "orthoepists" (the word refers to the part of grammar dealing with pronunciation) concentrated on pronunciation, arguing that only a small number of speakers possessed accents of acceptable purity and that everyone should aspire to speak a hypercorrect English modeled on the written language. In contrast, most of the orthographers believed that in preference to forcing everyone to speak as a few select authors wrote, spelling should instead be reformed to reflect norms of pronunciation. In spite of the conceptual divide, though, wherein writers on orthography (especially those committed to the more extreme kinds of spelling reform) preferred using the spoken language as a basis for the written one, while orthoepists embraced a more prescriptive or interventionist desire to force the spoken language into the mold of writing, both groups found themselves able to agree that speech was both historically antecedent and aesthetically and philosophically preferable to writing. Thus Sheridan, aligning nature with spoken English and culture with the written language, deplores writing as "the invention of man, a mere work of art, . . . [with] no natural power,"[59] a sentiment shared by many of his contemporaries.[60]

But Sheridan's definition of speech as natural and good and writing as artificial and bad (his writing is not noted for its nuance!) coexists alongside a very powerful desire to force speech into closer alignment with writing, rather than the other way around. This tendency, already conspicuous in Sheridan's writings on elocution, would become more generally dominant in early nineteenth-century English theory and practice. The pronunciation given for the word *falcon* by eighteenth-century authorities ("fawkn") includes no audible "l," for instance, but a "graphemic logic" (I borrow the phrase from Lynda Mugglestone) would directly affect pronunciation: one 1825 authority finds the old familiar pronunciation "vicious," and by the end of the nineteenth century, the standard middle-class English pronunciation audibly reflects the presence of the letter "l," a historical transformation further instanced in the realignment of the pronunciation of any number of words with their actual spelling: *waistcoat* (formerly pronounced "weskit"), *forehead* ("for-ed"), *cucumber* ("cowcumber").[61] Despite "the manifest incompatibility of grapheme and phoneme in English," as Mugglestone puts it, speech would become increasingly "literate" from the end of the eighteenth century onward.[62]

At the beginning of the century Jonathan Swift had proposed that the English language should be improved by means of Britain instituting an academy modeled on the French one, to correct and regulate the language as it was spoken and written.[63] But British xenophobia and hostility toward French absolutism, a hostility that would later on be folded (however illogically) into the passionate hatred many British commentators felt toward the Jacobins and their successors, made this goal increasingly unpopular.[64] British attitudes toward language are characterized toward the end of the century by a combination of nostalgia and passivity, as when John Fell (writing in 1784) rejects any desire to legislate the customs of speech in the manner of the French Academy with the statement that "the republic of letters is a true republic, in its disregard to the arbitrary decrees of usurped authority. . . . The laws of our speech, like the laws of our country, should breathe a spirit of liberty: they should check licentiousness, without restraining freedom."[65]

Published the same year, Robert Nares's *Elements of Orthoepy* (1784), conceived in part as "a monument of the pronunciation which prevailed in England towards the end of the 18th century," offers a more melancholy expression of a similar sentiment: "Could we hope by such an effort to fix what we thus delineate, there might indeed be reason to exult. The mutability of human speech has been perceived and lamented by every nation that has had a language worth improving, or one so far improved as to deserve perpetuating. But the evil is perhaps too inherent in the nature of language to be removed entirely by any care."[66] Nares's hands-off attitude is linked to a kind of social conservatism: in cases where he has "opposed [his] author," he says, "it is generally for the sake of preventing, not of introducing, innovation."[67] Nares is at once irritated by "corruptions . . . established by custom" and aware that "to deviate from them is affectation," a kind of resignation that takes the fangs out of his statement that "it is to be wished that the custom could be reformed" and that also leads him to provide a lengthy list of colloquial corruptions of written English ("leftenant" for *lieutenant,* "ha'penny" for *halfpenny,* "sparrowgrass" for *asparagus,* and so forth) while simultaneously refusing to assert "that all the above words ought to be spoken according to the propriety here noted."[68]

Nares' willingness to tolerate a custom at odds with propriety certainly did not mean that the hostility toward nonstandard forms of English had abated. Such hostility often arises in response to social transformations: English mockery of the Scots snowballed in the 1750s, for instance, with the political dominance of Scottish minister Lord Bute and the increasing prominence of Scots in England's professional classes, a development that contributed to the centrality of regional distinctions to new discussions of pronunciation.[69] Though Sheridan himself showed little awareness of the extent to which his plan—tailored first and foremost for well-educated Scottish and Irish men and women who wanted to blend into polite metropolitan society—might have facilitated an upward mobility he was far from endorsing, his contemporaries were quite aware that his lectures opened up the possibility that large numbers of lower-class speakers might learn to talk just like their social betters. The comedian Samuel Foote's theatrical parody *The Orators,* staged in direct response to Sheridan's popular lectures, pillories the character of the "Cit" bent on coming up in the world: "My wife Alice—for you must know my name is Ephraim Suds, I am a soap-boiler in the city," says one attendee at the oratorical lecture, "took it into her head, and nothing would serve her turn, but that I must be a common-council man this year; for says Alice, *says she,* It is the *onliest* way to rise in the world."[70] His verbal solecisms are revealed to be a matter of syntax as well as accent, and Foote implies that it is just as well that the elocutionist enterprise is doomed (as he believes) to fail.

As a prediction, this would turn out to say more about Foote's dislike for certain kinds of social mobility than about the way events would really unfold: the values of the elocutionists would soon squeeze out defenses of custom and established practice. History would deal less kindly with the movement to reform spelling, stigmatized then (especially during a wild burst of spelling-related activity in the 1780s) as now with the charge of being both impractical and visually barbaric. The grammarian William Kenrick, writing in 1784, disparages the vogue for "vocabularies, containing all the words in our language, so horribly metamorphosed as to be equally unintelligible both to the eye and ear."[71] Any number of seventeenth-century British writers had expressed discomfort at obvious gaps between written and spoken language, often fantasizing about the possibility of casting language into "visible letters" to close the gap between the two.[72] But later eighteenth-century writers put a different inflection on such discussions, showing new willingness to move from philology and philosophy to more overtly political or sociological questions. Writers interested in such questions mostly share a credo that spelling reform will ameliorate social ills, although they do not all subscribe to a shared set of beliefs about language and politics. The Newcastle-based writer Thomas Spence wants to enfranchise regional speakers by developing a system of writing that allows for local differences, for instance, while James Elphinston is a wholehearted metropolitan royalist whose phonetic spelling is designed to give the cultural provinces a happy conduit to metropolitan English. Here is Elphinston's mission statement:

> FROM long and attentive discrimminacion ov livving speech, in dhe center ov Inglish purity: haz been at last completed a picture, hwich TRUITH can stamp widh dhe name ov INGLISH ORTHOGGRAPHY: dhat sacred depozzit, hware LONDON, in prime pollish, first sees hwat she says, and hwat dherfore she haz onely to' prezerv; but hware dhoze, hoo cannot hear her, may also see it; and, confiding in a delinneacion so authenticated; may speedily imbibe in dhe remotest corners a purity, hwich Coarts doo not always bestow. Hwile all endowed widh speech, ar dhus interested in propriety; such members ov dhe Metroppolis, az hav had dhe good-fortune, (hweddher from dellicate edducacion, or from incorruptibel taste) ov keeping equally free from grocenes, and from affectacion; hav doutles a chance, if stil but a chance, for purity. But dhe distant hav no possibel chance, unles from repprezentacion. If dherfore a few cood, az non can, be sure ov edher acquiring or prezerving Propriety, widhout an attested Picture; widhout dhat *Theory*, strictly so called, hwich can alone emboddy livving *Practice;* indispensabel wood be such Picture or Theory, to' dhe grait majorrity, even ov dhe Brittish Cappital.[73]

Elphinston's program is centered on a desire to fix the language in its present form, forestalling the decline that Samuel Johnson bemoaned (though Johnson himself was rather skeptical about the advantages of altering spelling) when he wrote that "it is incident to words, as to their authours, to degenerate from their ancestors, and to change their manners when they change their country."[74] Preoccupied with purity and its discrimination, Elphinston's treatment of language reveals a wish to make propriety a moral as well as an aesthetic value.

In an interesting aside, however, Elphinston hedges as to what constitutes purity, attributing the good luck of Londoners whose speech remains untainted *either* to delicate education *or* to incorruptible taste. By "dellicate edducacion," he presumably means something above the common touch, but the phrase "incorruptibel taste" offers an equivocally democratic impulse, one in which "taste"—detached now from the court—may reside in the breast of a natural aristocrat, a concept that at once defies the usual social distinctions and reinscribes them in a different guise. The extent to which writing itself is valorized within Elphinston's system can be seen in the fact that the easiest words to recognize at first glance—the words whose spelling has undergone the least change—are those borrowed from Greek and Latin (*authenticated, imbibe, sacred, propriety*). Striking, too, is the emptying-out of meaning from words that might be considered political in another setting: the representation that will give regional speakers their only chance of achieving purity isn't parliamentary, just a new way of writing English words.[75] Elphinston's orthographic program endorses polite standardization, not democratic leveling or the toleration of linguistic difference, and his nonstandard spellings thus work to very different ends from the Scottish dialect transcriptions of Robert Burns, Sir Walter Scott, and many others, writers whose twentieth-century successors would continue to assert the power of nonstandard Englishes, as in the Glaswegian poet Tom Leonard's use of phonetic transcription to mount a scathing critique of what he identifies as Britain's "essentially acquisitive attitude to culture, 'education', and 'a good accent.'"[76]

Despite Elphinston's willingness to locate the fountain of speech in London, eighteenth-century commentators remain divided as to the rights and wrongs of allowing a small group of speakers to set the tone for the rest of the country. Joseph Priestley was perhaps eighteenth-century Britain's most insightful commentator on the relationship between language and political structures.[77] In his *Course of Lectures on the Theory of Language* (1762), based on the curriculum of the Dissenting Academy at Warrington, Priestley observes that regional differences in modern English (between Scottish and English speakers, for example) find a precedent in the various dialects of ancient Greece. What prevented Greek dialects from giving way to one standard form, he goes on to suggest, was the fact that "in *Greece*, every seperate [sic] community looking upon itself as in no respect inferior to its neighbours in point of antiquity, dignity, intelligence, or any other qualification; and being constantly rivals for power, wealth, and influence, would no more submit to receive the laws of language from another than the laws of government."[78] In contrast, a perfect uniformity in writing (toward which current British practice seemed to be moving) would arise only in a hierarchical society in which "all writers, ambitious to draw the attention of the leading men in the state, would studiously throw aside the particular forms of speaking they might happen to have been brought up in, and conform to that of their superiors."

The Scottish scholar James Beattie sees language as being governed by a Lockean tacit consent, arguing that the forms of language—arbitrary in the first place—are made binding on communities of speakers by way of convention and custom: "To speak as others speak," he writes, "is one of those tacit obligations, annexed to the condition of living in society, which we are bound in conscience to fulfil, though we have never ratified them by any express promise; because, if they were disregarded, society would be impossible, and human happiness at an end."[79] In his *Dissertations on the English Language* (1789), the American grammarian Noah Webster expresses outrage at the British elocutionists' conviction of their own "authority to make changes at pleasure, and palm their novelties upon a nation under the idea of *custom*," deploring the rise of "individuals, who dictate to a nation the rules of speaking, with the same imperiousness as a tyrant gives laws to his vassals": "And, strange as it may appear," Webster continues, "even well bred people and scholars, often surrender their right of private judgement to these literary governors. The *ipse dixit* of a Johnson, a Garrick, or a Sheridan, has the force of law; and to contradict it, is rebellion."[80] Webster hopes to persuade his American readers of their patriotic duty to reject the prescriptions of the British elocutionists, though Webster's extensive and uncredited borrowing from Sheridan's writings injects that rejection with a healthy shot of opportunism.

In the earlier *Grammatical Institute, of the English Language* (1783–1784), Webster took a less extreme stance on custom and its political valence, observing that "when a sentiment has acquired the stamp of time and the authority of general custom, it is too firm to be shaken by the efforts of an individual": "Even errour becomes too sacred to be violated by the assaults of innovation," he concludes, relegating to a footnote his discussion of "odious distinctions of provincial dialects" ("The inhabitants of New England and Virginia have a peculiar pronunciation which affords much diversion to their neighbours," Webster observes) along with his wish that Americans would "unite in destroying provincial and local distinctions."[81] The *Grammatical Institute* also disavows an interest in reforming spelling, given that the spoken language is always in fluctuation: "[T]o attempt a total change at once, is equally idle and extravagant, as it would render the language unintelligible," Webster writes. "We may better labour to speak our language with propriety and elegance, as we have it, than to attempt a reformation without advantage or probability of success."[82] But by the late 1780s, Webster (partly influenced by Benjamin Franklin's interest in reforming spelling) was ready to reverse his position, embracing orthographic reform along with a new kind of elocutionary practice. "I once believed that a reformation of our othography [sic] would be unnecessary and impracticable," he writes in the preface to the *Dissertations*. "This opinion was hasty; being the result of a slight examination of the subject. I now believe with Dr. Franklin that such a reformation is practicable and highly *necessary*."[83] His motive is pragmatic to the point of being somewhat mercenary: "The alteration, however small, would encourage the publication of books in our own country. It would render it, in some measure, necessary that all books should be printed in America. The English would never copy our orthography for their own use; and consequently the same impressions of books would not answer for both countries. The inhabitants of the present generation would read the English impressions; but posterity, being taught a different spelling, would prefer the American orthography."[84]

Webster runs hot and cold on reformed spelling, and he would quietly lay aside his experiments in later years when he realized how much they irritated mainstream readers. His main interest is in making the case that American identity will be most powerfully consolidated by means of a truly national language, one enshrined and perpetuated in schools and books rather than legislation. "A sameness of pronunciation is of considerable consequence in a political view," Webster writes; "for provincial accents are disagreeable to strangers and sometimes have an unhappy effect upon the social affections. All men have local attachments, which lead them to believe their own practice to be the least exceptionable. Pride and prejudice incline men to treat the practice of their neighbors with some degree of contempt."[85] Political harmony depends on a "uniformity of language," for "social intercourse" goes smoothly only if people aren't tempted to make fun of each other because of small differences in how they speak. Webster argues that the present time offers "the fairest opportunity of establishing a national language, and of giving it uniformity and perspicuity, in North America, that ever presented itself to mankind":

Now is the time to begin the plan. The minds of the Americans are roused by the events of a revolution; the necessity of organizing the political body and of forming constitutions of government that shall secure freedom and property, has called all the faculties of the mind into exertion; and the danger of losing the benefits of independence, has disposed every man to embrace any scheme that shall tend, in its future operation, to reconcile the people of America to each other, and weaken the prejudices which oppose a cordial union.[86]

While Webster consistently juxtaposes the egalitarian uniformity of American speech (or at least his idealizing projection of such) to the reinforcement of social distinctions in the words and actions of the British elocutionists, few in Britain shared his objections to the top-down nature of the elocution movement. Indeed, even those most directly inconvenienced by the imposition of a metropolitan standard seem remarkably placid in the face of pressure to conform. Speaking about the standard of pronunciation to a class of Scottish university students in the 1760s, for instance, Adam Smith gives voice to a new consensus on speech: "Our words must not only be English and agreable [sic] to the custom of the country but likewise to the custom of some particular part of the nation. This part undoubtedly is formed of the men of rank and breeding."[87] Webster hates this kind of argument. "The Authors, who have attempted to give us a standard, make the practice of the court and stage in London the sole criterion of propriety in speaking," he notes. "An attempt to establish a standard on this foundation is both *unjust* and *idle*. It is unjust, because it is abridging the nation of its rights: The *general practice* of a nation is the rule of propriety, and this practice should at least be consulted in so important a matter, as that of making laws for speaking. While all men are upon a footing and no singularities are accounted vulgar or ridiculous, every man enjoys perfect liberty."[88]

In contrast to his British rivals, then, Webster insists that language is "a democratical state" and that the standard should be fixed not on the habits of a few eminent speakers, but on the "*general practice of the nation*": "when a particular set of men, in exalted stations, undertake to say, 'we are the standards of propriety and elegance, and if all men do not conform to our practice, they shall be accounted vulgar and ignorant,' they take a very great liberty with the rules of the language and the rights of civility," he concludes.[89] Language also represents an indisputable means for achieving national unity, and Webster generates more than one different argument in favor of American English parting ways with its progenitor, postulating that "[c]ustoms, habits, and *language,* as well as government should be national" and that "America should have her *own* distinct from all the world," then adding the clincher: that "the people of America, in particular the English descendants, speak the most *pure English* now known in the world."[90] The ideal of purity, though, easily topples over into xenophobia, and Webster's desire to erase distinctions between, say, northerners and southerners is counterbalanced by a strong desire to reinscribe the differences between English-speaking nations.

A different critique of elocution can be found in the writings of dialect speakers who hold on to regional difference for political and cultural reasons that include national pride and/or a sneaking awareness that wholesale reinvention isn't as classy as more subtle forms of self-improvement. But the national pride argument often falls back on a strain of nativism that uneasily straddles the birth-upbringing divide, as when the self-conscious Scot James Boswell tries to persuade Edmund Burke of the "strange proposition" that it is better (because more natural) for Scottish and Irish speakers "to preserve so much of their native accent and not to be quite perfect in English."[91] "I would have all the birds of the air to retain somewhat of their own notes," Boswell tells Burke: "a blackbird to sing like a blackbird, and a thrush like a thrush, and not a blackbird and other birds to sing all like some other bird." Doesn't the metaphor hint that the difference between, say, a Scottish person and an English one is a species difference like that between a blackbird and a thrush? Boswell clearly preferred Scottish speakers to retain quite a bit of their accent: in a personal aside during his discussion of Johnson's indignation at Sheridan's receiving a pension, Boswell writes that Sheridan was one of the instructors who assisted Alexander Wedderburne to "[get] rid of the coarse part of his Scotch accent, retaining only as much of the 'native wood-note wild,' as to mark his country; which, if any Scotchman should affect to forget, I should heartily despise him."[92] Elsewhere Boswell breaks off from quoting Johnson's praise of his own pronunciation ("Sir, your pronunciation is not offensive") to address the Scottish reader directly:

> [L]et me give my countrymen of North-Britain an advice not to aim at absolute perfection in this respect; not to speak *High English,* as we are apt to call what is far removed from the *Scotch,* but which is by no means *good English,* and makes 'the fools who use it,' truly ridiculous. . . . A studied and factitious pronunciation, which requires perpetual attention, and imposes perpetual constraint, is exceedingly disgusting. A small intermixture of provincial peculiarities may, perhaps, have an agreeable effect, as the notes of different birds concur in the harmony of the grove, and please more than if they were all exactly alike.[93]

As a matter of manners, of course, Boswell's argument makes a lot of sense. Then as now, an accent with its rough edges sanded off but still recognizably regional is viewed as being more attractive (certainly more tasteful, if the word may be allowed) than a more drastic alteration to the way one speaks, which would imply an overly strong desire to please others as well as a chameleonic willingness to abandon the claims of an "authentic" self inside, one whose history is marked above all in its speech. Many speakers of nonstandard English are audibly torn between the desire to assimilate, thereby gaining all the advantages associated with speaking and writing standard English, and the need to hold on to a cultural identity more often framed in terms of birth than breeding.

———————

Though some would take the writings of the elocutionists as more travesty than exemplification of Enlightenment values—Johnson likened Sheridan's attempt to influence the language by these "narrow exertions" to "burning a farthing candle at Dover, to shew light at Calais"[94]—the linguistic wing of Enlightenment thought contains its own critique. The witty argument for linguistic tolerance and cultural union offered by Irish novelist Maria Edgeworth and her father and coauthor Richard Lovell Edgeworth in *An Essay on Irish Bulls* (1802) is at once a comment on the 1801 Act of Union incorporating Ireland into a new entity called the United Kingdom of Great Britain and Ireland and a more self-reflexive intervention into the conversation about nature and culture. Writing in the aftermath of the trauma and bloodshed of the 1798 Rebellion, acutely aware of national disparities that threaten to fracture the recent union, the Edgeworths promote an ecumenical tolerance of difference, albeit a difference that tends to vanish toward the higher end of the social scale: the essay itself is narrated in an urbane and metropolitan voice that bears no obvious stylistic traces of its Anglo-Irish or female ownership (Maria Edgeworth is known to have done most of the actual writing here, though she and her father collaborated on the compilation of material).

The Edgeworths' central point about the comic expressions known as bulls—defined as verbal formulations displaying a "*laughable confusion of ideas*"—is that it's unfair to laugh at the Irish for producing so many of them when these solecisms inevitably crop up around *any* careless use of figurative language.[95] "Many bulls, reputed to be bred and born in Ireland, are of foreign extraction," the Edgeworths write near the outset, playing on the word's double meaning in linguistics and husbandry.[96] Presenting their reasoning as the only fair reading of the Act of Union, they proclaim: "The blunders of men of all countries, except Ireland, do not affix an indelible stigma upon individual or national character. A free pardon is, and ought to be, granted by every Englishman to the vernacular and literary errors of those who have the happiness to be born subjects of Great Britain. What enviable privileges are annexed to the birth of an Englishman! and what a misfortune it is to be a native of Ireland!"[97] (Literally, of course, Britain's new Irish subjects have not been "born" so much as "made," a fact the essay does not really acknowledge.)

The authors disavow the extreme argument in favor of cultural difference promoted by their Scottish contemporary James Adams, here dubbed "our philological Quixote" for his advocacy of the Scottish accent.[98] Their own position is to value assimilation rather than difference, and the essay culminates in an imagined conversation between an Englishman, a Scot, and an Irishman in a Bath coach. The conversation between these three men is characterized by their generosity toward each others' countries as well as by the fact that they seem to speak a more-or-less uniform version of the English language. It is the Irishman rather than either of his interlocutors who introduces a classic Irish bull. "But, gentlemen, I have just recollected an example of an Irish bull in which are all the happy requisites, incongruity, confusion, and laughable confusion, both in thought and expression," he says. "When sir Richard Steele was asked, how it happened that his countrymen made so many bulls, he replied, 'It is the effect of climate, sir; if an Englishman were born in Ireland, he would make as many.'"[99] This happy infelicity highlights the contradiction that dogs so many eighteenth-century invocations of the power of climate or culture. The Irish playwright and political writer Steele wants to have it both ways, exonerating the Irish on the grounds of "climate" and simultaneously reinscribing both Englishness and Irishness with the oxymoronic—and politically suggestive—counterfactual "if an Englishman were born in Ireland."

In response to the puzzle about birth and culture offered by the Irishman, the Scot contributes another bull whose phrasing is not so much interesting in itself as it is notable for being taken from the "celebrated preface to Shakspeare [sic]" written by "our friend Dr. Johnson, the leviathan of English literature." The tactfulness of the citation lies in its demonstration that bulls are by no means unique to the Irish: that even the two writers most strongly identified with English literary culture (examples of Shakespeare's bulls have been instanced throughout the essay, and Johnson's name is by this point virtually synonymous with literature) commit verbal solecisms when they're not paying attention. Thus the case for tolerating national difference rests on the assumption that even the most distinctive traits associated with any given nationality will always be better understood as manifestations of a universal human nature. If we can live with an imperfect uniformity, the essay suggests, we may find that a fine balance between sameness and difference (or between nurture and nature) is ultimately a better guarantee for human safety and human happiness than a philosophy of difference, for though nationalism may promote kinds of autonomy and self-determination largely unavailable to the United Kingdom's Irish subjects, it does so only by introducing the logic of shibboleth.

## Blots on the Landscape

5

What do blots on the landscape have to do with blotted copybooks and educational processes gone awry? My way into the next bit involves a backward approach to writings on population and development by Thomas Jefferson and William Godwin, through Mary Shelley's *Frankenstein; or, The Modern Prometheus* (1818).

Victor Frankenstein's mind runs on reproduction, but it is a form of reproduction remote from the ordinary forces of sexual generation.[1] Having discovered "the cause of generation and life," Victor becomes himself (and with no female assistance) "capable of bestowing animation upon lifeless matter" (36). He performs his experiments—preparing a frame "of a gigantic stature," because "the minuteness of the parts formed a great hindrance to [his] speed" (37)—in the grip of a fantasy of omnipotence:

> A new species would bless me as its creator and source; many happy and excellent natures would owe their being to me. No father could claim the gratitude of his child so completely as I should deserve theirs. Pursuing these reflections, I thought, that if I could bestow animation upon lifeless matter, I might in process of time (although I now found it impossible) renew life where death had apparently devoted the body to corruption. (37)

The fantasy of circumventing the processes of sexual reproduction by creating life from dead flesh (a fantasy bound up, it has been assumed, with Shelley's own recent loss of a child) is twinned with the hope that assuming the Creator's powers will allow Victor to achieve the ultimate goal of eradicating death itself, his vision of immortality distinctly reminiscent of the heady speculations of Mary Shelley's father, William Godwin, in the revolutionary years of the 1790s.

Afterward Victor would prefer to forget the basis of the creature's relationship to him: "Why do you call to my remembrance circumstances, of which I shudder to reflect, that I have been the miserable origin and author?" he asks (75). Authorship is not literally the same thing as paternity, of course, and the creature's self-examination upon coming into his intellectual maturity, as he recounts it to Victor, centers on the puzzle of his species identity:

> And what was I? Of my creation and creator I was absolutely ignorant; but I knew that I possessed no money, no friends, no kind of property. I was, besides, endowed with a figure hideously deformed and loathsome; I was not even of the same nature as man. I was more agile than they, and could subsist upon coarser diet; I bore the extremes of heat and cold with less injury to my frame; my stature far exceeded their's. When I looked around, I saw and heard of none like me. Was I then a monster, a blot upon the earth, from which all men fled, and whom all men disowned? (90)

A monster, a blot: this is the language of eighteenth-century deformities, the language of Thomas Jefferson's account of slavery. His creator's papers, the journal of the months preceding the great experiment, will transmit to the creature disgust-turned-self-disgust:

> Every thing is related in them which bears reference to my accursed origin; the whole detail of that series of disgusting circumstances which produced it is set in view; the minutest description of my odious and loathsome person is given, in language which painted your own horrors, and rendered mine ineffaceable. I sickened as I read. 'Hateful day when I received life!' I exclaimed in agony. 'Cursed creator! Why did you form a monster so hideous that even you turned from me in disgust? God in pity made man beautiful and alluring, after his own image; but my form is a filthy type of your's, more horrid from its very resemblance. Satan had his companions, fellow-devils, to admire and encourage him; but I am solitary and detested.' (97)

The language of "a filthy type" and "resemblance" invokes older discourses on generation even as it signals a uniquely modern and highly technological de-

formation of the generative processes. The creature's morphology departs profoundly enough from his creator's that he comes to think of himself (Victor certainly thinks of him) as belonging to another species. After his expulsion from the
pastoral idyll of the cottage where he has taken refuge, indeed, the creature's
orientation toward humanity becomes more fully malevolent: "There was none
among the myriads of men that existed who would pity or assist me; and should I
feel kindness towards my enemies? No: from that moment I declared everlasting
war against the species, and, more than all, against him who had formed me, and
sent me forth to this insupportable misery" (102).

Resentment of his single status finally prompts the creature to frame to Frankenstein a request for companionship, one phrased as an entitlement: "I am alone,
and miserable; man will not associate with me; but one as deformed and horrible
as myself would not deny herself to me. My companion must be of the same
species, and have the same defects. This being you must create" (107). Though
Victor can imagine the violent rampage that might ensue upon his creation of a
female counterpart with whom the creature's "joint wickedness might desolate the
world" (108), he decides at first to comply with the request, on condition that the
creature swear to quit Europe forever. Victor seems in this respect at once unduly
disgusted by the prospect of the creature's sexual coupling and disproportionately
attracted to it, at least so far as he allows the prospect of his own generation of a
female creature (by nonsexual means) to defer and to a considerable extent dis-
place the bonds of matrimony into which he himself is supposed to enter. His
feelings seem to run more strongly for his male friend Clerval than for his lovely
cousin Elizabeth; moreover, though he professes his love for his cousin and his
wish to marry her, Victor's promise to the creature becomes a reason to put off the
happy occasion—for two years! (*Frankenstein* might be set alongside Austen's *Persuasion*, published the same year, as a novel interested in making the case against
long engagements.) All the evidence suggests that Victor leans toward the kind of
perfectibility that to some extent precludes an interest in sex, or at least in making
a conventional marriage.

Traveling to England to pursue his covert goal of creating a mate for the monster, though, Victor embarks on a train of reflection that leads to a swerve in his
intentions:

> Three years before I was engaged in the same manner, and had created a fiend
> whose unparalleled barbarity had desolated my heart, and filled it for ever with
> the bitterest remorse. I was now about to form another being, of whose disposi-
> tions I was alike ignorant; she might become ten thousand times more malig-

nant than her mate, and delight, for its own sake, in murder and wretchedness. He had sworn to quit the neighbourhood of man, and hide himself in deserts; but she had not; and she, who in all probability was to become a thinking and reasoning animal, might refuse to comply with a compact made before her creation. They might even hate each other; the creature who already lived loathed his own deformity, and might he not conceive a greater abhorrence for it when it came before his eyes in the female form? She also might turn with disgust from him to the superior beauty of man; she might quit him, and he be again alone, exasperated by the fresh provocation of being deserted by one of his own species.

Even if they were to leave Europe, and inhabit the deserts of the new world, yet one of the first results of those sympathies for which the dæmon thirsted would be children, and a race of devils would be propagated upon the earth, who might make the very existence of the species of man a condition precarious and full of terror. Had I a right, for my own benefit, to inflict this curse upon everlasting generations? (128)

The specters of miscegenation and of a conjectural population explosion that might threaten the very existence of humanity contribute to persuade Victor to destroy his latest work. The monster responds with a threat: "[R]emember, I shall be with you on your wedding-night," he says, a promise Victor almost willfully misunderstands (130). In a fever following his dear friend Henry Clerval's death at the monster's hands, Victor describes himself to his father as "the assassin of those most innocent victims" (143). He would have "shed [his] own blood, drop by drop, to have saved their lives," he continues, pleading for his father's understanding, "but . . . could not sacrifice the whole human race" (143). Shelley shows especially clearly the confusion Victor experiences when he tries to negotiate the space between his obligation to individuals and his obligation to his species—a sharp diagnosis of the ills of identifying oneself as a member of a species or a race that may serve as a guide to the writings of the revolutionary generation to which both Shelley's parents belonged, and of which Jefferson may be considered a kind of harbinger.

## "This blot in our country increases"

Jefferson's *Notes on the State of Virginia* (1785) offers a more passionate and all-encompassing celebration of the virtues of the middle state, of husbandry, and of cultivation than the highly equivocal georgics of a Rousseau or a Smollett. Yet *Notes on Virginia* is vexed by some of the same doubts that perplexed Smollett in *Humphry Clinker*, particularly those concerning whether societies can be prevented from traveling beyond appropriate and admirable levels of cultivation toward the kinds of corruption associated with luxury. Jefferson's commitment to republican political ideals also intensifies his fears of corruption, his praise of America as a nation of cultivators always tinged with a pessimistic sense of republican virtue's precarious hold over the passions of the animal called man. Slavery poses for Jefferson a more extensive and immediately pressing set of questions about the limits of culture and the facts of natural degeneracy. Leo Marx wrote of *Notes on Virginia* that American literature has no "more appealing, vivid, or thorough statement of the case for the pastoral ideal," yet his discussion of Jefferson in *The Machine in the Garden* leaves out everything to do with slavery and race: an omission (though very much a function of the time and place of the book's composition) that has come to seem increasingly troubling, given the extent to which the problem of slavery is intimately bound up with Jefferson's arguments about how the cultivated nation he envisages is to be populated.[2] The most serious questions in *Notes on Virginia* are left largely unresolved, perhaps in part as a consequence of the work's relatively loose structure (it was written during the early 1780s in response to a set of queries from the secretary of the French legation to the United States).[3]

Jefferson often adopts a defensive position. Based on European examples, he admits, America may look deficient in manufactures and trade. But manufacture in Europe is "resorted to of necessity not of choice, to support the surplus of their people," as Europe's "lands are either cultivated, or locked up against the cultivator."[4] America, on the other hand, has "an immensity of land courting the industry of the husbandman," rendering it wholly unnecessary to make artisans out of the citizens presently "employed in its improvement":

> Those who labour in the earth are the chosen people of God, if ever he had a chosen people, whose breasts he has made his peculiar deposit for substantial and genuine virtue. It is the focus in which he keeps alive that sacred fire, which otherwise might escape from the face of the earth. Corruption of morals in the mass of cultivators is a phaenomenon of which no age nor nation has furnished an example. (19/170)

Jefferson offers substantive political reasons for maintaining the status quo, whatever dependence on European trade that may entail:

Carpenters, masons, smiths, are wanting in husbandry: but, for the general operations of manufacture, let our work-shops remain in Europe. It is better to carry provisions and materials to workmen there, than bring them to the provisions and materials, and with them their manners and principles. The loss by the transportation of commodities across the Atlantic will be made up in happiness and permanence of government. The mobs of great cities add just so much to the support of pure government, as sores do to the strength of the human body. It is the manners and spirit of a people which preserve a republic in vigour. A degeneracy in these is a canker which soon eats to the heart of its laws and constitution. (19/171)

This is only one of the ways in which Jefferson's America will diverge from European models: Jefferson also hopes that American surplus wealth will be used to build roads, to improve the arts and sciences, and so forth rather than to wage war, for this "would turn all our citizens to the cultivation of the earth; and, I repeat it again, cultivators of the earth are the most virtuous and independant [sic] citizens" (22/180).

The kinds of cultivation Jefferson envisages include education as well as tilling fields, and he elaborates a detailed scheme for schools that will "diffuse knowledge more generally through the mass of the people" (14/152). Despite the public nature of this education, however, it is designed to select a new natural aristocracy (a class to which Jefferson is passionately committed). By choosing from each local school "the boy, of best genius" and sending him on to one of twenty grammar schools from each of which "the best genius of the whole [will be] selected, and continued six years, and the residue dismissed," "twenty of the best geniuses will be raked from the rubbish annually," says Jefferson, in a memorable phrase that reveals the more ruthless aspect of his projected meritocracy (14/152–153). The school curriculum will foreground the study of history, arming students to defeat the views of ambitious men striving to deform American government: "In every government on earth is some trace of human weakness, some germ of corruption and degeneracy, which cunning will discover, and wickedness insensibly open, cultivate, and improve. Every government degenerates when trusted to the rulers of the people alone. The people themselves therefore are its only safe depositories. And to render even them safe their minds must be improved to a certain degree" (14/155). Such warnings punctuate the *Notes on Virginia:* in the previous query, which considers the constitution that will best suit the state's needs, Jefferson warns that the state assembly "should look forward to a time, and that not a distant one, when corruption in this, as in the country from which we derive our origin, will have seized the heads of government, and be spread by them through the body of the people; when they will purchase the voices of the people, and make them pay the price. Human nature is the same on every side of the Atlantic, and will be alike influenced by the same causes. The time to guard against corruption and tyranny, is before they shall have gotten hold on us. It is better to keep the wolf out of the fold, than to trust to drawing his teeth and talons after he shall have entered" (13/127).

Jefferson's conviction that all governments must degenerate partly undermines his eager refutation of Buffon's arguments about the degeneration of animals in the New World, a sustained defense of the vigor of the plants, animals, and people of America that represents one of the most persistent motifs of *Notes on Virginia*. Jefferson compiles numerous facts and figures and explains away any information that would seem to confirm Buffon's hypothesis.[5] The small size of American domesticated animals compared to their European counterparts, for instance, can be attributed to the fact of America being richer in land than labor, the farmer "find[ing] it more convenient to receive them from the hand of nature in that indifferent state, than to keep up their size by a care and nourishment which would cost him much labour," but it "would be erring therefore against that rule of philosophy, which teaches us to ascribe like effects to like causes, should we impute this diminution of size in America to any imbecility or want of uniformity in the operations of nature" (6/59). Eighteenth-century animal breeders were always concerned to prevent their stock from degenerating under the influence of damaging environmental conditions, and Jefferson clearly shares such a belief in the power of external influences over animals' properties.[6] In *The Gentleman Farmer* (1776), Lord Kames lays out the importance of environment for the constitution of plants and animals (everything from Arabian horses to melons): "Every species of animals has a climate adapted to it, where it flourishes, where it grows to perfection, and where it never degenerates. Propagation will go on in a less proper climate; but the species degenerates, if not kept up by frequent recruits from the original climate."[7] "Artful culture will do much," concludes Kames; "but it is not alone sufficient to prevail over the laws of nature." But coexisting with this notion of "rearing" animals to improve them was a strong suspicion—especially marked in the writings of Buffon (one of Jefferson's intellectual heroes) and those he influenced—that domestication degraded animals and eroded their natural nobility. Many writers, including Buffon himself, accept these two very different accounts of domestication despite their apparent incompatibility; accommodating both at once necessarily requires considerable rhetorical agility and a willingness to contradict oneself.

Jefferson puts the environmentalist account to good use when he suggests the peculiar suitability of the Virginia climate for rearing certain animals: "Experience has shewn that ours is the particular climate of America where [the Arabian horse] may be raised without degeneracy. Southwardly the heat of the sun occasions a deficiency of pasture, and northwardly the winters are too cold for the short and fine hair, the particular sensibility and constitution of that race. Animals transplanted into unfriendly climates, either change their nature and acquire new fences against the new difficulties in which they are placed, or they multiply poorly and become extinct" (20/174). Beyond his tabulations of the size of various species, Jefferson's most substantive case against Buffon rests on the argument that the supposed cold and moisture of the New World cannot have been "the agents of nature for diminishing the races of animals," given that there is no evidence of their affecting "the physical man of the new world," despite widespread acceptance of the idea that weather or climate affects the "moral faculties": "by what inconceivable process has their action been directed on his mind alone?" Jefferson asks (6/66). Even when it seems that Buffon's claims for New World degeneracy may be borne out, Jefferson argues, such appearances are deceptive. In an extended analogy between the effects of the environment on animals and on people, Jefferson attributes Indian women's having fewer children than their white counterparts to causes "found, not in a difference of nature, but of circumstance":

> With all animals, if the female be badly fed, or not fed at all, her young perish: and if both male and female be reduced to like want, generation becomes less active, less productive. To the obstacles then of want and hazard, which nature has opposed to the multiplication of wild animals, for the purpose of restraining their numbers within certain bounds, those of labour and of voluntary abortion are added with the Indian. No wonder then if they multiply less than we do. Where food is regularly supplied, a single farm will shew more of cattle, than a whole country of forests can of buffaloes. The same Indian women, when married to white traders, who feed them and their children plentifully and regularly, who exempt them from excessive drudgery, who keep them stationary and unexposed to accident, produce and raise as many children as the white women. (6/65)

His language emphasizes the notional animality of the Indian women; it is also striking that Jefferson does not attribute improvements in breeding to racial mixing between whites and Indians, but rather isolates a circumstantial or environmental deficiency to account for the supposed lack of offspring.

Later in query 6 Jefferson takes this argument a step further. The general conviction that the environment of the New World has shaped Indians' minds rather
than primarily their bodies is a contradiction in terms, he says: "To judge of the
truth of this, to form a just estimate of [the Indians'] genius and mental powers,
more facts are wanting, and great allowance to be made for those circumstances of
their situation which call for a display of particular talents only. This done, we shall
probably find that they are formed in mind as well as in body, on the same module
with the *'Homo sapiens Europaeus.' [Linn. Syst. Definition of a Man]" (6/66).
Making allowances for differences in the "circumstances of their situation" is a
way of acknowledging—though not necessarily endorsing—cultural difference.
Jefferson compares the Indians in their present unlettered state to "the Europeans
North of the Alps, when the Roman arms and arts first crossed those mountains,"
but with the difference that Europe at that time was far more heavily populated
than North America, and "numbers produce emulation, and multiply the chances
of improvement, and one improvement begets another" (6/68). Even so, Northern
Europe at that time produced no great poets, mathematicians, or inventors: "I do
not mean to deny, that there are varieties in the race of man," Jefferson continues,
"distinguished by their powers both of body and mind. I believe there are, as I
see to be the case in the races of other animals. I only mean to suggest a doubt,
whether the bulk and faculties of animals depend on the side of the Atlantic on
which their food happens to grow, or which furnishes the elements of which they
are compounded? Whether nature has enlisted herself as a Cis or Trans-Atlantic
partisan?" (6/68). Jefferson's defense of the Indian potential for culture thus slides
imperceptibly into a defense of American culture as a whole. Given the brevity
of America's existence (English-speaking America, Jefferson seems to mean), it is
not fair to expect the nation to have produced a poet of the first eminence: Jefferson instances Benjamin Franklin and David Rittenhouse as exemplary Americans, and suggests that the name of George Washington "will in future ages assume its just station among the most celebrated worthies of the world, when that
wretched philosophy shall be forgotten which would have arranged him among
the degeneracies of nature" (6/69). In this sense, culture or civilization is more
important than climate strictly conceived, as Dror Wahrman has recently argued:
"Whereas climatic and environmental views . . . had been around long before
the eighteenth century," he observes, "secular human agency—in the forms of
education, custom, and civilization—appears to have been a more peculiarly eighteenth-century addition to the mix."[8] "[C]ulture—be it religion, dress, education,
or level of civilization," he concludes, is "privileged above all other markers of
difference."[9]

In the *Notes on Virginia*, legal, political, and cultural elements are closely interwoven with natural phenomena. Jefferson observes of the new country's laws that they "have also descended to the preservation and improvement of the races of useful animals, such as horses, cattle, deer; to the extirpation of those which are noxious, as wolves, squirrels, crows, blackbirds; and to the guarding our citizens against infectious disorders, by obliging suspected vessels coming into the state, to perform quarantine, and by regulating the conduct of persons having such disorders within the state" (14/142). The country is also acting to expand its population, though Jefferson questions whether the method commonly proposed—"as great importations of foreigners as possible" (8/90)—is wise in terms of either policy or principle. He estimates by way of actuarial calculations that doubling the present "stock" will lead to the target population of four and a half million "only 27 years and 3 months sooner than if we proceed on our single stock":

> But are there no inconveniences to be thrown into the scale against the advantage expected from a multiplication of numbers by the importation of foreigners? It is for the happiness of those united in society to harmonize as much as possible in matters which they must of necessity transact together. Civil government being the sole object of forming societies, its administration must be conducted by common consent. Every species of government has its specific principles. Ours perhaps are more peculiar than those of any other in the universe. It is a composition of the freest principles of the English constitution, with others derived from natural right and natural reason. To these nothing can be more opposed than the maxims of absolute monarchies. Yet, from such, we are to expect the greatest number of emigrants. They will bring with them the principles of the governments they leave, imbibed in their early youth; or, if able to throw them off, it will be in exchange for an unbounded licentiousness, passing, as is usual, from one extreme to another. It would be a miracle were they to stop precisely at the point of temperate liberty. These principles, with their language, they will transmit to their children. In proportion to their numbers, they will share with us the legislation. They will infuse into it their spirit, warp and bias its direction, and render it a heterogeneous, incoherent, distracted mass. I may appeal to experience, during the present contest, for a verification of these conjectures. But, if they be not certain in event, are they not possible, are they not probable? Is it not safer to wait with patience 27 years and three months longer, for the attainment of any degree of population desired, or expected? May not our government be more homogeneous, more peaceable, more durable? (8/91)

The element of xenophobia here reveals a blurring of boundaries between the natural and the cultural, though Jefferson's vocabulary doesn't foreground such terms. America's legislation is robust, but not altogether impervious to the corruption of other political cultures carried by Old World emigrants who "imbibed in their early youth" principles of government now become a second nature that will (strikingly) be "transmit[ted] to their children," another instance of the eighteenth-century tendency to make culture or custom so strong a force as to be indistinguishable from what modern American readers would be more likely to conceive as natural or "genetic" means.

Jefferson's calculations concerning population are also vexed by the problem of how to represent America's enslaved inhabitants versus its free ones, and his language noticeably blurs together the slaves themselves and the institution of slavery. "Under the mild treatment our slaves experience, and their wholesome, though coarse, food," writes Jefferson, "this blot in our country increases as fast, or faster, than the whites" (8/94). It is a revealing solecism, the slippage between "blot" as slavery and "blot" as the frightening mass of black slaves evoked by the last word of the sentence. Jefferson laments the fact that under George III the importation of slaves came near to being outlawed, a change that was thwarted in part by the British king's intervention: the republican assembly has now voted to prohibit the importation of slaves, Jefferson continues, which "will in some measure stop the increase of this great political and moral evil, while the minds of our citizens may be ripening for a complete emancipation of human nature" (8/94).

The complexity of Jefferson's position on slavery is not my subject here; I am really interested in the arguments about population and human difference that cluster around slavery in the *Notes on Virginia,* not least for what they tell us about the matter of culture. Jefferson's starting premise is that the institution of slavery corrupts republican manners (Adam Smith had laid out a similar critique in *The Wealth of Nations* [1776]) and thus must be abolished on social or political rather than primarily compassionate grounds. Query 18, on Virginia's "*particular* customs and manners," prompts a brief and troubled meditation on slavery's "unhappy influence" on the manners and morals of white Americans: "The whole commerce between master and slave is a perpetual exercise of the most boisterous passions, the most unremitting despotism on the one part," Jefferson writes, "and degrading submissions on the other. Our children see this, and learn to imitate it; for man is an imitative animal. This quality is the germ of all education in him. From his cradle to his grave he is learning to do what he sees others do" (18/168). Slavery leads to an abuse of that quality—"imitative" is one word for it, but it is akin to what Rousseau means when he writes of perfectibility—that makes man human;

it is precisely because of (white) men's susceptibility to culture that their manners can be corrupted. The child who sees a parent "storm[ing]" at a slave "catches the lineaments of wrath . . . and thus nursed, educated, and daily exercised in tyranny, cannot but be stamped by it with odious peculiarities. The man must be a prodigy who can retain his manners and morals undepraved by such circumstances" (18/168).

Jefferson's paragraph in conclusion displays an extraordinarily dense and conflicted set of ideas:

> Indeed I tremble for my country when I reflect that God is just: that his justice cannot sleep for ever: that considering numbers, nature and natural means only, a revolution of the wheel of fortune, an exchange of situation, is among possible events: that it may become probable by supernatural interference! The Almighty has no attribute which can take side with us in such a contest.—But it is impossible to be temperate and to pursue this subject through the various considerations of policy, of morals, of history natural and civil. We must be contented to hope they will force their way into every one's mind. I think a change already perceptible, since the origin of the present revolution. The spirit of the master is abating, that of the slave rising from the dust, his condition mollifying, the way I hope preparing, under the auspices of heaven, for a total emancipation, and that this is disposed, in the order of events, to be with the consent of the masters, rather than by their extirpation. (18/169)

As a (qualified) supporter of emancipation, Jefferson sets himself apart from a country that has chosen not to get rid of slavery, yet his membership in the class of masters makes for considerable linguistic uneasiness. The construction "his condition mollifying" downplays agency—who is going to make this happen?— and the aside "I hope" in the phrase "the way I hope preparing" surely sounds more cautious than optimistic. In the opening sentences Jefferson invokes God's justice as clearly aligned with slaves rather than slave-owners, but though God's values or "attributes" align him with the slaves—presumably Jefferson is thinking of Jesus' compassion for the enslaved and the disenfranchised—the whole tone of the passage suggests a harsher God, less the kind shepherd of the New Testament than the arbitrary all-powerful deity of Genesis or Job.

The final word, *extirpation,* reveals what is surely Jefferson's real fear, the prospect of a complete rooting-out of the whites by the blacks. The specter of violent revolution stands behind his conviction that emancipation must be accompanied by a drastic program of resettlement, the population lost in the process to be replaced with "an equal number of white inhabitants" induced to emigrate by "proper encouragements":

> It will probably be asked, Why not retain and incorporate the blacks into the state, and thus save the expence of supplying, by importation of white settlers, the vacancies they will leave? Deep rooted prejudices entertained by the whites; ten thousand recollections, by the blacks, of the injuries they have sustained; new provocations; the real distinctions which nature has made; and many other circumstances, will divide us into parties, and produce convulsions which will probably never end but in the extermination of the one or the other race. (14/145)

But the political fears that motivate this policy (more particularly, the vision of "the extermination of the one or the other race," an echo of the debate about the extermination of the Yahoos in *Gulliver's Travels* [4.9]) are compounded by other objections, "physical and moral," to allowing blacks and whites to live alongside each other. Whether the difference in color resides in the skin or the blood or the bile, Jefferson writes (alluding to contemporary scientific debates), "the difference is fixed in nature, and is as real as if its seat and cause were better known to us" (14/145). In asserting the superior beauty of whites over blacks, Jefferson makes a eugenic argument that explicitly aligns people with the domestic animals that have long been subject to breeding: "The circumstance of superior beauty, is thought worthy attention in the propagation of our horses, dogs, and other domestic animals," he observes; "why not in that of man?" (14/145–146).

The ensuing discussion of the races of man (like Hume's notorious discussion of Africans in the 1753 footnote to the essay "Of National Characters" [1748]) is the element of *Notes on Virginia* most likely to produce outrage or disgust in modern readers, but I want to look closely and without excessive squeamishness at Jefferson's arguments for what they reveal of his understanding of culture.[10] After observing that blacks are equal to whites in memory but "in reason much inferior," Jefferson adds the following: "It would be unfair to follow them to Africa for this investigation. We will consider them here, on the same stage with the whites, and where the facts are not apocryphal on which a judgment is to be formed. It will be right to make great allowances for the difference of condition, of education, of conversation, of the sphere in which they move" (14/146–147). These sentences contain an element of bad faith, at least to twenty-first-century ears. Why is it "unfair" to follow them to Africa? And the statement about allowances sounds rather a token gesture of acknowledgment, and one scarcely borne out in the subsequent discussion. Jefferson suggests that the evidence of black intellectual and artistic inferiority is significant despite differences of condition, education, and so on, because "[s]ome have been liberally educated, and all have lived in countries where the arts and sciences are cultivated to a considerable degree, and have had before their eyes samples of the best works from abroad" (14/147). In contrast, he continues, "The Indians, with no advantages of this kind, will often carve figures on their pipes not destitute of design and merit. They will crayon out an animal, a plant, or a country, so as to prove the existence of a germ in their minds which only wants cultivation. They astonish you with strokes of the most sublime oratory; such as prove their reason and sentiment strong, their imagination glowing and elevated. But never yet could I find that a black had uttered a thought above the level of plain narration; never see even an elementary trait of painting or sculpture."

The metaphor of the germ is Jefferson's way of talking about an organic difference (recall his use of the same term in the assertion about imitation as "the germ of all education"), a quality of receptiveness to cultivation that resides in the structure of the mind. The derogatory remarks about Phyllis Wheatley that follow conclude with an even odder analogy of bodily difference: "The heroes of the Dunciad are to her," he says, "as Hercules to the author of that poem" (14/147). This is itself a typically mock-heroic trope, not just because of its invocation of Pope's *Dunciad* but structurally as well: it follows the practice of Milton's epic similes as they were adapted by Pope, Swift, and the Augustans, a form of comparison that resembles the miniaturizing language of "The Rape of the Lock" (1714) or the disorienting perspectival shifts of Lilliput and Brobdingnag. There is something crude, though, about invoking Pope's tiny stature and bodily deformity in contrast to Hercules as a way of figuring Wheatley's insignificance; the mention of Pope comes to seem especially jarring when Jefferson, a few pages later, offers a Homeric quotation on slavery in Pope's translation.

After criticizing the letters of Ignatius Sancho and suggesting that they may not have been his own work, Jefferson concludes thus: "The improvement of the blacks in body and mind, in the first instance of their mixture with the whites, has been observed by every one, and proves that their inferiority is not the effect merely of their condition of life. We know that among the Romans, about the Augustan age especially, the condition of their slaves was much more deplorable than that of the blacks on the continent of America" (14/148). Jefferson's use of the term *improvement* reveals the wide range of meanings this word could have for eighteenth-century writers; like the term *rearing*, which included selective breeding as well as upbringing in the strict sense, *improvement* refers to techniques or practices that would now be categorized as breeding or genetic modification. Another peculiar effect of his use of the word here is to highlight the self-contradictory aspect of Jefferson's own treatment of race and slavery.[11] His evidence for the innate as opposed to conditional nature of black inferiority is drawn from precisely the thing he most fears and deplores, "their mixture with the whites." Fear of mixing, indeed, is the other motive (combined with the fear of insurrection) behind Jefferson's conviction that there can be no place for blacks in the post-emancipation republic: "Among the Romans emancipation required but one effort. The slave, when made free, might mix with, without staining the blood of his master. But with us a second is necessary, unknown to history. When freed, he is to be removed beyond the reach of mixture" (14/151). There is no need to rehearse here Jefferson's hypocrisy in this instance, but in private letters he would continue to make similar or even stronger pronouncements, as when he wrote of blacks, in a letter of 25 August 1814 to Edward Coles, that "[t]heir amalgamation with the other color produces a degradation to which no lover of his country, no lover of excellence in the human character can innocently consent."[12]

The discourse of natural history grounds these discussions of racial difference, as the earlier citation of Linnaeus attests,[13] and Jefferson invokes the language of species and genus in his tentative, rather defensive-sounding justification of his conclusions about blacks in America:

> The opinion, that they are inferior in the faculties of reason and imagination, must be hazarded with great diffidence. To justify a general conclusion, requires many observations, even where the subject may be submitted to the Anatomical knife, to Optical glasses, to analysis by fire, or by solvents. How much more then where it is a faculty, not a substance, we are examining; where it eludes the research of all the senses; where the conditions of its existence are various and variously combined; where the effects of those which are present or absent bid defiance to calculation; let me add too, as a circumstance of great tenderness, where our conclusion would degrade a whole race of men from the rank in the scale of beings which their Creator may perhaps have given them. To our reproach it must be said, that though for a century and a half we have had under our eyes the races of black and of red men, they have never yet been viewed by us as subjects of natural history. I advance it therefore as a suspicion only, that the blacks, whether originally a distinct race, or made distinct by time and circumstances, are inferior to the whites in the endowments both of body and mind. It is not against experience to suppose, that different species of the same genus, or varieties of the same species, may possess different qualifications. Will

not a lover of natural history then, one who views the gradations in all the races of animals with the eye of philosophy, excuse an effort to keep those in the department of man as distinct as nature has formed them? (14/150–151)

"The anatomical knife," "the analysis by fire" do a metaphorical violence to Jefferson's subjects. His refusal to admit conclusions—to follow his intellectual mentor Lord Kames, for instance, in arguing explicitly that the human races do not share a single origin in the Creation—and his self-proclaimed diffidence and unwillingness to aver anything more than "a suspicion only" are belied by his self-reproach about the failure to make the other races "subjects of natural history."[14] The self-justificatory question at the end of the passage given here is followed by the observation that "[t]his unfortunate difference of colour, and perhaps of faculty, is a powerful obstacle to the emancipation of these people," the qualification "perhaps" sounding more wary than convinced.

A conviction of the inferiority of blacks, then, may mark the limits of Jefferson's belief in culture and its power to alter the natural world, an assertion of innate difference that rhetorically and thematically undercuts the celebration of cultivation in the *Notes on Virginia*. The fear of mixture and corruption expressed not just when Jefferson writes about race, but also in his discussions of the constitution and the American population more generally, can be seen as eruptions of georgic doubt about culture, analogous to the doubts about culture in Virgil's poem or in the strange and haunting fantasia of the precultural life that is Rousseau's *Discourse on Inequality*. In contrast to Rousseau or Smollett, though, Jefferson's discussions reveal a greater dependence on and interest in hereditary factors, and in this he is very much a person of his time. Gianna Pomata describes the movement from the eighteenth to the nineteenth century as a transition from "soft to hard hereditarianism":

> In late 18th century medicine, nature and nurture, though increasingly distinct, were not yet seen as mutually exclusive. The boundary between them remained elusive because nature was still understood first of all as a prescriptive, not a descriptive concept. Nature still meant a *telos*, an intention never fully realized in actuality. . . . [A]rt could improve on nature by seconding and furthering nature's own goal. Nature therefore did not imply destiny: it was understood as a pliable set of potentialities (like the humoralist notion of temperament), rather than a reality inexorably, unalterably fixed. Like nature, so heredity: both were conceived as malleable, susceptible to improvement or deterioration brought about by behaviour.[15]

As climate theory came to seem outdated and culture's meanings aggregated around a few nodes, nurture would lose some of its sway over the imagination, and the consequences of heredity's new hold would include a narrowing-down of opportunities for some kinds of transformation and an opening-up of others.

## "The incessant improveableness of the human species"

Although William Godwin is almost certainly eighteenth-century Britain's most perceptive and original writer on education and the human mind, he is disconcertingly capable of moving in the blink of an eye from striking insight to complete wackiness: indeed, the science-fictional quality of his imagination is part of what makes his insights so memorable. With the publication of *An Enquiry Concerning Political Justice, and Its Influence on General Virtue and Happiness* in 1793, Godwin suffered the historical misfortune of becoming known as the country's greatest advocate of human perfectibility just as perfectibility became stained by the September massacres, and though he continued to write over the course of a remarkably long career, we tend still to think of Godwin as a writer of the 1790s. He himself seems to have understood his political and educational writings more as part of a single lifelong project than as a sequence of individual works conforming to a developmental narrative, and in the discussion that follows (although I am aware of the potential methodological pitfalls) I will invoke writings from different periods when necessary in order to clarify the conceptual outlines of Godwin's thought on populations and perfectibility.[16]

The word *perfectibility* seems to have been coined by Turgot and popularized by Rousseau's *Discourse on Inequality* (1755).[17] Chemist and political theorist Joseph Priestley was one of Britain's first exponents of perfectibility, arguing in *An Essay on the First Principles of Government* (1771) that the "human species itself is capable of . . . unbounded improvement," with the consequence that just as individuals may advance in intellect, so does mankind progress toward a state of increasing perfection:

No horse of this age seems to have any advantage over other horses of former ages; and if there be any improvement in the species, it is owing to our manner of breeding and training them. But a man at this time, who has been tolerably well educated, in an improved christian country, is a being possessed of much greater power, to be, and to make happy, than a person of the same age, in the same, or any other country, some centuries ago. And, for this reason, I make no doubt, that a person some centuries hence will, at the same age, be as much superior to us.[18]

For Priestley, human nature cannot be "brought to perfection" without the indulgence of "unbounded liberty, and even caprice in conducting [education]":

> The power of nature in producing plants cannot be shown to advantage, but in all possible circumstances of culture. The richest colours, the most fragrant scents, and the most exquisite flavours, which our present gardens and orchards exhibit, would never have been known, if florists and gardeners had been confined in the processes of cultivation; nay if they had not been allowed the utmost licentiousness of fancy in the exercise of their arts. Many of the finest productions of modern gardening have been the result of casual experiment, perhaps of undesigned deviation from established rules. Observations of a similar nature may be made on the methods of breeding cattle, and training animals of all kinds. And why should the rational part of the creation be deprived of that opportunity of diversifying and improving itself, which the vegetable and animal world enjoy? (44)

Priestley's rationale is that education "is properly that which *makes the man*" (original emphasis), and that the present system "of endeavouring, by uniform and fixed systems of education, to keep mankind always the same" should be supplanted by giving "free scope to every thing which may bid fair for introducing more variety among us" (45). His case rests on what he believes to be a fundamental distinction between people and animals:

> Uniformity is the characteristic of the brute creation. Among them every species of birds build their nests with the same materials, and in the same form; the genius and disposition of one individual is that of all; and it is only the education which men give them that raises any of them much above others. But it is the glory of human nature, that the operations of reason, though variable, and by no means infallible, are capable of infinite improvement. (45)

That sense of there being no limits on human improvement was a crucial characteristic of utopian political thought in the last decades of the eighteenth century, and would elicit the mockery of skeptics in the early years of the nineteenth. Condorcet's aim in the *Sketch for a Historical Picture of the Progress of the Human Mind*, which he wrote in 1793 while in hiding (he died in 1794 in prison, and the book was first published in 1795), was "to show by appeal to reason and fact that nature has set no term to the perfection of human faculties; that the perfectibility of man is truly indefinite; and that the progress of this perfectibility, from now onwards independent of any power that might wish to halt it, has no other limit than the duration of the globe upon which nature has cast us."[19] The tenth and final stage of Condorcet's philosophical history is characterized by the rise of "the doctrine of the indefinite perfectibility of the human race" (he calls Turgot, Richard Price, and Priestley its "first and . . . most brilliant apostles"), and of course the elements Condorcet lays out here—"the abolition of inequality between nations, the progress of equality within each nation, and the true perfection of mankind"—remain immensely appealing.[20] One of the inequalities Condorcet wishes to abolish is that between men and women; beyond that, he observes that "a well directed system of education rectifies natural inequality in ability instead of strengthening it, just as good laws remedy natural inequality in the means of subsistence[.]"[21]

*Political Justice* is certainly indebted to political writers whose broadly radical politics Godwin shares (Priestley, Richard Price) and to a host of continental commentators on human psychology and improvement (he credits Holbach, Rousseau, and Helvétius by name, with Locke standing over their shoulders), but it is perhaps slightly more surprising that Godwin should affiliate himself so strongly with Swift, to whose political writings he expresses a significant debt. (Elsewhere he explicitly acknowledges the debt to Plato's *Republic*, More's *Utopia*, and *Gulliver's Travels*, the last of which comes up again and again throughout his writings.[22]) In a letter to an American student that he wrote and had printed in 1818, Godwin would go so far as to single out Swift as the greatest of the Augustan writers, and *Gulliver* as his masterpiece: "There is not a page of that book that you may not read six times before you see all that is in it. And this is rendered more surprising by the unaffected simplicity and plainness, with which he delivers himself there, and in all his writings" (5:335).

Perhaps the book's single most important passage for Godwin is Gulliver's description of war. Essential to the success of Swift's satire is a dynamic allowing Gulliver to utter devastating truths whose full meaning remains inaccessible to him, a literary choice that sometimes teeters on the edge of psychological implausibility. When Gulliver defines a soldier as "a *Yahoo* hired to kill in cold Blood as many of his own Species, who have never offended him, as possibly he can" (4.5/11:230–231), it sounds either as though he has gone off the deep end or as though the author behind the scenes has augmented the savage humor at the expense of the consistency of Gulliver's own voice and character. Something has to have changed in Gulliver, at any rate, for him to put forward such a sarcastic definition (or is it simple literal-mindedness?), though Gulliver is back in a more familiar vein a moment later when he begins to describe European warfare (war being a practice wholly unknown to the Houyhnhnms) with a naïve deadpan pride, establishing his countrymen's accomplishments in this respect by bragging of having "seen them blow up a Hundred Enemies at once in a Siege, and as many in a Ship; and beheld the dead Bodies drop down in Pieces from the Clouds, to the great Diversion of all the Spectators" (4.5/II:231). This discourse increases Gulliver's master's "Abhorrence of the whole Species" and leads him to distinguish the lower brutalities of Yahoos from human beings' "higher" ones: "although he hated the *Yahoos* of this Country, yet he no more blamed them for their odious Qualities, than he did a *Gnnayh* (a Bird of Prey) for its Cruelty, or a sharp Stone for cutting his Hoof. But, when a Creature pretending to Reason, could be capable of such Enormities, he dreaded lest the Corruption of that Faculty might be worse than Brutality itself" (4.5/II:232). It was a commonplace in the eighteenth century to refer to man as the only animal with no instincts. Violence in Yahoos may be exculpated as instinctual, but its coexistence with reason in Gulliver's kind renders it a vice; Gulliver's master exonerates the Yahoos on the grounds that their nastiness is an intrinsic quality, while men ("pretending to Reason") freely choose to sin.[23]

Godwin quotes the lines on war unironically, in support of a hard-line antiwar position. The passages he invokes had already proved useful to other writers: throughout the century, Swift's misanthropy had offered a convenient way of defining and defending a position on original sin or human perfectibility. Swift stands as chief stylistic inspiration behind Edmund Burke's *A Vindication of Natural Society* (1756; 2nd ed., 1757), for instance, a parody of Bolingbroke's providential deism and Rousseau's primitivist thought experiments that operates by taking their conclusions to the furthest possible extreme, in passionate visionary prose. Burke gives voice in this work to an argument that is antithetical to the beliefs he is later known to have held concerning custom, convention, and established government—the rhetorical instabilities of the irony mean that though it intermittently signals satirical intentions, the piece's affiliations might puzzle a reader who came to it without any context—and that can be summed up in the proposition "that Political Society is justly chargeable with much the greatest Part of [the] Destruction of the Species" associated with war and its consequences:

> From the earliest Dawnings of Policy to this Day, the Invention of Men has been sharpening and improving the Mystery of Murder, from the first rude Es-

says of Clubs and Stones, to the present Perfection of Gunnery, Cannoneering, Bombarding, Mining, and all these Species of artificial, learned, and refined Cruelty, in which we are now so expert, and which make a principal Part of what Politicians have taught us to believe is our principal Glory.[24]

"In vain you tell me that Artificial Government is good, but that I fall out only with the Abuse," says the narrator later in the piece. "The Thing! The Thing itself is the Abuse!"[25]

A roughly contemporary invocation, altogether different in style and purpose, can be found in John Wesley's intensely literary *Doctrine of Original Sin* (1757), which relies heavily (in support of an argument about human depravity) on quotations from the classics and from one or two eighteenth-century British writers as well. Wesley is especially concerned to show that not just heathens and Catholics but Protestants partake of fallen human nature, and he introduces the first excerpt from Book Two of *Gulliver's Travels* with the polemical question "ARE *Protestant* Nations nothing concerned in that humourous, but terrible Picture drawn by a late eminent Hand?"[26] It is impossible, of course, to say to what extent Swift might have conceived of book 4 of *Gulliver's Travels* as an account of the problem of original sin, and scholars of eighteenth-century British literature will perhaps breathe a sigh of relief when I confess that I have no intention of digging into this convoluted controversy, conducted over many years in countless essays and monographs, the letters column of *PMLA,* and the dustier corners of the *Journal of the History of Ideas.*[27] We can be relatively confident, though, in saying that *Gulliver's Travels* came to serve as a kind of secular scripture for writers who wished to consider the problem of human depravity, and it clearly appealed to Godwin on just such grounds.

The revolution in France provided the occasion for *Political Justice* but was far from being its chief prompt or most material substance, although revolutionary perfectibility formed a crucial part of Godwin's conception of human improvement. Godwin emphasized the dependence of men's "moral characters" on their perceptions (an associationist view), also arguing "that perfectibility is one of the most unequivocal characteristics of the human species, so that the political, as well as the intellectual state of man, may be presumed to be in a course of progressive improvement" (3:9). Godwin's vision of perfectibility runs from the individual to the entire globe—it is man's distinguishing characteristic, but societies as a whole are also subject to improvement. "Mind has a perpetual tendency to rise," he writes (3:468), and yet, though "[i]t is one of the most unquestionable properties of mind to be susceptible of perpetual improvement" (3:322), this may always be thwarted by government's wish to keep things as they are. Thus the desirability of an anarchic absence of regulatory mechanisms: we should "look for the moral improvement of the species, not in the multiplying of regulations, but in their repeal," Godwin says (3:323). He stakes his hopes on the exercise of private judgment, not the uniformity imposed from the top down by governments concerned about political and religious orthodoxy but rather a new and distinctive uniformity by which all right-thinking men will arrive independently but inexorably at the same conclusion. "Law tends no less than creeds, catechisms and tests, to fix the human mind in a stagnant condition," Godwin argues, "and to substitute a principle of permanence, in the room of that unceasing perfectibility which is the only salubrious element of mind" (3:413).

In response to readers' objections to the strand of his argument concerning man's perfectibility, Godwin would clarify the point in a subsequent edition:

> By perfectible it is not meant that he is capable of being brought to perfection. But the word seems sufficiently adapted to express the faculty of being continually made better and receiving perpetual improvement; and in this sense it is here to be understood. The term perfectible, thus explained, not only does not imply the capacity of being brought to perfection, but stands in express opposition to it. If we could arrive at perfection, there would be an end of our improvement. (4:44)

The concept of perfectibility as a capacity for improvement owes something to the associationist psychology that had grown out of Locke's writings on mind. Following Hartley and Helvétius, Godwin is outspoken in favor of the argument that "the moral characters of men originate in their perceptions," man bringing into the world "no innate principles" or "pre-established ideas" (3:13n, 3:10). Published posthumously in France under the title *De l'homme* (1772), Claude-Adrien Helvétius's *A Treatise on Man; His Intellectual Faculties and His Education* probably represents the eighteenth century's most extreme sequel to Locke's arguments about the power of education to form the human mind. For Helvétius, "organisation" means nothing and education everything. "Education makes us what we are," he writes. "If the Savoyard, from the age of six or seven years, be frugal, active, laborious, and faithful, it is because he is poor and hungry, and because he lives, as I have before said, with those that are endowed with the qualities required in him; in short, it is because he has for instructors example and want, two imperious masters whom all obey."[28] "Understanding and talents being never any thing more in men than the produce of their desires and particular situation," he concludes, "the science of education may be reduced perhaps to the placing a man in that situation which will force him to attain the talents and virtues required in him."[29]

Godwin hewed closely to a Helvetian line throughout the 1780s as he considered character in relation to education. In *An Account of the Seminary That will be opened On Monday the Fourth Day of August, At Epsom in Surrey, For the Instruction of Twelve Pupils in The Greek, Latin, French, and English Languages* (1783), a prospectus for the school he planned to open (a project subsequently abandoned for lack of students and funds), Godwin begins by identifying government and education as the "principal objects of human power," then asserts that while government is "very limited in its power of making men either virtuous or happy . . . our moral dispositions and character depend very much, perhaps entirely, upon education" (5:5). Showing clear debts to Hartley, Rousseau, and Locke, Godwin describes children's minds as being "like a sheet of white paper, . . . susceptible to every impression" (5:19), the corollary being that young people's vices, rather than springing "from nature, who is equally the kind and blameless mother of all her children," arise "from the defects of education" (5:21).

Godwin is particularly perceptive in his articulation of what's at stake in arguments about climate's effects on human character, the relative importance of innate qualities of "organisation" versus the effects of education and the relationship between "physical" and "moral" causes. He is also blunt about the extent to which one's position on such questions must be associated with a position on freedom and necessity. Godwin does not believe that climate ("weather," in his dismissive synonym) affects man's nature, most obviously because it affects individuals in such dramatically different ways (it would take near-uniformity among the population of a given region to support such a thesis) but also because what we think on this matter leads us to conclusions about "whether those persons act wisely who prescribe to themselves a certain discipline and are anxious to enrich their minds with science, or whether on the contrary it be better to trust every thing to the mercy of events" (3:35). This is not to say, however, that Godwin aligns himself with those of his predecessors who would like to think of man as altogether immune to physical causes. Here is his response to the controversial proposal that man is analogous to the other animals, and that "[b]reed"—or at least "this or certain other brute and occult causes"—may "be equally efficacious in the case of men":

> I answer, that the existence of physical causes cannot be controverted. In the case of man their efficacy is swallowed up in the superior importance of reflection and science. In animals on the contrary they are left almost alone. If a race of negroes were taken, and maintained each man from his infancy, except so far

as was necessary for the propagation of the species, in solitude; or even if they were excluded from an acquaintance with the improvements and imaginations of their ancestors, though permitted the society of each other, the operation of breed might be rendered as conspicuous among them, as in the different classes of horses and dogs. But the ideas they would otherwise receive from their parents and civilised or half-civilised neighbours would be innumerable: and, if the precautions above mentioned were unobserved, all parallel between the two cases would cease. . . . He that would change the character of the individual, would miserably misapply his efforts, if he principally sought to effect this purpose by the operation of heat and cold, dryness and moisture upon the animal frame. The true instruments of moral influence, are desire and aversion, punishment and reward, the exhibition of general truth, and the development of those punishments and rewards, which wisdom and error by the very nature of the thing constantly bring along with them. (3:36)

In the chilling human experiment imagined here, education neutralizes the effects of physical causes on organisms, and Godwin's political egalitarianism is in this sense directly entwined with his educational psychology. Insofar as differences between men are induced rather than innate, Britain's current system of rank expresses the deepest injustice:

A principle deeply interwoven with both monarchy and aristocracy in their most flourishing state, but most deeply with the latter, is that of hereditary preheminence. No principle can present a deeper insult upon reason and justice. Examine the new born son of a peer and a mechanic. Has nature designated in different lineaments their future fortune? Is one of them born with callous hands and an ungainly form? Can you trace in the other the early promise of genius and understanding, of virtue and honour? . . . [M]ankind will not soon again be persuaded, that one lineage of human creatures produces beauty and virtue, and another vice. (3:250)

Godwin relies on sarcasm to get his point across in the sentences that follow. "What are the sensations that the lord experiences in his mother's womb," he asks, "by which his mind is made different from that of the peasant? Is there any variation in the finer reticulated substance of the brain, by which the lord is adapted to receive clearer and stronger impressions than the husbandman or the smith?" (3:250). (Here he perhaps responds to Hume's observation in the chapter on liberty and necessity in *A Treatise of Human Nature* [1739–1740]: "The skin, pores, muscles, and nerves of a day-labourer are different from those of a man of quality: So are his sentiments, actions and manners. The different stations of life influence the whole fabric, external and internal. . . . Government makes a distinction of property, and establishes the different ranks of men."[30])

Yet while Godwin shares some of Hume's assumptions about the operation of moral and physical causes, he arrives at markedly different conclusions. Where Hume sees government, not unreasonably, as a necessary condition of human life, Godwin thinks it can and should be abolished; where Hume affects a calmly descriptive tone in the passage on rank, Godwin expresses a rather Swiftian horror at the fact that "the noblest families so often produce the most degenerate sons" (3:251). In one of *Political Justice*'s most eloquently over-the-top passages on the injustice entailed by the institution of aristocracy, Godwin contrasts the position of a Polish prince with an annual income of three hundred thousand pounds to a man "born a manorial serf or a Creolian negro": "[d]oomed by the law of [his] birth to wait at the gates of the palace [he] must never enter, to sleep under a ruined weather-beaten roof, while [his] master sleeps under canopies of state, to feed on putrefied offals while the world is ransacked for delicacies for his table, to labour without moderation or limit under a parching sun while he basks in perpetual sloth, and to be rewarded at last with contempt, reprimand, stripes and mutilation" (3:256). "Is all this necessary for the maintenance of civil order?" Godwin asks. "Let it be recollected that for this distinction there is not the smallest foundation in the nature of things, that, as we have already said, there is no particular mould for the construction of lords, and that they are born neither better nor worse than the poorest of their dependents" (3:256).

One intriguing contradiction inherent in Godwin's thought lies in his simultaneous embrace of a belief in the transformative potential of education and a highly necessitarian understanding of human nature.[31] It offers a salutary corrective to the views of those who think of eighteenth-century climate theory as somehow more liberating or less restrictive than the hereditarian accounts of human difference that would come to dominate nineteenth-century racial science. As I have said before, for many eighteenth-century British writers, climate and custom and education had the binding force that our own culture reserves for the idea of genetic inheritance (though genes too may now be subject to human manipulation). In the passage that follows, Godwin can be seen at once refuting the idea of original sin and rewriting supposedly inborn sin as an almost inescapable function of institutions and environments:

Is there any innate perverseness in man that continually hurries him to his own destruction? This is impossible; for man is thought, and, till thought began, he had no propensities either to good or evil. My propensities are the fruit of the impressions that have been made upon me, the good always preponderating, because the inherent nature of things is more powerful than any human institutions. The original sin of the worst men, is in the perverseness of these institutions, the opposition they produce between public and private good, the monopoly they create of advantages which reason directs to be left in common. (3:381)

Yet *Political Justice*'s uncompromising position on the natural equality of men would be modified by Godwin in subsequent editions of the book, a retraction that speaks to Godwin's intellectual honesty in the face of his experience as an educator of real children (as opposed to a pure theorist of education).

In an unpublished manuscript that probably dates from the later 1790s, Godwin explicitly withdrew his support for the principle of equality: "I am desirous of retracting the opinions I have given favourable to Helvetius' doctrine of equality of intellectual beings as they are born into the world, and subscribing to the received opinion, that, though education is a most powerful instrument, yet there exist differences of the highest importance between human beings from the period of their birth."[32] This is a staggering turnabout, which is probably why the scrupulous Godwin takes the trouble to be so explicit about it (much as it must have pained him to embrace "received opinion"!). The published record shows Godwin wrestling with these questions, though he is not always so explicit there in his disavowal of his own earlier position. The 1793 edition of *Political Justice* contains an important chapter, titled "The Moral Characters of Men Originate in their Perceptions," whose material was rewritten for the second edition (and revised again for the third). The new chapter, titled "The Characters of Men Originate in Their External Circumstances," now sets out to show "that the characters and dispositions of mankind are the offspring of circumstances and events, and not of any original determination that they bring into the world" (4:16–17). Godwin dismisses innate principles, instincts, and "the original differences of our structure, together with the impressions we receive in the womb" as possible explanations for human inequality (4:17). But in a long added passage, Godwin recasts his own earlier arguments and draws surprising new conclusions:

What is born into the world is an unfinished sketch, without character or decisive feature impressed upon it. In the sequel there is a correspondence between the physiognomy and the intellectual and moral qualities of the mind. But is it not reasonable to suppose that this is produced, by the continual propensity of the mind to modify its material engine in a particular way? There is for the most part no essential difference between the child of the lord and of the porter. Provided he do not come into the world infected with any ruinous distemper, the child of the lord, if changed in the cradle, would scarcely find any greater difficulty than the other, in learning the trade of his foster father, and becoming a carrier of burthens. The muscles of those limbs which are most frequently called into play, are always observed to acquire peculiar flexibility or strength. It is not improbable, if it should be found that the capacity of the scull of a wise man is greater than that of a fool, that this enlargement should be produced by the incessantly repeated action of the intellectual faculties, especially considering of how flexible materials the sculls of infants are composed, and at how early an age persons of eminent intellectual merit acquire some portion of their future characteristics.

In the mean time it would be ridiculous to question the real differences that exist between children at the period of their birth. Hercules and his brother, the robust infant whom scarcely any neglect can destroy, and the infant that is with difficulty reared, are undoubtedly from the moment of parturition very different beings. (4:21)

Godwin supplements the romance trope of the child exchanged in the cradle with the rather wonderful example of the mind modifying its own "material engine" in the case of the large-skulled intellectual, but the twist that chiefly concerns us here comes in the following paragraph. The common-sense tone with which Godwin delivers the provocative Hercules example differs markedly from the abstractions of Hartley and Helvétius. (A comparable coexistence of pragmatic acknowledgment of difference with an almost millennial belief in the power of education can be seen in Locke's writings.)

Godwin further pursues the topic of difference or inequality in the pages that follow: "[A]t the moment of birth man has really a certain character, and each man a character different from his fellows. . . . If there have been philosophers that have asserted otherwise, and taught that all minds from the period of birth were precisely alike, they have reflected discredit by such an incautious statement upon the truth they proposed to defend" (4:23). It remains clear, though, that for Godwin the "disposition" is less important than the "understanding" (perhaps roughly aligned with what we might call personality and intelligence, though it will not do to force an equivalence). "How long has the jargon imposed upon the world, which would persuade us that in instructing a man you do not add to, but unfold his stores?" asks the unrepentant educator in conclusion (4:23). In sum, differences of bodily structure don't have any obvious connection to mental differences (the ones in which Godwin is chiefly interested); moreover, his belief that the "efficiency [of moral causes] is nearly unlimited" (4:22) always takes us back again into the realm of environment:

> Among the inferior animals breed is a circumstance of considerable importance, and a judicious mixture and preservation in this point is found to be attended with the most unequivocal results. But nothing of that kind appears to take place in our own species. A generous blood, a gallant and fearless spirit is by no means propagated from father to son. When a particular appellation is granted, as is usually practised in the existing governments of Europe, to designate the descendants of a magnanimous ancestry, we do not find, even with all the arts of modern education to assist, that such descendants are the legitimate representatives of departed heroism. (4:22)

Recasting some of the material discussed above, Godwin proposes in the new edition that differences between individuals would probably be more conspicuous among savages than in civilized society:

> It is not unlikely that, if men, like brutes, were withheld from the more considerable means of intellectual improvement, if they derived nothing from the discoveries and sagacity of their ancestors, if each individual had to begin absolutely *de novo* in the discipline and arrangement of his ideas, blood or whatever other circumstances distinguish one man from another at the period of his nativity, would produce as memorable effects in man, as they now do in those classes of animals that are deprived of our advantages. Even in the case of brutes education and care on the part of man seems to be nearly indispensible, if we would not have the foal of the finest racer degenerate to the level of the cart-horse. In plants the peculiarities of soil decide in a great degree upon the future properties of each. But who would think of forming the character of a human being by the operations of heat and cold, dryness and moisture upon the animal frame? With us moral considerations swallow up the effects of every accident. (4:23)

Like Hume, then, Godwin sees moral causes dramatically overriding what might otherwise nonetheless be quite pronounced physical ones.

In the preface to *The Enquirer. Reflections on Education, Manners, and Literature. In a Series of Essays* (1797), Godwin describes the method of investigating truth practiced in these essays as complementary to that of *Political Justice*, which had appeared four years earlier. Unlike the philosophical enquiry, the essay recurs incessantly "to experiment and actual observation" (5:77), the shift from treatise to essay also more-or-less self-consciously recalling Hume's choice, following the failure of the *Treatise of Human Nature* (1739–1740) to find a suitable readership, to adopt the essay as his preferred mode of enquiry. Character's dependence on birth or on education is one of the collection's central subjects, and Godwin's positions here are modified by various concessions to difference in the name of common sense. "What may be the precise degree of difference with respect to capacity that children generally bring into the world with them, is a problem that it is perhaps impossible completely to solve," Godwin writes in "Of Awakening the Mind" (5:84). "But, if education cannot do every thing, it can do much. . . . The more inexperienced and immature is the mind of the infant, the greater is its pliability. It is not to be told how early, habits, pernicious or otherwise, are acquired. Children bring some qualities, favourable or adverse to cultivation, into the world with them. But they speedily acquire other qualities in addition to these, and which are probably of more moment than they." Again, in the first of two essays titled "Of the Sources of Genius" (no. 3), Godwin identifies it as "a question which has but lately entered into philosophical disquisition, whether genius be born with a man, or may be subsequently infused" (5:87), the earlier consensus having been in favor of birth rather than education, and offers a measured case for nurture:

> In infancy the mind is peculiarly ductile. We bring into the world with us nothing that deserves the name of habit; are neither virtuous nor vicious, active nor idle, inattentive nor curious. The infant comes into our hands a subject, capable of certain impressions and of being led on to a certain degree of improvement. His mind is like his body. What at first was cartilage, gradually becomes bone. Just so the mind acquires its solidity; and what might originally have been bent in a thousand directions, becomes stiff, unmanageable and unimpressible. (5:88)

Thus the seven-year-old child of peasants is likely to show a quickness and delicacy whose "very traces . . . are obliterated at the age of fourteen" (5:89). But in the subsequent essay, which bears an identical title, Godwin forwards an alternative view:

> That the accidents of body and mind should regularly descend from father to son, is a thing that daily occurs, yet is little in correspondence with the systems of our philosophers.

How small a share, accurately speaking, has the father in the production of the son? How many particles is it possible should proceed from him, and constitute a part of the body of the child descended from him? Yet how many circumstances they possess in common?

It has sometimes been supposed that the resemblance is produced by the intercourse which takes place between them after their birth. But this is an opinion which the facts by no means authorise us to entertain.

The first thing which may be mentioned as descending from father to son is his complexion; fair, if a European; swarthy or black, if a negro. Next, the son frequently inherits a strong resemblance to his father's distinguishing features. He inherits diseases. He often resembles him in stature. Persons of the same family are frequently found to live to about the same age. Lastly, there is often a striking similarity in their temper and disposition.

It is easy to perceive how these observations will apply to the question of genius. If so many other things be heritable, why may not talents be so also? They have a connection with many of the particulars above enumerated; and especially there is a very intimate relation between a man's disposition and his portion of understanding. Again; whatever is heritable, a man must bring into the world with him, either actually, or in the seminal germ from which it is afterwards to be unfolded. Putting therefore the notion of inheritance out of the question, it should seem that complexion, features, diseases, stature, age and temper, may be, and frequently are, born with a man. Why may not then his talents in the same sense be born with him? (5:91–92)

The irony is that Godwin should have been so perfectly positioned to see and to articulate the workings of hereditary causes in spite of—because of?—his early adherence to an extreme Helvetian position. In the end, he argues for balance: "It is the madness of philosophy only, that would undertake to account for every thing, and to trace out the process by which every event in the world is generated" (5:92). Man "brings a certain character into the world with him," but not "an immutable character," although elsewhere in the same collection the older position resurfaces: "Every incident of our lives contributes to form our temper, our character and our understanding; and the mass thus formed modifies every one of our actions. All in man is association and habit."[33]

Godwin would return to these questions throughout his career. In the years following the publication of *The Enquirer*, which coincided with his becoming a parent, he sank a great deal of his resources in a doomed enterprise involving the production and publication of children's books. In *Thoughts on Man, His Nature,*

*Productions, and Discoveries* (1831), Godwin's summing-up of his own thinking on a wide range of issues he had explored throughout his career, he returns to the question of whether the inequality of talents is natural or artificial and falls down this time on the side of what he often calls "the equality of man with man": "[M]an is more like and more equal to man, deformities of body and abortions of intellect excepted, than the disdainful and fastidious censors of our common nature are willing to admit" (6:53). Apparent inequalities, he suggests, result in many cases from the fact that we "take the inexhaustible varieties of man, as he is given into our guardianship by the bountiful hand of nature, and train him in one uniform exercise" (6:53). Godwin writes nostalgically of the Spartan practice of elders visiting every baby boy as soon as he is born "to decide whether he was to be reared, and would be made an efficient member of the commonwealth," though he admits it is a question of great difficulty to make such a determination at a young age. Even should we be so lucky as to ascertain the most suitable calling for a given child, he says, "a thousand extrinsical circumstances will often prevent that from being the calling chosen. Nature distributes her gifts without any reference to the distinctions of artificial society" (6:54–55).

There is no doubt that Godwin allows here for some considerable natural difference. "Human creatures are born into the world with various dispositions," he writes:

The subtle network of the brain, or whatever else it is, that makes a man more fit for, and more qualified to succeed in, one occupation than another, can scarcely be followed up and detected either in the living subject or the dead one. But, as in the infinite variety of human beings no two faces are so alike that they cannot be distinguished, nor even two leaves plucked from the same tree, so it may reasonably be presumed, that there are varieties in the senses, the organs, and the internal structure of the human species, however delicate, and to the touch of the bystander evanescent, which may give to each individual a predisposition to rise to a supreme degree of excellence in some certain art or attainment, over a million of competitors. (6:55–56)

In the pages that follow, Godwin definitively rejects the extreme associationist position, arriving at an interesting synthesis that reconciles the existence of innate qualities with the hypothesis of perfectibility:

Those persons who favour the opinion of the incessant improveableness of the human species, have felt strongly prompted to embrace the creed of Helvetius, who affirms that the minds of men, as they are born into the world, are in a state of equality, alike prepared for any kind of discipline and instruction that may be afforded them, and that it depends upon education only, in the largest sense of that word, including every impression that may be made upon the mind, intentional or accidental, from the hour of our birth, whether we shall be poets or philosophers, dancers or singers, chemists or mathematicians, astronomers or dissectors of the faculties of our common nature.

But this is not true. It has already appeared in the course of this Essay, that the talent, or, more accurately speaking, the original suitableness of the individual for the cultivation, of music or painting, depends upon certain peculiarities that we bring into the world with us. The same thing may be affirmed of the poet. . . .

And this view of things, if well considered, is as favourable, nay, more so, to the hypothesis of the successive improveableness of the human species, as the creed of Helvetius. According to that philosopher, every human creature that is born into the world, is capable of becoming, or being made, the equal of Homer, Bacon or Newton, and as easily and surely on the one as the other. This creed, if sincerely embraced, no doubt affords a strong stimulus to both preceptor and pupil, since, if true, it teaches us that any thing can be made of any thing, and that, wherever there is mind, it is within the compass of possibility, not only that that mind can be raised to a high pitch of excellence, but even to a high pitch of that excellence, whatever it is, that we shall prefer to all others, and most earnestly desire. (6:61–62)

But such a premise is "too vast and indefinite": really, Godwin says, we are "presented in every individual human creature with a subject better fitted for one sort of cultivation than another" and "excited to an earnest study of the individual, that we may the more unerringly discover what pursuit it is for which his nature and qualifications especially prepare him." And "it should be the aim of those persons, who from their situation have more or less the means of looking through the vast assemblage of their countrymen, of penetrating 'into the seeds' of character, and determining 'which grain will grow, and which will not,' to apply themselves to the redeeming such as are worthy of their care from the oblivious gulph into which the mass of the species is of necessity plunged" (6:108). "When a genuine philosopher holds a new-born child in his arms, and carefully examines it," he writes elsewhere (in direct contravention of the disdain he expresses at times for the "jargon" of unfolding), "he perceives in it various indications of temper and seeds of character. It was all there, though folded up and confused, and not ob-truding itself upon the remark of every careless spectator" (6:185–186).

Education is thus the greatest moral end—and here Godwin is very much in the spirit of the age of European Romanticism, a period whose innovations would continue to set the terms of progressive education for many years to come (even in some respects down to the present day). Godwin describes the philosopher-educator's interest in the growing infant in a rather delightful image:

> His little eye begins to sparkle with meaning; his tongue tells a tale that may be understood; his very tones, and gestures, and attitudes, all inform me concern-ing what he shall be. I am like a florist, who has received a strange plant from a distant country. At first he sees only the stalk, and the leaves, and the bud having yet no other colour than that of the leaves. But as he watches his plant from day to day, and from hour to hour, the case with [sic] contains the flower divides, and betrays first one colour and then another, till the shell gradually subsides more and more towards the stalk, and the figure of the flower begins now to be seen, and its radiance and its pride to expand itself to the ravished observer.—Every lesson that the child learns, every comment that he makes upon it, every sport that he pursues, every choice that he exerts, the demeanour that he adopts to his playfellows, the modifications and character of his little fits of authority or submission, all make him more and more an individual to me, and open a wider field for my sagacity or my prophecy, as to what he prom-ises to be, and what he may be made. (6:189)

This certainty, however, coexists with a renewed commitment to the power of education and does not negate the possibility of human liberty. In a perceptive late section of the *Thoughts on Man*, on phrenology, Godwin deems the new sci-ence of physiognomy "all a system of fatalism" (the first sentence quoted below is sarcastic summary):

> Independently of ourselves, and far beyond our control, we are reserved for good or for evil by the predestinating spirit that reigns over all things. Unhappy is the individual who enters himself in this school. He has no consolation, ex-cept the gratified wish to know distressing truths, unless we add to this the pride of science, that he has by his own skill and application purchased for himself the discernment which places him in so painful a preeminence. The great triumph of man is in the power of education, to improve his intellect, to

sharpen his perceptions, and to regulate and modify his moral qualities. But craniology reduces this to almost nothing, and exhibits us for the most part as the helpless victims of a blind and remorseless destiny. (6:239)

One of the intellectual reasons to reject a set of (pseudo-)scientific arguments about human nature, in other words, involves articulating the psychological and ethical costs of adopting them and making them a sort of bellwether for the theory as a whole.

## "Encumbering the world with useless and wretched beings"

At least in his philosophical writings, Godwin expresses an almost intractable dislike for human reproduction. In the first edition of *Political Justice,* Godwin's reimagining of human sexual arrangements seems as important a component of the social transformations he conceives as the abolition of other, more public institutions. A taste of his millennial optimism about the defeat of irrationality in its incarnation as sex is given by the following passage. "Reasonable men now eat and drink, not from the love of pleasure, but because eating and drinking are essential to our healthful existence," he writes. "Reasonable men then [in the distant utopian future] will propagate their species, not because a certain sensible pleasure is annexed to this action, but because it is right the species should be propagated; and the manner in which they exercise this function will be regulated by the dictates of reason and duty" (3:454).

It is not surprising that so many of his contemporaries should have found absurdity in Godwin's insistence that future sex would be motivated by rational rather than sensual aims, as well as his strange detachment from what he elsewhere calls "the mere animal function" of sex (3:465). Godwin had a seriously science-fictional (but also an Augustinian) vision of futurity, one that would find twentieth- and twenty-first-century echoes in the novels of Aldous Huxley and Michel Houellebecq. "The men therefore who exist when the earth shall refuse itself to a more extended population, will cease to propagate," he writes, "for they will no longer have any motive, either of error or duty, to induce them. In addition to this they will perhaps be immortal. The whole will be a people of men, and not of children. Generation will not succeed generation, nor truth have in a certain degree to recommence her career at the end of every thirty years" (3:465). Godwin also argued, notoriously and uncompromisingly, against the bonds of familial love:

"I ought to prefer no human being to another, because that being is my father, my wife or my son, but because, for reasons which equally appeal to all understandings, that being is entitled to preference" (3:455).

Condorcet, too, displays a characteristic utopian doubtfulness about the merits of producing offspring when he suggests in the *Sketch of the History of the Progress of the Human Mind* that in mankind's lofty future "men will know that, if they have a duty towards those who are not yet born, that duty is not to give them existence but to give them happiness; their aim should be to promote the general welfare of the human race or of the society in which they live or of the family to which they belong, rather than foolishly to encumber the world with useless and wretched beings."[34] Such arguments are easily skewered by antagonists with a sense of humor. Think of pioneering geneticist J. B. S. Haldane's words in his 1923 lecture *Daedalus; or, Science and the Future:* "The eugenic official, a compound, it would appear, of the policeman, the priest and the procurer, is to hale us off at suitable intervals to the local temple of Venus Genetrix with a partner chosen, one gathers, by something of the nature of a glorified medical board. To this prophecy I should reply that it proceeds from a type of mind as lacking in originality as in knowledge of human nature. Marriage 'by numbers', so to speak, was a comparatively novel idea when proposed by Plato 2,300 years ago."[35] A telling symptom of the depth of the Augustinian background of questions about man's malleability can be seen in the fact of eighteenth-century perfectibility theory—otherwise so profoundly Pelagian in its contours—containing this deep hostility toward sexual reproduction. (This is one of the things that Godwin's surprising indebtedness to Swift also tells us.) Such hostility also owes something to the Platonic tradition, as Haldane's allusion suggests, but the belief of a Godwin or a Condorcet that sex will fall away from future existence more directly calls to mind Augustine's Edenic fantasy of a sexual desire altogether subject to reason.

It is not always remembered that Malthus's first *Essay on Population* (1798) responds directly to Godwin and Condorcet's writings on perfectibility, but Malthus lays out the need for various measures of population control in a withering tone that makes Godwin sound soft-hearted and sentimental by contrast. Depopulation and food shortages may "prevent population from increasing beyond the means of subsistence," writes the implacable Malthus; "and, if I may use an expression which certainly at first appears strange, supercede the necessity of great and ravaging epidemics to repress what is redundant."[36] "Were a wasting plague to sweep off two millions in England, and six millions in France," he continues, the voice a masterwork of bland provocation, "there can be no doubt whatever, that after the inhabitants had recovered from the dreadful shock, the proportion of births to burials would be much above what it is in either country at present." Malthus is particularly scathing about the idea (shared by Godwin and Condorcet, and according to Malthus the logical corollary of a passionate secular belief in the perfectibility of man, with its incompatibility with any religious conception of an afterlife) that man may in future become immortal:

> I am told that it is a maxim among the improvers of cattle, that you may breed to any degree of nicety you please, and they found this maxim upon another, which is, that some of the offspring will possess the desirable qualities of the parents in a greater degree. In the famous Leicestershire breed of sheep, the object is to procure them with small heads and small legs. Proceeding upon these breeding maxims, it is evident, that we might go on till the heads and legs were evanescent quantities; but this is so palpable an absurdity, that we may be quite sure that the premises are not just, and that there really is a limit, though we cannot see it, or say exactly where it is. In this case, the point of the greatest degree of improvement, or the smallest size of the head and legs, may be said to be undefined, but this is very different from unlimited, or from indefinite, in Mr. Condorcet's acceptation of the term. Though I may not be able, in the present instance, to mark the limit, at which further improvement will stop, I can very easily mention a point at which it will not arrive. I should not scruple to assert, that were the breeding to continue for ever, the head and legs of these sheep would never be so small as the head and legs of a rat.
>
> It cannot be true, therefore, that among animals, some of the offspring will possess the desirable qualities of the parents in a greater degree; or that animals are indefinitely perfectible.[37]

What rouses Malthus' ire is not the claim that humans may be improved as animals are so much as the associated suggestion that this can be carried forward without limit:

> It does not . . . seem impossible, that by an attention to breed, a certain degree of improvement, similar to that among animals, might take place among men. Whether intellect could be communicated may be a matter of doubt: but size, strength, beauty, complexion, and perhaps even longevity are in a degree transmissible. The error does not seem to lie, in supposing a small degree of

improvement possible, but in not discriminating between a small improvement, the limit of which is undefined, and an improvement really unlimited. As the human race however could not be improved in this way, without condemning all the bad specimens to celibacy, it is not probable, that an attention to breed should ever become general; indeed, I know of no well-directed attempts of the kind, except in the ancient family of the Bickerstaffs, who are said to have been very successful in whitening the skins, and increasing the height of their race by prudent marriages, particularly by that very judicious cross with Maud, the milk-maid, by which some capital defects in the constitutions of the family were corrected.[38]

Citing that *Tatler* passage on the Bickerstaff lineage is part of Malthus' broader tactic of mockery, just as harping on the analogy between schemes of human and animal or vegetable improvement in this case makes the whole enterprise ridiculous.

In a more serious vein, Malthus uses the analogy between human and vegetable improvement to show how unreasonable it is to believe that experimentation will yield superior rather than simply monstrous products. Speaking of the gardener, for instance, he argues as follows, in an uncharacteristically forced metaphor that tells us something about what is really at stake in his argument:

By endeavouring to improve one quality, he may impair the beauty of another. The richer mould which he would employ to increase the size of his plant, would probably burst the calyx, and destroy at once its symmetry. In a similar manner, the forcing manure used to bring about the French revolution, and to give a greater freedom and energy to the human mind, has burst the calyx of humanity, the restraining bond of all society; and, however large the separate petals have grown; however strongly, or even beautifully a few of them have been marked; the whole is at present a loose, deformed, disjointed mass, without union, symmetry, or harmony of colouring.[39]

A striking hostility can be heard here toward forms of environmental influence ("forcing manure," in a phrase that calls to mind that use of improvement as a euphemism for excrement), though Malthus in many respects displays considerable sensitivity to the interplay of nature and nurture. "It is probable that no two grains of wheat are exactly alike," he writes elsewhere in the *Essay*, sounding—strange to say—a little like Godwin himself. "Soil undoubtedly makes the principal difference in the blades that spring up; but probably not all. It seems natural to suppose some sort of difference in the original germs that are afterwards awakened into thought; and the extraordinary difference of susceptibility in very young children seems to confirm the supposition" (382). The supposition of difference has by now been inscribed as a character strongly associated with political conservatism, as Godwin himself acknowledges.

Godwin's first extended response to Malthus—though he would return to questions of population at considerably greater length in 1820—can be found in his *Thoughts Occasioned by the Perusal of Dr. Parr's Spital Sermon* (1801). Godwin concedes that human prosperity depends on checking the growth of population and points to the strange reversal this represents of the conventional wisdom, so that it is no longer the celibate but "the man who rears a numerous family, that has in some degree transgressed the consideration he owes to the public welfare" (2:198). He goes on to point out a moral shortcoming in the approach taken by the anonymous author of the *Essay on Population,* in which misery and vice are preferred to abortion and the exposure of children as means of population control. In contrast, Godwin (though he "hope[s], and trust[s], that no such expedient will be necessary to be resorted to") refuses to "regard a new-born child with any superstitious reverence"—given that "the globe of earth affords room for only a certain number of human beings to be trained to any degree of perfection"—and would choose rather that "such a child should perish at the first hour of its existence, than that a man should spend seventy years of life in a state of misery and vice" (2:199–200).[40] Godwin smells hypocrisy in Malthus's desire to control population, at least in the light of his unwillingness to give voice to the actual measures such a goal would necessitate, and the argument harks back to the Houyhnhnms' debate on the extermination of the Yahoos in book 4 of *Gulliver's Travels* as well as to *A Modest Proposal.* Yet the contrast between Godwin and Malthus is strangely blurred by what they have in common. Godwin seems genuinely to have believed in man's perfectibility, even to the extent of imagining a future in which the passion that precipitates sex becomes so attenuated in man as to wither away altogether; Malthus found such an idea ludicrous beyond belief. But both Godwin and Malthus share with Swift an element of disgust at the idea of propagation, or at least of its necessary consequences, and a stark longing for a planet unsullied by human copulation.

———

An afterthought on perfectibility: the strain of interventionist or proto-eugenicist thought continues to look strikingly agnostic on the question of environmental versus innate influence, just as it would remain agnostic on the question of whether moral or physical causes had greater power to shape men's bodies. Samuel Stanhope Smith, in *An Essay on the Causes of the Variety of Complexion and Figure in the Human Species* (first published in 1787, then reissued in a revised edition in 1810), speculated along these lines: "If men, in the union of the sexes, were as much under control as some of the inferior animals, their persons might be moulded, in the course of a few generations, to almost any standard, making due allowance for the influence of climate, and the necessary operation of other causes which may be connected with it."[41] This suggests the need for a fine balance between selective breeding and the countervailing force of the environment. (I am not making a historical argument here so much as following an intriguing and often quite disturbing strain in later eighteenth- and early nineteenth-century thought on human nature, a body of writing increasingly preoccupied with questions about racial difference.)

James Cowles Prichard's *Researches into the Physical History of Man* (1813) includes a similar gesture, though he credits "moral causes" with greater real-world influence over reproduction than conscious top-down intervention: "If the same constraint were exercised over men, which produces such remarkable effects among the brute kinds, there is no doubt that its influence would be as great. But no despot has ever thought of amusing himself in this manner, or at least such an experiment has never been carried on upon that extensive scale, which might lead to important results. Certain moral causes however, have an influence on mankind, which appears in some degree to lead to similar ends."[42] Though he notes in a footnote the attempts of the kings of Prussia to breed taller soldiers, Prichard means by the phrase "moral causes" to evoke, for instance, the way that the human attraction to beauty works unofficially "as a constant principle of improvement," beauty corresponding in turn to "health and perfect organization"; human repugnance to deformity works to similar ends, and Prichard notes with implicit approval (for it "prevents the hereditary transmission of such peculiarities, which would probably in many cases happen, if deformed persons were generally married") the custom among savage tribes "to destroy children which are imperfect in their figure."[43] Indeed, reading these books, one comes to suspect that the invocation of animal breeding as a way of calling for greater control over human reproduction has become reflexive. I close with the observation of physiologist Pierre-Jean-George Cabanis in his brilliant and maddening *Rapports du physique et du moral de l'homme* (1802; 2nd ed., 1805):

After we have so ingeniously occupied ourselves with the means of making the races of animals more appealing and suitable, or the plants more useful and pleasant; after having a hundred times reshaped the races of horses and of dogs; after having transplanted, grafted, worked in all ways on fruits and flowers, how shameful it is totally to neglect the human race! as though it did not affect us more closely! as though it were more essential to have large and strong bulls than to have vigorous and healthy men; sweet-smelling peaches or well-speckled tulips, than wise and good citizens![44]

6

# Shibboleths

One lesson of the twentieth century is that linguistic difference within communities of all sizes often provides a cover story for discrimination and violence, a topic explored with great subtlety in the Haitian-American writer Edwidge Danticat's novel *The Farming of Bones* (1998). Taking the "shibboleth" passage from Judges 12:4–6 as its epigraph, Danticat's novel about the 1937 massacre of Haitians at the prompting of a Dominican general, Rafael Trujillo, foregrounds the dictator's use of a verbal test to detect an ethnic difference not always visible on the skin, a test earlier memorialized in Rita Dove's poem "Parsley" (1983). One recent historian of the massacre gives this description: "[The soldiers] would accost any person with dark skin. Holding up sprigs of parsley, Trujillo's men would query their prospective victims: '*¿Cómo se llama ésto?*' What is this thing called? The terrified victim's fate lay in the pronunciation of the answer. Haitians, whose Kreyol uses a wide, flat *r*, find it difficult to pronounce the trilled *r* in the Spanish word for parsley, *perejil*. If the word came out as the Haitian *pe'sil*, or a bastardized Spanish *pewehi*, the victim was condemned to die."[1] Danticat highlights the absurdity of equating language with race, an equation motivated in context by Trujillo's paranoia about racial mixing. The novel's Haitian narrator, Amabelle Désir, comments frequently on speech that defies the racist stereotypes of Trujillo and his henchmen: in the novel as in the real world, Dominicans may speak Kreyòl, Haitian refugees may speak only Spanish, and Spanish-speaking Dominicans may bear the wounds of the machete in cases where their dark skin has led soldiers to take them for Haitians.[2] The linguistic test is thus shown to be nothing more than a cloak for violence driven by fear of the other. When the narrator herself comes up against the parsley test in her attempt to escape over the border to Haiti, she isn't even given the chance to say the word:

> The young toughs waved parsley sprigs in front of our faces.
>
> "Tell us what this is," one said. "Que diga perejil."
>
> At that moment I did believe that had I wanted to, I could have said the word properly, calmly, slowly, the way I often asked "Perejil?" of the old Dominican women and their faithful attending granddaughters at the roadside gardens and markets, even though the trill of the *r* and the precision of the *j* was sometimes too burdensome a joining for my tongue. It was the kind of thing that if you were startled in the night, you might forget, but with all my senses calm, I could have said it. But I didn't get my chance. Yves and I were shoved down onto our knees. Our jaws were pried open and parsley stuffed into our mouths. My eyes watering, I chewed and swallowed as quickly as I could, but not nearly as fast as they were forcing the handfuls into my mouth.[3]

Even in the face of brutality and devastating loss, the narrator refuses to abandon her belief that a shared language can facilitate communication between members of different groups, a belief represented here in the vision of conversation in the roadside markets and the linguistic "joining" of the Spanish utterance.

## Shibboleths

Language is inherently both a biological and a cultural phenomenon, a fact that can produce revealing rhetorical and conceptual contradictions. An especially telling instance of the slippage between language's cultural aspects and its biological ones, an ambiguity enshrined in everyday usage when we describe someone as a "native" speaker of a particular language (nobody, after all, actually emerges from the womb at birth capable of speaking any language at all), can be found in Alexander Walker's 1839 tract *Intermarriage; or, The Natural Laws by Which Beauty, Health and Intellect, Result from Certain Unions, and Deformity, Disease and Insanity, From Others.* Dedicated to Thomas Andrew Knight, the president of the Royal Horticultural Society, *Intermarriage* argues that biological inheritance can be miraculously assisted or augmented by culture. "[T]he whelps of well-trained dogs are, almost at birth, more fitted for sporting purposes than others," Walker asserts. "[A]ny particular art or trick acquired by these animals, [is] readily practised by their progeny, without the slightest instruction."[4] He goes on to provide a lengthy extract from a letter in which Knight shows how a person's ancestry may be deduced from his or her appearance and accomplishments. On seeing a little girl (one "wholly unknown" to him, he says) repeat her catechism in church "in less than half the time that her companions did, and without missing, or hesitating about, a single word," Knight whispers to his wife, "'That girl is a gentleman's natural daughter;' and so she proved to be."[5]

Knight goes on to assert "that the kind of language used by any people through many successive generations, might change and modify the organs of speech, though not to an extent cognizable by the anatomist":

A celebrated French civil engineer, M. Polonceau, visited me some years ago, bringing with him a young French gentleman, who spoke English eloquently, and perfectly like an Englishman, though he had been in England only two years, and, as he assured me, knew nothing of the language previously, nor had ever heard it spoken. I asked him whether he could pronounce the English name Thistlethwaite, and he instantly pronounced it most distinctly and perfectly. The next day, when talking of other matters, he said that he had some Irish relations; and it appeared that his grandmother, on the female side, whom he had never seen, was an Irishwoman. Hence arose, I do not at all doubt, his power of so readily pronouncing the word I had prescribed. A French gentleman at Paris boasted to me that he could pronounce correctly any English word. I proposed Thistlethwaite to him, when, instead of trying, he exclaimed, "Ah barbare!"[6]

It is tempting to poke fun at this readiness to believe that a person might inherit the power of speaking "perfectly like an Englishman" from a grandmother he'd never met (Knight accounts for it as a case of the inheritance of acquired traits), but the story's sheer preposterousness masks a belief in the connection between cultural and ethnic difference that is disturbing partly because of the persistence with which it lingers in contemporary writing about language and identity, as language continues to provide a ready battleground for debates about human nature.[7]

In his best-selling *The Language Instinct* (1994), Steven Pinker describes the work of geneticist Luigi Cavalli-Sforza, who has used the genes of modern human populations to uncover the history of human migrations and construct a genetic family tree that roughly corresponds to the main human language groupings, and then clarifies his assertion about the relationship between genes and language in a characteristically breezy manner:

A correlation between language families and human genetic groupings does *not,* by the way, mean that there are genes that make it easier for some kinds of people to learn some kinds of languages. This folk myth is pervasive, like the claim of some French speakers that only those with Gallic blood can truly master the gender system, or the insistence of my Hebrew teacher that the assimilated Jewish students in his college classes innately outperformed their Gentile classmates. As far as the language instinct is concerned, the correlation between genes and languages is a coincidence. People store genes in their gonads and pass them to their children through their genitals; they store grammars in their brains and pass them to their children through their mouths. Gonads and brains are attached to each other in bodies, so when bodies move, genes and grammars move together. That is the only reason that geneticists find any correlation between the two. We know that the connection is easily severed, thanks to the genetic experiments called immigration and conquest, in which children get their grammars from the brains of people other than their parents.[8]

Despite this strong assertion of culture's independence from genetics, though, the passage appears in the context of a broader discussion in which Pinker takes every opportunity to lambaste Stephen Jay Gould, Richard Lewontin, and other opponents of sociobiology, attributing to them as a group the "secular ideology" (supremely unreasonable, in Pinker's view) that "[w]hereas animals are rigidly controlled by their biology, human behavior is determined by culture . . . [f]ree from biological constraints, cultures can vary from one another arbitrarily and without limit," a view that Pinker has devoted much of his career to exploding.[9]

In an intellectual climate where the prestige of genetics has never been greater, Pinker's claim to speak for the underdog sounds more than a little disingenuous. Just as troubling as this disregard for intellectual history is Pinker's cavalier reference to the linguistic dislocations produced by immigration and empire as "genetic experiments." While Pinker would presumably justify the phrase as a rhetorical flourish, his desire to flout certain norms of political correctness makes him insensitive to many of contemporary America's most serious concerns about language and ethnicity, particularly with regard to the relationship between nonstandard English dialects and access to education and other social and economic goods. The irony of Pinker's dismissal of such questions as peripheral to his inquiry is that issues about language and power have been central to the work of Noam Chomsky, without whose redefinition of language as an innate capacity rather than a system of habits established by means of education Pinker's work would not have been possible. Indeed, Chomsky's work was welcomed by activists for nonstandard Englishes: "For those of us in the language-rights struggle," Geneva Smitherman writes, "Chomsky's theory of language and the research tradition that he launched have been an invaluable weapon in putting the lie to notions of 'inferior' languages or speakers. Rather, language is the purview of *all* men and women, and all acquire it in the same way, and go through similar stages in this acquisition process, regardless of culture, race/ethnicity, gender, nationality."[10]

A brief consideration of the Ebonics controversy of the mid-1990s may illustrate the cost of assuming, as Pinker does, that "folk myths" about language and biology no longer have the power to harm. In December 1996, in the face of disastrous underachievement by mostly inner-city-dwelling African-American students, the Oakland school board—impressed by one elementary school's success using Black English in the classroom to help students learn to read and write standard English—passed a resolution to develop a plan "for imparting instruction to African-American students in their primary language for the combined purposes of maintaining the legitimacy and richness of such language . . . and to facilitate their acquisition and mastery of English language skills."[11] The media responded to what was perceived as "an attempt to elevate 'street slang' to the level of Shakespeare" with "mockery, ridicule, and outrage," in the words of one commentator.[12] Although the measure's school-board supporters understood it as offering seriously disadvantaged students their best chance of mastering standard English, the Oakland resolution was widely misinterpreted as an attempt to relegate black inner-city students to second-class linguistic citizenship, and the resolution drew particular scorn from high-profile African-Americans, including Bill Cosby and Brent Staples. Further fanning the flames of the controversy, one passage of the resolution (the wording would be revised later on) included an odd-sounding assertion about genetic relationships:

> WHEREAS, numerous validated scholarly studies demonstrate that African-American students as a part of their culture and history as African people possess and utilize a language described in various scholarly approaches as "Ebonics" (literally Black sounds) or "Pan-African Communication Behaviors" or "African Language Systems"; and
>
> WHEREAS, these studies have also demonstrated that African Language Systems are genetically based and not a dialect of English. . . . [13]

The word *genetically* encouraged many people following the story in the media to attribute to the document's framers a racist belief in genetic disparities between whites and blacks of the kind associated with the discussions of race and IQ by

A. R. Jensen and Richard Herrnstein in the late 1960s and early 1970s, as well as with the newer incarnation of the debate that coalesced around Herrnstein and Charles Murray's *The Bell Curve: Intelligence and Class Structure in American Life* (1994). Though the words "are genetically based" would be replaced in the final draft with "have origins in West [African] and Niger-Congo languages,"[14] many wondered how the word came to appear in the first place and speculated as to what it said about the document's framers.

In a history of Black English titled *Spoken Soul* (2000), John Russell Rickford and Russell John Rickford comment on the strangest feature of the resolution's first clause, its omission of the common terms "Black English" or "Black English Vernacular" as well as their successor, "African American Vernacular English" (AAVE). These terms were coined by white sociolinguists such as William Labov and Walt Wolfram in the 1960s and adopted by the majority of linguists—black and white—who entered the field from the 1970s to the 1990s, but were later deemed (as the Rickfords put it) "derogatory and insufficiently suggestive of African origins by Afrocentric scholars such as psychologist Robert L. Williams and social studies professor Robert Twiggs, who created alternatives in the 1970s."[15] Given that most linguists believe AAVE to be a dialect of English, why did the resolution's authors affirm that Ebonics (one of those Afrocentric alternative terms) was "not a dialect of English"?[16] The Rickfords show that the phrasing most likely came from the Afrocentric African-American linguist Ernie Smith, who argued in a 1995 paper that many African-American children are bilingual in English and Ebonics, two quite different languages if you accept the Africanist premise "that Ebonics is not genetically related to English."[17]

While offering a clearer paraphrase of Smith's meaning, however ("Ebonics was genetically related to West African languages in the sense that linguists use the word to denote descent from a common origin"), the Rickfords also point out that "the original phrasing that the resolution's framers chose ('are genetically based') was unusual even in linguistics, and was wide open to misinterpretation."[18] Linguist John Baugh puts his finger on the most counterproductive aspect of the resolution's reinvention of linguistic history.[19] By choosing to use the term "Black Language" rather than "Black English," Baugh points out, the legislators posited the existence of "linguistic interpretations that are inclusive of all black people—regardless of language background."[20] Even a cursory consideration of the languages spread by colonialism (English, French, Russian, Portuguese, Spanish, and so on), he continues, will show "that speech communities and racial communities are not coincident": "The fundamental premise of Afrocentric scholarship, which focuses exclusively on people with complete or partial African ancestry, flies in the face of the fundamental linguistic principle that a language never be equated with a single racial group."[21]

But decoupling language from race altogether can also lead to distortion, even if the two are mapped onto each other as a contingency of history rather than biology. *Spoken Soul* elsewhere describes a charged moment in the O.J. Simpson trial when prosecutor Christopher Darden asked a white male witness to confirm his earlier statement that one of the voices he heard near Nicole Brown Simpson's house on the night of the murder sounded as though it belonged to a black man. Defense attorney Johnnie Cochran objected (an objection sustained by Judge Lance Ito): "You can't tell by somebody's voice whether they sounded black," the Rickfords report Cochran as saying. "I resent that [as] a racist statement. . . . This statement about whether he sounds black or white is racist and I resent it and that is why I stood and objected. And I think it is totally improper in America [that] at this time . . . we have to hear and endure this.'"[22] The Rickfords point to the hypocrisy of this assertion, invoking more than a dozen different studies that show that "[m]ost Americans, and especially black ones, can almost always tell that a person is black even on the phone, and even when the speaker is using standard English sentences."[23]

Many speakers do not conform to expectation, of course, a fact foregrounded in Patricia Cornwell's first novel about medical examiner Kay Scarpetta. At least in the world of the fictional thriller, serial killers are supposed to target victims of their own race rather than crossing racial boundaries: thus the presence of one black victim among a number of white women presents Cornwell's protagonist with a puzzle that will be resolved only when she looks skeptically at her own assumptions about race and language. Scarpetta gains the crucial clue to the murderer's identity when she talks to the dead woman's sister on the telephone, realizes she has a "cultured and Virginian" voice—i.e., that "*black* people can talk *white*," in the black woman's angry summary—and deduces that he must target his victims over the telephone.[24] Certain features of Black English—perhaps most notoriously, the pronunciation of the word "ask" as "aks"/"axe"—continue to operate as "shibboleths of vernacular black speech": "In a March 1995 segment of *60 Minutes*," the Rickfords recount, "television news reporter Morley Safer asked Arch Whitehead, a well-suited African American who recruits corporate executives, what would happen if a black man applying for a Wall Street job were to say, 'May I *aks* you a question?' versus 'May I *ask* you a question?' Whitehead laughed and said, 'He won't get to *aks* that very often, I'll tell ya,' and the two men agreed that he wouldn't even 'get a foot in the door.'"[25] There is nothing inherently wrong about the use of "aks" for ask; in fact, it was widespread in earlier British English, both written and spoken. It is frequently spelled "axen" in Middle English, and the transformation of "ask" into "axe" also offers also a textbook example of a common linguistic phenomenon called "metathesis," in which two consonants are switched to make articulation easier. Yet the real-world consequences of speaking an English that includes this feature can be quite harmful, as Safer and Whitehead's discussion shows.

The history of the elocution movement in eighteenth-century Britain touches on similar issues about access and entitlement, and the vacillations of the elocutionists about the extent to which language could be considered a wholly cultural phenomenon tell a cautionary tale about breeding and its shibboleths, one that remains highly relevant to our own time.

## The Blackmail of Enlightenment

The conditions that led to the 1937 massacre Danticat's novel chronicles are very clearly the consequence of colonialism, conquest, and the African slave trade—in other words, historical ideologies and processes often identified as the dark side of the Enlightenment. But I want to follow Michel Foucault here in his refusal to participate in what he calls the "blackmail" of the Enlightenment.[26] In an essay entitled "What Is Enlightenment?" (a response to Kant's 1784 essay on the same question), Foucault argues that although we ourselves are "historically determined, to a certain extent, by the Enlightenment," that does not mean "that one has to be 'for' or 'against'" it:

> It even means precisely that one has to refuse everything that might present itself in the form of a simplistic and authoritarian alternative: you either accept the Enlightenment and remain within the tradition of its rationalism (this is considered a positive term by some and used by others, on the contrary, as a reproach); or else you criticize the Enlightenment and then try to escape from its principles of rationality (which may be seen once again as good or bad). And we do not break free of this blackmail by introducing "dialectical" nuances while seeking to determine what good and bad elements there may have been in the Enlightenment.[27]

Viewed in this light, questions about the rise of hereditary explanation in later eighteenth- and nineteenth-century writing—and whether it represents rupture or sequel vis-à-vis the eighteenth-century history this book has recounted—come clean, as it were, as to their own unanswerability. The nineteenth- and twentieth-century ramifications of eugenic science, for instance, are so grotesque as to make it virtually impossible to give eighteenth-century discussions of the genetic modification of human beings anything like a fair hearing—and we are not, in any case, putting the Enlightenment on trial. The inverse to this kind of blackmail of Enlightenment, I might add, is a kind of wishful thinking—most eighteenth-century scholars have been guilty of it at one time or another, myself certainly included—in which one idealizes the eighteenth century as a favorable alternate to the nineteenth: it was less prudish about women's sexuality, less racist, etc.[28]

I had an interesting experience with these sentences of Foucault's on the first day of a graduate seminar I taught at Columbia on the idea of culture. As I asked the students to unpack the meaning of the words, it slowly dawned on me that my questions were being greeted with the silence not of reticence but of utter incomprehension. What had seemed to me like a fairly straightforward statement of a well-known problem that affects scholars across the humanities and social sciences was completely opaque to them: they had *no idea* what Foucault was talking about. This led me to start thinking about what happens when those of us educated, perhaps, in the seventies and eighties (and in a particular set of departments at a particular set of universities) assume that every new set of students will have read exactly the same things we have. New English Ph.D. students, even those specializing in eighteenth-century studies, are likely to have read only a tiny handful of works written in the eighteenth century and to have spent little time contemplating the legacies of Enlightenment. Those who come to the eighteenth century by way of history or political philosophy or postcolonial theory will be more likely to have some familiarity with Kant and Foucault's arguments about Enlightenment, but may well be ignorant of the writings of Pope and Swift. In this kaleidoscopic world of reading, it seems to me very risky to make assumptions about a shared language or body of texts. Critical writing necessarily places demands on its readers that many readers either do not choose to undertake or may even be incapable of undertaking. That is the nature of the enterprise. But there are many reasons one might nonetheless contemplate making it more hospitable, in particular by not shying away from discussing works that may seem hyper-canonical but with which, when taken as a group, few readers are likely to be thoroughly and universally familiar.

To speak bluntly, how many college students read even those eighteenth-century texts most widely accepted as canonical: *Gulliver's Travels,* say, or Locke's *Essay*? How many students doing doctoral degrees in English who are not specializing in the eighteenth century are likely to know Rousseau's *Discourse on In-*

*equality*? I do not ask these questions to indict the American educational system. I believe many different routes can be followed to knowledge, and I am temperamentally averse to calls for canon-making and canon-restoration. (But I also believe that it is condescending and hypocritical to suggest that we do not expect our strongest students to acquire some body of knowledge that may as well be made publicly and institutionally accessible to all students in the form of lists and curricula.)

I write from and for eighteenth-century studies, but I am concerned to make my discussion hospitable to those outside that subfield—or outside of literary study—who might prefer just to visit for a while. I offer these thoughts in a spirit diametrically opposed to the deliberate amateurism of David Denby's *Great Books: My Adventures With Homer, Rousseau, Woolf, and Other Indestructible Writers of the Western World* (1996). I want to keep all the intensity and the precision of academic writing, and the virtues of specialization, but to make what I write at least potentially open to readers in other disciplines, or in other walks of life. Mary Midgley argues that the topic of human nature "must necessarily be discussed in plain language," partly because it cuts across so many different disciplines but also because there is already a quite sophisticated everyday human terminology for talking about motives: "Of course it needs refining and expanding," she writes, "but to by-pass it and start again as if it were all ignorant babble is arrogant and wasteful."[29] "Jargon always tends to make unwelcome facts unstatable," she adds. "We can all see this when we look at other people's jargon. It is just as true of our own." The *New Yorker* practices a form of description—"Arnold Schwarzenegger, the California governor"—that has been affectionately parodied by one long-time senior editor at the magazine in the happy formulation "God, the well-known Judeo-Christian deity." But there is something admirable about this desire to invite the reader in, and if we hope to write across time and across space—and what else is writing but a technology for doing both of those things?—such gestures are essential.

CONCLUSION
The Promise of Perfection

In a series of letters exchanged during the summer and fall of 1813, John Adams and Thomas Jefferson fell to debating the relative merits of aristocracy and democracy. Adams maintained that a genuinely republican government "over five and twenty millions people, when four and twenty millions and five hundred thousands of them could neither write nor read" should be considered "as unnatural irrational and impracticable; as it would be over the Elephants Lions Tigers Panthers Wolves and Bears in the Royal Menagerie, at Versailles":

> Inequalities of Mind and Body are so established by God Almighty in his constitution of Human Nature that no Art or policy can ever plain them down to a Level. I have never read Reasoning more absurd, Sophistry more gross, in proof of the Athanasian Creed, or Transubstantiation, than the subtle labours of Helvetius and Rousseau to demonstrate the natural Equality of Mankind.[1]

The rest of the letter conveys Adams' powerfully elegiac sense of opportunities lost. Having seen the European nations from 1778 to 1785 "to be advancing by slow but sure Steps towards an Amelioration of the condition of Man," Adams claims to have "dreaded" the French Revolution because he knew that it would "not only arrest the progress of Improvement, but give it a retrograde course, for at least a Century, if not many Centuries": "Let me now ask you, very seriously my Friend," he entreats Jefferson, "Where are now in 1813, the Perfection and perfectability of human Nature? Where is now, the progress of the human Mind? Where is the Amelioration of Society?"[2]

In subsequent letters Adams frames human inequality in terms of breeding, offering his own translation of a maxim attributed to the poet Theognis (writing in Greek during the sixth century BCE)—"'When We want to purchase, Horses, Asses or Rams, We inquire for the Wellborn. And every one wishes to procure, from the good Breeds. A good Man, does not care to marry a Shrew, the Daughter of a Shrew; unless They give him, a great deal of Money with her'"—and asking "how far advanced We were in the Science of Aristocracy, since Theognis's Stallions Jacks and Rams?"[3] In response, Jefferson suggests that the passage from Theognis "has an Ethical, rather than a political object," serving as "a reproof to man, who, while with his domestic animals he is curious to improve the race by employing always the finest male, pays no attention to the improvement of his own race."[4] Such improvements might be highly desirable, Jefferson continues, and yet precluded by the circumstances of democratic government:

> The selecting the best male for a Haram of well chosen females also, which Theognis seems to recommend from the example of our sheep and asses, would doubtless improve the human, as it does the brute animal, and produce a race of veritable [aristocrats]. For experience proves that the moral and physical qualities of man, whether good or evil, are transmissible in a certain degree from father to son. But I suspect that the equal rights of men will rise up against this privileged Solomon, and oblige us to continue acquiescence under the [degeneration of the race of men] which Theognis complains of, and to content ourselves with the accidental aristoi produced by the fortuitous concourse of breeders.[5]

By lingering on the idea of a natural aristocracy among men, both men express a shared sense that the century of perfectibility has come to an end, the French Revolution having spelled the death or at least the general discrediting of a notion of human malleability that had flourished in the conditions created by Locke's writings on education and the human mind.

Twentieth-century history has offered in every respect a far more devastating indictment than the French Revolution did of state-administered efforts in aid of human perfectibility, but do such developments provide reason to give up on the idea altogether? This is the question John Passmore contemplates at the end of his history of perfectibility:

In spite of these reflections, which might lead us to reject perfectibilism in any of its forms, it is very hard to shake off the feeling that man is capable of becoming something much superior to what he now is. This feeling, if it is interpreted in the manner of the more commonsensical Enlighteners, is not in itself irrational. There is certainly no *guarantee* that men will ever be any better than they now are; their future is not, as it were, underwritten by Nature. Nor is there any device, whether skilful government, or education, which is certain to ensure the improvement of man's condition. To that extent the hopes of the developmentalists or the governmentalists or the educators must certainly be abandoned. There is not the slightest ground for believing, either, with the anarchist, that if only the State could be destroyed and men could start afresh, all would be well. But we know from our own experience, as teachers or parents, that individual human beings can come to be better than they once were, given care, and that wholly to despair of a child or a pupil is to abdicate what is one's proper responsibility. We know, too, that in the past men have made advances, in science, in art, in affection. Men, almost certainly, are capable of more than they have ever so far achieved. But what they achieve, or so I have suggested, will be a consequence of their remaining anxious, passionate, discontented human beings.[6]

The ethical core here lies in the sentence where Passmore turns to the experience of being a teacher or a parent. There is something at once modest and stubborn in this gesture, and it harks back to a turn that can also be seen in the writings of Locke and Godwin when they consider the call of education. Individual human beings can come to be better than they once were—one reason we do not relish Prospero's description of Caliban as "[a] devil, a born devil, on whose nature/Nurture can never stick."[7]

Perfection has been much in the news recently, as a consequence both of ongoing scandals concerning athletes' use of performance-enhancing drugs and of an array of therapeutic possibilities in genetic engineering that seem now on the cusp of coming into being. In a recent book called *The Case Against Perfection*, Michael Sandel comes down strongly against the notion that it might be appropriate for parents to obtain genetic enhancements for their children. His case depends in part on the idea that such enhancements will deform relations between parents and children (an argument that was also prominent in discussions of reproductive cloning in the late 1990s, where many were inclined to argue that parental expectations of a cloned child would prove disabling in a qualitatively different fashion from the ordinary way of things). Sandel invokes the theologian William F. May's phrase "'openness to the unbidden,'" a phrase that "describes a quality of character and heart that restrains the impulse to mastery and control and prompts a sense of life as gift," in support of an argument that "the deepest moral objection to enhancement lies less in the perfection it seeks than in the human disposition it expresses and promotes," and he links enhancement to a kind of hubris that will disfigure the relationship between parent and child.[8]

I am not an ethicist, but I am skeptical about this kind of assertion, partly in this case because I simply don't see how we can know where to draw the line. The will to mastery seems to me just as likely to deform a human relationship entirely unaffected by new technologies of enhancement, and genetic enhancements exist on a spectrum of techniques of remediation that include things as uncontroversial as, say, finding a workaround to help a severely dyslexic child learn to read. (Pretty quickly, of course, we come to more complicated and controversial instances, but these need not be genetic enhancements in order to provoke profound disagreement: consider the case of cochlear implants.)

Slavoj Žižek offers a provocative argument about perfection that captures more of the flavor of its dilemmas, in any case, than Sandel's perhaps overly clear-cut judgment, and I will quote it here at some length:

> Imagine the following scenario: I am to take part in a quiz, but instead of working away at getting up the facts, I use drugs to enhance my memory. The self-esteem I acquire by winning the competition is still based on a real achievement: I performed better than my opponent who had spent night after night trying to memorise the relevant data. The intuitive counter-argument is that only my opponent has the right to be proud of his performance, because his knowledge, unlike mine, was the result of hard work. There's something inherently patronising in that.
>
> Again, we see it as perfectly justified when someone with a good natural singing voice takes pride in his performance, although we're aware that his singing has more to do with talent than with effort and training. If, however, I were to improve my singing by the use of a drug, I would be denied the same recognition (unless I had put a lot of effort into inventing the drug in question before testing it on myself). The point is that both hard work and natural talent are considered 'part of me', while using a drug is 'artificial' enhancement because it is a form of external manipulation. Which brings us back to the same problem: once we know that my 'natural talent' depends on the levels of certain chemicals in my brain, does it matter, morally, whether I acquired it

from outside or have possessed it from birth? To further complicate matters, it's possible that my willingness to accept discipline and work hard itself depends on certain chemicals. What if, in order to win a quiz, I don't take a drug which enhances my memory but one which 'merely' strengthens my resolve? Is this still 'cheating'?[9]

Žižek's deliberate tabling of origins, his refusal to entertain the idea that we can reasonably distinguish things that are a part of us from "cheating" surrogates, finds an interesting complement in Stephen J. Dubner and Steven D. Levitt's argument that "the trait we commonly call talent is highly overrated":

> Or, put another way, expert performers—whether in memory or surgery, ballet or computer programming—are nearly always made, not born. And yes, practice does make perfect. These may be the sort of clichés that parents are fond of whispering to their children. But these particular clichés just happen to be true.
>
> [Anders] Ericsson's research [on talents and learning] suggests a third cliché as well: when it comes to choosing a life path, you should do what you love— because if you don't love it, you are unlikely to work hard enough to get very good. Most people naturally don't like to do things they aren't 'good' at. So they often give up, telling themselves they simply don't possess the talent for math or skiing or the violin. But what they really lack is the *desire* to be good and to undertake the deliberate practice that would make them better.[10]

It undoubtedly takes a certain facility with mental gymnastics to think about talent as a product of desire rather than luck, but the great appeal of Dubner and Levitt's argument derives from the way it might be seen to provide ballast for an ethical exhortation to improve others and oneself.

We often associate such arguments with the age of Enlightenment, but they have a history that goes back to the ancient world, in particular to the Greeks. In his treatise "The Affections and Errors of the Soul," the physician Galen (writing long after Plato, in the second century of the common era) offers an especially compelling account of the call for self-transformation:

> For becoming a perfect man is a goal which requires in each of us a discipline that will continue through practically the whole of his life. One should not put aside the possibility of improving oneself even at the age of fifty, if one is aware of some defect one's soul has sustained, provided that defect is not in-

curable or irremediable. If one's body were in a bad state at that age, one would not give oneself up to the bad condition; one would by all means attempt to improve it, even if one were not able to achieve a Heraclean sort of good condition. No more, then, should we refrain from efforts to achieve a better state of the soul. Even if that of the wise man is beyond us—though we should have a high hope of attaining even that state, if we have taken care of our soul from early youth—then at least we should exert ourselves that our soul be not utterly disgusting, as was Thersites' body.

If it had lain in our power before being born to meet the one responsible for our birth, we would have asked him to let us have the finest type of body. If he had refused this, we would have requested of him the second, third, or fourth from the first in good condition. It would be a highly desirable outcome, even if we could not get the body of a Heracles, to have at least that of an Achilles, and failing that, that of an Ajax, a Diomedes, an Agamemnon, a Patroclus; and failing those, the body of some other fine hero. It is just the same with the soul. If one were unable to attain the most perfect good condition, one would surely accept the second, third, or fourth from the top. Such a goal is quite achievable for one who is prepared to exert himself over a long period in a process of constant discipline.[11]

To borrow and misapply another phrase that's been in the news recently, what Galen offers us—and what I would argue should stop us from altogether giving up on perfectibility, for in spite of Foucault's suggestion about holding oneself back from position-taking on Enlightenment, each of us has some orientation in regard to it, a deep temperamental and intellectual investment in or antagonism toward its values—is indeed a way of throwing off the tyranny of low expectations, for ourselves as well as for others. This offsets the versions of determinism that provide cover stories for moral inertia of various kinds, a point made perceptively by the psychiatrist Leslie Farber:

The realm of causation is treacherous ground for a man interested in the truth about himself. Although it is certainly probable that most phenomena of this world, human and otherwise, do have causes of one sort or another, an absorption with the role of causation in human affairs may lead to an habitual reduction of any human event to its postulated cause. It is apparent how such reduction promises refuge to a man beset by the necessity to "confess": once he turns his attention to cause, his personal responsibility (whether he acknowledges it or not) is diminished, along with any undue stress or discomfort he may have felt in facing what he believes to be his absolute worst. No matter what scandalous detail about himself he may reveal, he follows such revelation with "I am this way because . . . ," and everyone relaxes.[12]

Farber's point is not that ascriptions of causes are factually inaccurate, though certainly causes identified in this way might often be described as more plausible than truthful, but rather that explaining ourselves in this fashion can lead to ethical falsification. A hard-core commitment to nature-based explanation, a hard-core advocacy of nurture: either one of these "because" modes may, as Godwin said of phrenology, "[exhibit] us for the most part as the helpless victims of a blind and remorseless destiny" (6:239). Those of us who are educators may tend, like Passmore, to align ourselves with nurture, but to insist too strongly on its powers is to allow for an erosion of moral autonomy, in ourselves and others, that is in the end difficult to distinguish from the kinds of deterministic thinking we shrink from when they are associated with genes.

# NOTES

## Introduction. Breeding Before Biology

1. While Johnson's definitions of the verb *breed* move from the biological to the educational, the three meanings he gives for the noun *breeding* relate solely to education: "Education; instruction; qualifications"; "Manners; knowledge of ceremony"; "Nurture; care to bring up from the infant state." See Samuel Johnson, *A Dictionary of the English Language,* 2 vols. (London: W. Strahan, 1755). The text of the authoritative fourth edition is substantially the same; see *A Dictionary of the English Language,* 4th ed., 2 vols. (London: W. Strahan, 1773).

2. On the long persistence of the belief that one grain might be transformed into another by cultivation, see Conway Zirkle, *The Beginnings of Plant Hybridization* (Philadelphia: University of Pennsylvania Press, 1935), 64–65; the quotation on resemblance is from [Anon.], *Aristoteles Master-Piece; or, The Secrets of Generation displayed in all the parts thereof* (London: J. How, 1684), 25.

3. The dates are admittedly approximate; the noun *heredity* can be found in earlier writing, for instance, though not in its modern sense. On the term *biology,* see Michel Foucault, *The Order of Things: An Archeology of the Human Sciences* (1966), trans. Alan Sheridan (New York: Vintage, 1973), 160–162; Jacques Roger, "The Living World," in *The Ferment of Knowledge: Studies in the Historiography of Eighteenth-Century Science,* ed. G.S. Rousseau and Roy Porter (Cambridge: Cambridge University Press, 1980), 255–283, esp. 258; and Evelyn Fox Keller, *The Century of the Gene* (Cambridge, MA: Harvard University Press, 2000), 106 and 163 n. 6. On Bateson's coinage of the name "genetics," see Hans Stubbe, *History of Genetics: From Prehistoric Times to the Rediscovery of Mendel's Laws,* rev. ed., trans. T.R.W. Waters (1965; Cambridge, MA: MIT Press, 1972), 272; and Miles Hadfield, *A History of British Gardening,* 3rd ed. (1960; London: John Murray, 1979), 395.

4. Roger Smith, "The Language of Human Nature," in *Inventing Human Science: Eighteenth-Century Domains,* ed. Christopher Fox, Roy Porter, and Robert Wokler (Berkeley: University of California Press, 1995), 88–111, esp. 89.

5. Gillian Beer, "Has Nature a Future?," in *The Third Culture: Literature and Science,* ed. Elinor S. Shaffer (Berlin: de Gruyter, 1998), 15–27 (the quotation is on 16); Raymond Williams, *Keywords: A Vocabulary of Culture and Society,* rev. ed. (1976; New York: Oxford University Press, 1983), entries for *culture* and *nature.*

6. Hans-Jörg Rheinberger and Staffan Müller-Wille, "Introduction," in *A Cultural History of Heredity II: Eighteenth and Nineteenth Centuries,* Max Planck Institute for the History of Science, preprint 247 (2003): 3–6; the quotation is on 3. The papers on which they base this claim can be found in *A Cultural History of Heredity I: Seventeenth and Eighteenth Centuries,* Max Planck Institute for the History of Science, preprint 222 (2002). The classic history of the science of heredity is François Jacob, *The Logic of Life: A History of Heredity,* trans. Betty E. Spillman (1970; Princeton: Princeton University Press, 1973).

7. John Arbuthnot, *An Essay Concerning the Effects of Air on Human Bodies* (London: J. Tonson, 1733), 146–147.

8. [Richard Steele and Joseph Addison], *The Tatler,* ed. Donald F. Bond, vol. 1 (Oxford: Clarendon, 1987), no. 75, 1 Oct. 1709, pp. 512–517.

9. Discussing the theory and practice of sheep-breeding in eighteenth-century Britain, Roger J. Wood identifies the central debate as concerning "the extent to which the blood could be moderated by rearing, i.e. by the farmer's system of management": "rearing could include selective breeding, as well as the control of living conditions and the provision of special food to replace or supplement the natural diet," he writes, meaning that *rearing* is "obviously a more inclusive concept than that which Francis Galton would later define as 'nurture'" (Roger J. Wood, "The Sheep Breeders' View of Heredity [1723–1843]," in *A Cultural History of Heredity II,* 21–46; the quotation is on 24). John Goodridge offers a useful discussion of heredity and environment in sheep-breeding in *Rural Life in Eighteenth-Century English Poetry* (Cambridge: Cambridge University Press, 1995), esp. 125ff.; and see also the extended discussions in Roger J. Wood and Vitezslav Orel, *Genetic Prehistory in Selective Breeding: A Prelude to Mendel* (Oxford: Oxford University Press, 2001), 38–56, 88–94.

10. Antoine-Nicolas de Condorcet, *Sketch for a Historical Picture of the Progress of the Human Mind* (1795), trans. June Barraclough, intro. Stuart Hampshire (London: Weidenfeld and Nicolson, 1955), 201.

11. Daniel J. Kevles, *In the Name of Eugenics: Genetics and the Uses of Human Heredity* (New York: Knopf, 1985), 86. Galton left forty-five thousand pounds to UCL in his will to establish the Galton Eugenics Professorship, but in the aftermath of World War II, eugenics permanently tarnished, the incumbent Lionel Penrose lobbied to remove the institutional name and affiliation (38, 251–252). Vidyanand Nanjundiah provides a thoughtful recap of Kevles' history in "Dangerous Muddle," *Journal of Genetics* 76.2 (1997): 161–165.

12. Dorinda Outram, "The Enlightenment Our Contemporary," in *The Sciences in Enlightened Europe,* ed. William Clark, Jan Golinski, and Simon Schaffer (Chicago: Uni-

versity of Chicago Press, 1999), 32–40. Because of the essay's brevity, I will not give page references for specific quotations.

13. A word like *temperament* still interestingly straddles the nature-nurture divide, but the tendency in recent years has been to inscribe temperament as a strongly genetically determined quality; see Jerome Kagan (with Nancy Snidman, Doreen Arcus, and J. Steven Reznick), *Galen's Prophecy: Temperament in Human Nature* (New York: Basic Books, 1994).

14. Evelyn Fox Keller, "Nature, Nurture, and the Human Genome Project," in *The Code of Codes: Scientific and Social Issues in the Human Genome Project,* ed. Daniel J. Kevles and Leroy Hood (Cambridge, MA: Harvard University Press, 1992), 281–299; the quotation is on 285.

15. On Lysenko's pseudoscience, see David Joravesky, *The Lysenko Affair* (Cambridge, MA: Harvard University Press, 1970), 214–217.

16. Eve Kosofsky Sedgwick, *Epistemology of the Closet* (Berkeley: University of California Press, 1990), 40.

17. Mary Midgley, *Beast and Man: The Roots of Human Nature* (Ithaca: Cornell University Press, 1978), xviii.

18. "Airs, Waters, Places," in *Hippocratic Writings,* ed. G.E.R. Lloyd, trans. J. Chadwick and W. Mann (1950; London: Penguin, 1983), 161; and see also Jacques Jouanna, *Hippocrates,* trans. M.B. DeBevoise (1992; Baltimore: Johns Hopkins University Press, 1999), esp. 220–224, 364.

19. August Weismann, "On Heredity" (1883), in *Essays Upon Heredity and Kindred Biological Problems,* trans. and ed. Edward B. Poulton et al. (Oxford: Clarendon, 1889), 67–105, 84. My guide on this set of questions has been Conway Zirkle, "The Early History of the Idea of the Inheritance of Acquired Characters and of Pangenesis," *Transactions of the American Philosophical Society* 35.2 (1946): 91–151.

20. For two perceptive essays by literary scholars on the language of genes, see Priscilla Wald, "Future Perfect: Grammar, Genes, and Geography," *New Literary History* 31 (2000): 681–708; and Jay Clayton, "Genome Time," in *Time and the Literary,* ed. Karen Newman, Jay Clayton, and Marianne Hirsch (New York: Routledge, 2002), 31–59.

21. Jacques Roger, *The Life Sciences in Eighteenth-Century French Thought,* ed. Keith R. Benson, trans. Robert Ellrich (1963, rev. ed. 1993; Stanford: Stanford University Press, 1997), xlii–xliii; and see also the discussion in George W. Stocking Jr., "On the Limits of 'Presentism' and 'Historicism,'" in *Race, Culture, and Evolution: Essays in the History of Anthropology,* rev. ed. (1968; Chicago: University of Chicago Press/Free Press, 1982), 1–12; and the foreword and introduction to *Languages of Nature: Critical Essays on Science and Literature,* ed. L.J. Jordanova, intro. Raymond Williams (New Brunswick, NJ: Rutgers University Press, 1986).

22. Jürgen Pieters offers some interesting reflections on associated concepts and methodology in *Speaking with the Dead: Explorations in Literature and History* (Edinburgh: Edinburgh University Press, 2005). For further thoughts on such voices, see W.G. Sebald, "Between History and Natural History: On the Literary Description of Total Destruc-

tion," in *Campo Santo,* trans. Anthea Bell (New York: Random House, 2005), 65–95; Svetlana Alexievich, *Voices from Chernobyl,* trans. Keith Gessen (Normal: Dalkey Archive Press, 2005); and the discussion of the "parliament of things" at the end of Bruno Latour, *We Have Never Been Modern* (1991), trans. Catherine Porter (Cambridge, MA: Harvard University Press, 1993), 142–145.

23. Clifford Geertz, "Thick Description: Toward an Interpretive Theory of Culture," in *The Interpretation of Cultures* (New York: Basic Books, 1973), 3–30; the quotation is on 29. On the possibility that "the idea of culture has been in crisis from the moment it began to take distinct shape and that it has embarrassed as much as it has empowered its users," see Christopher Herbert, *Culture and Anomie: Ethnographic Imagination in the Nineteenth Century* (Chicago: University of Chicago Press, 1991), 17–18; and for an interesting assessment of methodological challenges facing cultural historians, see Peter Mandler, "The Problem with Cultural History," *Cultural and Social History* 1 (2004): 94–117.

24. Georges Perec, "Attempt at an Inventory of the Liquid and the Solid Foodstuffs Ingurgitated by Me in the Course of the Year Nineteen Hundred and Seventy-Four," trans. John Sturrock, *Granta* 52 (1995): 87–92; the quotation is on 89.

25. Primo Levi, *The Periodic Table* (1975), trans. Raymond Rosenthal, intro. Neal Ascherson (New York and Toronto: Knopf/Everyman, 1996); and see also Paul Strathern, *Mendeleyev's Dream: The Quest for the Elements* (New York: St. Martin's/Thomas Dunne, 2000).

26. W.G. Sebald, *The Rings of Saturn* (1995), trans. Michael Hulse (New York: New Directions, 1999), 43.

27. Sebald, *The Rings of Saturn,* 98.

28. I will always remember Wayne Koestenbaum reading out loud, circa 1996 and to his students' great delight and edification, the magical passage from the autobiographical text titled *Roland Barthes* which opens with the line "Here is what I did with my body one day" and proceeds to describe the fate of the "rib chop" that was removed from the author's chest in 1945 as part of "an extrapleural pneumothorax operation," was given to him to take home, and languished for many years afterward in a drawer whose function it was "to ease, to acclimate the death of objects by causing them to pass through a sort of pious site, a dusty chapel where, in the guise of keeping them alive, we allow them a decent interval of dim agony"; finally, Barthes says, "I flung the rib chop and its gauze from my balcony, as if I were romantically scattering my own ashes, into the rue Servandoni, where some dog would come and sniff them out" (Roland Barthes, *Roland Barthes* [1975], trans. Richard Howard [New York: Hill and Wang, 1977], 61).

29. Roland Barthes, *The Neutral: Lecture Course at the Collège de France (1977–1978),* trans. Rosalind E. Krauss and Denis Hollier (New York: Columbia University Press, 2005), 8–9.

30. Barthes, *The Neutral,* 130.

31. Jane Austen, "The History of England from the reign of Henry the 4th to the death of Charles the 1st," in *Catharine and Other Writings,* ed. Margaret Anne Doody and Douglas Murray (1993; Oxford: Oxford University Press, 1998), 134.

32. On the concept of breeding, see also Walter Benn Michaels, "The Souls of White Folk," in *Literature and the Body: Essays on Populations and Persons. Selected Papers from the English Institute, 1986,* ed. Elaine Scarry (Baltimore: Johns Hopkins University Press, 1990), 185–209; and Benn Michaels, *Our America: Nativism, Modernism, and Pluralism* (Durham: Duke University Press, 1995), esp. 119–121, 129, 133.

# 1. The Rules of Resemblance

1. See for instance Franco Moretti, "Conjectures on World Literature," *New Left Review* 1 (2000): 54–68; Wai Chee Dimock, "Planetary Time and Global Translation: 'Context' in Literary Studies," *Common Knowledge* 9.3 (2003): 488–507; and Dimock, "Genre as World System: Epic and Novel on Four Continents," *Narrative* 14.1 (2006): 85–101.

2. Between 1700 and 1750, it was staged only a few more times than such perennially unpopular plays as *Coriolanus, The Comedy of Errors, Troilus and Cressida,* and *Pericles;* Charles Beecher Hogan, *Shakespeare in the Theatre, 1701–1800,* 2 vols. (Oxford: Clarendon, 1952–1957), 1:457–458. In terms of stage performance, Shakespeare's popularity remained roughly the same in the second half of the eighteenth century as it had been in the first half: approximately one-sixth of all documented plays performed in London were by Shakespeare (2:715).

3. It was roughly comparable in popularity to *Twelfth Night* or *Henry V;* Hogan, *Shakespeare in the Theatre,* 2:716–719. The number refers to total performances, not separate productions; for purposes of comparison, during the same period, *Romeo and Juliet* was acted 399 times, *Hamlet* 343, and *Antony and Cleopatra* only six.

4. Most notoriously, the happy ending to *King Lear;* Nahum Tate, *The History of King Lear* (1681), ed. James Black (Lincoln: University of Nebraska Press, 1975), 5.6.135–137. Samuel Johnson writes in his preface to Lear that he was "many years ago so shocked by Cordelia's death, that I know not whether I ever endured to read again the last scenes of the play till I undertook to revise them as an editor"; *Johnson on Shakespeare,* ed. Arthur Sherbo, vol. 8 of *The Yale Edition of the Works of Samuel Johnson* (New Haven: Yale University Press, 1968), 704.

5. Today a number of Shakespeare's late plays are grouped together under the generic rubric of romance, but that heading did not appear in the 1623 folio edition of the plays, which groups all the plays as comedies, histories, or tragedies (with *The Winter's Tale* in the first group). Many thanks to Ivan Lupić for his helpful clarification of matters Shakespearean and otherwise. For a thoughtful account of romance and its vagaries, see Patricia A. Parker, *Inescapable Romance: Studies in the Poetics of a Mode* (Princeton: Princeton University Press, 1979).

6. William Shakespeare, *The Winter's Tale,* in *The Riverside Shakespeare,* ed. G. Blakemore Evans et al., 2nd ed. (Boston: Houghton Mifflin, 1997), 4.4.92–95. Subsequent references are to this edition and will be given parenthetically in the text.

7. The essays collected in *The Character of Kinship*, ed. Jack Goody (Cambridge: Cambridge University Press, 1973) provide an excellent starting point for further reading; see especially J.A. Barnes, "Genetrix : Genitor :: Nature : Culture" (61–73).

8. The concordance gives fourteen uses of *issue* and the variant-spelling *yssue* in the play's earliest printing, the First Folio (1623); *Oxford Shakespeare Concordance: The Winter's Tale* (Oxford: Clarendon, 1969). The play also includes eight uses of *breed* and its cognates *bred* and *breeding*. On reproduction in *The Winter's Tale*, see especially Janet Adelman, *Suffocating Mothers: Fantasies of Maternal Origin in Shakespeare's Plays* (London: Routledge, 1992), 193–236.

9. Edmund Burke, *Reflections on the Revolution in France, and on the Proceedings in Certain Societies in London Relative to that Event* (1790), ed. Conor Cruise O'Brien (1968; London: Penguin, 1986), 171.

10. The quotations in this paragraph are from *The Winter's Tale*, 1.2.119–135.

11. *OED*, 2nd ed., 1989.

12. In her invaluable treatment of the stamp metaphor in "theories of both knowledge and generation," Margreta de Grazia points to the pervasiveness of the trope of child as imprint of the father and the ways it was affected by the introduction of printing; "Imprints: Shakespeare, Gutenberg, and Descartes," in *Alternative Shakespeare*, vol. 2, ed. Terrence Hawkes (London: Routledge, 1996), 63–94. The essay can also be found in *Printing and Parenting in Early Modern England*, ed. Douglas A. Brooks (Burlington, VT: Ashgate, 2005), 29–58. Thanks to David Kastan for this reference. For two suggestive later examples of play on the back-and-forth between the issue of the body and the issue of print, see Nich. Culpeper, *A Directory for Midwives; or, A Guide for Women, In their Conception, Bearing, And Suckling their Children* (London: Peter Cole, 1651), 219; and Martin Lluelyn's dedicatory poem in preface to William Harvey, *Anatomical Exercertations, Concerning the Generation of Living Creatures*, [trans. Martin Lluelyn] (1651; London: James Young for Octavian Pulleyn, 1653).

13. See F.J. Cole, *Early Theories of Sexual Generation* (Oxford: Clarendon, 1930), 133; and Joseph Needham, *A History of Embryology*, 2nd ed., rev. with Arthur Hughes (1934; Cambridge: Cambridge University Press, 1959), 74. On Fabricius, see Jane M. Oppenheimer, *Essays in the History of Embryology and Biology* (Cambridge, MA: MIT Press, 1967), 124–125; and the useful discussion in Howard B. Adelmann, "Introduction: A Brief Sketch of the History of Embryology Before Fabricius," in *The Embryological Treatises of Hieronymus Fabricius of Acquapendente*, ed. Adelmann (Ithaca: Cornell University Press, 1942), 36–70.

14. Aristotle, *Generation of Animals*, trans. A.L. Peck (1942; Cambridge, MA: Harvard University Press, 1990), 1.20 (109). Thomas Laqueur offers a broad treatment of sex and gender in early modern British writing; see especially the first chapter of *Making Sex: Body and Gender from the Greeks to Freud* (Cambridge, MA: Harvard University Press, 1990).

15. Aristotle, *Generation of Animals*, 1.21 (113).

16. Aristotle, *Generation of Animals*, 1.22 (121). On the idea (shared by the Egyptians and the Greeks) that the father is the sole parent of the child, see Needham, *History of*

*Embryology,* 43–46. Perhaps the best-known exposition of this theory can be found in the *Oresteia,* where Orestes is absolved of the blood guilt for killing his mother on the grounds (in Apollo's words) that "[t]he mother is no parent of that which is called/her child, but only nurse of the new-planted seed/that grows. The parent is he who mounts," in *Eumenides* (ca. 458 BCE), ll. 658–660, *Oresteia,* trans. Richmond Lattimore (Chicago: University of Chicago Press, 1953).

17. See Aristotle, *Generation of Animals,* 4.3 (401–403). In conjunction with an argument that "anyone who does not take after his parents is really in a way a monstrosity," he notoriously goes on to identify "[t]he first beginning of this deviation [as] when a female is formed instead of a male"; and see also the assertion that "we should look upon the female state as being as it were a deformity, though one which occurs in the ordinary course of nature" (4.6 [461]).

18. On sixteenth- and seventeenth-century debates over female semen, see Ian Maclean, *The Renaissance Notion of Woman: A Study in the Fortunes of Scholasticism and Medical Science in European Intellectual Life* (Cambridge: Cambridge University Press, 1980), 35–38.

19. For what remains an excellent survey of primary sources on maternal impression, see J.W. Ballantyne, *Teratogenesis: An Inquiry Into the Causes of Monstrosities* (Edinburgh: Oliver and Boyd, 1897), esp. 24–46 and the bibliography given at 47–62. More recent discussions of maternal impression and its effects on children, mostly concentrating on the special case of the monstrous birth, include G.S. Rousseau, "Pineapples, Pregnancy, Pica, and *Peregrine Pickle,*" in *Tobias Smollett: Bicentennial Essays Presented to Lewis M. Knapp,* ed. G.S. Rousseau and Paul-Gabriel Boucé (New York: Oxford University Press, 1971), 79–109; Katharine Park and Lorraine J. Daston, "Unnatural Conceptions: The Study of Monsters in Sixteenth- and Seventeenth-Century France and England," *Past and Present* 92 (1981): 20–54, and the elaboration of that argument in *Wonders and the Order of Nature, 1150–1750* (New York: Zone Books; Cambridge: MIT Press, 1998); Paul-Gabriel Boucé, "Imagination, Pregnant Women, and Monsters, in Eighteenth-Century England and France," in *Sexual Underworlds of the Enlightenment,* ed. G.S. Rousseau and Roy Porter (Chapel Hill: University of North Carolina Press, 1988), 86–100; Barbara Maria Stafford, *Body Criticism: Imaging the Unseen in Enlightenment Art and Medicine* (Cambridge, MA: MIT Press, 1991), 313; Marie-Hélène Huet, *Monstrous Imagination* (Cambridge, MA: Harvard University Press, 1993); Roy Porter and Lesley Hall, "Medical Folklore in High and Low Culture: *Aristotle's Masterpiece,*" in *The Facts of Life: The Creation of Sexual Knowledge in Britain, 1650–1950,* ed. Porter and Hall (New Haven: Yale University Press, 1995), 33–53, esp. 48; Dennis Todd, *Imagining Monsters: Miscreations of the Self in Eighteenth-Century England* (Chicago: University of Chicago Press, 1995), esp. 45–48, 282–283; Valeria Finucci, "Maternal Imagination and Monstrous Birth: Tasso's *Gerusalemme liberata,*" in *Generation and Degeneration: Tropes of Reproduction in Literature and History from Antiquity Through Early Modern Europe,* ed. Valeria Finucci and Kevin Brownlee (Durham: Duke University Press, 2001), 41–77; Philip K. Wilson, "Eighteenth-Century Monsters and Nineteenth-Century 'Freaks': Reading the Maternally Marked Child," *Literature and Medicine* 21.1 (2002): 1–25;

Rachel Adams, *Sideshow U.S.A.: Freaks and the American Cultural Imagination* (Chicago: University of Chicago Press, 2001), 186–189; and Julie Crawford, *Marvellous Protestantism: Monstrous Births in Post-Reformation England* (Baltimore: Johns Hopkins University Press, 2005).

20. Valerie A. Fildes, *Breasts, Bottles, and Babies: A History of Infant Feeding* (Edinburgh: Edinburgh University Press, 1986), 189.

21. See Valerie Fildes, *Wet Nursing: A History from Antiquity to the Present* (Oxford: Basil Blackwell, 1988), 68, 88. On breastfeeding, see Nina Adriane Prytula, "'The soul stark naked': The Female Breast and the Anatomy of Character in the Eighteenth-Century Novel" (Ph.D. diss., Yale University, 2001), 15–17; Randolph Trumbach, *The Rise of the Egalitarian Family: Aristocratic Kinship and Domestic Relations in Eighteenth-Century England* (New York: Academic Press, 1978), 197–208; and Mitzi Myers, "'Servants as They are now Educated': Women Writers and Georgian Pedagogy," *Essays in Literature* 16 (1989): 51–69, esp. 56.

22. On the language of bastardy in the play, see Aaron Kitch, "Bastards and Broadsides in *The Winter's Tale,*" *Renaissance Drama* 30 (2001): 43–71.

23. Ambroise Paré, *On Monsters and Marvels* (1573), trans. Janis L. Pallister (Chicago: University of Chicago Press, 1982), 38, 54. The treatise was first published in 1573; this translation follows the text given in the posthumous 1598 edition of Paré's *Oeuvres complètes,* but also refers to the 1585 edition (see Pallister's note on the text at xxvii). For another contemporary discussion, see Michel de Montaigne, "Of the force of Imagination" (1580), in *The essays of Montaigne done into English by John Florio anno 1603,* ed. George Saintsbury, 3 vols. (London: David Nutt, 1892; New York: AMS, 1967), 1:90–102, 1:100.

24. Genesis 30:37–39, quoted from Literature Online's The Bible in English (990–1970) (subscription-only database at http://collections.chadwyck.com.bie, consulted on 15 Dec. 2003). Shylock invokes the story of Jacob and Laban's sheep as a metaphor for his own generation of money in *The Merchant of Venice,* 1.3.77–90 (first performed ca. 1598 and published in quarto in 1600).

25. Henry Bracken, *The Midwife's Companion; or, A Treatise of Midwifery* (London: J. Clarke and J. Shuckburgh, 1737), 40.

26. Nicolas Malebranche, *The Search After Truth,* trans. and ed. Thomas M. Lennon and Paul J. Olscamp (Cambridge: Cambridge University Press, 1997), 2.1.7 (117). For a late seventeenth-century translation of Malebranche, see *Father Malebranche's Treatise concerning The Search after Truth,* trans. T. Taylor (Oxford: L. Lichfield for Thomas Bennet, 1694), esp. the chapter on maternal imagination (56–63). The passage quoted above is given there in much more lively language: the theory is necessary to "explain why a Mare does not produce a Calf, and a Hen an Egg which contains a little Partridge, or some other Bird of a new *Species*" (59).

27. See for instance *Aristoteles Master-Piece; or, The Secrets of Generation displayed in all the parts thereof* (London: J. How, 1684), 25. For other instances of the argument that a child's resemblance to his or her supposed father need not prove legitimacy, see Nicolas

Venette, "Si les enfans sont bâtards ou legitimes quand ils ressemblent à leur pere ou à leur mere," *De la generation de l'homme, ou tableau de l'amour conjugal,* 7th ed. (1686; Cologne: Claude Joly, 1696), 521–549, esp. 525; and John Maubray, *The Female Physician, Containing all the Diseases incident to that Sex, in Virgins, Wives, and Widows* (London: James Holland, 1724), 64–65.

28. *Aristoteles Master-Piece,* 25. On the sources of *Aristotle's Master-Piece,* see Needham, *History of Embryology,* 92–93; and see also the references given by Boucé, "Imagination, Pregnant Women, and Monsters," 99 n. 5.

29. *Aristoteles Master-Piece,* 29.

30. A note on terminology: "In this world where like did not necessarily breed like, and where mice could be generated from wheat, there was no space for the idea of 'reproduction,'" writes Matthew Cobb. "The word literally means the copying of an individual through the process of generation, and was not used in its current sense until the second half of the eighteenth century" (*Generation: The Seventeenth-Century Scientists Who Unraveled the Secrets of Sex, Life, and Growth* [London: Bloomsbury, 2006], 10).

31. For a more detailed chronology, see the timeline in Elizabeth B. Gasking, *Investigations Into Generation, 1651–1828* (Baltimore: Johns Hopkins University Press, [1967]), 174–180; and on the interpretation of the chronology, see Jacques Roger, *The Life Sciences in Eighteenth-Century French Thought,* ed. Keith R. Benson, trans. Robert Ellrich (1963, rev. ed. 1993; Stanford: Stanford University Press, 1997), 369.

32. Quoted in Needham, *History of Embryology,* 170.

33. Clara Pinto-Correia, *The Ovary of Eve: Egg and Sperm and Preformation* (Chicago: University of Chicago Press, 1997), 10.

34. Cole, *Early Theories,* provides a translation of the letter in its entirety (9–12; the quotation is on 11); for the original Latin text, see "*Observationes D.* Anthonii Lewenhoeck, *de Natis è semine genitali Animalculis,*" in *Philosophical Transactions of the Royal Society* 12.142 (1677): 1040–1046.

35. See Gasking, *Investigations Into Generation,* 136. For a more detailed account of Spallanzani and his experiments, see Pinto-Correia's chapter "Frogs with Boxer Shorts," *Ovary of Eve,* 183–210; and Abbé Spallanzani, *An Essay on Animal Reproductions,* [trans. M. Maty] (London: T. Becket and P. A. De Hondt, 1766), 43.

36. John Mason Good, *The Nature of Things: A Didactic Poem,* 2 vols. (London: Longman et al., 1805), 2:196–199, esp. 2:197. I owe this reference to Cole, *Early Theories,* 122.

37. On the problems posed by resemblance and by the existence of hybrids for the theory of preformation, see especially Roger, *Life Sciences,* 308–312.

38. Gasking, *Investigations Into Generation,* 107.

39. Pinto-Correia, *Ovary of Eve,* 4. For another imaginative account of embryology in relation to the culture and politics of the late seventeenth century, see Eve Keller, "Embryonic Individuals: The Rhetoric of Seventeenth-Century Embryology and the Construction of Early-Modern Identity," *Eighteenth-Century Studies* 33.3 (2000): 321–348.

40. Ruth Perry, *Novel Relations: The Transformation of Kinship in English Literature and Culture, 1748–1818* (Cambridge: Cambridge University Press, 2004), esp. 40–41. And on the relationship between preformation and political theories of individualism, see Karen Newman, *Fetal Positions: Individualism, Science, Visuality* (Stanford: Stanford University Press, 1996), 66. Perhaps most striking is the tension between increasingly ideologically freighted and often conceptually incompatible systems; for an interesting discussion of Welsh farmers' "almost blind faith in sire lines" during exactly this period, see R.J. Moore-Colyer, "Horses and Equine Improvement in the Economy of Modern Wales," *Agricultural History Review* 39.2 (1991): 126–142, phrase above on 132.

41. For a comparable contemporary use of grafting, see the exchange in John Webster, *The Duchess of Malfi* (performed ca. 1614, published in 1623), ed. Brian Gibbons, 4th ed. (1964; London: Black; New York: Norton, 2001), 2.1.148–151.

42. Edward William Tayler, *Nature and Art in Renaissance Literature* (New York: Columbia University Press, 1964), 21–22, 30, 134–138; the quotation is on 136. For an important recent discussion of the social implications of grafting, including a discussion of this passage in *The Winter's Tale,* see Rebecca Bushnell, *Green Desire: Imagining Early Modern English Gardens* (Ithaca: Cornell University Press, 2003), 132–160, esp. 148–149.

43. On this topic, see Frances Dolan, "Taking the Pencil out of God's Hand: Art, Nature, and the Face-Painting Debate in Early Modern England," *PMLA* 108 (1993): 224–239, esp. 227–228.

44. Older discussions of Shakespeare's use of horticultural material include the following: Joseph Hunter, *New Illustrations of the Life, Studies, and Writings of Shakespeare,* 2 vols. (London: J.B. Nichols, 1845), 1:421–422; Henry N. Ellacombe, *The Plant-Lore and Garden-Craft of Shakespeare,* 2nd ed. (London: W. Satchell and Co., 1884), 353–354; Horace Howard Furness, ed., *A New Variorum Edition of Shakespeare: The Winter's Tale,* 6th ed. (New York: J.B. Lippincott, 1889; New York: Dover, 1964), 189–192; R.E. Prothero, "Agriculture and Gardening," in *Shakespeare's England: An Account of the Life and Manners of His Age* (1916; Oxford: Clarendon, 1962), 1:346–380; Esther Singleton, *The Shakespeare Garden* (New York: William Farquhar Payson, 1931), x–xi and 181–189; Sir Arthur Quiller-Couch and John Dover Wilson, eds., *The Winter's Tale* (Cambridge: Cambridge University Press, 1931), 167–168; and J.H.P. Pafford, ed., *The Winter's Tale* (1963; London: Arden Shakespeare, 2001), 93–94n and 169–170.

45. *The Tempest* (staged in 1611, published in 1623), 4.1.188–189; and see also the discussion of this play and *The Winter's Tale* in Leo Marx, *The Machine in the Garden: Technology and the Pastoral Ideal in America* (1964; New York: Oxford University Press, 2000), 54–67.

46. Bushnell, *Green Desire,* 137; and see also the more extended discussion in Bushnell, *A Culture of Teaching: Early Modern Humanism in Theory and Practice* (Ithaca: Cornell University Press, 1996), 73–116, esp. 107–108.

47. William Lawson, *A New Orchard and Garden* (London: Alsop, 1618; New York: Garland, 1982), 27–28; the volume also contains John Marriott's *Knots for Gardens* (1625)

and Ralph Austen's *A Treatise of Fruit-Trees Together with the Spirituall Use of an Orchard* (1653).

48. Michael Pollan, *The Botany of Desire: A Plant's-Eye View of the World* (2001; New York: Random House, 2002), 10; and on the domestication of plants more generally, see Jared Diamond, *Guns, Germs, and Steel: The Fates of Human Societies* (1997; New York: Norton, 1999), 114–156.

49. Elizabeth A. Clark, "Generation, Degeneration, Regeneration: Original Sin and the Conception of Jesus in the Polemic Between Augustine and Julian of Eclanum," in *Generation and Degeneration,* ed. Finucci and Brownlee, 17–40; the quotation is on 22. In Romans 11:17–24, Paul envisions Gentiles grafted into the original (Jewish) olive trees; see Clark, "Generation," 22 n. 20.

50. Jane Sharp, *The Midwives Book; or, The Whole Art of Midwifry Discovered. Directing Childbearing Women how to behave themselves In their Conception, Breeding, Bearing, and Nursing of Children* (London: Simon Miller, 1671), 120, 122.

51. Sharp, *Midwives Book,* 123–124.

52. Vol. 4 of *The Plays of William Shakspeare. In ten volumes. With the corrections and illustrations of various commentators; to which are added notes by Samuel Johnson and George Steevens. The second edition, revised and augmented* (London: C. Bathurst et al., 1778), 377.

53. See Charles Marsh, *The Winter's Tale, a Play. Alter'd from* SHAKESPEAR (London: Charles Marsh, 1756), 33–34. There are no documented performances of this adaptation, and it resembles a reading version more than a play text. Morgan keeps Perdita's lines on "nature's bastards" but skips directly from 4.4.84 to 4.4.103 (I follow the line numbering of the Riverside edition), leaving out the core of the debate between Perdita and Polixenes; Garrick goes even further, skipping directly from 4.4.79 to 4.4.103, so that the entire exchange is missing: [Macnamara Morgan], *The Sheep-Shearing; or, Florizel and Perdita. A Pastoral Comedy Taken from Shakespear* (London: J. Truman, 1762; London: Cornmarket, 1969), 12; David Garrick, *Florizel and Perdita: A Dramatic Pastoral in Three Acts. Alter'd from The Winter's Tale of Shakespear* (London: J. and R. Tonson, 1758; London: Cornmarket, 1969), 21. Subsequent references are to these editions and are given parenthetically in the text.

54. See Maurice Hunt, "The Critical Legacy," introduction to *The Winter's Tale: Critical Essays* (New York: Garland, 1995), 3–61, esp. 7; and Dennis Bartholomeusz, *The Winter's Tale in Performance in England and America, 1611–1976* (Cambridge: Cambridge University Press, 1982), 45, 134–135, 168, 195. For Kemble's adaptation, see the facsimile edition of *Shakespeare's Winter's Tale; A Play; Adapted to the Stage by J. P. Kemble; and Now First Published as it is Acted at The Theatre Royal in Covent Garden* (London, 1811), 50–51, as given in vol. 9 of *John Philip Kemble Promptbooks,* 11 vols., ed. Charles H. Shattuck (Charlottesville: University Press of Virginia, 1974).

55. Harold Wilson, "'Nature and Art' in *Winter's Tale* IV.iv.86ff," *Shakespeare Association Bulletin* 18.3 (1943): 114–120.

56. See for instance F.C. Tinkler, "*The Winter's Tale*," *Scrutiny* 5.4 (March 1937): 344–364; and E.M. Tillyard, *Shakespeare's Last Plays* (London: Chatto and Windus, 1938).

57. S.L. Bethell, *The Winter's Tale: A Study* (London: Staples, [1947]), 27, 93–94; G. Wilson Knight, "'Great Creating Nature': An Essay on *The Winter's Tale*," in *The Crown of Life* (London: Oxford University Press, 1947), 76–128, esp. 104–105; F. David Hoeniger, "The Meaning of *The Winter's Tale*," in *University of Toronto Quarterly* 20.1 (1950): 11–26; and Northrop Frye, "Recognition in *The Winter's Tale*," in *Essays on Shakespeare and Elizabethan Drama in Honor of Hardin Craig*, ed. Richard Hosley (Columbia: University of Missouri Press, 1962), 235–246, esp. 240–242.

58. See H.F. Roberts, *Plant Hybridization Before Mendel* (Princeton: Princeton University Press, 1929); and Conway Zirkle, *The Beginnings of Plant Hybridization* (Philadelphia: University of Pennsylvania Press, 1935).

59. [George Colman], *The Sheep-Shearing: A Dramatic Pastoral in Three Acts. Taken from Shakespeare. As it is performed at the Theatre Royal in the Haymarket* (London: G. Kearsly, 1777). Full references for Morgan and Garrick are given in note 53. On dates and adaptations, see Michael Dobson, *The Making of the National Poet: Shakespeare, Adaptation, and Authorship, 1660–1769* (Oxford: Clarendon, 1992), 188; and for a more general discussion of eighteenth-century attitudes toward Shakespeare, see also Jonathan Brody Kramnick, *Making the English Canon: Print-Capitalism and the Cultural Past, 1700–1770* (Cambridge: Cambridge University Press, 1998), esp. 107–136.

60. Bartholomeusz, *The Winter's Tale in Performance*, 31.

61. Dobson, *Making of the National Poet*, 190, 192. On Garrick's alterations to the original, and on the responses of his contemporaries, see *Garrick's Adaptations of Shakespeare, 1744–1756*, ed. Harry William Pedicord and Fredrick Louis Berhmann (Carbondale: Southern Illinois University Press, 1981), 431–435.

62. On Perdita's likeness to Hermione, though, see for instance 5.1.225–227 and 5.2.30–39.

63. See Nancy Tuana, "The Weaker Seed: The Sexist Bias of Reproductive Theory," in *Feminism and Science*, ed. Nancy Tuana (Bloomington: Indiana University Press, 1989), 147–171. Galen's views were more hospitable than Aristotle's to the consideration of female influence on forms, and several passages in *The Faerie Queene* seem to attribute a forming capacity to the female partner (Venus, in this case); see Edmund Spenser, *The Faerie Queene*, ed. A.C. Hamilton (Harlow: Pearson, 2001), book 3, canto 6, stanzas 9, 12, and 46–47. The Spenser passage receives brief discussion in C.S. Lewis, *Spenser's Images of Life*, ed. Alastair Fowler (Cambridge: Cambridge University Press, 1967), 53; Humphrey Tonkin, "Spenser's Garden of Adonis and Britomart's Quest," *PMLA* 88.3 (1973): 408–417, 409; and Pamela Joseph Benson, *The Invention of the Renaissance Woman: The Challenge of Female Independence in the Literature and Thought of Italy and England* (University Park: Pennsylvania State University Press, 1992), 254. Thanks to Blair Hoxby for the Spenser reference and to Matt Zarnowiecki for helping me to unravel it.

64. Ivan Lupić points me to Shakespeare's sonnet 3, especially lines 9–10: "Thou art thy *mother*'s glass, and she in thee / Calls back the lovely April of her prime" (emphasis

added). Other instances of authors pointing out either a son's or a daughter's resemblance to the mother abound, but in this case as in many others the word "glass" is primarily a descriptive rather than an explanatory metaphor, whereas the notion of "printing" a child off a parent seems significantly closer to offering not simply an analogy but an account of how the resemblance might have been achieved. An excellent discussion of the significance of such metaphors can be found in Ann Thompson and John O. Thompson, "Meaning, 'Seeing', Printing," in *Printing and Parenting in Early Modern England,* ed. Brooks, 59–86, esp. 70–73.

65. See also the discussion in de Grazia, "Imprints," esp. 34–36.

66. Perry, *Novel Relations,* 2, 8; and see also Christopher Flint, *Family Fictions: Narrative and Domestic Relations in Britain, 1688–1798* (Stanford: Stanford University Press, 1998), 1–22, 249–252. For James Boswell's active defense of primogeniture and female disinheritance (against his father's "predilection for heirs general, that is, males and females indiscriminately"), see *Boswell's Life of Johnson,* ed. George Birkbeck Hill, rev. L. F. Powell, 6 vols. (Oxford: Clarendon, 1934–1964), 2:414ff.

67. Raymond Williams, *The Country and the City* (1973; New York: Oxford University Press, 1975) remains an excellent introduction to the literary and cultural consequences of the enclosure movement and other social transformations. For further treatment of changing notions of inheritance (legal and otherwise) in Britain, see the essays in *Family and Inheritance: Rural Society in Western Europe, 1200–1800,* ed. Jack Goody, Joan Thirsk, and E. P. Thompson (Cambridge: Cambridge University Press, 1976); Susan Staves, *Married Women's Separate Property in England, 1660–1833* (Cambridge, MA: Harvard University Press, 1990); and the essays in *Early Modern Conceptions of Property,* ed. John Brewer and Susan Staves (London: Routledge, 1996).

68. See, for instance, Georges Louis Leclerc, Count de Buffon, *Natural History, General and Particular,* 9 vols., trans. William Smellie, intro. Aaron V. Garrett (London: A. Strahan and T. Cadell, 1791; Bristol: Thoemmes, 2000), 2:59ff; and Pierre-Louis Moreau de Maupertuis, *The Earthly Venus,* trans. Simone Brangier Boas, intro. George Boas (New York: Johnson Reprint Corporation, 1966), 1.12.41 (the numbers refer to part, chapter, page number). Subsequent references are to this edition and will be given parenthetically in the text.

69. It is very likely that Garrick knew the rough outlines of Buffon's celebrated theories, whether or not he had himself read the Natural History. Prints from Buffon's *Natural History* were catalogued in Garrick's collections, and he had a taste for natural history; George Winchester Stone Jr. and George M. Kahrl, *David Garrick: A Critical Biography* (Carbondale: Southern Illinois University Press; London: Fetter and Simons, Inc., 1979), 456.

70. On the resemblance motif, see Susan C. Greenfield, *Mothering Daughters: Novels and the Politics of Family Romance, Frances Burney to Jane Austen* (Detroit: Wayne State University Press, 2002), 35–56, esp. 51–56; and Perry, *Novel Relations,* 77–78. Male protagonists can also be likened to their mothers, with interesting consequences for gender and masculinity; see Jill Campbell, "'The Exact Picture of his Mother': Recognizing Joseph Andrews," *ELH* 55 (1988): 643–664, esp. 654–656.

71. Fanny [Frances] Burney, *Evelina; or, The History of a Young Lady's Entrance Into the World* (1778), ed. Edward A. Bloom with Lillian D. Bloom (1968; Oxford: Oxford University Press, 1984), 3.17 (372–374).

72. Burney, *Evelina*, 3.18 (377).

73. Elizabeth Inchbald, *A Simple Story* (1791), ed. Pamela Clemit (London: Penguin, 1996), 3.6 (207). It is possible that the word *moulds* invokes Buffon's controversial but influential suggestion that reproduction worked by a mechanism of *moules intérieures,* or interior molds; on this theory of Buffon's, see Jacques Roger, *Buffon: A Life in Natural History* (1989), trans. Sarah Lucille Bonnefoi, ed. L. Pearce Williams (Ithaca: Cornell University Press, 1997), 129–131, 133–134.

74. The play resonated in all sorts of other ways also: on the relationship between the Prince Regent and Mary "Perdita" Robinson, and the widespread use of the names "Florizel" and "Perdita" to describe the pair (the Prince first saw Robinson as she performed the role), see Paula Byrne, "A Maniac for Perdita," *TLS,* 6 Aug. 2004, 11–12; and on the appeal of the Florizel-Perdita motif to contemporary caricaturists, see Jonathan Bate, *Shakespearean Constitutions: Politics, Theatre, Criticism, 1730–1830* (Oxford: Clarendon, 1989), 75.

75. Darwin's reading list for 1840 is quoted in Gillian Beer, *Darwin's Plots: Evolutionary Narrative in Darwin, George Eliot, and Nineteenth-Century Fiction,* 2nd ed. (1983; Cambridge: Cambridge University Press, 2000), 27; and see also the discussion of Darwin's reading of Montaigne and Shakespeare in Beer, "Darwin's Reading and the Fictions of Development," in *The Darwinian Heritage,* ed. David Kohn with Malcolm J. Kottler (Princeton: Princeton University Press, 1985), 543–588, esp. 551–552, 587.

76. Gasking, *Investigations Into Generation,* 164. On the relative lack of exchange between breeders and scientists (and on Darwin's ability to bridge the gap), see James A. Secord, "Darwin and the Breeders: A Social History," in *Darwinian Heritage,* ed. Kohn, 519–542, esp. 522; and Secord's delightful article "Nature's Fancy: Charles Darwin and the Breeding of Pigeons," *Isis* 72.2 (1981): 162–186.

77. See the long chapter on pangenesis in Charles Darwin, vol. 2 of *The Variation of Animals and Plants Under Domestication* (1868), 2nd ed., intro. Harriet Ritvo (New York: D. Appleton and Co., 1883; Baltimore: Johns Hopkins University Press, 1998), 349–399; the quotation is on 350.

78. L. C. Dunn, *A Short History of Genetics: The Development of Some of the Main Lines of Thought, 1864–1939* (1965; Ames: Iowa State University Press, 1991), 215.

79. August Weismann, "On the Supposed Transmission of Mutilations" (1888), in *Essays Upon Heredity and Kindred Biological Problems,* trans. and ed. Edward B. Poulton et al. (Oxford: Clarendon, 1889), 419–448. On the continued sway of Lamarckian theory in France post-Weismann and post-Mendel, see William Schneider, "Toward the Improvement of the Human Race: The History of Eugenics in France," *Journal of Modern History* 54.2 (1982): 268–291, esp. 271–274. There is no place here for an extended treatment of the topic, but for a particularly lovely early instance of the argument that mutilations may be passed on to offspring, see Nathaniel Highmore, *The History of Generation* (London:

R.N., 1651), 31–32. John Ray also suggests that "indeed every part of the Body seems to club and contribute to the Seed, else why should Parents that are born Blind or Deaf, or that want a Finger or any other Part, or have one superfluous, sometimes generate Children that have the same defects or imperfections," in John Ray, *The Wisdom of God Manifested in the Works of the Creation* (London: Samuel Smith, 1691), 218. Weismann was not the first to refute the idea, of course; see for instance James Cowles Prichard, *Researches Into the Physical History of Man* (1813; Chicago: University of Chicago Press, 1973), 199.

80. Weismann, "Supposed Transmission of Mutilations," 434; the results of the mouse experiment are on 431–434.

## 2. Bent

1. Steven Pinker, *The Blank Slate: The Modern Denial of Human Nature* (New York: Viking, 2002), 372.

2. Roger Shattuck, *The Forbidden Experiment: The Story of the Wild Boy of Aveyron* (New York: Farrar Straus Giroux, 1980), 58; and see also Ullica Segerstråle, *Defenders of the Truth: The Battle for Science in the Sociobiology Debate and Beyond* (Oxford: Oxford University Press, 2000).

3. See, for instance, Steven Pinker, *The Language Instinct* (New York: Morrow, 1994), 407–408.

4. See, for instance, the very different account in Paul R. Ehrlich, *Human Natures: Genes, Cultures, and the Human Prospect* (Washington, DC, and Covelo, CA: Island Press/Shearwater Books, 2000).

5. John Locke, *Some Thoughts Concerning Education* (1693), ed. John W. Yolton and Jean S. Yolton (Oxford: Clarendon, 1989), 265, 122.

6. John Lawson, *Lectures Concerning Oratory. Delivered in Trinity College, Dublin* (Dublin: George Faulkner, 1758; Menston: Scolar, 1969), 10.

7. *Boswell's Life of Johnson*, ed. George Birkbeck Hill, rev. L. F. Powell, 6 vols. (Oxford: Clarendon, 1934–1964), 2:436.

8. For a perceptive critique of Pinker's "relentless parodying of the Blank Slate," see H. Allen Orr, "Darwinian Storytelling," *New York Review of Books,* 27 Feb. 2003, 17–20. Pinker's response to Orr (and Orr's response to the response) appeared in the issue of 1 May 2003 (pp. 48–49); for a relevant earlier exchange in the letters column of the *NYRB,* between Pinker and Stephen Jay Gould, see the issue of 9 Oct. 1997 (pp. 55–58). On what eighteenth-century writing on perfectibility shows us about Pinker and the nature-nurture debates, see also Michael E. Winston, *From Perfectibility to Perversion: Meliorism in Eighteenth-Century France* (New York: Lang, 2005), vii, 20–21.

9. Adam Kuper, *The Chosen Primate: Human Nature and Cultural Diversity* (Cambridge, MA: Harvard University Press, 1994), 17; and see also, for instance, Jonathan Harwood,

"Heredity, Environment, and the Legitimation of Social Policy," in *Natural Order: Historical Studies of Scientific Culture,* ed. Barry Barnes and Steven Shapin (Beverly Hills: Sage Publications, 1979), 231–248.

10. Jonah Lehrer, *Proust Was a Neuroscientist* (Boston: Houghton Mifflin, 2007), 191–192.

11. John Locke, *An Essay Concerning Human Understanding* (1690; 4th ed., 1700), ed. Peter H. Nidditch (Oxford: Oxford University Press, 1975), 1.3.67. All references are to this edition and will be given parenthetically in the text by volume, chapter, and page number.

12. The emphasis on experience leads to a kind of cultural relativism: "Had you or I been born at the Bay of *Soldania,* possibly our Thoughts, and Notions, had not exceeded those brutish ones of the *Hotentots* that inhabit there: And had the *Virginia* King *Apochancana,* been educated in *England,* he had, perhaps, been as knowing a Divine, and as good a Mathematician, as any in it. The difference between him, and a more improved *English-* man, lying barely in this, That the exercise of his Faculties was bounded within the Ways, Modes, and Notions of his own Country" (1.4.92).

13. [Anon.], *The Bird-Fancier's Delight* (London: Thomas Ward, 1714), 33; [Anon.], *A New Treatise of Canary-Birds. Containing The manner of Breeding and Coupling them, that they may have Beautiful Young Ones. With Curious Remarks relating to the Signs and Causes of their Distempers, and the Method of Curing Them. Written in French by Mr. Hervieux, and Translated into English* (London: Bernard Lintot, 1718), 50.

14. Erving Goffman, *The Presentation of Self in Everyday Life* (Garden City, NY: Doubleday, 1959).

15. This language is used by Locke's contemporaries as well, and should certainly not be attributed to him alone. Timothy Nourse, for instance, alludes to "the Bent and Genius" of a particular person and suggests that a person drawn to a particular vice may be tempted to its opposite, which "by drawing him to the contrary side, 'tis probable he may stay at the Golden Mean, like a crooked Stick which is made much more easy to stand streight, by being bent as much the other way"; Tim. Nourse, Gent., *A Discourse Upon the Nature and Faculties of Man, in Several Essayes* (London: Jacob Tonson, 1686), 33–34.

16. Tatha Wiley, *Original Sin: Origins, Developments, Contemporary Meanings* (New York: Paulist Press, 2002), 65.

17. S. Trooster, S.J., *Evolution and the Doctrine of Original Sin,* trans. John A. Ter Haar (Glen Rock, NJ: Newman Press, 1968), 12–13.

18. Henri Rondet, S.J., *Original Sin: The Patristic and Theological Background,* trans. Cajetan Finegan, O.P. (Shannon: Ecclesia Press, 1972), 141.

19. John Passmore, *The Perfectibility of Man* (London: Duckworth, 1970), 149. No single book I have discovered in the last ten years has produced in me such a strong feeling of outrage at not having known it sooner, and I commend to the reader's attention the recent Liberty Press reissue of what is surely one of the twentieth century's great works of scholarship in the humanities.

20. Passmore, *Perfectibility of Man,* 163–164.

21. Andrew Biswell, *The Real Life of Anthony Burgess* (London: Picador, 2005), 127.

22. W.M. Spellman, "Locke and the Latitudinarian Perspective on Original Sin," *Revue Internationale de Philosophie* 42:2 (1988): 215–228; the quotation is on 216.

23. W.M. Spellman, *John Locke and the Problem of Depravity* (Oxford: Clarendon, 1988), 124.

24. John Marshall, *John Locke: Resistance, Religion, and Responsibility* (Cambridge: Cambridge University Press, 1994), 27, 345–346. See also 135, 388, 414–415, 432, and the critique of Spellman's argument at 397 n. 24: "Socinians and Pelagians did not deny that men were extremely sinful in practice; they disagreed about its genesis and whether it was essential to men."

25. Victor Hilts, "Enlightenment Views on the Genetic Perfectibility of Man," in *Transformation and Tradition in the Sciences: Essays in Honor of I. Bernard Cohen,* ed. Everett Mendelsohn (Cambridge: Cambridge University Press, 1984), 255–271; the quotation is on 267–268. This rich and fascinating essay served as my initial guide to eighteenth-century eugenic thought.

26. Timothy Nourse, *Campania Fœlix; or, A Discourse of the Benefits and Improvements of Husbandry* (London: Tho. Bennet, 1700; New York: Garland, 1982), 2. Subsequent references are to this edition and will be given parenthetically in the text.

27. Nourse, *Campania,* 203–204. On the popular call for the government to counter the threat of luxury by means of stringent sumptuary laws, see John Sekora, *Luxury: The Concept in Western Thought, Eden to Smollett* (Baltimore: Johns Hopkins University Press, 1977), 51–62.

28. Nourse, *Campania,* 203–204.

29. See for instance W.D., *Æsop's Fables, With their Morals: In Prose and Verse,* 16th ed. (ca. 1650; London: J. Phillips et al., 1706), 79; Francis Barlow, *Æsop's Fables with his Life: In English, French and Latin* (1666; London: H. Hills, 1687), 143; Sir Roger L'Estrange, *Fables, of Æsop And other Eminent Mythologists: With Morals and Reflexions* (London: R. Sare et al., 1692), 60–61; and [John Toland, trans.], *The Fables of Æsop. With the Moral Reflexions of Monsieur Baudoin* (London: Tho. Leigh and Dan. Midwinter, 1704), 374–375. On the use of the form of the fable by seventeenth-century British political writers, see Annabel Patterson, *Fables of Power: Aesopian Writing and Political History* (Durham: Duke University Press, 1991), esp. 52–54.

30. Sir Francis Bacon, "Of Nature in Men," in *The Essayes or Counsels, Civill and Morall,* ed. Michael Kiernan (1995; Oxford: Clarendon, 2000), 118–120.

31. *The Concise Oxford Dictionary of Proverbs,* 2nd ed., ed. John Simpson and Jennifer Speake (Oxford: Oxford University Press, 1992), 104. The textual sources for the proverb date only as far back as the nineteenth century, but the concept was current in the early modern period.

# 3. Cultures of Improvement

1. Eve Kosofsky Sedgwick, *Epistemology of the Closet* (Berkeley: University of California Press, 1990), 41.

2. John Dryden, trans., *Virgil's Georgics* (1697), in vol. 5 of *The Works of John Dryden*, ed. William Frost and Vinton A. Dearing (Berkeley: University of California Press, 1987), 137. Subsequent references are to this edition and will be given parenthetically in the notes by book and line number.

3. Addison, "An Essay on the Georgics," in vol. 5 of *The Works of John Dryden*, ed. William Frost and Vinton A. Dearing, 145–153; the quotation is on 146.

4. Kurt Heinzelman, "Roman Georgic in the Georgian Age: A Theory of Romantic Genre," in *Texas Studies in Literature and Language* 33.2 (1991): 182–214; the quotation is on 187.

5. The observation is in vol. 6 of *The Works of John Dryden*, ed. William Frost, Vinton A. Dearing, and Alan Roper (Berkeley: University of California Press, 1987), 887; the editors estimate that Dryden's translation contains 44 percent more lines than Virgil's original (p. 882) and that twenty-four editions had appeared by the end of the eighteenth century, with fifty or more published in the nineteenth (p. 886). A particularly nice example of Dryden's elaboration of a metaphor not found in Virgil's poem can be found at 3.259–278, which describes the calf "Set . . . betimes to School" (p. 930). The Latin text is from the Loeb Classical Library's edition; Virgil, *Eclogues, Georgics, Aeneid I–VI,* trans. H. Rushton Fairclough, rev. G. P. Goold (Cambridge, MA: Harvard University Press, 1999).

6. *Georgics* 1.91–95; "continuo has leges aeternaque foedera certis/imposuit natura locis, quo tempore primum/Deucalion vacuum lapides iactavit in orbem,/unde homines nati, durum genus" (1.60–64).

7. *Georgics* 1.288–289; "sic omnia fatis/in peius ruere ac retro sublapsa referri" (1.199–200).

8. *Georgics* 2.580–583; "iam vinctae vites, iam falcem arbusta reponunt,/iam canit effectos extremus vinitor antes:/sollicitanda tamen tellus pulvisque movendus,/et iam maturis metuendus Iuppiter uvis" (2.416–419).

9. *Georgics* 2.45–50; "Quare agite o proprios generatim discite cultus,/agricolae, fructusque feros mollite colendo,/neu segnes iaceant terrae" (2.35–37).

10. *Georgics* 2.71–74; "tamen haec quoque, si quis/inserat aut scrobibus mandet mutata subactis,/exuerint silvestrem animum, cultuque frequenti/in quascumque voles artes haud tarda sequentur" (2.49–52).

11. John Dryden, *The State of Innocence, and Fall of Man* (1677), in vol. 12 of *The Works of John Dryden*, ed. Vinton A. Dearing (Berkeley: University of California Press, 1994), 110.

12. *Georgics* 2.323–236; "salsa autem tellus et quae perhibetur amara/(frugibus infelix ea, nec mansuescit arando/nec Baccho genus aut pomis sua nomina servat)" (2.238–240).

13. *Georgics* 3.204–205 ("ne blando nequeat superesse labori/invalidique patrum referant ieiunia nati" [3.127–128]); 3.420, 439–441 ("et saepe sine ullis/coniugiis vento gravidae

(mirabile dictu) . . ./hippomanes vero quod nomine dicunt/pastores, lentum destillat ab inguine virus" [3.274–275, 280–281]).

14. *Georgics* 3.598 ("reice, ne maculis infuscet vellera pullis/nascentum" [3.389–390]); 3.712–715 ("serpant contagia vulgus" [3.469]; "nec singula morbi/corpora corripuint, sed tota aestiva repente,/spemque gregemque simul cunctamque ab origine gentem" [3.471–473]).

15. *Georgics* 4.435–442; "interea teneris tepefactus in ossibus umor/aestuat, et visenda modis animalia miris,/trunca pedum primo, mox et stridentia pinnis,/miscentur, tenuemque magis magis aëra carpunt,/donec ut aestivis effusus nubibus imber/erupere" (4.308–313).

16. *Georgics* 4.807–810; "Haec super arvorum cultu pecorumque canebam/et super arboribus, Caesar dum magnus ad altum/fulminat Euphraten bello" (4.559–561).

17. *Georgics* 2.641–642; 2.715–716 ("quos rami fructus, quos ipsa volentia rura/sponte tulere sua, carpsit" [2.500–501]).

18. *Georgics* 2.688–691; "rura mihi et rigui placeant in vallibus amnes,/flumina amem silvasque inglorius" (2.485–486).

19. *Georgics* 2.777, 780; Virgil gives simply "veteres" (2.532).

20. [Walter Harte], *Essays on Husbandry* (Bath: W. Frederick; London: J. Hinton et al., 1764), 6.

21. [Jethro Tull], *The New Horse-Houghing Husbandry; or, An Essay on the Principles of Tillage and Vegetation* (London, 1731), xi, and see also xiii, xvi, 115–116.

22. Anthony Low, *The Georgic Revolution* (Princeton: Princeton University Press, 1985), 12. It is not within my scope to address Low's arguments about English history and poetic form, but for a thoughtful critique, see Alastair Fowler, "Georgic and Pastoral: Laws of Genre in the Seventeenth Century," in *Culture and Cultivation in Early Modern England: Writing and the Land,* ed. Michael Leslie and Timothy Raylor (Leicester: Leicester University Press, 1992), 81–88; and Rachel Crawford, "English Georgic and British Nationhood," *ELH* 65.1 (1998): 123–158.

23. Rachel Crawford, *Poetry, Enclosure, and the Vernacular Landscape, 1700–1830* (Cambridge: Cambridge University Press, 2002), 99. On the georgic mode in eighteenth-century writing more generally, see especially Clifford Siskin, *The Work of Writing: Literature and Social Change in Britain, 1700–1830* (Baltimore: Johns Hopkins University Press, 1998), 118–124; two important articles by Frans De Bruyn, "The Classical Silva and the Generic Development of Scientific Writing in Seventeenth-Century England," *New Literary History* 32 (2001): 347–373, and "Reading Virgil's *Georgics* as a Scientific Text: The Eighteenth-Century Debate Between Jethro Tull and Stephen Switzer," *ELH* 71 (2004): 661–689; and a trio of pieces by Kevis Goodman: her review of Siskin in *Modern Language Quarterly* 61.3 (2000): 545–551; an article on Virgil and Milton, "'Wasted Labor'? Milton's Eve, the Poet's Work, and the Challenge of Sympathy," *ELH* 64.2 (1997): 415–446; and the book-length development of her complex thesis about modernity and the georgic mode, *Georgic Modernity and British Romanticism: Poetry and the Mediation of History* (Cambridge: Cambridge University Press, 2004), 1–16.

24. John Locke, *Some Thoughts Concerning Education*, ed. John W. Yolton and Jean S. Yolton (Oxford: Clarendon, 1989), 122.

25. On georgic across genres, see John Chalker, *The English Georgic: A Study in the Development of a Form* (Baltimore: Johns Hopkins University Press, 1969), 12–13; and Richard Feingold, *Nature and Society: Later Eighteenth-Century Uses of the Pastoral and Georgic* (New Brunswick, NJ: Rutgers University Press, 1978).

26. Letter of 16 Aug. 1764, given in *The Autobiography of Arthur Young, with Selections from his Correspondence*, ed. M. Betham-Edwards (London: Smith, Elder and Co., 1898), 34.

27. Harte, *Essays on Husbandry*, 36–37.

28. Edward Lisle, *Observations in Husbandry* (London: J. Hughs, 1757), xi; [Henry Home, Lord Kames], *The Gentleman Farmer. Being an Attempt to improve Agriculture, By Subjecting it to the Test of Rational Principles* (Edinburgh: W. Creech; London: T. Cadell, 1776), xv; *Autobiography of Arthur Young*, 131, 217–218. Elizabeth Heckendorn Cook offers a rich reading of later eighteenth-century georgic writing in "Crown Forests and Female Georgic: Frances Burney and the Reconstruction of Britishness," in *The Country and the City Revisited: England and the Politics of Culture, 1550–1850*, ed. Gerald MacLean et al. (Cambridge: Cambridge University Press, 1999), 197–212.

29. All citations are to Daniel Defoe, *Robinson Crusoe* (1719), ed. Michael Shinagel, 2nd ed. (New York: Norton, 1994), and will be given parenthetically in the text.

30. Jean-Jacques Rousseau, *Émile* (1762), trans. Barbara Foxley, intro. P.D. Jimack (London: J.M. Dent; North Clarendon, VT: Tuttle, 1993), 176. Subsequent references are to this edition and will be given parenthetically in the text.

31. Arthur Young, vol. 2 of *Annals of Agriculture, and Other Useful Arts* (London: for the editor, 1784), 132.

32. The information here is drawn from the editor's introduction to [Daniel Defoe], *Mere Nature Delineated; or, A Body without a Soul* (1726), in vol. 5 of *Writings on Travel, Discovery, and History by Daniel Defoe*, ed. Andrew Wear (London: Pickering and Chatto, 2002); the quotation is from the *St. James's Evening Post* of 14 Dec. 1725, as given on p. 17. All quotations are to this edition and will be given parenthetically in the text. The attribution to Defoe has been questioned, but most recent critics seem to accept it. Richard Nash offers a useful discussion of this and other issues in *Wild Enlightenment: The Borders of Human Identity in the Eighteenth Century* (Charlottesville: University of Virginia Press, 2003), 67ff., 192 n. 2; and Michael Newton gives an excellent account of Peter of Hanover in *Savage Girls and Wild Boys: A History of Feral Children* (New York: St. Martin's/Thomas Dunne, 2002), 16–72.

33. On feral children and the Enlightenment, see especially Harlan Lane, *The Wild Boy of Aveyron* (Cambridge, MA: Harvard University Press, 1976), 19; and, for more general discussions, H.W. Janson, *Apes and Ape Lore in the Middle Ages and the Renaissance* (London: Warburg Institute, 1952; Nendeln: Kraus Reprint, 1976), 327–354; Roger Bartra, *The Artificial Savage: Modern Myths of the Wild Man*, trans. Christopher Follett (Ann Arbor: University of Michigan Press, 1997); the essays (described by the editors as a sort of

sequel to Lovejoy and Boas's first volume on primitivism) in *The Wild Man Within: An Image in Western Thought from the Renaissance to Romanticism,* ed. Edward Dudley and Maximillian E. Novak (Pittsburgh: University of Pittsburgh Press, 1972); and Clarence J. Glacken, *Traces on the Rhodian Shore: Nature and Culture in Western Thought from Ancient Times to the End of the Eighteenth Century* (1967; Berkeley: University of California Press, 1976).

34. The Reverend J.A.L. Singh and Professor Robert M. Zingg, *Wolf-Children and Feral Man* (New York: Harper and Brothers, 1942), xxvii.

35. Singh and Zingg, *Wolf-Children and Feral Man,* 178.

36. The anthropologist Lucien Malson, for instance, begins his investigation of human nature (published in French in 1964, and in English translation in 1972) with the statement that "[t]he idea that man has no nature is now beyond dispute. He has or rather is a history"; *Wolf Children and the Problem of Human Nature, with Jean Itard, The Wild Boy of Aveyron,* trans. Edmund Fawcett, Peter Ayrton, and Joan White (New York: Monthly Review Press, 1972), 9. Another translation is Jean-Marc-Gaspard Itard, *The Wild Boy of Aveyron* (*Rapports et memoires sur le sauvage de l'Aveyron*), trans. George Humphrey and Muriel Humphrey (New York: Century Co., 1932); see also the collection of primary-source documents in Thierry Gineste, *Victor de l'Aveyron: Dernier enfant sauvage, premier enfant fou* (Paris: Le Sycomore, 1981).

37. Roger Shattuck, *The Forbidden Experiment: The Story of the Wild Boy of Aveyron* (New York: Farrar Straus Giroux, 1980), 41.

38. Swift's writings are quoted in the edition of *The Prose Works of Jonathan Swift,* ed. Herbert Davis et al., 14 vols. (Oxford: Blackwell/Shakespeare Head, 1939–1974); references are given parenthetically in the text by volume and page number. For *Gulliver's Travels,* I also give volume and chapter numbers based on Swift's divisions.

39. The *OED* notes the use of the phrase "species being" from Marx's *Gattungswesen,* perhaps a sort of sequel to Enlightenment arguments about human nature. I am grateful to my colleague Gayatri Spivak for illuminating my understanding of the term *Gattung* (and see also note 50).

40. On the relationship between the terms *race* and *species,* see the excellent essay by Nicholas Hudson, "From 'Nation' to 'Race': The Origin of Racial Classification in Eighteenth-Century Thought," *Eighteenth-Century Studies* 29.3 (1996): 247–264, esp. 253–254.

41. On men and monkeys, see M.F. Ashley Montagu, "Tyson's *Orang-Outang, Sive Homo Sylvestris* and Swift's *Gulliver's Travels,*" *PMLA* 59.1 (1944): 84–89; and also the chapter on *Gulliver's Travels* in Bartra, *Artificial Savage,* 175–200.

42. In an influential essay on the "hard" and "soft" schools of interpretation of Gulliver's fourth voyage, James Clifford outlined the wide range of possibilities (tragic, shocking, comic, satirical, didactic, . . .) offered by Swift's satire and the absence of any consensus as to the significance of the Houyhnhnms; see James L. Clifford, "Gulliver's Fourth Voyage: 'Hard' and 'Soft' Schools of Interpretation," in *Quick Springs of Sense: Studies in the Eighteenth Century* (Athens: University of Georgia Press, 1974), 33–49, esp. 42.

43. Claude Rawson has traced the history and implications of the dangling breast imagery, and in general my discussion of Swift is indebted to his consideration of how Swift "is to be uncoupled . . . from the imputation of being an apologist for mass-slaughter while showing every sign of endorsing (or at least not disowning) the Houyhnhnm scheme"; Claude Rawson, *God, Gulliver, and Genocide: Barbarism and the European Imagination, 1492–1945* (Oxford: Oxford University Press, 2001), 92ff. (the quotation is on ix).

44. For a passage on nose-flattening that may have been one of Swift's sources, see Edward Tyson, *Orang-Outang, sive Homo Sylvestris; or, The Anatomy of a Pygmie Compared with that of a Monkey, an Ape, and a Man* (London: Thomas Bennet and Daniel Brown, 1699), 9.

45. On the distinction between man as a rational animal (*animal rationale*) versus merely an animal capable of reason (*rationis capax*), see the classic essay by R.S. Crane, "The Houyhnhnms, the Yahoos, and the History of Ideas," in *Reason and the Imagination: Studies in the History of Ideas, 1600–1800,* ed. J.A. Mazzeo (New York: Columbia University Press; London: Routledge and Kegan Paul, 1962), 231–253. The bibliography concerning this topic is copious to the point of excess, but other relevant discussions include Betsy Bowden, "Before the Houyhnhnms: Rational Horses in the Late Seventeenth Century," *Notes and Queries* 39.1 (1992): 38–40; Ronald Knowles, *Gulliver's Travels: The Politics of Satire* (New York: Twayne, 1996), 118–138; and Margaret Olofson Thickstun, "The Puritan Origins of Gulliver's Conversion in Houyhnhnmland," *Studies in English Literature, 1500–1900* 37.3 (1997): 517–534. On the importance of Swift's Yahoos for later eighteenth- and nineteenth-century accounts of sin and human nature, see Roland Mushat Frye, "Swift's Yahoo and the Christian Symbols for Sin," *Journal of the History of Ideas* 15.2 (1954): 201–217, esp. 203–204.

46. Bentley Glass, "The Germination of the Idea of Biological Species," in *Forerunners of Darwin, 1745–1859,* ed. Bentley Glass, Owsei Temkin, and William L. Straus Jr. (Baltimore: Johns Hopkins University Press, 1959), 30–48; the point is made on 31. See also the discussion of *Gulliver's Travels* and species definitions in Nash, *Wild Enlightenment,* 26.

47. John Ray, *The Wisdom of God Manifested in the Works of the Creation* (London: Samuel Smith, 1691), 5.

48. John Ray, "A discourse on the specific differences of plants" (a paper delivered to the Royal Society in 1674), in Thomas Birth, *The History of the Royal Society of London for Improving of Natural Knowledge,* 4 vols. (London: A. Millar, 1756–1757), 3:169–173; the quotation is on 3:171. I am indebted for this reference to Phillip R. Sloan, "The Idea of Racial Degeneracy in Buffon's *Histoire Naturelle,*" in *Studies in Eighteenth-Century Culture 3: Racism in the Eighteenth Century,* ed. Harold E. Pagliaro (Cleveland: Press of Case Western Reserve University, 1973), 293–321; as Sloan observes, "The interbreeding criterion, stating that fertile interbreeding takes precedence over morphological or behavioral distinctions in defining the unity of a natural species of organisms, was in rising ascendancy in scientific circles in the early eighteenth century, and had been applied specifically to the question of the unity of the human species by John Ray in 1674" (298, 314 n. 21). Also relevant are sev-

eral essays in *Histoire du concept d'espèce dans les sciences de la vie* (Paris: Fondations Singer-Polignac, 1985), especially Anto Leikola's "The Development of the Species Concept in the Thinking of Linnaeus" (45–59, esp. 52–55) and Phillip R. Sloan's "From Logical Universals to Historical Individuals: Buffon's Idea of Biological Species" (101–140, esp. 122, 126).

49. Quoted in Jacques Roger, *Buffon: A Life in Natural History*, trans. Sarah Lucille Bonnefoi, ed. L. Pearce Williams (Ithaca: Cornell University Press), 127 (and see, for instance, Georges Louis Leclerc, Count de Buffon, *Natural History, General and Particular*, trans. William Smellie, intro. Aaron V. Garrett, 9 vols. [London: A. Strahan and T. Cadell, 1791; Bristol: Thoemmes, 2000], 4:9–10). Roger provides a useful miniature history of the definition of species, observing that Locke questioned the abstraction of the species concept as it had been inherited from Aristotle—where should the lines between species be drawn?—and that Ray responded to Locke by abandoning the search for the "essential characteristic" of species; see esp. 313–317, 328–330, 340. The early nineteenth-century surgeon William Lawrence would observe in his *Lectures on Physiology, Zoology, and the Natural History of Man* (1822) that "[t]he transmission of specific forms by generation, and the aversion to unions with those of other kinds, soon led naturalists to seek for a criterion of species in breeding," glossing the last word with an interesting footnote: "The principle has not escaped common observation: it is expressed in the English word *breed*, and in the German *gattung*, (species) which signifies copulation"; W. Lawrence, *Lectures on Physiology, Zoology, and the Natural History of Man* (London: Benbow, 1822), 229n.

50. *Examiner* 40, 10 May 1711 (*Prose Works*, 3:150).

51. *Prose Works*, 3:151.

52. [A. S. Gent.], *The Gentleman's Compleat Jockey: With The Perfect Horse-man and Experienc'd Farrier* (London: T. Norris, [1715?]), 17–18.

53. Plato, *The Republic*, ed. G. R. F. Ferrari, trans. Tom Griffith (Cambridge: Cambridge University Press, 2000), 52. Subsequent references are to this edition and will be given parenthetically in the text. David J. Galton offers useful background in "Greek Theories on Eugenics," *Journal of Medical Ethics* 24.4 (1998): 263–267. On Swift and Plato, see also John F. Reichert, "Plato, Swift, and the Houyhnhnms," *Philological Quarterly* 47.2 (1968): 179–192; and Frank T. Boyle, "Chinese Utopianism and Gulliverian Narcissism in Swift's *Travels*," in *Locating Swift: Essays from Dublin on the 250th Anniversary of the Death of Jonathan Swift, 1667–1745*, ed. Aileen Douglas, Patrick Kelly, and Ian Campbell Ross (Dublin: Four Courts Press, 1998), 117–128, esp. 124.

54. Quoted in John Jeremiah Sullivan, *Blood Horses: Notes of a Sportswriter's Son* (New York: Farrar Straus Giroux, 2004), 90.

55. Thomas More, *Utopia* (1516), ed. and trans. George M. Logan and Robert M. Adams, rev. ed. (Cambridge: Cambridge University Press, 2002), 79. Gulliver complains in the introductory letter to his cousin that some readers "are so bold as to think my Book of Travels a meer Fiction out of mine own Brain; and have gone so far as to drop Hints, that the *Houyhnhnms* and *Yahoos* have no more Existence than the Inhabitants of *Utopia*" (11:xxxvi). On Swift and More, see especially Brian Vickers, "The Satiric Structure of

*Gulliver's Travels* and More's *Utopia,*" in *The World of Jonathan Swift: Essays for the Tercentenary,* ed. Vickers (Oxford: Blackwell, 1968), 233–257; and Jenny Mezciems, "Swift's Praise of Gulliver: Some Renaissance Background to the *Travels,*" in *The Character of Swift's Satire: A Revised Focus,* ed. Claude Rawson (Newark: University of Delaware Press; London: Associated University Presses, 1983), 245–281.

56. Plutarch, *On Sparta,* rev. ed., trans. Richard J.A. Talbert (London: Penguin, 2005), 19.

57. Tim. Nourse, Gent., *A Discourse Upon the Nature and Faculties of Man, in Several Essayes* (London: Jacob Tonson, 1686), 358–359.

58. [Richard Steele and Joseph Addison], *The Tatler,* ed. Donald F. Bond, vol. 1 (Oxford: Clarendon, 1987), no. 75, 1 Oct. 1709, 513. Swift shows a general skepticism about the notion of improvement, agricultural or otherwise; one of the absurd agricultural improvers of book 3 hopes "by a certain Composition of Gums, Minerals, and Vegetables outwardly applied, to prevent the Growth of Wool upon two young Lambs; and . . . in a reasonable Time to propagate the Breed of naked Sheep all over the Kingdom" (3.5/11:166).

59. See also *Prose Works,* 11:182–183. This represents a persistent theme in Swift's work. Writing satirically in Ireland in 1728 about the inverse relationship between wealth and education, he first celebrates the fact of the sons of the new rich "bred in Sloth and Idleness" leaving the world as beggars, as their fathers came into it—"The Dunghil having raised a huge Mushroom of short Duration, is now spread to enrich other Mens Lands"—and then considers the decay of noble families whose titles outlast their estates: "But even here, God hath likewise prescribed some Remedy in the Order of Nature; so many great Families coming to an End by the Sloth, Luxury, and abandoned Lusts, which enervated their Breed through every Succession, producing gradually a more effeminate Race, wholly unfit for Propagation" (*Intelligencer* no. 9 [*Prose Works,* 12:53]).

60. *Prose Works,* 12:110; and see also Louis A. Landa's 1942 essay "*A Modest Proposal* and Populousness," reprinted in *Eighteenth-Century English Literature: Modern Essays in Criticism,* ed. James L. Clifford (New York: Oxford University Press, 1959), 102–111.

61. Richard Nash, "'Honest English Breed': The Thoroughbred as Cultural Metaphor," in *The Culture of the Horse: Status, Discipline, and Identity in the Early Modern World,* ed. Karen Raber and Treva J. Tucker (New York: Palgrave Macmillan, 2005), 245–272, 252; and see also the chapter on equestrian art in Lisa Jardine and Jerry Brotton, *Global Interests: Renaissance Art Between East and West* (Ithaca: Cornell University Press, 2000), 132–185; and Keith Thomas, *Man and the Natural World: Changing Attitudes in England, 1500–1800* (1983; New York: Oxford University Press, 1996), 59.

62. On Osmer and Wall, see Nicholas Russell, *Like Engendr'ing Like: Heredity and Animal Breeding in Early Modern England* (Cambridge: Cambridge University Press, 1986), 105–110. On the holdover into the eighteenth century (despite Osmer's case) of the idea—associated in particular with the prolific sixteenth-century husbandry writer Gervase Markham—of notions of blood, see R. J. Moore-Colyer, "Horses and Equine Im-

provement in the Economy of Modern Wales," *Agricultural History Review* 39.2 (1991): 134–135.

63. William Osmer, *A Dissertation on Horses: Wherein it is demonstrated, by Matters of Fact, as well as from the Principles of Philosophy, that* INNATE QUALITIES *do not exist, and that the excellence of this Animal is altogether mechanical and not in the Blood* (London: T. Waller, 1756), 10, 16.

64. Osmer, *Dissertation on Horses,* 27, 29–30.

65. Osmer, *Dissertation on Horses,* 52–53, 55–56.

66. Richard Wall, *A Dissertation on Breeding of Horses, upon Philosophical and Experimental Principles; Being An attempt to promote thereby an Improvement in the present manner of Breeding Racers, And Horses in general* (London: G. Woodfall et al., [1760]), 23–24. See also Osmer, *Dissertation,* 23–24 and Wall, *Dissertation,* 42–43; "[I]f providence had intended it as a general rule that the offspring should partake more of the female than the male," concludes Wall (he clearly finds this the clincher), "then certainly no species could have continued its existence, because in length of time they would have degenerated into the lowest degree of effeminacy" (52).

67. Richard Bradley, *The Gentleman and Farmer's Guide For the Increase and Improvement of Cattle,* 2nd ed. (London: G. S., 1732), 268.

68. Bradley, *Gentleman and Farmer's Guide,* 271.

69. Bradley, *Gentleman and Farmer's Guide,* 275.

70. Quoted in Joseph Needham, *A History of Embryology,* 2nd ed., rev. with Arthur Hughes (1934; Cambridge: Cambridge University Press, 1959), 170.

71. Abbé Spallanzani, *Dissertations Relative to the Natural History of Animals and Vegetables,* 2 vols. (London: J. Murray, 1784), 2:242.

72. Spallanzani, *Dissertations,* 2:377–378. Buffon shared this interest in the possibility of farfetched hybrids; see Roger, *Buffon,* 317–318. At one point the French naturalist actually quotes an extract from a letter from a member of the Dijon Academy about a dog who suckled "two young cats, one of which participated so much of the nature of its nurse, that its cries had more resemblance to the barking of a dog, than to the mewing of a cat" (Buffon, *Natural History, General and Particular,* 4:43). The cat's resistance to any form of education made it an object of equal fascination and horror to eighteenth-century natural historians.

73. For Voltaire's attack, see *Histoire du Docteur Akakia et du Natif de St-Malo* (1753), ed. Jacques Tuffet (Paris: A.G. Nizet, 1967).

74. See the important essays by Arthur O. Lovejoy, "Some Eighteenth-Century Evolutionists I," *Popular Science Monthly* 65 (1904): 238–251, esp. 245; and Bentley Glass, "Maupertuis, Pioneer of Genetics and Evolution," in *Forerunners of Darwin: 1745–1859,* 51–83, esp. 62–67. For somewhat corrective recalibrations of Maupertuis' significance, however, see Iris Sandler, "Pierre Louis Moreau de Maupertuis—A Precursor of Mendel?," *Journal of the History of Biology* 16.1 (1983): 101–136; Anne Fagot, "Le 'transformisme' de Maupertuis,"

in *Actes de la journée Maupertuis 1973* (Paris: J. Vrin, 1975), 163–181; H.O. Lancaster, "Mathematicians in Medicine and Biology. Genetics Before Mendel: Maupertuis and Réaumur," *Journal of Medical Biography* 3 (1995): 84–89; and David Beeson, *Maupertuis: An Intellectual Biography*, Studies on Voltaire and the Eighteenth Century 299 (Oxford: Voltaire Foundation, 1992), 2–3, 182, 268.

75. George W. Stocking Jr., introduction to James Cowles Prichard, *Researches Into the Physical History of Man* (1813; Chicago: University of Chicago Press, 1973), lii.

76. François Jacob, *The Logic of Life: A History of Heredity*, trans. Betty E. Spillman (1970; Princeton: Princeton University Press, 1973), 139.

77. For a detailed chronology and the (complex) publication history of Maupertuis' writings on heredity, see Mary Terrall's excellent biography, *The Man Who Flattened the Earth: Maupertuis and the Sciences in the Enlightenment* (Chicago: University of Chicago Press, 2002), 208–209, 311 n. 1. A number of these works are available in facsimile reprints; see especially the reprint of the sixth edition (1751) of *Venus Physique* in *Bernier, Linnaeus, and Maupertuis*, ed. Robert Bernasconi, vol. 1 of *Concepts of Race in the Eighteenth Century* (Bristol: Thoemmes, 2001).

78. "Sur la génération des animaux," in *Lettres*, in *Oeuvres de Maupertuis*, 4 vols., rev. ed. (Lyon: Jean-Marie Bruyset, 1768), 2:299–314, 2:307.

79. Pierre-Louis Moreau de Maupertuis, *The Earthly Venus*, trans. Simone Brangier Boas, intro. George Boas (New York: Johnson Reprint Corporation, 1966), 2.3.71–73.

80. Buffon, *Natural History of the Horse. To which is added, that of the Ass, Bull, Cow, Ox, Sheep, Goat, and Swine. With Accurate Descriptions of their several Parts. And full Directions for Breeding, Chusing, Feeding, and Improving, those useful Creatures* (London: R. Griffith, 1756), 152.

81. Lawrence, *Lectures on Physiology*, 253–254. On Linnaean beliefs about hybridization and species, see Peter J. Bowler, *Evolution: The History of an Idea* (Berkeley: University of California Press, 1984), 52.

82. E.C. Spary, *Utopia's Garden: French Natural History from Old Regime to Revolution* (Chicago: University of Chicago Press, 2000), 117.

83. Julien Offray de la Mettrie, *Machine Man and Other Writings*, trans. and ed. Ann Thomson (Cambridge: Cambridge University Press, 1996), 37, 82.

84. Vandermonde, *Essai sur la manière de perfectionner l'espèce humaine*, 2 vols. (Paris: Vincent, 1756), 1:94 ["Seeing as we've arrived at perfecting the breed of horses, dogs, cats, chickens, pigeons, songbirds, why shouldn't there be a similar effort for mankind?"].

85. Anne Carol, *Histoire de l'eugénisme en France: Les médecins et la procréation XIXᵉ–XXᵉ siècle* (Paris: Seuil, 1995), 19–20. The contrast is clear when Vandermonde's book is considered alongside something like the anonymous *Callipædiæ; or, An Art how to have Handsome Children: Written in Latin By the Abbot Quillet. To which is Added, Pædotrophiæ; or, The Art of Nursing and Breeding up Children: Written in Latin By Monsieur St. Marthe, Physician to Henry III. of France. Now done into* English *Verse* (London: John Morphew, 1710).

86. John Gregory, *A Comparative View of the State and Faculties of Man with those of the Animal World*, 6th ed., 2 vols. (London: J. Dodsley, 1774; London: Routledge/Thoemmes, 1994), 1:27. Subsequent references are to this edition and will be given parenthetically in the text.

87. Robert Bakewell, *Observations on the Influence of Soil and Climate upon Wool* (London: J. Harding, 1808), 114; for a contemporary description, see for instance Redhead, Laing, and Marshall, *Observations on the Different Breeds of Sheep* (Edinburgh: W. Smellie, 1792), 37; and also the valuable discussions in Harriet Ritvo, "Possessing Mother Nature: Genetic Capital in Eighteenth-Century Britain," in *Early Modern Conceptions of Property*, ed. John Brewer and Susan Staves (London: Routledge, 1996), 413–426; and Roger J. Wood and Vitezslav Orel, *Genetic Prehistory in Selective Breeding: A Prelude to Mendel* (Oxford: Oxford University Press, 2001), 57ff.

88. John Luccock, *The Nature and Properties of Wool, Illustrated: With a Description of the English Fleece* (Leeds: Edward Baines and J. Heaton; London: J. Harding, 1805), 105.

89. Russell, *Like Engendr'ing Like*, esp. 197–198. On the cultural significance of livestock breeding in late eighteenth-century Britain, see especially Harriet Ritvo, *The Animal Estate: The English and Other Creatures in the Victorian Age* (Cambridge, MA: Harvard University Press, 1987).

90. Bradley, *Gentleman and Farmer's Guide*, 2.

91. James Bate, *A Rationale of the Literal Doctrine of Original Sin; or, A Vindication of God's permitting the Fall of Adam, And the Subsequent Corruption of our Human Nature* (London: J. Dodsley et al., 1766), 222–223.

92. Glacken describes Arbuthnot's *An Essay Concerning the Effects of Air on Human Bodies* (1731) as a sort of counterpart to Montesquieu's work on climate; *Traces on the Rhodian Shore*, 563, 567.

93. David Hartley, *Observations on Man, His Frame, His Duty, and His Expectations*, 2 vols. (London: S. Richardson, 1749), 2:109.

94. The bibliography on this topic is copious, but see Emmanuel C. Eze, "Hume, Race, and Human Nature," *Journal of the History of Ideas* 61.4 (2000): 691–698.

95. David Hume, "Of National Characters," in *Essays Moral, Political, and Literary*, ed. Eugene F. Miller, rev. ed. (Indianapolis: Liberty Fund, 1987), 198. The date is given in this edition's foreword (xiii); it was one of three essays published under the title *Three Essays, Moral and Political* (the first work to bear Hume's name), all of which were incorporated into the third edition of the *Essays, Moral and Political*, published the same year. Subsequent references are to the Liberty Fund edition.

96. Hume, "Of National Characters," 207–208. The note was first added to the essay in the four-volume *Essays and Treatises on Several Subjects* of 1753–1754; the 1777 edition featured a revised version of the note which begins instead with the words "I am apt to suspect the negroes, and in general all the other species of men (for there are four or five different kinds) to be naturally inferior to the whites" (629).

97. Hume, "Of National Characters," 215.

98. Blumenbach, *On the Natural Variety of Mankind* (1775, 1795), in *Anthropological Treatises,* trans. and ed. Thomas Bendyshe (1865; Boston: Longwood, [1978]), 190–191.

99. Blumenbach, *Anthropological Treatises,* 340.

100. On the population debate, see Glacken, "Environment, Population, and the Perfectibility of Man," *Traces on the Rhodian Shore,* 623–654.

101. Hume, "Of the Populousness of Ancient Nations," 386, 387–388.

102. Hume, "Of the Populousness of Ancient Nations," 392–393.

103. [Robert Wallace], *Various Prospects of Mankind, Nature, and Providence* (1758), 2nd ed. (London: A. Millar, 1761; New York: Augustus M. Kelley, 1969), 114.

104. Wallace, *Various Prospects,* 119.

105. Robert Wallace, *A Dissertation on the Numbers of Mankind, in Ancient and Modern Times* (1753), 2nd ed. (Edinburgh: Archibald Constable and Co.; London: Constable, Hunter, Park, and Hunter, 1809), 149.

106. Denis Diderot, *Supplément au Voyage de Bougainville* (drafted 1771, expanded in 1772, and circulated in manuscript in 1773, the text was first published in 1796), in Diderot, *Political Writings,* trans. and ed. John Hope Mason and Robert Wokler (Cambridge: Cambridge University Press, 1992), 63–64. Thanks to Sunil Agnani for first bringing this passage to my attention.

107. Robert Crawford, *Devolving English Literature* (Oxford: Clarendon, 1992), 16.

108. See for instance John Locke, *Observations upon the Growth and Culture of Vines and Olives: The Production of Silk: The Preservation of Fruits* (London: W. Sandby, 1766), 7.

109. See Alistair M. Duckworth, "Fiction and Some Uses of the Country House Setting from Richardson to Scott," in *The Country Myth: Motifs in the British Novel from Defoe to Smollett,* ed. H. George Hahn (Frankfurt: Lang, 1991), 221–254; and Michael Rosenblum, "Smollett's *Humphry Clinker,*" in *The Cambridge Companion to the Eighteenth-Century Novel,* ed. John Richetti (Cambridge: Cambridge University Press, 1996), 175–197.

110. Smollett uses *breeding* and its cognates in both senses. See the passage in which Tabitha Bramble is said to have "become so indifferent to Chowder [her lapdog], as to part with him in a present to lady Griskin, who proposes to bring the breed of him into fashion" (99); and Matt's reference to Lismahago having "been bred to the law," in contrast to Matt himself, who has "been bred to nothing" (200). All references are to Tobias Smollett, *The Expedition of Humphry Clinker,* intro. and notes by Thomas R. Preston, ed. O.M. Brack Jr. (Athens: University of Georgia Press, 1990). Subsequent references are given parenthetically in the text.

111. Raymond Williams, *The Country and the City* (1973; New York: Oxford University Press, 1975), 29–30.

112. For Smollett's own review of "Lyle" (Lisle's *Observations in Husbandry*), see *Critical Review* 3 (Jan. 1757): 1–20.

113. Thanks to Alastair Duckworth for pointing out this ambiguity.

# 4. A Natural History of Inequality

1. Jean-Jacques Rousseau, in *The Discourses and Other Early Political Writings,* ed. Victor Gourevitch (Cambridge: Cambridge University Press, 1997). All references are to this edition and will be given parenthetically in the text. For reasons of space, I will not give the original French, but the full text can be found in vol. 3 of *Œuvres completes,* ed. Bernard Gagnebin and Marcel Raymond (Paris: Pléiade, 1964).

2. See the entries for *perfectibilité* in *Trésor de la langue française* (Paris: Gallimard, 1988) and *Dictionnaire historique de la langue française* (Paris: Dictionnaires le Robert, 1993); the word comes into much more widespread use during the 1790s. My thinking on this topic has also been greatly assisted by Julia V. Douthwaite, *The Wild Girl, Natural Man, and the Monster: Dangerous Experiments in the Age of Enlightenment* (Chicago: University of Chicago Press, 2002), 20.

3. *Discourse on this Question proposed by the Academy: Whether the restoration of the Sciences and Arts has contributed to the purification of morals* (1750), in *Discourses and Other Early Political Writings,* 7.

4. Leo Marx, *The Machine in the Garden: Technology and the Pastoral Idea in America* (1964; New York: Oxford University Press, 2000), 101.

5. Marx, *Machine in the Garden,* 102.

6. Jacques Derrida, *Of Grammatology,* trans. Gayatri Chakravorty Spivak (Baltimore: Johns Hopkins University Press, 1976), 145–146.

7. Terry Eagleton, *The Idea of Culture* (Malden: Blackwell, 2000), 6.

8. See Jacques Roger, *Buffon: A Life in Natural History,* trans. Sarah Lucille Bonnefoi, ed. L. Pearce Williams (Ithaca: Cornell University Press), 299–304.

9. Some recent researchers have ardently disputed the notion that animals have no culture, but the distinction between people and animals has been surprisingly durable, despite the efforts of advocates—Peter Singer prominent among them—for changing the legal status of animals. For a summary of recent scientific work on whether animals also have culture, see Frans de Waal, *The Ape and the Sushi Master: Cultural Reflections by a Primatologist* (New York: Basic Books, 2001), esp. 213–271; and on man's ethical relations with animals more generally, see *Animal Rights: A Historical Anthology,* ed. Andrew Linzey and Paul Barry Clarke (New York: Columbia University Press, 2004).

10. The material that would support such a view is mostly contained in the notes affixed to the end of the *Discourse* (218–221); for further discussion of this point, see Felicity Baker, "Rousseau and the Colonies," *Eighteenth-Century Life* 22.1 (1998): 172–189.

11. Sigmund Freud, *Civilization and Its Discontents* (1930), trans. James Strachey (New York: Norton, 1989), 38.

12. Jean-Jacques Rousseau, *Émile* (1762), trans. Barbara Foxley, intro. P.D. Jimack (London: J.M. Dent; North Clarendon, VT: Tuttle, 1993), xx–xxi.

13. On eighteenth-century thought concerning the environment's effect on female bodies, including the ways in which habit and custom induced "physiological changes . . .

with the result that each human body was a tangled composite of nature and culture," see Ludmilla Jordanova, *Sexual Visions: Images of Gender in Science and Medicine Between the Eighteenth and Twentieth Centuries* (New York: Harvester Wheatsheaf, 1989), 26.

14. On accent and class, see especially Lynda Mugglestone, *"Talking Proper": The Rise of Accent as Social Symbol* (Oxford: Clarendon, 1995), 5. Some early dictionaries did note aspects of regional use; for further discussion of this topic, see Carey McIntosh, "Eighteenth-Century English Dictionaries and the Enlightenment," *Yearbook of English Studies* 28 (1998): 3–18. I am immensely grateful to Carey for reading an earlier version of this material and giving me the very great benefit of his knowledge on these matters.

15. Wilbur Samuel Howell, *Eighteenth-Century British Logic and Rhetoric* (Princeton: Princeton University Press, 1971), 156; and for another important discussion of the elocution movement, see Peter DeBolla, *The Discourse of the Sublime: Readings in History, Aesthetics, and the Subject* (Oxford: Blackwell, 1989), 146–182. On the more general rise of a standard of polite pronunciation—and its ideological implications—see Mugglestone, *"Talking Proper,"* 7–57; and, on language and social class in eighteenth-century British writing, Carey McIntosh, *Common and Courtly Language: The Stylistics of Social Class in Eighteenth-Century British Literature* (Philadelphia: University of Pennsylvania Press, 1986), esp. 1–11; and McIntosh, *The Evolution of English Prose: Style, Politeness, and Print Culture* (Cambridge: Cambridge University Press, 1998).

16. See for instance John Mason, *An Essay on Elocution; or, Pronunciation* (London: M. Cooper, 1748; Menston: Scolar, 1968). Howell discusses these overlapping terms in *Eighteenth-Century British Logic and Rhetoric*, 147–151.

17. John Walker, *Elements of Elocution*, 2 vols. (London: T. Cadell et al., 1781; Menston: Scolar, 1969), 2:10–11. For an example of the earlier sense of *accent*, see Isaac Watts, *The Art of Reading and Writing English* (London: John Clark et al., 1721; Menston: Scolar, 1972), 55.

18. Samuel Johnson, *The Plan of a Dictionary of the English Language*, in *Johnson on the English Language*, ed. Gwin J. Kolb and Robert DeMaria Jr., vol. 18 of *The Yale Edition of the Works of Samuel Johnson* (New Haven: Yale University Press, 2005), 37–38. On Johnson's practice in the dictionary, see especially Allen Reddick, *The Making of Johnson's Dictionary, 1746–1773* (Cambridge: Cambridge University Press, 1990).

19. "Preface," in *Johnson on the English Language*, 109. On "the eighteenth-century slippage between the tongue as language and the tongue as organ of speech, a slippage central to the belief that language and national character were indissolubly linked," see Michèle Cohen, *Fashioning Masculinity: National Identity and Language in the Eighteenth Century* (London: Routledge, 1996), 1.

20. Thomas Sheridan, *A Rhetorical Grammar of the English Language. Calculated solely for the Purposes of Teaching Propriety of Pronunciation, and Justness of Delivery, in that Tongue, by the Organs of Speech* (Dublin: Price et al., 1781), vii.

21. Rev. Peter Peckard, Master of Magdalen College, Cambridge, quoted in W. Benzie, *The Dublin Orator: Thomas Sheridan's Influence on Eighteenth-Century Rhetoric and Belles Lettres* (Leeds: University of Leeds School of English, 1972), 110 n. 47. For a wide-ranging

treatment of the role of oratory in mid-eighteenth-century political thought, see Adam Potkay, *The Fate of Eloquence in the Age of Hume* (Ithaca: Cornell University Press, 1994), 24–58.

22. For a contemporary account, see Thomas Somerville, D.D., *My Own Life and Times, 1741–1814* (Edinburgh: Edmonston and Douglas, 1861), 56–57. More details can be found in Mugglestone, *"Talking Proper,"* 43–44; Benzie, *Dublin Orator,* 27–28; H. Lewis Ulman, *Things, Thoughts, Words, and Actions: The Problem of Language in Late Eighteenth-Century British Rhetorical Theory* (Carbondale: Southern Illinois University Press, 1994), 147–175; and R.C. Alston, *A Bibliography of the English Language from the Invention of Printing to the Year 1800,* rev. ed. (Ilkey: Janus Press, 1974). Alston was also responsible for publishing facsimiles of virtually all the major works on language printed in English between 1500 and 1800, a superb resource for scholars.

23. Thomas Sheridan, *A Course of Lectures on Elocution: Together With Two Dissertations on Language; and Some other Tracts relative to those Subjects* (London: W. Strahan et al., 1762), xiv.

24. Sheridan, *Lectures on Elocution,* 247.

25. Sheridan, *Lectures on Elocution,* 205, 261–262.

26. Thomas Sheridan, *A Discourse Delivered in the Theatre at Oxford, in the Senate-House at Cambridge, and at Spring-Garden in London* (London: A. Millar et al., 1759), 12.

27. For a more detailed discussion of the debate about sermon delivery, see Jenny Davidson, "Professional Education and Female Accomplishments: Gender and Education in Maria Edgeworth's *Patronage,*" in *Eighteenth-Century Women* 4 (2006): 259–285.

28. Sheridan, *Rhetorical Grammar,* xv–xvi.

29. Robert Crawford, *Devolving English Literature* (Oxford: Clarendon, 1992), 16, 22–23, 44; and on the relation between Scottish and English pronunciation during this period, see also Charles Jones, *A Language Suppressed: The Pronunciation of the Scots Language in the Eighteenth Century* (Edinburgh: John Donato, 1996), 1–21. For an example of the interpenetration of the languages of agricultural and personal improvement, see for instance Hugh Blair, *Lectures on Rhetoric and Belles Lettres* (1783), 2 vols., ed. Harold F. Harding, intro. David Potten (Carbondale: Southern Illinois University Press, 1965), 1:7, 1:11.

30. James Buchanan, *An Essay Towards Establishing a Standard for an Elegant and Uniform Pronunciation of the English Language, Throughout the British Dominions, As practised by the Most Learned and Polite Speakers* (London: Edward and Charles Dilly, 1764), xi–xii.

31. Thomas P. Miller, *The Formation of College English: Rhetoric and Belles Lettres in the British Cultural Provinces* (Pittsburgh: University of Pittsburgh Press, 1997), 138, 119.

32. [Anon.], *A Vocabulary of Such Words in the English Language as are of Dubious or Unsettled Accentuation* (London: F. and C. Rivington et al., 1797), ii. For a defense by one Scottish authority of his own right to publish on pronunciation, see William Angus, *A Pronouncing Vocabulary of the English Language* (Glasgow: D. Niven, 1800; Menston: Scolar, 1969), 4.

33. Sheridan, *Rhetorical Grammar,* xxi.

34. Thomas Sheridan, *Lectures on the Art of Reading; First Part* (London: J. Dodsley et al., 1775), 144–146.

35. Sheridan, *Art of Reading,* 146.

36. Sheridan, *Rhetorical Grammar,* 165 (original emphasis). On the difference between contemporary and eighteenth-century understandings of the term *nature,* see especially Joseph Roach's chapter "Nature Still, But Nature Mechanized," in *The Player's Passion: Studies in the Science of Acting* (1985; Ann Arbor: University of Michigan Press, 1993), 58–92.

37. Though I concentrate here primarily on practical rather than philosophical treatments of language by eighteenth-century writers, there is obviously some overlap between the two: for a useful survey, see Nalina Jain, "Ideas of the Origin of Language in the Eighteenth Century: Johnson vs. the Philosophers," in *Aberdeen and the Enlightenment,* ed. Jennifer J. Carter and Joan H. Pittock (Aberdeen: Aberdeen University Press, 1987), 291–297.

38. Etienne Bonnot de Condillac, *Essay on the Origin of Human Knowledge* (1746), trans. Hans Aarsleff (Cambridge: Cambridge University Press, 2001), 85.

39. J.H. [James Harris], *Hermes; or, A Philosophical Inquiry Concerning Language and Universal Grammar* (London: H. Woodfall for J. Nourse and P. Vaillant, 1751; Menston: Scolar, 1968), 425.

40. Blair, *Lectures on Rhetoric,* 1:19.

41. John Herries, *The Elements of Speech* (London: Edward and Charles Dilly, 1773; Menston: Scolar, 1968), 82.

42. Herries, *Elements of Speech,* 85–86; and on the cultural aspects of birdsong, see de Waal, *The Ape and the Sushi Master,* 153–161.

43. Thomas Sheridan, *An Oration, Pronounced before a Numerous Body of the Nobility and Gentry, Assembled at the Musick-Hall in* Fishamble-Street, *On* Tuesday *the 6th of this instant* December, *And now first Published at their unanimous Desire,* 2nd ed. (Dublin: M. Williamson, 1757), 7.

44. Sheridan, *An Oration,* 13.

45. Sheridan, *An Oration,* 30.

46. Jay Fliegelman, *Declaring Independence: Jefferson, Natural Language, and the Culture of Performance* (Stanford: Stanford University Press, 1993), 149.

47. Daniel Cottom, *The Civilized Imagination: A Study of Ann Radcliffe, Jane Austen, and Sir Walter Scott* (Cambridge: Cambridge University Press, 1985), 14.

48. Cottom, *Civilized Imagination,* 16, 17; John Barrell, *English Literature in History, 1730–80: An Equal, Wide Survey* (London: Hutchinson, 1983), esp. 111, 142; and Olivia Smith, *The Politics of Language, 1791–1819* (Oxford: Clarendon, 1984), viii. On gender, rhetoric, and identity, see especially Patricia Parker, "Motivated Rhetorics: Gender, Order, Rule," in *Literary Fat Ladies: Rhetoric, Gender, Property* (London: Methuen, 1987), 97–125; and Janet Sorensen, *The Grammar of Empire in Eighteenth-Century British Writing* (Cambridge: Cambridge University Press, 2000), 77.

49. Sheridan, *Lectures on Elocution,* 2–3.

50. On eighteenth-century European references to foot-binding, see David Porter, *Ideographia: The Chinese Cipher in Early Modern Europe* (Stanford: Stanford University Press, 2001), 217.

51. [James Burnett, Lord Monboddo], *Antient Metaphysics*, 6 vols. (London and Edinburgh: T. Cadell, J. Balfour et al., 1779–1799; New York: Garland, 1977), 3:239, 1:216 (original emphasis). Subsequent references are to this edition and will be given parenthetically in the text.

52. John Baptista Porta, *Natural Magick*, ed. Derek J. Price (London: Thomas Young and Samuel Speed, 1658; New York: Basic Books, 1959), 50–51. I am indebted for this reference to Conway Zirkle, "The Early History of the Idea of the Inheritance of Acquired Characters and of Pangenesis," *Transactions of the American Philosophical Society* 35.2 (1946): 93–94.

53. Sheridan, *Lectures on Elocution*, 24. For another writer's readiness to liken linguistic to biological differentiation in isolated communities, see T. Batchelor, *An Orthoëpical Analysis of the English Language; or, An Essay on the Nature of its Simple and Combined Sounds; The Manner of their Formation by the Vocal Organs; the Minute Varieties which Constitute a Depraved or Provincial Pronunciation; and the Inadequacy of attempting to explain by means of the English Alphabet* (London: P. Da Ponte for Didier and Tebbet, 1809), 21.

54. Thomas Sheridan, *British Education; or, The Source of the Disorders of Great Britain* (London: R. and J. Dodsley, 1756), 365–366.

55. Jacques Derrida, "Plato's Pharmacy," in *Dissemination*, trans. Barbara Johnson (Chicago: University of Chicago Press, 1981), 61–84.

56. For the well-known passage in which Boswell (in a conversation of 30 September 1769) prods Johnson to make reflections on Monboddo, see *Boswell's Life of Johnson*, ed. George Birkbeck Hill, rev. L. F. Powell, 6 vols. (Oxford: Clarendon, 1934–1964), 1:73–74.

57. The full reference for *Antient Metaphysics* has already been given; quotations from Monboddo's other major work are from [James Burnett, Lord Monboddo], *Of the Origin and Progress of Language*, 6 vols. (Edinburgh and London: A. Kincaid, W. Creech, T. Cadell et al., 1773–1792; Menston: Scolar, 1967). Subsequent references will be given parenthetically in the text.

58. The term *blood* would itself provide an interesting keyword for future investigation; Clarissa, for instance, playfully asks Anna Howe whether "[she really thinks] Mr Lovelace can have a *very* bad heart? Why should not there be something in *blood* in the human creature, as well as in the ignobler animals?" (Samuel Richardson, *Clarissa; or, The History of A Young Lady* [1747–1748], ed. Angus Ross [London: Penguin, 1985], letter 36, p. 169).

59. Sheridan, *British Education*, 85.

60. See Potkay, *Hume and the Age of Eloquence*; Penny Fielding, *Writing and Orality: Nationality, Culture, and Nineteenth-Century Scottish Fiction* (Oxford: Clarendon, 1996), esp. 12; and Nicholas Hudson, *Writing and European Thought, 1600–1830* (Cambridge: Cambridge University Press, 1994), 92–93, 111–112. For a broader view of the study of orality and literacy in the second half of the twentieth century, see Eric A. Havelock, *The Muse Learns*

*to Write: Reflections on Orality and Literacy from Antiquity to the Present* (New Haven: Yale University Press, 1986), as well as his essay "The Oral-Literate Equation: A Formula for the Modern Mind," in *Essays in Literacy and Orality,* ed. David R. Olson and Nancy Torrance (Cambridge: Cambridge University Press, 1991), 11–27.

61. Mugglestone, *"Talking Proper,"* 104 n. 152.

62. Mugglestone, *"Talking Proper,"* 208.

63. See Jonathan Swift, "A Proposal for Correcting, Improving and Ascertaining the English Tongue" (1712), in *The Prose Works of Jonathan Swift,* ed. Herbert Davis et al., 14 vols. (Oxford: Blackwell/Shakespeare Head, 1939–1974), 4:5–21.

64. For English ambivalence toward the French Academy, see especially Johnson's famous response to a friend's skeptical remark about whether Johnson could complete the *Dictionary* in three years, given that "the French Academy, which consists of forty members, took forty years to compile their Dictionary": "Sir, thus it is," said Johnson. "This is the proportion. Let me see; forty times forty is sixteen hundred. As three to sixteen hundred, so is the proportion of an Englishman to a Frenchman" (*Boswell's Life of Johnson,* 1:186).

65. [John Fell], *An Essay Towards an English Grammar* (London: C. Dilly, 1784; Menston: Scolar, 1967), xi–xii.

66. R. Nares, *Elements of Orthoepy* (London: T. Payne and Son, 1784; Menston: Scolar, 1968), xix.

67. Nares, *Elements of Orthoepy,* 271.

68. Nares, *Elements of Orthoepy,* 267.

69. See Linda Colley, *Britons: Forging the Nation, 1707–1837* (New Haven: Yale University Press, 1992), 122–128.

70. Samuel Foote, *The Orators* (London: J. Coote et al., 1762), 6, reprinted in vol. 1 of *The Plays of Samuel Foote,* ed. Paula R. Backscheider and Douglas Howard (New York: Garland, 1983).

71. William Kenrick, *A Rhetorical Grammar of the English Language* (London: R. Cadell and W. Longman, 1784; Menston: Scolar, 1972), ii. For a friendly criticism of Elphinston's attempt to reform spelling, see William Smith, *An Attempt to Render the Pronunciation of the English Language More Easy to Foreigners* (London: C. Dilly et al. and Edinburgh: W. Creech, 1795; Menston: Scolar, 1969), v; and see also Edward Search [Abraham Tucker], *Vocal Sounds* (London: T. Jones and T. Payne, 1773; Menston: Scolar, 1969), 3.

72. See for instance Robert Robinson, *The Art of Pronuntiation [sic]* (London: Nicholas Okes, 1617; Menston: Scolar, 1969), n. p.

73. James Elphinston, *Propriety Ascertained in her Picture; or, Inglish Speech and Spelling Rendered Mutual Guides* (London: Jon Walter, 1787), vol. 1, xii–xiii.

74. Johnson, "Preface" in *Johnson on the English Language,* 83.

75. The trivializing of political vocabularies can be seen in many different places, as when the grammarian Duncan Mackintosh—writing in Martinique in the last years of the century—observes playfully that "etymology, analogy and euphony may be called the

*parliament,* accent the *monarch,* and our standard accent rules the *magna charta* of English pronunciation"; Duncan Mackintosh and his two Daughters, *A Plain, Rational Essay on English Grammar: The main object of which is to point out a plain, rational and permanent standard of pronunciation* (Boston: Manning and Loring, 1797; Menston: Scolar, 1969), xi.

76. Tom Leonard, "The Proof of the Mince Pie" (1973), in *Intimate Voices: Selected Work, 1965–1983* (1984; London: Vintage, 1995), 65; and see also Crawford's discussion in *Devolving English Literature.* On language and nation, see Tom Paulin, "A New Look at the Language Question," in Field Day Theatre Company, *Ireland's Field Day* (1983–1984; London: Hutchinson, 1985), 3–17; and Tony Crowley, "Language, History, and the Formation of Cultural Identity," in *Proper English? Readings in Language, History, and Cultural Identity* (London: Routledge, 1991), 1–12.

77. The political implications of the early history of the study of English language and literature have attracted rich discussion in recent years: see especially Franklin E. Court, *Institutionalizing English Literature: The Culture and Politics of Literary Study, 1750–1900* (Stanford: Stanford University Press, 1992); Miller, *Formation of College English;* Gauri Viswanathan, *Masks of Conquest: Literary Study and British Rule in India* (1989; New Delhi: Oxford University Press, 1998); the essays collected in *The Lie of the Land: English Literary Studies in India,* ed. Rajeswari Sunder Rajan (New Delhi: Oxford University Press, 1993); and Ian Duncan, "Adam Smith, Samuel Johnson, and the Institutions of English," in *The Scottish Invention of English Literature,* ed. Robert Crawford (Cambridge: Cambridge University Press, 1998), 37–54.

78. Joseph Priestley, *A Course of Lectures on the Theory of Language, and Universal Grammar* (Warrington: W. Eyres, 1762; Menston: Scolar, 1970), 136–137.

79. James Beattie, *The Theory of Language* (London: A. Strahan and T. Cadell; Edinburgh: W. Creech, 1788; Menston: Scolar, 1968), 53.

80. Noah Webster, *Dissertations on the English Language* (Boston: Isaiah Thomas, 1789; Menston: Scolar, 1967), 166–168.

81. Noah Webster, *A Grammatical Institute, of the English Language,* 2 vols. (Hartford: Hudson and Goodwin, [1783]–1784; Menston: Scolar, 1968), 1:3, 1:6–7n. For another early American attack on regional dialects, see James Carrol, *The American Criterion of the English Language; containing the Elements of Pronunciation; in Five Sections. For the use of English schools and foreigners* (New-London: Samuel Green, 1795), iii.

82. Webster, *Grammatical Institute,* 1:12n.

83. Webster, *Dissertations,* xi; and see also Franklin's letter of 26 Dec. 1789 thanking Webster for sending a copy of the *Dissertations,* in *A Benjamin Franklin Reader,* ed. Nathan G. Goodman (New York: Thomas Y. Crowell, 1945), 265–272. An excellent discussion of Webster's career as a spelling reformer can be found in David Micklethwait, *Noah Webster and the American Dictionary* (Jefferson, NC: McFarland, 2000), 93–104; and for Webster's most radical experiments with reformed spelling, see *A Collection of Essays and Fugitiv [sic] Writings* (Boston: I. Thomas and E.T. Andrews, 1790).

84. Webster, *Dissertations*, 397.

85. Webster, *Dissertations*, 19–20.

86. Webster, *Dissertations*, 36.

87. Adam Smith, *Lectures on Rhetoric and Belles Lettres,* ed. J.C. Bryce (Oxford: Clarendon, 1983), 4. The lectures were transcribed by a student around the year 1763 but not published until the twentieth century.

88. Webster, *Dissertations*, 24. On the power of actors to define the standard, see [Anon.], *A Vocabulary of Such Words,* entry on *authority;* and Sheridan's criticisms of Garrick's Staffordshire inflection in *Elements of English* (London: C. Dilly, 1786), 28–29.

89. Webster, *Dissertations*, 167, 27 (original emphasis), 25.

90. Webster, *Dissertations*, 179, 288.

91. Quoted by Pat Rogers, "Boswell and the Scotticism," in *New Light on Boswell,* ed. Greg Clingham (Cambridge: Cambridge University Press, 1991), 56–71 (the quotation is on p. 63, and the original reference can be found in James Boswell, *The Ominous Years: 1774–1776,* ed. Charles Ryskamp and Frederick A. Pottle [New York: McGraw-Hill, 1963], 124–125); and see the discussion in *Boswell's Life of Johnson,* 2:158–159. In a May 1795 letter, Edmund Burke—seeking teachers to staff a school for the children of French exiles—requested "a Scholar as to Latin &c.—and who can read English, in Prose and Verse, in a firm, manly, natural manner—a triffle [sic] of our Country accent, provided it was not gross and enormous, would be no serious Objection"; vol. 9 of *The Correspondence of Edmund Burke,* ed. R.B. McDowell and John A. Woods (Cambridge: Cambridge University Press; Chicago: University of Chicago Press, 1970), 21. Thanks to Dermot Ryan for the reference.

92. *Boswell's Life of Johnson,* 1:386–387.

93. *Boswell's Life of Johnson,* 2:159–160.

94. *Boswell's Life of Johnson,* 1:453–454.

95. Maria Edgeworth and Richard Lovell Edgeworth, *An Essay on Irish Bulls* (1802), in vol. 1 of *The Novels and Selected Works of Maria Edgeworth,* ed. Jane Desmarais, Tim McLoughlin, and Marilyn Butler (London: Pickering and Chatto, 1999), 74 (original emphasis).

96. Edgeworth, *Essay on Irish Bulls,* 76.

97. Edgeworth, *Essay on Irish Bulls,* 89.

98. Edgeworth, *Essay on Irish Bulls,* 124; and see the discussion of *nature* and Scottish accents in James Adams, *Euphonologia Linguae Anglicanae* (London: R. White, 1794; Menston: Scolar, 1968), 11–12.

99. Edgeworth, *Essay on Irish Bulls,* 133–134. The example is actually borrowed from Adams, though he is not credited here; for his version, see Reverend James Adams, *The Pronunciation of the English Language Vindicated From Imputed Anomaly & Caprice . . . With an Appendix, on the Dialects of Human Speech in All Countries, and an Analytical Discussion and Vindication of the Dialect of Scotland* (Edinburgh: J. Moir et al., 1799), 146.

## 5. Blots on the Landscape

1. Quotations are from Mary Shelley, *Frankenstein; or, The Modern Prometheus*, vol. 1 of *The Novels and Selected Works of Mary Shelley*, ed. Nora Crook, intro. Betty T. Bennett (London: Pickering, 1996). Page numbers will be given parenthetically in the text. The critical literature on *Frankenstein* is copious enough to defy selection, but especially worth considering, in the light of the topics I discuss here, are Lee Sterrenburg, "Mary Shelley's Monster: Politics and Psyche in *Frankenstein*," in *The Endurance of* Frankenstein*: Essays on Mary Shelley's Novel*, ed. George Levine and U.C. Knoepflmacher (Berkeley: University of California Press, 1979), 143–171; Margaret Homans, *Bearing the Word: Language and Female Experience in Nineteenth-Century Women's Writing* (Chicago: University of Chicago Press, 1986); Anne K. Mellor, *Mary Shelley: Her Life, Her Fiction, Her Monsters* (New York: Routledge, 1988); and David A. Hedrich Hirsch, "Liberty, Equality, Monstrosity: Revolutionizing the Family in Mary Shelley's *Frankenstein*," in *Monster Theory: Reading Culture*, ed. Jeffrey Jerome Cohen (Minneapolis: University of Minnesota Press, 1996), 115–140. See also Maureen N. McLane, *Romanticism and the Human Sciences: Poetry, Population, and the Discourse of the Species* (Cambridge: Cambridge University Press, 2000); and two books that have clarified my notion of the meanings of the term *reproduction* during this period: Lisa Forman Cody's *Birthing the Nation: Sex, Science, and the Conception of Eighteenth-Century Britons* (Oxford: Oxford University Press, 2005); and Eve Keller's *Generating Bodies and Gendered Selves: The Rhetoric of Reproduction in Early Modern England* (Seattle: University of Washington Press, 2007).

2. Leo Marx, *The Machine in the Garden: Technology and the Pastoral Idea in America* (1964; New York: Oxford University Press, 2000), 118. On Jefferson as practical agriculturalist, see *The Garden and Farm Books of Thomas Jefferson*, ed. Robert C. Baron (Golden, CO: Fulcrum, 1987).

3. On the form in which Jefferson chose to write, see Robert A. Ferguson, *Law and Letters in American Culture* (Cambridge, MA: Harvard University Press, 1984), 34–58.

4. Thomas Jefferson, *Notes on the State of Virginia* (1785), ed. Frank Shuffelton (London: Penguin, 1999), 19/170. Subsequent references are to this edition and will be given parenthetically in the text, by query and page number.

5. See Jacques Roger, *Buffon: A Life in Natural History*, trans. Sarah Lucille Bonnefoi, ed. L. Pearce Williams (Ithaca: Cornell University Press); Phillip R. Sloan, "The Idea of Racial Degeneracy in Buffon's *Histoire Naturelle*," in *Studies in Eighteenth-Century Culture 3: Racism in the Eighteenth Century*, ed. Harold E. Pagliaro (Cleveland: Press of Case Western Reserve University, 1973); Clarence J. Glacken, *Traces on the Rhodian Shore: Nature and Culture in Western Thought from Ancient Times to the End of the Eighteenth Century* (1967; Berkeley: University of California Press, 1976), 681–685; and I. Bernard Cohen, *Science and the Founding Fathers: Science in the Political Thought of Jefferson, Franklin, Adams, and Madison* (New York: Norton, 1995), 72–88.

6. See Nicholas Russell, *Like Engend'ring Like: Heredity and Animal Breeding in Early Modern England* (Cambridge: Cambridge University Press, 1986), 11–12; and John Goodridge, *Rural Life in Eighteenth-Century English Poetry* (Cambridge: Cambridge University Press, 1995), esp. 125–143.

7. [Henry Home, Lord Kames], *The Gentleman Farmer. Being an Attempt to improve Agriculture, By Subjecting it to the Test of Rational Principles* (Edinburgh: W. Creech; London: T. Cadell, 1776), 309–311.

8. Dror Wahrman, *The Making of the Modern Self: Identity and Culture in Eighteenth-Century England* (New Haven: Yale University Press, 2004), 101. For a useful introduction to climate theory, see Glacken, *Traces on the Rhodian Shore,* 551–662; and part 3 of Montesquieu, *The Spirit of the Laws* (1748), trans. Anne M. Cohler, Basia Carolyn Miller, and Harold Samuel Stone (Cambridge: Cambridge University Press, 1989).

9. Wahrman, *Making of the Modern Self,* 103.

10. David Hume, "Of National Characters," in *Essays Moral, Political, and Literary,* ed. Eugene F. Miller, rev. ed. (Indianapolis: Liberty Fund, 1987), 197–215 (the note is on 208 and was added in edition K of 1753–1754 [xiii, 629n]). On Jefferson's treatment of human nature and racial identity, see Charles A. Miller, *Jefferson and Nature: An Interpretation* (Baltimore: Johns Hopkins University Press, 1988), 56–87.

11. On climate theory and racial ideology, see especially Roxann Wheeler, *The Complexion of Race: Categories of Difference in Eighteenth-Century British Culture* (Philadelphia: University of Pennsylvania Press, 2000), 21. I believe that Wheeler tends to overstate the malleability of cultural influence according to eighteenth-century writers, downplaying the extent to which climate theory becomes another route to determinism; see also the discussion in chapter 6, note 28 below.

12. The text of the letter is printed as an appendix to *Notes on Virginia,* 284–287. Jefferson made a number of comments in private letters that add to our understanding of his racial theories; the relevant letters are provided in Shuffelton's edition. See especially the letter of 7 June 1785 to the Marquis de Chastellux; Benjamin Banneker's letter to Jefferson of 19 August 1791 and Jefferson's response of 30 August; Jefferson's to Condorcet on 30 August 1791; and Jefferson to James Monroe on 24 November 1801.

13. For two fascinating reflections on the legacies of Linnaean racial thinking, see Jamaica Kincaid, "In History," *Callaloo* 20.1 (1997): 1–7; and M. T. Anderson, *The Astonishing Life of Octavian Nothing, Traitor to the Nation: The Pox Party* (Cambridge: Candlewick, 2006), 46.

14. On polygenesis, see [Henry Home, Lord Kames], *Sketches of the History of Man,* 2 vols. (Edinburgh: W. Creech; London: W. Strahan and T. Cadell, 1774); and Robert Bernasconi's introduction to *American Theories of Polygenesis* (Bristol: Thoemmes, 2002), v–xiii.

15. Gianna Pomata, "Comments on the Papers Given by Phillip Wilson, John C. Waller, and Laure Cartron," *A Cultural History of Heredity II: 18th and 19th Centuries,* Max Planck Institute for the History of Science, preprint 247, ed. Hans-Jörg Rheinberger and Staffan Müller-Wille (2003), 145–151; the quotation is on 151.

16. All quotations from Godwin's prose are drawn from *Political and Philosophical Writings of William Godwin*, ed. Mark Philp et al., 7 vols. (London: William Pickering, 1993); citations will be given parenthetically in the text by volume and page number. On Godwin's revisions to the second and third editions of *Political Justice*, see Mark Philp's discussion in the introduction to *PPWWG*, 1:38.

17. See chapter 4, note 2.

18. Joseph Priestley, *An Essay on the First Principles of Government, and on the Nature of Political, Civil, and Religious Liberty*, 2nd ed. (1771), in *Political Writings*, ed. Peter N. Miller (Cambridge: Cambridge University Press, 1993), 9.

19. Antoine-Nicolas de Condorcet, *Sketch for a Historical Picture of the Progress of the Human Mind* (1795), trans. June Barraclough, intro. Stuart Hampshire (London: Weidenfeld and Nicolson, 1955), 4. For a more detailed treatment of French arguments about human perfectibility, see Michael E. Winston, *From Perfectibility to Perversion: Meliorism in Eighteenth-Century France* (New York: Lang, 2005); and Virginia L. Muller, *The Idea of Perfectibility* (Lanham, MD: University Press of America, 1985).

20. Condorcet, *Sketch*, 142, 173.

21. Condorcet, *Sketch*, 184.

22. *PPWWG* 3:iv, 3:430n; and see also 3:7–8, 6:104, 5:137, and 5:223. On Godwin's debt to Swift (and particularly on the relationship between Godwin's utopia and Swift's Houyhnhnms), see James A. Preu, *The Dean and the Anarchist* (Tallahassee: Florida State University, 1959), esp. 48–49 and 66–67; and C.J. Rawson, *Gulliver and the Gentle Reader: Studies in Swift and Our Time* (London and Boston: Routledge and Kegan Paul, 1973), 148.

23. And see Claude Rawson, "*Gulliver's Travels* and Some Modern Fictions," in *Order From Confusion Sprung: Studies in Eighteenth-Century Literature from Swift to Cowper* (London: George Allen and Unwin, 1985), 68–120.

24. Edmund Burke, *A Vindication of Natural Society* (1756; 2nd ed., 1757), in *Pre-Revolutionary Writings*, ed. Ian Harris (Cambridge: Cambridge University Press, 1993), 27.

25. Burke, *Vindication of Natural Society*, 42.

26. John Wesley, *The Doctrine of Original Sin: According to Scripture, Reason, and Experience* (Bristol: E. Farley, 1757), 53.

27. Valuable older discussions include Roland Mushat Frye, "Swift's Yahoo and the Christian Symbols for Sin," *Journal of the History of Ideas* 15.2 (1954): 201–217; John J. McManmon, "The Problem of a Religious Interpretation of Gulliver's Fourth Voyage," *Journal of the History of Ideas* 27.1 (1966): 59–72; and (more recently) Richard Webster's discussion in *Why Freud Was Wrong: Sin, Science, and Psychoanalysis* (1995), excerpted online as "The Diminutive Insect: *Gulliver's Travels*, Original Sin, and the Imagery of Size," at http://www.richardwebster.net/gulliverstravelsandoriginalsin.html. Also relevant, though excessively polemical, is Donald Greene's essay "Augustinianism and Empiricism: A Note on Eighteenth-Century English Intellectual History," *Eighteenth-Century Studies* 1.1 (1967): 33–68. The problem, really, is that the argument is at once old-fashioned-sounding and

rather intellectually pressing—not to mention unprovable one way or another, barring the discovery of some miraculously revelatory letter by Swift or one of his intimates.

28. Helvétius, *A Treatise on Man; His Intellectual Faculties and His Education* (1772), trans. W. Hooper, 2 vols. (1810; New York: Burt Franklin, 1969), 2:405.

29. Helvétius, *Treatise on Man*, 2:406–407.

30. David Hume, *A Treatise of Human Nature*, ed. L.A. Selby-Bigge, 2nd ed., rev. P.H. Nidditch (Oxford: Clarendon, 1978), 2.3.1 (the quotation is on 402). In his anthology of early writings on human nature, J.S. Slotkin provides extensive quotations from Scottish discussions of the question of natural difference; in general (Kames is the great exception), thinkers such as Adam Smith, William Robertson, Adam Ferguson, and John Millar tend to emphasize the importance of social or environmental factors rather than birth in creating the appearance of natural differences between men. The tendency can be summed up in a passage from *The Wealth of Nations* in which Smith calls the "difference of natural talents in different men . . . in reality, much less than we are aware of" and "[not] so much the cause, as the effect of the division of labour. The difference between the most dissimilar characters, between a philosopher and a common street porter, for example, seems to arise not so much from nature, as from habit, custom, and education" (J.S. Slotkin, ed., *Readings in Early Anthropology*, Viking Fund Publications in Anthropology 40 (Japan: Wenner-Gren Foundation for Anthropological Research, 1965), 418n; see also 427, 434, 443, 454, 457). Darwin seems to have liked Francis Galton's *Hereditary Genius* (1869) very much, and wrote to his cousin that he had "made a convert of an opponent in one sense, for I have always maintained that, excepting fools, men did not differ much in intellect, only in zeal and hard work; and I still think this is an *eminently* important difference" (the text of the letter, drawn from the third edition of Galton's *Memories of My Life*, is given by Nicholas Wright Gillham, *A Life of Sir Francis Galton: From African Exploration to the Birth of Eugenics* [Oxford: Oxford University Press, 2001], 169). The desirability of Darwin's imprimatur was obvious; on the first page of Karl Pearson's biography of Galton appeared another quotation from Darwin (again, as quoted by Gillham), "I am inclined to agree with Francis Galton in believing that education and environment produce only a small effect on the mind of anyone, and that most of our qualities are innate" (155).

31. On necessity and perfectibility (and the compatibility of Godwin's views with those of Hartley and Priestley), see Mark Philp's useful discussion in *Godwin's Political Justice* (London: Duckworth, 1986), 89–90. For Godwin's own thoughts on the moral and psychological necessity of the sentiment of free will, see especially *Thoughts on Man*, 6:165–166; and *The Genius of Christianity Unveiled*, published posthumously in 1873 in *Essays Never Before Published*, esp. 7:127. On Godwin and the idea of genetic perfectibility, see Burton Ralph Pollin, *Education and Enlightenment in the Works of William Godwin* (New York: Las Americas Publishing Company, 1962), 91–94.

32. The quotation is given in Philp, *Godwin's Political Justice*, 213 (and for an apt summary of the inconsistencies in Godwin's position on the equality as opposed to the distinction of individuals, see 210–213). On Godwin's shift from an environmental to a loosely

hereditary emphasis, see especially Alan Richardson, "Of Heartache and Head Injury: Reading Minds in *Persuasion*," *Poetics Today* 23.1 (2002): 141–160, 143.

33. *PPWWG* 5:215; and see also 3:11.

34. Condorcet, *Sketch,* 189; and see also Godwin's development of the argument about population in passages added to the third edition of *Political Justice* (4:342–343).

35. J. B. S. Haldane, *Daedalus; or, Science and the Future* (New York: E. P. Dutton and Co., 1924), 40–41.

36. [Thomas Robert Malthus], *An Essay on the Principle of Population, As It Affects the Future Improvement of Society, with Remarks on the Speculations of Mr. Godwin, M. Condorcet, and Other Writers* (London: J. Johnson, 1798; New York: Augustus M. Kelley, 1965), 126.

37. Malthus, *Essay on Population* (1798), 163–165. The afterlife interpretation can be found on 241.

38. Malthus, *Essay on Population* (1798), 170–171.

39. Malthus, *Essay on Population* (1798), 273–274.

40. Malthus expanded the initial essay on population a number of times, and Godwin's last major response to it can be found in *Of Population. An Enquiry concerning the Power of Increase in the Numbers of Mankind, being an Answer to Mr. Malthus's Essay on that Subject* (1820); here again he isolates the contradiction internal to Malthus' argument by pointing out that "it would be better upon this hypothesis, that we could cut off, in a summary way, a proper number of children in the first stage of their existence, as the cultivator of the earth sets himself to hoe his turnips, clearing the ground round each favoured plant, that it may have room enough for growth and subsistence," but that "this is not consistent with Mr Malthus's ideas of Christian morality" (2:273).

41. Samuel Stanhope Smith, *An Essay on the Causes of the Variety of Complexion and Figure in the Human Species,* ed. Winthrop D. Jordan (Cambridge, MA: Harvard University Press, 1965), 115.

42. James Cowles Prichard, *Researches into the Physical History of Man* (1813; Chicago: University of Chicago Press, 1973), 40–41.

43. Prichard, *Researches,* 41–42. William Lawrence would produce an argument along very similar lines a few years later: "As, on the one hand, a particular form may be perpetuated by confining the intercourse of the sexes to individuals in whom it exists; so, again, it may be changed by introducing into the breed those remarkable for any other quality. Connexions in marriage will generally be formed on the idea of human beauty in any country; an influence, this, which will gradually approximate the countenance towards one common standard. If men, in the affair of marriage, were as much under management as some animals are in the exercise of their generative functions, an absolute ruler might accomplish, in his dominions, almost any idea of the human form" (*Lectures on Physiology, Zoology, and the Natural History of Man* [London: Benbow, 1822], 392–393).

44. Pierre-Jean-George Cabanis, *Rapports du physique et du moral de l'homme* (1802; 2nd ed., 1805), in the translation of Margaret Duggan Saidi, *On the Relations Between the Physi-*

*cal and Moral Aspects of Man,* 2 vols., ed. George Mora, intro. Sergio Moravia and George Mora (Baltimore: Johns Hopkins University Press, 1981), 1:308–309.

# 6. Shibboleths

1. Michele Wucker, *Why the Cocks Fight: Dominicans, Haitians, and the Struggle for Hispaniola* (New York: Farrar Straus Giroux, 1999), 49; and see Rita Dove's poem "Parsley," in *Museum* (Pittsburgh, PA: Carnegie-Mellon University Press, 1983), 75–77, as well as the discussion in Stan Sanvel Rubin and Judith Kitchen, "Riding That Current as Far as It'll Take You" (1985), in *Conversations with Rita Dove,* ed. Earl G. Ingersoll (Jackson: University Press of Mississippi, 2003), 3–14.

2. Edwidge Danticat, *The Farming of Bones* (New York: Soho, 1998), 140, 176, 217. The novel is written in English—another turn of the screw.

3. Danticat, *The Farming of Bones,* 193.

4. Alexander Walker, *Intermarriage; or, The Natural Laws by Which Beauty, Health and Intellect, Result from Certain Unions, and Deformity, Disease and Insanity, From Others* (1839), 2nd ed. (London: John Churchill, 1841), 175–176. On the relationship between hereditarian arguments and the idea that acquired characteristics were passed on from parent to offspring, see Conway Zirkle, "The Early History of the Idea of the Inheritance of Acquired Characters and of Pangenesis," *Transactions of the American Philosophical Society* 35.2 (1946).

5. Walker, *Intermarriage,* 178.

6. Walker, *Intermarriage,* 178–179. Earlier references to the English shibboleth of "th" can be found in Monboddo, *Of the Origin and Progress of Language,* 6 vols. (Edinburgh and London: A. Kincaid, W. Creech, T. Cadell et al., 1773–1792; Menston: Scolar, 1967), 1:176, 4:181; and B.H. Smart, *A Practical Grammar of English Pronunciation, on Plain and Recognised Principles, Calculated to Assist in Removing every objectionable peculiarity of utterance, arising either from Foreign, Provincial, or Vulgar Habits; or from a defective use of the organs of speech* (London: John Richardson and J. Johnson, 1810), 41.

7. See for instance the essays given under the heading "Identities" in *The State of the Language,* ed. Leonard Michaels and Christopher Ricks (Berkeley: University of California Press, 1980).

8. Steven Pinker, *The Language Instinct* (New York: Morrow, 1994), 258; and see also Luigi Luca Cavalli-Sforza, *Genes, Peoples, and Languages,* trans. Mark Seielstad (Berkeley: University of California Press, 2000).

9. Pinker, *The Language Instinct,* 406.

10. Smitherman comments here on her own review of Chomsky's book *Language and Responsibility,* a review written shortly after the *King* "Black Language" decision in 1979 and published in 1983; see Geneva Smitherman, *Talkin That Talk: Language, Culture, and Education in African America* (London: Routledge, 2000), 18. Pinker departs from Chom-

sky in a number of important ways: for Chomsky's skepticism about the idea of language as the result of biological evolution, for instance, see "An Interview on Minimalism," in Noam Chomsky, *On Nature and Language,* ed. Adriana Belletti and Luigi Rizzi (Cambridge: Cambridge University Press, 2002), 92–161, esp. 146–151. Like Pinker, however, Chomsky drastically misrepresents Locke's arguments about innateness and language; see the discussion in Hans Aarsleff, *From Locke to Saussure: Essays on the Study of Language and Intellectual History* (Minneapolis: University of Minnesota Press, 1982), 114–115, 172.

11. The full text of the Oakland Ebonics Resolution and its subsequent revisions is given (along with other relevant documents) in *The Real Ebonics Debate: Power, Language, and the Education of African-American Children,* ed. Theresa Perry and Lisa Delpit (Boston: Beacon Press, 1998), 143–147; this quotation appears on p. 145.

12. Wayne O'Neil, "If Ebonics Isn't a Language, Then Tell Me, What Is?," in *The Real Ebonics Debate,* 38–47; the quotation appears on p. 38.

13. "Oakland Ebonics Resolution," in *The Real Ebonics Debate,* 143.

14. "Ebonics Resolution Revisions," in *The Real Ebonics Debate,* 146.

15. John Russell Rickford and Russell John Rickford, *Spoken Soul: The Story of Black English* (New York: Wiley, 2000), 169.

16. On the origins of African-American English, see especially Salikoko S. Mufwene, "Some Sociohistorical Inferences About the Development of African American English," in *The English History of African American English,* ed. Shana Poplack (Oxford: Blackwell, 2000), 233–263; and John R. Rickford, "The Creole Origins of African-American Vernacular English: Evidence from Copula Absence," in *African-American English: Structure, History, and Use,* ed. Salikoko S. Mufwene, John R. Rickford, Guy Bailey, and John Baugh (London: Routledge, 1998), 154–200.

17. Rickford and Rickford, *Spoken Soul,* 170.

18. Rickford and Rickford, *Spoken Soul,* 170–171.

19. John Baugh, *Beyond Ebonics: Linguistic Pride and Racial Prejudice* (New York: Oxford University Press, 2000); and see also Baugh, *Out of the Mouths of Slaves: African American Language and Educational Malpractice* (Austin: University of Texas Press, 1999), esp. 152–155; and the introduction added in response to the controversy in Eleanor Wilson Orr, *Twice As Less: Black English and the Performance of Black Students in Mathematics and Science,* 2nd ed. (1987; New York: Norton, 1997), 3–7.

20. Baugh, *Beyond Ebonics,* 68–69.

21. Baugh, *Beyond Ebonics,* 85; and see also Baugh, *Out of the Mouths of Slaves,* 7.

22. Trial transcript, quoted in Rickford and Rickford, *Spoken Soul,* 101.

23. Rickford and Rickford, *Spoken Soul,* 101.

24. Patricia Daniels Cornwell, *Postmortem* (New York: Scribner's, 1990), 246–247.

25. Rickford and Rickford, *Spoken Soul,* 102–103.

26. Michel Foucault, "What Is Enlightenment?," trans. Catherine Porter, in *The Foucault Reader,* ed. Paul Rabinow (New York: Pantheon Books, 1984), 32–50; the quotation appears on p. 42.

27. Foucault, "What Is Enlightenment?," 43; and see also Immanuel Kant, "Answer to the Question: What Is Enlightenment?" (1784), trans. Thomas K. Abbott, in *Basic Writings of Kant,* ed. Allen W. Wood (New York: Modern Library, 2001), 135–141. These essays come front-and-center for historians and social scientists in a way that they do not necessarily do for literary critics; see, for instance, Dorinda Outram, *The Enlightenment* (Cambridge: Cambridge University Press, 1995), 1–3.

28. A good example of this can be found in Roxann Wheeler, *The Complexion of Race: Categories of Difference in Eighteenth-Century British Culture* (Philadelphia: University of Pennsylvania Press, 2000). Wheeler makes a strong case for the possibility that the "four-stages" theory, or progress theory, of the Scottish Enlightenment "offered a more significant form of racialization of the body politic than the categories concerning the physical body found in natural history" (7). The book's language, though, sometimes expresses a kind of ethical muddle around the implications of four-stages theory (with its emphasis on "climate") for theories of human differences and the practices—very often violent, almost always offensive to us now—associated with such theories. Here is Wheeler on the ways that writings on civil society "functioned as a racial ideology": "With its emphasis on material culture, four-stages theory provided a conception of human difference that was, on the face of it, antipathetic to the implications of physical typology. By offering an alternative explanatory system, it also forestalled the trend to make notions of race bone deep through the study of comparative anatomy. In this paradigm, like its religious counterpart Christianity, what people do and how they live is important—not what people look like" (182). A "racial ideology" is surely a bad thing, something we want to get away from; to argue that "four-stages theory" is a racial ideology is by definition to find it ethically culpable, though Wheeler's book does not offer a framework in which such "meta"-questions can be treated. But an ideology that is "antipathetic to the implications of physical typology" (at least "on the face of it"—an odd use of the metaphor of surfaces, given the context of Wheeler's attack on the dominance of skin color as an explanatory factor in accounts of eighteenth-century racism) is surely preferable to one that is not—and doesn't forestalling "the trend to make notions of race bone deep through the study of comparative anatomy" also sound like a good thing, even a kind of fantasy or wish-fulfillment in which the eighteenth century can be exonerated from the sins of the nineteenth? Thanks to Jennifer Thorn for organizing the MLA special session on four-stages theory that first prompted me to consider these questions.

29. Mary Midgley, *Beast and Man: The Roots of Human Nature* (Ithaca: Cornell University Press, 1978), xv–xvi.


## Conclusion. The Promise of Perfection

1. *The Adams-Jefferson Letters: The Complete Correspondence Between Thomas Jefferson and Abigail and John Adams,* ed. Lester J. Cappon, 2 vols. (Chapel Hill: University of North Carolina Press, 1959), 2:355.

2. *Adams-Jefferson Letters,* 2:357–358.

3. *Adams-Jefferson Letters,* 2:365, 2:376.

4. *Adams-Jefferson Letters,* 2:387.

5. *Adams-Jefferson Letters,* 2:387–388.

6. John Passmore, *The Perfectibility of Man* (London: Duckworth, 1970), 326.

7. Shakespeare, *The Tempest,* 4.1.188–189.

8. Michael J. Sandel, *The Case Against Perfection: Ethics in the Age of Genetic Engineering* (Cambridge, MA: Harvard University Press, 2007), 46.

9. Slavoj Žižek, "Bring Me My Philips Mental Jacket," *London Review of Books* 25.10 (22 May 2003): 5. See also the related observations in Eve Kosofsky Sedgwick, *Epistemology of the Closet* (Berkeley: University of California Press, 1990), 43.

10. Stephen J. Dubner and Steven D. Levitt, "A Star Is Made," *New York Times,* 7 May 2006.

11. Galen, "The Affections and Errors of the Soul," *Selected Works,* trans. P. N. Singer (Oxford: Oxford University Press, 1997), 106.

12. Leslie H. Farber, "Schizophrenia and the Mad Psychotherapist" (1963), *The Ways of the Will: Selected Essays,* rev. ed., ed. Robert Boyers and Anne Farber (New York: Basic Books, 2000), 21–45; the quotation is on 36–37.

# BIBLIOGRAPHY OF WORKS CITED

Aarsleff, Hans. *From Locke to Saussure: Essays on the Study of Language and Intellectual History.* Minneapolis: University of Minnesota Press, 1982.

Adams, James. *Euphonologia Linguae Anglicanae.* London: R. White, 1794. Menston: Scolar, 1968.

———. *The Pronunciation of the English Language Vindicated From Imputed Anomaly & Caprice . . . With an Appendix, on the Dialects of Human Speech in All Countries, and an Analytical Discussion and Vindication of the Dialect of Scotland.* Edinburgh: J. Moir et al., 1799.

Adams, John, Abigail Adams, and Thomas Jefferson. *The Adams-Jefferson Letters: The Complete Correspondence Between Thomas Jefferson and Abigail and John Adams.* Ed. Lester J. Cappon. 2 vols. Chapel Hill: University of North Carolina Press, 1959.

Adams, Rachel. *Sideshow U.S.A.: Freaks and the American Cultural Imagination.* Chicago: University of Chicago Press, 2001.

Adelman, Janet. *Suffocating Mothers: Fantasies of Maternal Origin in Shakespeare's Plays.* London: Routledge, 1992.

Adelmann, Howard B. "Introduction: A Brief Sketch of the History of Embryology Before Fabricius." In *The Embryological Treatises of Hieronymus Fabricius of Acquapendente.* Ed. Adelmann. Ithaca: Cornell University Press, 1942.

Aeschylus. *Oresteia.* Trans. Richmond Lattimore. Chicago: University of Chicago Press, 1953.

Alexievich, Svetlana. *Voices from Chernobyl.* Trans. Keith Gessen. Normal: Dalkey Archive Press, 2005.

Alston, R.C. *A Bibliography of the English Language from the Invention of Printing to the Year 1800.* Rev. ed. Ilkey: Janus Press, 1974.

Anderson, M.T. *The Astonishing Life of Octavian Nothing, Traitor to the Nation: The Pox Party.* Cambridge: Candlewick, 2006.

Angus, William. *A Pronouncing Vocabulary of the English Language.* Glasgow: D. Niven, 1800. Menston: Scolar, 1969.

[Anon.]. *A New Treatise of Canary-Birds. Containing The manner of Breeding and Coupling them, that they may have Beautiful Young Ones. With Curious Remarks relating to the Signs and Causes of their Distempers, and the Method of Curing Them. Written in French by Mr. Hervieux, and Translated into English.* London: Bernard Lintot, 1718.

[Anon.]. *Aristoteles Master-Piece; or, The Secrets of Generation displayed in all the parts thereof.* London: J. How, 1684.

[Anon.]. *A Vocabulary of Such Words in the English Language as are of Dubious or Unsettled Accentuation.* London: F. and C. Rivington et al., 1797

[Anon.]. *Callipædiæ; or, An Art how to have Handsome Children: Written in Latin By the Abbot Quillet. To which is Added, Pædotrophiæ; or, The Art of Nursing and Breeding up Children: Written in Latin By Monsieur St. Marthe, Physician to Henry III. of France. Now done into* English *Verse.* London: John Morphew, 1710.

[Anon.]. *The Bird-Fancier's Delight.* London: Thomas Ward, 1714.

Arbuthnot, John. *An Essay Concerning the Effects of Air on Human Bodies.* London: J. Tonson, 1733.

Aristotle. *Generation of Animals.* Trans. A.L. Peck. 1942. Cambridge, MA: Harvard University Press, 1990.

[A.S. Gent.]. *The Gentleman's Compleat Jockey: With The Perfect Horse-man and Experienc'd Farrier.* London: T. Norris, [1715?].

Austen, Jane. "The History of England from the reign of Henry the 4th to the death of Charles the 1st." In *Catharine and Other Writings,* ed. Margaret Anne Doody and Douglas Murray, 134–144. 1993. Oxford: Oxford University Press, 1998.

Bacon, Sir Francis. *The Essayes or Counsels, Civill and Morall.* Ed. Michael Kiernan. 1995. Oxford: Clarendon, 2000.

Baker, Felicity. "Rousseau and the Colonies." *Eighteenth-Century Life* 22.1 (1998): 172–189.

Bakewell, Robert. *Observations on the Influence of Soil and Climate upon Wool.* London: J. Harding, 1808.

Ballantyne, J.W. *Teratogenesis: An Inquiry Into the Causes of Monstrosities.* Edinburgh: Oliver and Boyd, 1897.

Barlow, Francis. *Æsop's Fables with his Life: In English, French and Latin.* 1666. London: H. Hills, 1687.

Barnes, J.A. "Genetrix : Genitor :: Nature : Culture." In *The Character of Kinship,* ed. Goody, 61–73.

Barrell, John. *English Literature in History, 1730–80: An Equal, Wide Survey.* London: Hutchinson, 1983.

Barthes, Roland. *The Neutral: Lecture Course at the Collège de France (1977–1978).* Trans. Rosalind E. Krauss and Denis Hollier. New York: Columbia University Press, 2005.

——. *Roland Barthes.* 1975. Trans. Richard Howard. New York: Hill and Wang, 1977.

Bartholomeusz, Dennis. *The Winter's Tale in Performance in England and America, 1611–1976.* Cambridge: Cambridge University Press, 1982.

Bartra, Roger. *The Artificial Savage: Modern Myths of the Wild Man.* Trans. Christopher Follett. Ann Arbor: University of Michigan Press, 1997.

Batchelor, T. *An Orthoëpical Analysis of the English Language; or, An Essay on the Nature of its Simple and Combined Sounds; The Manner of their Formation by the Vocal Organs; the Minute Varieties which Constitute a Depraved or Provincial Pronunciation; and the Inadequacy of attempting to explain by means of the English Alphabet.* London: P. Da Ponte for Didier and Tebbet, 1809.

Bate, James. *A Rationale of the Literal Doctrine of Original Sin; or, A Vindication of God's permitting the Fall of Adam, And the Subsequent Corruption of our Human Nature.* London: J. Dodsley et al., 1766.

Bate, Jonathan. *Shakespearean Constitutions: Politics, Theatre, Criticism, 1730–1830.* Oxford: Clarendon, 1989.

Baugh, John. *Beyond Ebonics: Linguistic Pride and Racial Prejudice.* New York: Oxford University Press, 2000.

——. *Out of the Mouths of Slaves: African American Language and Educational Malpractice.* Austin: University of Texas Press, 1999.

Beattie, James. *The Theory of Language.* London: A. Strahan and T. Cadell; Edinburgh: W. Creech, 1788. Menston: Scolar, 1968.

Beer, Gillian. *Darwin's Plots: Evolutionary Narrative in Darwin, George Eliot, and Nineteenth-Century Fiction.* 2nd ed. 1983. Cambridge: Cambridge University Press, 2000.

——. "Darwin's Reading and the Fictions of Development." In *The Darwinian Heritage,* ed. David Kohn with Malcolm J. Kottler, 543–588. Princeton: Princeton University Press, 1985.

——. "Has Nature a Future?" In *The Third Culture: Literature and Science,* ed. Elinor S. Shaffer, 15–27. Berlin: de Gruyter, 1998.

Beeson, David. *Maupertuis: An Intellectual Biography.* Studies on Voltaire and the Eighteenth Century 299. Oxford: Voltaire Foundation, 1992.

Benson, Pamela Joseph. *The Invention of the Renaissance Woman: The Challenge of Female Independence in the Literature and Thought of Italy and England.* University Park: Pennsylvania State University Press, 1992.

Benzie, W. *The Dublin Orator: Thomas Sheridan's Influence on Eighteenth-Century Rhetoric and Belles Lettres.* Leeds: University of Leeds School of English, 1972.

Bernasconi, Robert. Introduction. *American Theories of Polygenesis,* v–xiii. Bristol: Thoemmes, 2002.

Bethell, S. L. *The Winter's Tale: A Study.* London: Staples, [1947].

Biswell, Andrew. *The Real Life of Anthony Burgess.* London: Picador, 2005.

Blair, Hugh. *Lectures on Rhetoric and Belles Lettres.* 1783. 2 vols. Ed. Harold F. Harding. Intro. David Potten. Carbondale: Southern Illinois University Press, 1965.

Blumenbach. *On the Natural Variety of Mankind.* 1775. 1795. In *Anthropological Treatises,* trans. and ed. Thomas Bendyshe. 1865. Boston: Longwood, [1978].

Boswell, James. *Boswell's Life of Johnson.* Ed. George Birkbeck Hill. Rev. L.F. Powell. 6 vols. Oxford: Clarendon, 1934–1964.

———. *The Ominous Years: 1774–1776.* Ed. Charles Ryskamp and Frederick A. Pottle. New York: McGraw-Hill, 1963.

Boucé, Paul-Gabriel. "Imagination, Pregnant Women, and Monsters, in Eighteenth-Century England and France." In *Sexual Underworlds of the Enlightenment,* ed. G.S. Rousseau and Roy Porter, 86–100. Chapel Hill: University of North Carolina Press, 1988.

Bowden, Betsy. "Before the Houyhnhnms: Rational Horses in the Late Seventeenth Century." *Notes and Queries* 39.1 (1992): 38–40.

Bowler, Peter J. *Evolution: The History of an Idea.* Berkeley: University of California Press, 1984.

Boyle, Frank T. "Chinese Utopianism and Gulliverian Narcissism in Swift's *Travels.*" In *Locating Swift: Essays from Dublin on the 250th Anniversary of the Death of Jonathan Swift, 1667–1745,* ed. Aileen Douglas, Patrick Kelly, and Ian Campbell Ross, 117–128. Dublin: Four Courts Press, 1998.

Bracken, Henry. *The Midwife's Companion; or, A Treatise of Midwifery.* London: J. Clarke and J. Shuckburgh, 1737.

Bradley, Richard. *The Gentleman and Farmer's Guide For the Increase and Improvement of Cattle.* 2nd ed. London: G.S., 1732.

Brewer, John, and Susan Staves, eds. *Early Modern Conceptions of Property.* London: Routledge, 1996.

Brooks, Douglas, ed. *Printing and Parenting in Early Modern England.* Burlington, VT: Ashgate, 2005.

Buchanan, James. *An Essay Towards Establishing a Standard for an Elegant and Uniform Pronunciation of the English Language, Throughout the British Dominions, As practised by the Most Learned and Polite Speakers.* London: Edward and Charles Dilly, 1764.

Buffon, Georges Louis Leclerc, Count de. *Natural History, General and Particular.* 9 vols. Trans. William Smellie. Intro. Aaron V. Garrett. London: A. Strahan and T. Cadell, 1791. Bristol: Thoemmes, 2000.

Buffon. *Natural History of the Horse. To which is added, that of the Ass, Bull, Cow, Ox, Sheep, Goat, and Swine. With Accurate Descriptions of their several Parts. And full Directions for Breeding, Chusing, Feeding, and Improving, those useful Creatures.* London: R. Griffith, 1756.

Burke, Edmund. Vol. 9 of *The Correspondence of Edmund Burke.* Ed. R.B. McDowell and John A. Woods. Cambridge: Cambridge University Press; Chicago: University of Chicago Press, 1970.

———. *Reflections on the Revolution in France, and on the Proceedings in Certain Societies in London Relative to that Event.* 1790. Ed. Conor Cruise O'Brien. 1968. London: Penguin, 1986.

———. *A Vindication of Natural Society*. 1756. 2nd ed. 1757. In *Pre-Revolutionary Writings*, ed. Ian Harris. Cambridge: Cambridge University Press, 1993.

[Burnett, James, Lord Monboddo]. *Antient Metaphysics*. 6 vols. London and Edinburgh: T. Cadell, J. Balfour et al., 1779–1799. New York: Garland, 1977.

———. *Of the Origin and Progress of Language*. 6 vols. Edinburgh and London: A. Kincaid, W. Creech, T. Cadell et al., 1773–1792. Menston: Scolar, 1967.

Burney, Fanny [Frances]. *Evelina; or, The History of a Young Lady's Entrance Into the World*. 1778. Ed. Edward A. Bloom with Lillian D. Bloom. 1968. Oxford: Oxford University Press, 1984.

Bushnell, Rebecca. *A Culture of Teaching: Early Modern Humanism in Theory and Practice*. Ithaca: Cornell University Press, 1996.

———. *Green Desire: Imagining Early Modern English Gardens*. Ithaca: Cornell University Press, 2003.

Byrne, Paula. "A Maniac for Perdita." *TLS*, 6 August 2004, 11–12.

Cabanis, Pierre-Jean-George. *Rapports du physique et du moral de l'homme*. 1802. 2nd ed. 1805. Trans. Margaret Duggan Saidi as *On the Relations Between the Physical and Moral Aspects of Man*. Ed. George Mora. Intro. Sergio Moravia and George Mora. 2 vols. Baltimore: Johns Hopkins University Press, 1981.

Campbell, Jill. "'The Exact Picture of his Mother': Recognizing Joseph Andrews." *ELH* 55 (1988): 643–664.

Carol, Anne. *Histoire de l'eugénisme en France: Les médecins et la procréation XIX^e–XX^e siècle*. Paris: Seuil, 1995.

Carrol, James. *The American Criterion of the English Language; containing the Elements of Pronunciation; in Five Sections. For the use of English schools and foreigners*. New-London: Samuel Green, 1795.

Cavalli-Sforza, Luigi Luca. *Genes, Peoples, and Languages*. Trans. Mark Seielstad. Berkeley: University of California Press, 2000.

Chalker, John. *The English Georgic: A Study in the Development of a Form*. Baltimore: Johns Hopkins University Press, 1969.

Chomsky, Noam. *On Nature and Language*. Ed. Adriana Belletti and Luigi Rizzi. Cambridge: Cambridge University Press, 2002.

Clark, Elizabeth A. "Generation, Degeneration, Regeneration: Original Sin and the Conception of Jesus in the Polemic Between Augustine and Julian of Eclanum." In *Generation and Degeneration*, ed. Finucci and Brownlee, 17–40.

Clayton, Jay. "Genome Time." In *Time and the Literary*, ed. Karen Newman, Jay Clayton, and Marianne Hirsch, 31–59. New York: Routledge, 2002.

Clifford, James L. "Gulliver's Fourth Voyage: 'Hard' and 'Soft' Schools of Interpretation." In *Quick Springs of Sense: Studies in the Eighteenth Century*, 33–49. Athens: University of Georgia Press, 1974.

Cobb, Matthew. *Generation: The Seventeenth-Century Scientists Who Unraveled the Secrets of Sex, Life, and Growth*. London: Bloomsbury, 2006.

Cody, Lisa Forman. *Birthing the Nation: Sex, Science, and the Conception of Eighteenth-Century Britons.* Oxford: Oxford University Press, 2005.

Cohen, I. Bernard. *Science and the Founding Fathers: Science in the Political Thought of Jefferson, Franklin, Adams, and Madison.* New York: Norton, 1995.

Cohen, Michèle. *Fashioning Masculinity: National Identity and Language in the Eighteenth Century.* London: Routledge, 1996.

Cole, F.J. *Early Theories of Sexual Generation.* Oxford: Clarendon, 1930.

Colley, Linda. *Britons: Forging the Nation, 1707–1837.* New Haven: Yale University Press, 1992.

[Colman, George]. *The Sheep-Shearing: A Dramatic Pastoral in Three Acts. Taken from Shakespeare. As it is performed at the Theatre Royal in the Haymarket.* London: G. Kearsly, 1777.

Condillac, Etienne Bonnot de. *Essay on the Origin of Human Knowledge.* 1746. Trans. Hans Aarsleff. Cambridge: Cambridge University Press, 2001.

Condorcet, Antoine-Nicolas de. *Sketch for a Historical Picture of the Progress of the Human Mind.* 1795. Trans. June Barraclough. Intro. Stuart Hampshire. London: Weidenfeld and Nicolson, 1955.

Cook, Elizabeth Heckendorn. "Crown Forests and Female Georgic: Frances Burney and the Reconstruction of Britishness." In *The Country and the City Revisited: England and the Politics of Culture, 1550–1850,* ed. Gerald MacLean et al., 197–212. Cambridge: Cambridge University Press, 1999.

Cornwell, Patricia Daniels. *Postmortem.* New York: Scribner's, 1990.

Cottom, Daniel. *The Civilized Imagination: A Study of Ann Radcliffe, Jane Austen, and Sir Walter Scott.* Cambridge: Cambridge University Press, 1985.

Court, Franklin E. *Institutionalizing English Literature: The Culture and Politics of Literary Study, 1750–1900.* Stanford: Stanford University Press, 1992.

Crane, R.S. "The Houyhnhnms, the Yahoos, and the History of Ideas." In *Reason and the Imagination: Studies in the History of Ideas, 1600–1800,* ed. J.A. Mazzeo, 231–253. New York: Columbia University Press; London: Routledge and Kegan Paul, 1962.

Crawford, Julie. *Marvellous Protestantism: Monstrous Births in Post-Reformation England.* Baltimore: Johns Hopkins University Press, 2005.

Crawford, Rachel. "English Georgic and British Nationhood." *ELH* 65.1 (1998): 123–158.

——. *Poetry, Enclosure, and the Vernacular Landscape, 1700–1830.* Cambridge: Cambridge University Press, 2002.

Crawford, Robert. *Devolving English Literature.* Oxford: Clarendon, 1992.

Crowley, Tony. "Language, History, and the Formation of Cultural Identity." In *Proper English? Readings in Language, History, and Cultural Identity,* 1–12. London: Routledge, 1991.

Culpeper, Nich[olas]. *A Directory for Midwives; or, A Guide for Women, In their Conception, Bearing, And Suckling their Children.* London: Peter Cole, 1651.

Danticat, Edwidge. *The Farming of Bones.* New York: Soho, 1998.

Darwin, Charles. *The Variation of Animals and Plants Under Domestication.* 1868. 2 vols. 2nd ed. Intro. Harriet Ritvo. New York: D. Appleton and Co., 1883. Baltimore: Johns Hopkins University Press, 1998.

Davidson, Jenny. "Professional Education and Female Accomplishments: Gender and Education in Maria Edgeworth's *Patronage.*" *Eighteenth-Century Women* 4 (2006): 259–285.

DeBolla, Peter. *The Discourse of the Sublime: Readings in History, Aesthetics, and the Subject.* Oxford: Blackwell, 1989.

De Bruyn, Frans. "The Classical Silva and the Generic Development of Scientific Writing in Seventeenth-Century England." *New Literary History* 32 (2001): 347–373.

———. "Reading Virgil's *Georgics* as a Scientific Text: The Eighteenth-Century Debate Between Jethro Tull and Stephen Switzer." *ELH* 71 (2004): 661–689.

[Defoe, Daniel]. *Mere Nature Delineated; or, A Body without a Soul.* 1726. In vol. 5 of *Writings on Travel, Discovery, and History by Daniel Defoe,* ed. Andrew Wear. London: Pickering and Chatto, 2002.

Defoe, Daniel. *Robinson Crusoe.* 1719. Ed. Michael Shinagel. 2nd ed. New York: Norton, 1994.

de Grazia, Margreta. "Imprints: Shakespeare, Gutenberg, and Descartes." In vol. 2 of *Alternative Shakespeare,* ed. Terrence Hawkes, 63–94. London: Routledge, 1996. Repr. in *Printing and Parenting in Early Modern England,* ed. Brooks.

Derrida, Jacques. *Of Grammatology.* Trans. Gayatri Chakravorty Spivak. Baltimore: Johns Hopkins University Press, 1976.

———. "Plato's Pharmacy." In *Dissemination,* 61–84. Trans. Barbara Johnson. Chicago: University of Chicago Press, 1981.

de Waal, Frans. *The Ape and the Sushi Master: Cultural Reflections by a Primatologist.* New York: Basic Books, 2001.

Diamond, Jared. *Guns, Germs, and Steel: The Fates of Human Societies.* 1997. New York: Norton, 1999.

*Dictionnaire historique de la langue française.* Paris: Dictionnaires le Robert, 1993.

Diderot, Denis. *Supplément au Voyage de Bougainville.* 1796. In Diderot, *Political Writings.* Trans. and ed. John Hope Mason and Robert Wokler. Cambridge: Cambridge University Press, 1992.

Dimock, Wai Chee. "Genre as World System: Epic and Novel on Four Continents." *Narrative* 14.1 (2006): 85–101.

———. "Planetary Time and Global Translation: 'Context' in Literary Studies." *Common Knowledge* 9.3 (2003): 488–507.

Dobson, Michael. *The Making of the National Poet: Shakespeare, Adaptation, and Authorship, 1660–1769.* Oxford: Clarendon, 1992.

Dolan, Frances. "Taking the Pencil out of God's Hand: Art, Nature, and the Face-Painting Debate in Early Modern England." *PMLA* 108 (1993): 224–239.

Douthwaite, Julia V. *The Wild Girl, Natural Man, and the Monster: Dangerous Experiments in the Age of Enlightenment.* Chicago: University of Chicago Press, 2002.

Dove, Rita. *Museum*. Pittsburgh, PA: Carnegie-Mellon University Press, 1983.

Dryden, John. *The State of Innocence, and Fall of Man*. 1677. In vol. 12 of *The Works of John Dryden*, ed. Vinton A. Dearing. Berkeley: University of California Press, 1994.

———. Vol. 6 of *The Works of John Dryden*. Ed. William Frost, Vinton A. Dearing, and Alan Roper. Berkeley: University of California Press, 1987.

Dryden, John, trans. *Virgil's Georgics*. 1697. In vol. 5 of *The Works of John Dryden*, ed. William Frost and Vinton A. Dearing. Berkeley: University of California Press, 1987.

Dubner, Stephen J., and Steven D. Levitt. "A Star Is Made." *New York Times*, 7 May 2006.

Duckworth, Alistair M. "Fiction and Some Uses of the Country House Setting from Richardson to Scott." In *The Country Myth: Motifs in the British Novel from Defoe to Smollett*, ed. H. George Hahn, 221–254. Frankfurt: Lang, 1991.

Dudley, Edward, and Maximillian E. Novak, eds. *The Wild Man Within: An Image in Western Thought from the Renaissance to Romanticism*. Pittsburgh: University of Pittsburgh Press, 1972.

Duncan, Ian. "Adam Smith, Samuel Johnson, and the Institutions of English." In *The Scottish Invention of English Literature*, ed. Robert Crawford, 37–54. Cambridge: Cambridge University Press, 1998.

Dunn, L. C. *A Short History of Genetics: The Development of Some of the Main Lines of Thought, 1864–1939*. 1965. Ames: Iowa State University Press, 1991.

Eagleton, Terry. *The Idea of Culture*. Malden: Blackwell, 2000.

Edgeworth, Maria, and Richard Lovell Edgeworth. *An Essay on Irish Bulls*. 1802. In vol. 1 of *The Novels and Selected Works of Maria Edgeworth*, ed. Jane Desmarais, Tim McLoughlin, and Marilyn Butler. London: Pickering and Chatto, 1999.

Ehrlich, Paul R. *Human Natures: Genes, Cultures, and the Human Prospect*. Washington, DC, and Covelo, CA: Island Press/Shearwater Books, 2000.

Ellacombe, Henry N. *The Plant-Lore and Garden-Craft of Shakespeare*. 2nd ed. London: W. Satchell and Co., 1884.

Elphinston, James. *Propriety Ascertained in her Picture; or, Inglish Speech and Spelling Rendered Mutual Guides*. London: Jon Walter, 1787.

Eze, Emmanuel C. "Hume, Race, and Human Nature." *Journal of the History of Ideas* 61.4 (2000): 691–698.

Fagot, Anne. "Le 'transformisme' de Maupertuis." In *Actes de la journée Maupertuis 1973*, 163–181. Paris: J. Vrin, 1975.

Farber, Leslie H. "Schizophrenia and the Mad Psychotherapist." 1963. In *The Ways of the Will: Selected Essays*, 21–45. Rev. ed. Ed. Robert Boyers and Anne Farber. New York: Basic Books, 2000.

Feingold, Richard. *Nature and Society: Later Eighteenth-Century Uses of the Pastoral and Georgic*. New Brunswick, NJ: Rutgers University Press, 1978.

[Fell, John]. *An Essay Towards an English Grammar*. London: C. Dilly, 1784; Menston: Scolar, 1967.

# Bibliography

Ferguson, Robert A. *Law and Letters in American Culture.* Cambridge, MA: Harvard University Press, 1984.

Fielding, Penny. *Writing and Orality: Nationality, Culture, and Nineteenth-Century Scottish Fiction.* Oxford: Clarendon, 1996.

Fildes, Valerie A. *Breasts, Bottles, and Babies: A History of Infant Feeding.* Edinburgh: Edinburgh University Press, 1986.

——. *Wet Nursing: A History from Antiquity to the Present.* Oxford: Basil Blackwell, 1988.

Finucci, Valeria. "Maternal Imagination and Monstrous Birth: Tasso's *Gerusalemme liberata.*" In *Generation and Degeneration,* ed. Finucci and Brownlee, 41–77.

Finucci, Valeria, and Kevin Brownlee, eds. *Generation and Degeneration: Tropes of Reproduction in Literature and History from Antiquity Through Early Modern Europe.* Durham: Duke University Press, 2001.

Fliegelman, Jay. *Declaring Independence: Jefferson, Natural Language, and the Culture of Performance.* Stanford: Stanford University Press, 1993.

Flint, Christopher. *Family Fictions: Narrative and Domestic Relations in Britain, 1688–1798.* Stanford: Stanford University Press, 1998.

Foote, Samuel. *The Orators.* London: J. Coote et al., 1762. Repr. in vol. 1 of *The Plays of Samuel Foote,* ed. Paula R. Backscheider and Douglas Howard. New York: Garland, 1983.

Foucault, Michel. *The Order of Things: An Archeology of the Human Sciences.* 1966. Trans. Alan Sheridan. New York: Vintage, 1973.

——. "What Is Enlightenment?" Trans. Catherine Porter. In *The Foucault Reader,* ed. Paul Rabinow, 32–50. New York: Pantheon Books, 1984.

——. *The Order of Things: An Archeology of the Human Sciences.* 1966. [Trans. Alan Sheridan.] New York: Vintage, 1973.

Fowler, Alastair. "Georgic and Pastoral: Laws of Genre in the Seventeenth Century." In *Culture and Cultivation in Early Modern England: Writing and the Land,* ed. Michael Leslie and Timothy Raylor, 81–88. Leicester: Leicester University Press, 1992.

Franklin, Benjamin. *A Benjamin Franklin Reader.* Ed. Nathan G. Goodman. New York: Thomas Y. Crowell, 1945.

Freud, Sigmund. *Civilization and Its Discontents.* 1930. Trans. James Strachey. New York: Norton, 1989.

Frye, Northrop. "Recognition in *The Winter's Tale.*" In *Essays on Shakespeare and Elizabethan Drama in Honor of Hardin Craig,* ed. Richard Hosley, 235–246. Columbia: University of Missouri Press, 1962.

Frye, Roland Mushat. "Swift's Yahoo and the Christian Symbols for Sin." *Journal of the History of Ideas* 15.2 (1954): 201–217.

Furness, Horace Howard, ed. *A New Variorum Edition of Shakespeare: The Winter's Tale.* 6th ed. New York: J.B. Lippincott, 1889. New York: Dover, 1964.

Galen. "The Affections and Errors of the Soul." In *Selected Works,* trans. P.N. Singer. Oxford and New York: Oxford University Press, 1997.

Galton, David J. "Greek Theories on Eugenics." *Journal of Medical Ethics* 24.4 (1998): 263–267.

Garrick, David. *Florizel and Perdita: A Dramatic Pastoral in Three Acts. Alter'd from The Winter's Tale of Shakespear.* London: J. and R. Tonson, 1758. London: Cornmarket, 1969.

Gasking, Elizabeth B. *Investigations Into Generation, 1651–1828.* Baltimore: Johns Hopkins University Press, [1967].

Geertz, Clifford. *The Interpretation of Cultures.* New York: Basic Books, 1973.

Gillham, Nicholas Wright. *A Life of Sir Francis Galton: From African Exploration to the Birth of Eugenics.* Oxford: Oxford University Press, 2001.

Gineste, Thierry, ed. *Victor de l'Aveyron: Dernier enfant sauvage, premier enfant fou.* Paris: Le Sycomore, 1981.

Glacken, Clarence J. *Traces on the Rhodian Shore: Nature and Culture in Western Thought from Ancient Times to the End of the Eighteenth Century.* 1967. Berkeley: University of California Press, 1976.

Glass, Bentley. "The Germination of the Idea of Biological Species." In *Forerunners of Darwin: 1745–1859,* 30–48.

——. "Maupertuis, Pioneer of Genetics and Evolution." In *Forerunners of Darwin: 1745–1859,* 51–83.

Glass, Bentley, Owsei Temkin, and William L. Straus Jr., eds. *Forerunners of Darwin: 1745–1859.* Baltimore: Johns Hopkins University Press, 1959.

Godwin, William. *Political and Philosophical Writings of William Godwin.* Ed. Mark Philp et al. 7 vols. London: William Pickering, 1993.

Goffman, Erving. *The Presentation of Self in Everyday Life.* Garden City, NY: Doubleday, 1959.

Good, John Mason. *The Nature of Things: A Didactic Poem.* 2 vols. London: Longman et al., 1805.

Goodman, Kevis. *Georgic Modernity and British Romanticism: Poetry and the Mediation of History.* Cambridge: Cambridge University Press, 2004.

——. Review of Clifford Siskin, *The Work of Writing. Modern Language Quarterly* 61.3 (2000): 545–551.

——. "'Wasted Labor'? Milton's Eve, the Poet's Work, and the Challenge of Sympathy." *ELH* 64.2 (1997): 415–446.

Goodridge, John. *Rural Life in Eighteenth-Century English Poetry.* Cambridge: Cambridge University Press, 1995.

Goody, Jack, ed. *The Character of Kinship.* Cambridge: Cambridge University Press, 1973.

Goody, Jack, Joan Thirsk, and E. P. Thompson, eds. *Family and Inheritance: Rural Society in Western Europe, 1200–1800.* Cambridge: Cambridge University Press, 1976.

Greene, Donald. "Augustinianism and Empiricism: A Note on Eighteenth-Century English Intellectual History." *Eighteenth-Century Studies* 1.1 (1967): 33–68.

Greenfield, Susan C. *Mothering Daughters: Novels and the Politics of Family Romance, Frances Burney to Jane Austen.* Detroit: Wayne State University Press, 2002.

Gregory, John. *A Comparative View of the State and Faculties of Man with those of the Animal World.* 6th ed. 2 vols. London: J. Dodsley, 1774. London: Routledge/Thoemmes, 1994.

Hadfield, Miles. *A History of British Gardening.* 3rd ed. 1960. London: John Murray, 1979.

Haldane, J. B. S. *Daedalus; or, Science and the Future.* New York: E. P. Dutton and Co., 1924.

[Harte, Walter]. *Essays on Husbandry.* Bath: W. Frederick; London: J. Hinton et al., 1764.

Hartley, David. *Observations on Man, His Frame, His Duty, and His Expectations.* 2 vols. London: S. Richardson, 1749.

Harvey, William. *Anatomical Exercertations, Concerning the Generation of Living Creatures.* [Trans. Martin Lluelyn.] 1651. London: James Young for Octavian Pulleyn, 1653.

Harwood, Jonathan. "Heredity, Environment, and the Legitimation of Social Policy." In *Natural Order: Historical Studies of Scientific Culture,* ed. Barry Barnes and Steven Shapin, 231–248. Beverly Hills: Sage Publications, 1979.

Havelock, Eric A. *The Muse Learns To Write: Reflections on Orality and Literacy from Antiquity to the Present.* New Haven: Yale University Press, 1986.

——. "The Oral-Literate Equation: A Formula for the Modern Mind." In *Essays in Literacy and Orality,* ed. David R. Olson and Nancy Torrance, 11–27. Cambridge: Cambridge University Press, 1991.

Heinzelman, Kurt. "Roman Georgic in the Georgian Age: A Theory of Romantic Genre." *Texas Studies in Literature and Language* 33.2 (1991): 182–214.

Helvétius. *A Treatise on Man; His Intellectual Faculties and His Education.* 1772. Trans. W. Hooper. 2 vols. 1810. New York: Burt Franklin, 1969.

Herbert, Christopher. *Culture and Anomie: Ethnographic Imagination in the Nineteenth Century.* Chicago: University of Chicago Press, 1991.

Herries, John. *The Elements of Speech.* London: Edward and Charles Dilly, 1773. Menston: Scolar, 1968.

Highmore, Nathaniel. *The History of Generation.* London: R. N., 1651.

Hilts, Victor. "Enlightenment Views on the Genetic Perfectibility of Man." In *Transformation and Tradition in the Sciences: Essays in Honor of I. Bernard Cohen,* ed. Everett Mendelsohn, 255–271. Cambridge: Cambridge University Press, 1984.

[Hippocrates]. "Airs, Waters, Places." In *Hippocratic Writings,* ed. G. E. R. Lloyd, trans. J. Chadwick and W. Mann, 148–169. 1950. London: Penguin, 1983.

Hirsch, David A. Hedrich. "Liberty, Equality, Monstrosity: Revolutionizing the Family in Mary Shelley's *Frankenstein.*" In *Monster Theory: Reading Culture,* ed. Jeffrey Jerome Cohen, 115–140. Minneapolis: University of Minnesota Press, 1996.

*Histoire du concept d'espèce dans les sciences de la vie.* Paris: Fondations Singer-Polignac, 1985.

Hoeniger, F. David. "The Meaning of *The Winter's Tale.*" *University of Toronto Quarterly* 20.1 (1950): 11–26.

Hogan, Charles Beecher. *Shakespeare in the Theatre, 1701–1800.* 2 vols. Oxford: Clarendon, 1952–1957.

Homans, Margaret. *Bearing the Word: Language and Female Experience in Nineteenth-Century Women's Writing.* Chicago: University of Chicago Press, 1986.

[Home, Henry, Lord Kames]. *The Gentleman Farmer. Being an Attempt to improve Agriculture, By Subjecting it to the Test of Rational Principles.* Edinburgh: W. Creech; London: T. Cadell, 1776.

———. *Sketches of the History of Man.* 2 vols. Edinburgh: W. Creech; London: W. Strahan and T. Cadell, 1774.

Howell, Wilbur Samuel. *Eighteenth-Century British Logic and Rhetoric.* Princeton: Princeton University Press, 1971.

Hudson, Nicholas. "From 'Nation' to 'Race': The Origin of Racial Classification in Eighteenth-Century Thought." *Eighteenth-Century Studies* 29.3 (1996): 247–264.

———. *Writing and European Thought, 1600–1830.* Cambridge: Cambridge University Press, 1994.

Huet, Marie-Hélène. *Monstrous Imagination.* Cambridge, MA: Harvard University Press, 1993.

Hume, David. *Essays Moral, Political, and Literary.* Ed. Eugene F. Miller. Rev. ed. Indianapolis: Liberty Fund, 1987.

———. *A Treatise of Human Nature.* 1739–40. Ed. L.A. Selby-Bigge. 2nd ed. Rev. P.H. Nidditch. Oxford: Clarendon, 1978.

Hunt, Maurice. "The Critical Legacy." Introduction to *The Winter's Tale: Critical Essays*, 3–61. New York: Garland, 1995.

Hunter, Joseph. *New Illustrations of the Life, Studies, and Writings of Shakespeare.* 2 vols. London: J.B. Nichols, 1845.

Inchbald, Elizabeth. *A Simple Story.* 1791. Ed. Pamela Clemit. London: Penguin, 1996.

Itard, Jean-Marc-Gaspard. *The Wild Boy of Aveyron (Rapports et memoires sur le sauvage de l'Aveyron).* Trans. George Humphrey and Muriel Humphrey. New York: Century Co., 1932.

Jacob, François. *The Logic of Life: A History of Heredity.* 1970. Trans. Betty E. Spillman. Princeton: Princeton University Press, 1973.

Jain, Nalina. "Ideas of the Origin of Language in the Eighteenth Century: Johnson vs. the Philosophers." In *Aberdeen and the Enlightenment*, ed. Jennifer J. Carter and Joan H. Pittock, 291–297. Aberdeen: Aberdeen University Press, 1987.

Janson, H.W. *Apes and Ape Lore in the Middle Ages and the Renaissance.* London: Warburg Institute, 1952. Nendeln/Liechtenstein: Kraus Reprint, 1976.

Jardine, Lisa, and Jerry Brotton. *Global Interests: Renaissance Art Between East and West.* Ithaca: Cornell University Press, 2000.

Jefferson, Thomas. *Notes on the State of Virginia.* 1785. Ed. Frank Shuffelton. London: Penguin, 1999.

———. *The Garden and Farm Books of Thomas Jefferson.* Ed. Robert C. Baron. Golden, CO: Fulcrum, 1987.

J.H. [James Harris]. *Hermes; or, A Philosophical Inquiry Concerning Language and Universal Grammar.* London: H. Woodfall for J. Nourse and P. Vaillant, 1751. Menston: Scolar, 1968.

Johnson, Samuel. *A Dictionary of the English Language.* 2 vols. London: W. Strahan, 1755.

———. *A Dictionary of the English Language.* 4th ed. 2 vols. London: W. Strahan, 1773.

———. *Johnson on the English Language.* Vol. 18 of *The Yale Edition of the Works of Samuel Johnson.* Ed. Gwin J. Kolb and Robert DeMaria Jr. New Haven: Yale University Press, 2005.

———. *Johnson on Shakespeare.* Vol. 8 of *The Yale Edition of the Works of Samuel Johnson.* Ed. Arthur Sherbo. New Haven: Yale University Press, 1968.

Jones, Charles. *A Language Suppressed: The Pronunciation of the Scots Language in the Eighteenth Century.* Edinburgh: John Donato, 1996.

Joravesky, David. *The Lysenko Affair.* Cambridge, MA: Harvard University Press, 1970.

Jordanova, L.J., ed. *Languages of Nature: Critical Essays on Science and Literature.* Intro. Raymond Williams. New Brunswick, NJ: Rutgers University Press, 1986.

Jordanova, Ludmilla. *Sexual Visions: Images of Gender in Science and Medicine Between the Eighteenth and Twentieth Centuries.* New York: Harvester Wheatsheaf, 1989.

Jouanna, Jacques. *Hippocrates.* 1992. Trans. M.B. DeBevoise. Baltimore: Johns Hopkins University Press, 1999.

Kagan, Jerome, with Nancy Snidman, Doreen Arcus, and J. Steven Reznick. *Galen's Prophecy: Temperament in Human Nature.* New York: Basic Books, 1994.

Kant, Immanuel. "Answer to the Question: What Is Enlightenment?" 1784. Trans. Thomas K. Abbott. In *Basic Writings of Kant,* ed. Allen W. Wood, 135–141. New York: Modern Library, 2001.

Keller, Eve. "Embryonic Individuals: The Rhetoric of Seventeenth-Century Embryology and the Construction of Early-Modern Identity." *Eighteenth-Century Studies* 33.3 (2000): 321–348.

———. *Generating Bodies and Gendered Selves: The Rhetoric of Reproduction in Early Modern England.* Seattle: University of Washington Press, 2007.

Keller, Evelyn Fox. *The Century of the Gene.* Cambridge, MA: Harvard University Press, 2000.

———. "Nature, Nurture, and the Human Genome Project." In *The Code of Codes: Scientific and Social Issues in the Human Genome Project,* ed. Daniel J. Kevles and Leroy Hood, 281–299. Cambridge, MA: Harvard University Press, 1992.

Kemble, John Philip. *Shakespeare's Winter's Tale; A Play; Adapted to the Stage by J.P. Kemble; and Now First Published as it is Acted at The Theatre Royal in Covent Garden.* London, 1811. Repr. in vol. 9 of *John Philip Kemble Promptbooks.* 11 vols. Ed. Charles H. Shattuck. Charlottesville: University Press of Virginia, 1974.

Kenrick, William. *A Rhetorical Grammar of the English Language.* London: R. Cadell and W. Longman, 1784. Menston: Scolar, 1972.

Kevles, Daniel J. *In the Name of Eugenics: Genetics and the Uses of Human Heredity.* New York: Knopf, 1985.

Kincaid, Jamaica. "In History." *Callaloo* 20.1 (1997): 1–7.

Kitch, Aaron. "Bastards and Broadsides in *The Winter's Tale.*" *Renaissance Drama* 30 (2001): 43–71.

Knight, G. Wilson. "'Great Creating Nature': An Essay on *The Winter's Tale*." In *The Crown of Life*, 76–128. London: Oxford University Press, 1947.

Knowles, Ronald. *Gulliver's Travels: The Politics of Satire*. New York: Twayne, 1996.

Kohn, David, with Malcolm J. Kottler, eds. *The Darwinian Heritage*. Princeton: Princeton University Press, 1985.

Kramnick, Jonathan Brody. *Making the English Canon: Print-Capitalism and the Cultural Past, 1700–1770*. Cambridge: Cambridge University Press, 1998.

Kuper, Adam. *The Chosen Primate: Human Nature and Cultural Diversity*. Cambridge, MA: Harvard University Press, 1994.

la Mettrie, Julien Offray de. *Machine Man and Other Writings*. Trans. and ed. Ann Thomson. Cambridge: Cambridge University Press, 1996.

Lancaster, H.O. "Mathematicians in Medicine and Biology. Genetics Before Mendel: Maupertuis and Réaumur." *Journal of Medical Biography* 3 (1995): 84–89.

Landa, Louis A. "*A Modest Proposal* and Populousness." 1942. Repr. in *Eighteenth-Century English Literature: Modern Essays in Criticism*, ed. James L. Clifford, 102–111. New York: Oxford University Press, 1959.

Lane, Harlan. *The Wild Boy of Aveyron*. Cambridge, MA: Harvard University Press, 1976.

Laqueur, Thomas. *Making Sex: Body and Gender from the Greeks to Freud*. Cambridge, MA: Harvard University Press, 1990.

Latour, Bruno. *We Have Never Been Modern*. 1991. Trans. Catherine Porter. Cambridge, MA: Harvard University Press, 1993.

Lawrence, William. *Lectures on Physiology, Zoology, and the Natural History of Man*. London: Benbow, 1822.

Lawson, John. *Lectures Concerning Oratory. Delivered in Trinity College, Dublin*. Dublin: George Faulkner, 1758. Menston: Scolar, 1969.

Lawson, William. *A New Orchard and Garden*. London: Alsop, 1618. New York: Garland, 1982.

Lehrer, Jonah. *Proust Was a Neuroscientist*. Boston: Houghton Mifflin, 2007.

Leikola, Anto. "The Development of the Species Concept in the Thinking of Linnaeus." In *Histoire du concept d'espèce dans les sciences de la vie*, 45–59.

Leonard, Tom. "The Proof of the Mince Pie." 1973. In *Intimate Voices: Selected Work, 1965–1983*. 1984. London: Vintage, 1995.

L'Estrange, Sir Roger. *Fables, of Æsop And other Eminent Mythologists: With Morals and Reflexions*. London: R. Sare et al., 1692.

Levi, Primo. *The Periodic Table*. 1975. Trans. Raymond Rosenthal. Intro. Neal Ascherson. New York and Toronto: Knopf/Everyman, 1996.

Lewenhoeck, Anthonii. "*Observationes D.* Anthonii Lewenhoeck, *de Natis è semine genitali Animalculis*." *Philosophical Transactions of the Royal Society* 12.142 (1677): 1040–1046.

Lewis, C.S. *Spenser's Images of Life*. Ed. Alastair Fowler. Cambridge: Cambridge University Press, 1967.

Linzey, Andrew, and Paul Barry Clarke, eds. *Animal Rights: A Historical Anthology.* New York: Columbia University Press, 2004.

Lisle, Edward. *Observations in Husbandry.* London: J. Hughs, 1757.

Literature Online. The Bible in English (990–1970). http://collections.chadwyck.com/bie.

Locke, John. *An Essay Concerning Human Understanding.* 1690. 4th ed., 1700. Ed. Peter H. Nidditch. Oxford: Oxford University Press, 1975.

——. *Observations upon the Growth and Culture of Vines and Olives: The Production of Silk: The Preservation of Fruits.* London: W. Sandby, 1766.

——. *Some Thoughts Concerning Education.* 1693. Ed. John W. Yolton and Jean S. Yolton. Oxford: Clarendon, 1989.

Lovejoy, Arthur O. "Some Eighteenth-Century Evolutionists I." *Popular Science Monthly* 65 (1904): 238–251.

Low, Anthony. *The Georgic Revolution.* Princeton: Princeton University Press, 1985.

Luccock, John. *The Nature and Properties of Wool, Illustrated: With a Description of the English Fleece.* Leeds: Edward Baines and J. Heaton; London: J. Harding, 1805.

Mackintosh, Duncan, and his two Daughters. *A Plain, Rational Essay on English Grammar: The main object of which is to point out a plain, rational and permanent standard of pronunciation.* Boston: Manning and Loring, 1797. Menston: Scolar, 1969.

Maclean, Ian. *The Renaissance Notion of Woman: A Study in the Fortunes of Scholasticism and Medical Science in European Intellectual Life.* Cambridge: Cambridge University Press, 1980.

[Malebranche, Nicolas]. *Father Malebranche's Treatise concerning The Search after Truth.* Trans. T. Taylor. Oxford: L. Lichfield for Thomas Bennet, 1694.

Malebranche, Nicolas. *The Search After Truth.* Trans. and ed. Thomas M. Lennon and Paul J. Olscamp. Cambridge: Cambridge University Press, 1997.

Malson, Lucien. *Wolf Children and the Problem of Human Nature, with Jean Itard, The Wild Boy of Aveyron.* Trans. Edmund Fawcett, Peter Ayrton, and Joan White. New York: Monthly Review Press, 1972.

[Malthus, Thomas Robert]. *An Essay on the Principle of Population, As It Affects the Future Improvement of Society, with Remarks on the Speculations of Mr. Godwin, M. Condorcet, and Other Writers.* London: J. Johnson, 1798. New York: Augustus M. Kelley, 1965.

Mandler, Peter. "The Problem with Cultural History." *Cultural and Social History* 1 (2004): 94–117.

Marsh, Charles. *The Winter's Tale, a Play. Alter'd from* SHAKESPEAR. London: Charles Marsh, 1756.

Marshall, John. *John Locke: Resistance, Religion, and Responsibility.* Cambridge: Cambridge University Press, 1994.

Marx, Leo. *The Machine in the Garden: Technology and the Pastoral Ideal in America.* 1964. New York: Oxford University Press, 2000.

Mason, John. *An Essay on Elocution; or, Pronunciation.* London: M. Cooper, 1748. Menston: Scolar, 1968.

Maubray, John. *The Female Physician, Containing all the Diseases incident to that Sex, in Virgins, Wives, and Widows*. London: James Holland, 1724.

Maupertuis, Pierre-Louis Moreau de. *The Earthly Venus*. Trans. Simone Brangier Boas. Intro. George Boas. New York: Johnson Reprint Corporation, 1966.

Maupertuis. *Oeuvres de Maupertuis*. 4 vols. Rev. ed. Lyon: Jean-Marie Bruyset, 1768.

——. *Venus Physique*. 6th ed. 1751. Repr. in *Bernier, Linnaeus, and Maupertuis*, ed. Robert Bernasconi. Vol. 1 of *Concepts of Race in the Eighteenth Century*. Bristol: Thoemmes, 2001.

McIntosh, Carey. *Common and Courtly Language: The Stylistics of Social Class in Eighteenth-Century British Literature*. Philadelphia: University of Pennsylvania Press, 1986.

——. "Eighteenth-Century English Dictionaries and the Enlightenment." *Yearbook of English Studies* 28 (1998): 3–18.

——. *The Evolution of English Prose: Style, Politeness, and Print Culture*. Cambridge: Cambridge University Press, 1998.

McLane, Maureen N. *Romanticism and the Human Sciences: Poetry, Population, and the Discourse of the Species*. Cambridge: Cambridge University Press, 2000.

McManmon, John J. "The Problem of a Religious Interpretation of Gulliver's Fourth Voyage." *Journal of the History of Ideas* 27.1 (1966): 59–72.

Mellor, Anne K. *Mary Shelley: Her Life, Her Fiction, Her Monsters*. New York: Routledge, 1988.

Mezciems, Jenny. "Swift's Praise of Gulliver: Some Renaissance Background to the *Travels*." In *The Character of Swift's Satire: A Revised Focus*, ed. Claude Rawson, 245–281. Newark: University of Delaware Press; London: Associated University Presses, 1983.

Michaels, Leonard, and Christopher Ricks, eds. *The State of the Language*. Berkeley: University of California Press, 1980.

Michaels, Walter Benn. *Our America: Nativism, Modernism, and Pluralism*. Durham: Duke University Press, 1995.

——. "The Souls of White Folk." In *Literature and the Body: Essays on Populations and Persons. Selected Papers from the English Institute, 1986*, ed. Elaine Scarry, 185–209. Baltimore: Johns Hopkins University Press, 1990.

Micklethwait, David. *Noah Webster and the American Dictionary*. Jefferson, NC: McFarland, 2000.

Midgley, Mary. *Beast and Man: The Roots of Human Nature*. Ithaca: Cornell University Press, 1978.

Miller, Charles A. *Jefferson and Nature: An Interpretation*. Baltimore: Johns Hopkins University Press, 1988.

Miller, Thomas P. *The Formation of College English: Rhetoric and Belles Lettres in the British Cultural Provinces*. Pittsburgh: University of Pittsburgh Press, 1997.

Montagu, M. F. Ashley. "Tyson's *Orang-Outang, Sive Homo Sylvestris* and Swift's *Gulliver's Travels*." *PMLA* 59.1 (1944): 84–89.

Montaigne, Michel de. "Of the force of Imagination." 1580. In *The essays of Montaigne done into English by John Florio anno 1603,* ed. George Saintsbury, 1:90–102. 3 vols. London: David Nutt, 1892. New York: AMS, 1967.

Montesquieu. *The Spirit of the Laws.* 1748. Trans. Anne M. Cohler, Basia Carolyn Miller, and Harold Samuel Stone. Cambridge: Cambridge University Press, 1989.

Moore-Colyer, R.J. "Horses and Equine Improvement in the Economy of Modern Wales." *Agricultural History Review* 39.2 (1991): 126–142.

More, Thomas. *Utopia.* 1516. Ed. and trans. George M. Logan and Robert M. Adams. Rev. ed. Cambridge: Cambridge University Press, 2002.

Moretti, Franco. "Conjectures on World Literature." *New Left Review* 1 (2000): 54–68.

[Morgan, Macnamara]. *The Sheep-Shearing; or, Florizel and Perdita. A Pastoral Comedy Taken from Shakespear.* London: J. Truman, 1762. London: Cornmarket, 1969.

Mufwene, Salikoko S. "Some Sociohistorical Inferences About the Development of African American English." In *The English History of African American English,* ed. Shana Poplack, 233–263. Oxford: Blackwell, 2000.

Mugglestone, Lynda. *"Talking Proper": The Rise of Accent as Social Symbol.* Oxford: Clarendon, 1995.

Muller, Virginia L. *The Idea of Perfectibility.* Lanham, MD: University Press of America, 1985.

Myers, Mitzi. "'Servants as They are now Educated': Women Writers and Georgian Pedagogy." *Essays in Literature* 16 (1989): 51–69.

Nanjundiah, Vidyanand. "Dangerous Muddle." *Journal of Genetics* 76.2 (1997): 161–165.

Nares, R. *Elements of Orthoepy.* London: T. Payne and Son, 1784. Menston: Scolar, 1968.

Nash, Richard. "'Honest English Breed': The Thoroughbred as Cultural Metaphor." In *The Culture of the Horse: Status, Discipline, and Identity in the Early Modern World,* ed. Karen Raber and Treva J. Tucker, 245–272. New York: Palgrave Macmillan, 2005.

——. *Wild Enlightenment: The Borders of Human Identity in the Eighteenth Century.* Charlottesville: University of Virginia Press, 2003.

Needham, Joseph. *A History of Embryology.* 1934. 2nd ed. Rev. with Arthur Hughes. Cambridge: Cambridge University Press, 1959.

Newman, Karen. *Fetal Positions: Individualism, Science, Visuality.* Stanford: Stanford University Press, 1996.

Newton, Michael. *Savage Girls and Wild Boys: A History of Feral Children.* New York: St. Martin's/Thomas Dunne, 2002.

Nourse, Tim[othy]. *A Discourse Upon the Nature and Faculties of Man, in Several Essayes.* London: Jacob Tonson, 1686.

Nourse, Timothy. *Campania Fælix; or, A Discourse of the Benefits and Improvements of Husbandry.* London: Tho. Bennet, 1700. New York and London: Garland, 1982.

O'Neil, Wayne. "If Ebonics Isn't a Language, Then Tell Me, What Is?" In *The Real Ebonics Debate,* ed. Perry and Delpit, 38–47.

Oppenheimer, Jane M. *Essays in the History of Embryology and Biology.* Cambridge, MA: MIT Press, 1967.

Orr, Eleanor Wilson. *Twice As Less: Black English and the Performance of Black Students in Mathematics and Science.* 1987. 2nd ed. New York: Norton, 1997.

Orr, H. Allen. "Darwinian Storytelling." *New York Review of Books,* 27 February 2003, 17–20.

Osmer, William. *A Dissertation on Horses: Wherein it is demonstrated, by Matters of Fact, as well as from the Principles of Philosophy, that* INNATE QUALITIES *do not exist, and that the excellence of this Animal is altogether mechanical and not in the Blood.* London: T. Waller, 1756.

Outram, Dorinda. *The Enlightenment.* Cambridge: Cambridge University Press, 1995.

——. "The Enlightenment Our Contemporary." In *The Sciences in Enlightened Europe,* ed. William Clark, Jan Golinski, and Simon Schaffer, 32–40. Chicago: University of Chicago Press, 1999.

*Oxford English Dictionary.* 2nd ed. 1989.

*Oxford Shakespeare Concordance: The Winter's Tale.* Oxford: Clarendon, 1969.

Pafford, J.H.P., ed. *The Winter's Tale.* 1963. London: Arden Shakespeare, 2001.

Paré, Ambroise. *On Monsters and Marvels.* 1573. Trans. Janis L. Pallister. Chicago: University of Chicago Press, 1982.

Park, Katharine, and Lorraine J. Daston. "Unnatural Conceptions: The Study of Monsters in Sixteenth- and Seventeenth-Century France and England." *Past and Present* 92 (1981): 20–54.

——. *Wonders and the Order of Nature, 1150–1750.* New York: Zone Books; Cambridge: MIT Press, 1998.

Parker, Patricia A. *Inescapable Romance: Studies in the Poetics of a Mode.* Princeton: Princeton University Press, 1979.

——. *Literary Fat Ladies: Rhetoric, Gender, Property.* London: Methuen, 1987.

Passmore, John. *The Perfectibility of Man.* London: Duckworth, 1970.

Patterson, Annabel. *Fables of Power: Aesopian Writing and Political History.* Durham: Duke University Press, 1991.

Paulin, Tom. "A New Look at the Language Question." In Field Day Theatre Company, *Ireland's Field Day.* 1983–1984. London: Hutchinson, 1985.

Pedicord, Harry William, and Fredrick Louis Berhmann, eds. *Garrick's Adaptations of Shakespeare, 1744–1756.* Carbondale: Southern Illinois University Press, 1981.

Perec, Georges. "Attempt at an Inventory of the Liquid and the Solid Foodstuffs Ingurgitated by Me in the Course of the Year Nineteen Hundred and Seventy-Four." Trans. John Sturrock. *Granta* 52 (1995): 87–92.

Perry, Ruth. *Novel Relations: The Transformation of Kinship in English Literature and Culture, 1748–1818.* Cambridge: Cambridge University Press, 2004.

Perry, Theresa, and Lisa Delpit, eds. *The Real Ebonics Debate: Power, Language, and the Education of African-American Children.* Boston: Beacon Press, 1998.

Philp, Mark. *Godwin's Political Justice.* London: Duckworth, 1986.

Pieters, Jürgen. *Speaking with the Dead: Explorations in Literature and History.* Edinburgh: Edinburgh University Press, 2005.

Pinker, Steven. *The Blank Slate: The Modern Denial of Human Nature.* New York: Viking, 2002.

——. *The Language Instinct.* New York: Morrow, 1994.

Pinto-Correia, Clara. *The Ovary of Eve: Egg and Sperm and Preformation.* Chicago: University of Chicago Press, 1997.

Plato. *The Republic.* Ed. G. R. F. Ferrari. Trans. Tom Griffith. Cambridge: Cambridge University Press.

Plutarch. *On Sparta.* Trans. Richard J. A. Talbert. Rev. ed. London: Penguin, 2005.

Pollan, Michael. *The Botany of Desire: A Plant's-Eye View of the World.* 2001. New York: Random House, 2002.

Pollin, Burton Ralph. *Education and Enlightenment in the Works of William Godwin.* New York: Las Americas Publishing Company, 1962.

Pomata, Gianna. "Comments on the Papers Given by Phillip Wilson, John C. Waller, and Laure Cartron." In *A Cultural History of Heredity II,* ed. Rheinberger and Müller-Wille, 145–151.

Porta, John Baptista. *Natural Magick.* Ed. Derek J. Price. London: Thomas Young and Samuel Speed, 1658. New York: Basic Books, 1959.

Porter, David. *Ideographia: The Chinese Cipher in Early Modern Europe.* Stanford: Stanford University Press, 2001.

Porter, Roy, and Lesley Hall. "Medical Folklore in High and Low Culture: *Aristotle's Masterpiece.*" In *The Facts of Life: The Creation of Sexual Knowledge in Britain, 1650–1950,* ed. Porter and Hall, 33–53. New Haven: Yale University Press, 1995.

Potkay, Adam. *The Fate of Eloquence in the Age of Hume.* Ithaca: Cornell University Press, 1994.

Preu, James A. *The Dean and the Anarchist.* Tallahassee: Florida State University, 1959.

Prichard, James Cowles. *Researches Into the Physical History of Man.* 1813. Chicago: University of Chicago Press, 1973.

Priestley, Joseph. *A Course of Lectures on the Theory of Language, and Universal Grammar.* Warrington: W. Eyres, 1762. Menston: Scolar, 1970.

——. *An Essay on the First Principles of Government, and on the Nature of Political, Civil, and Religious Liberty.* 2nd ed. 1771. In *Political Writings,* ed. Peter N. Miller. Cambridge: Cambridge University Press, 1993.

Prothero, R. E. *Shakespeare's England: An Account of the Life and Manners of his Age.* 1916. Oxford: Clarendon, 1962.

Prytula, Nina Adriane. "'The soul stark naked': The Female Breast and the Anatomy of Character in the Eighteenth-Century Novel." Ph.D. diss., Yale University, 2001.

Quiller-Couch, Sir Arthur, and John Dover Wilson, eds. *The Winter's Tale.* Cambridge: Cambridge University Press, 1931.

Rajan, Rajeswari Sunder, ed. *The Lie of the Land: English Literary Studies in India*. New Delhi: Oxford University Press, 1993.

Rawson, Claude. *God, Gulliver, and Genocide: Barbarism and the European Imagination, 1492–1945*. Oxford: Oxford University Press, 2001.

———. "*Gulliver's Travels* and Some Modern Fictions." In *Order From Confusion Sprung: Studies in Eighteenth-Century Literature from Swift to Cowper*, 68–120. London: George Allen and Unwin, 1985.

Rawson, C.J. *Gulliver and the Gentle Reader: Studies in Swift and Our Time*. London and Boston: Routledge and Kegan Paul, 1973.

Ray, John. "A discourse on the specific differences of plants." In Thomas Birch, *The History of the Royal Society of London for Improving of Natural Knowledge*, 3:169–173. 4 vols. London: A. Millar, 1756–1757.

———. *The Wisdom of God Manifested in the Works of the Creation*. London: Samuel Smith, 1691.

Reddick, Allen. *The Making of Johnson's Dictionary, 1746–1773*. Cambridge: Cambridge University Press, 1990.

Redhead, Laing, and Marshall. *Observations on the Different Breeds of Sheep*. Edinburgh: W. Smellie, 1792.

Reichert, John F. "Plato, Swift, and the Houyhnhnms." *Philological Quarterly* 47.2 (1968): 179–192.

Rheinberger, Hans-Jörg, and Staffan Müller-Wille, eds. *A Cultural History of Heredity I: Seventeenth and Eighteenth Centuries*. Max Planck Institute for the History of Science, preprint 222 (2002).

———. *A Cultural History of Heredity II: Eighteenth and Nineteenth Centuries*. Max Planck Institute for the History of Science, preprint 247 (2003).

Richardson, Alan. "Of Heartache and Head Injury: Reading Minds in *Persuasion*." *Poetics Today* 23.1 (2002): 141–160.

Richardson, Samuel. *Clarissa; or, The History of A Young Lady*. 1747–1748. Ed. Angus Ross. London: Penguin, 1985.

Rickford, John R. "The Creole Origins of African-American Vernacular English: Evidence from Copula Absence." In *African-American English: Structure, History, and Use*, ed. Salikoko S. Mufwene, John R. Rickford, Guy Bailey, and John Baugh, 154–200. London: Routledge, 1998.

Rickford, John Russell, and Russell John Rickford. *Spoken Soul: The Story of Black English*. New York: Wiley, 2000.

Ritvo, Harriet. *The Animal Estate: The English and Other Creatures in the Victorian Age*. Cambridge, MA: Harvard University Press, 1987.

———. "Possessing Mother Nature: Genetic Capital in Eighteenth-Century Britain." In *Early Modern Conceptions of Property*, ed. Brewer and Staves, 413–426.

Roach, Joseph. *The Player's Passion: Studies in the Science of Acting*. 1985. Ann Arbor: Michigan University Press, 1993.

Roberts, H.F. *Plant Hybridization Before Mendel.* Princeton: Princeton University Press, 1929.

Robinson, Robert. *The Art of Pronuntiation [sic].* London: Nicholas Okes, 1617. Menston: Scolar, 1969.

Roger, Jacques. *Buffon: A Life in Natural History.* 1989. Trans. Sarah Lucille Bonnefoi. Ed. L. Pearce Williams. Ithaca: Cornell University Press, 1997.

———. *The Life Sciences in Eighteenth-Century French Thought.* Ed. Keith R. Benson. Trans. Robert Ellrich. 1963. Rev. ed. 1993. Stanford: Stanford University Press, 1997.

———. "The Living World." In *The Ferment of Knowledge: Studies in the Historiography of Eighteenth-Century Science,* ed. G.S. Rousseau and Roy Porter, 255–283. Cambridge: Cambridge University Press, 1980.

Rogers, Pat. "Boswell and the Scotticism." In *New Light on Boswell,* ed. Greg Clingham, 56–71. Cambridge: Cambridge University Press, 1991.

Rondet, Henri. *Original Sin: The Patristic and Theological Background.* Trans. Cajetan Finegan OP. Shannon: Ecclesia Press, 1972.

Rosenblum, Michael. "Smollett's *Humphry Clinker.*" In *The Cambridge Companion to the Eighteenth-Century Novel,* ed. John Richetti, 175–197. Cambridge: Cambridge University Press, 1996.

Rousseau, G.S. "Pineapples, Pregnancy, Pica, and *Peregrine Pickle.*" In *Tobias Smollett: Bicentennial Essays Presented to Lewis M. Knapp,* ed. Rousseau and Paul-Gabriel Boucé, 79–109. New York: Oxford University Press, 1971.

Rousseau, Jean-Jacques. *The Discourses and Other Early Political Writings.* Ed. Victor Gourevitch. Cambridge: Cambridge University Press, 1997.

———. *Émile.* 1762. Trans. Barbara Foxley. Intro. P.D. Jimack. London: J.M. Dent; North Clarendon, VT: Tuttle, 1993.

Rubin, Stan Sanvel, and Judith Kitchen. "Riding That Current as Far as It'll Take You." 1985. In *Conversations with Rita Dove,* ed. Earl G. Ingersoll, 3–14. Jackson: University Press of Mississippi, 2003.

Russell, Nicholas. *Like Engendr'ing Like: Heredity and Animal Breeding in Early Modern England.* Cambridge: Cambridge University Press, 1986.

Sandel, Michael J. *The Case Against Perfection: Ethics in the Age of Genetic Engineering.* Cambridge, MA: Harvard University Press, 2007.

Sandler, Iris. "Pierre Louis Moreau de Maupertuis—A Precursor of Mendel?" *Journal of the History of Biology* 16.1 (1983): 101–136.

Schneider, William. "Toward the Improvement of the Human Race: The History of Eugenics in France." *Journal of Modern History* 54.2 (1982): 268–291.

Search, Edward [Abraham Tucker]. *Vocal Sounds.* London: T. Jones and T. Payne, 1773. Menston: Scolar, 1969.

Sebald, W.G. "Between History and Natural History: On the Literary Description of Total Destruction." In *Campo Santo,* trans. Anthea Bell, 65–95. New York: Random House, 2005.

———. *The Rings of Saturn.* 1995. Trans. Michael Hulse. New York: New Directions, 1999.

Secord, James A. "Darwin and the Breeders: A Social History." In *The Darwinian Heritage,* ed. Kohn, 519–542.

———. "Nature's Fancy: Charles Darwin and the Breeding of Pigeons." *Isis* 72.2 (1981): 162–186.

Sedgwick, Eve Kosofsky. *Epistemology of the Closet.* Berkeley: University of California Press, 1990.

Segerstråle, Ullica. *Defenders of the Truth: The Battle for Science in the Sociobiology Debate and Beyond.* Oxford: Oxford University Press, 2000.

Sekora, John. *Luxury: The Concept in Western Thought, Eden to Smollett.* Baltimore: Johns Hopkins University Press, 1977.

Shakespeare, William. *The Riverside Shakespeare.* 2nd ed. Ed. G. Blakemore Evans et al. Boston and New York: Houghton Mifflin, 1997.

Sharp, Jane. *The Midwives Book; or, The Whole Art of Midwifry Discovered. Directing Childbearing Women how to behave themselves In their Conception, Breeding, Bearing, and Nursing of Children.* London: Simon Miller, 1671.

Shattuck, Roger. *The Forbidden Experiment: The Story of the Wild Boy of Aveyron.* New York: Farrar Straus Giroux, 1980.

Shelley, Mary. *Frankenstein; or, The Modern Prometheus.* Vol. 1 of *The Novels and Selected Works of Mary Shelley.* Ed. Nora Crook. Intro. Betty T. Bennett. London: Pickering, 1996.

Sheridan, Thomas. *British Education; or, The Source of the Disorders of Great Britain.* London: R. and J. Dodsley, 1756.

———. *A Course of Lectures on Elocution: Together With Two Dissertations on Language; and Some other Tracts relative to those Subjects.* London: W. Strahan et al., 1762.

———. *A Discourse Delivered in the Theatre at Oxford, in the Senate-House at Cambridge, and at Spring-Garden in London.* London: A. Millar et al., 1759.

———. *Elements of English.* London: C. Dilly, 1786.

———. *Lectures on the Art of Reading; First Part.* London: J. Dodsley et al., 1775.

———. *An Oration, Pronounced before a Numerous Body of the Nobility and Gentry, Assembled at the Musick-Hall in* Fishamble-Street, *On* Tuesday *the 6th of this instant* December, *And now first Published at their unanimous Desire.* 2nd ed. Dublin: M. Williamson, 1757.

———. *A Rhetorical Grammar of the English Language. Calculated solely for the Purposes of Teaching Propriety of Pronunciation, and Justness of Delivery, in that Tongue, by the Organs of Speech.* Dublin: Price et al., 1781.

Simpson, John, and Jennifer Speake, eds. *The Concise Oxford Dictionary of Proverbs.* 2nd ed. Oxford: Oxford University Press, 1992.

Singh, the Reverend J. A. L., and Professor Robert M. Zingg. *Wolf-Children and Feral Man.* New York: Harper and Brothers, 1942.

Singleton, Esther. *The Shakespeare Garden.* New York: William Farquhar Payson, 1931.

Siskin, Clifford. *The Work of Writing: Literature and Social Change in Britain, 1700–1830.* Baltimore: Johns Hopkins University Press, 1998.

Sloan, Phillip R. "From Logical Universals to Historical Individuals: Buffon's Idea of Biological Species." In *Histoire du concept d'espèce dans les sciences de la vie,* 101–140.

———. "The Idea of Racial Degeneracy in Buffon's *Histoire Naturelle.*" In *Studies in Eighteenth-Century Culture 3: Racism in the Eighteenth Century,* ed. Harold E. Pagliaro, 293–321. Cleveland: Press of Case Western Reserve University, 1973.

Slotkin, J.S., ed. *Readings in Early Anthropology.* Viking Fund Publications in Anthropology 40. Japan: Wenner-Gren Foundation for Anthropological Research, 1965.

Smart, B.H. *A Practical Grammar of English Pronunciation, on Plain and Recognised Principles, Calculated to Assist in Removing every objectionable peculiarity of utterance, arising either from Foreign, Provincial, or Vulgar Habits; or from a defective use of the organs of speech.* London: John Richardson and J. Johnson, 1810.

Smith, Adam. *Lectures on Rhetoric and Belles Lettres.* Ed. J.C. Bryce. Oxford: Clarendon, 1983.

Smith, Olivia. *The Politics of Language, 1791–1819.* Oxford: Clarendon, 1984.

Smith, Roger. "The Language of Human Nature." In *Inventing Human Science: Eighteenth-Century Domains,* ed. Christopher Fox, Roy Porter, and Robert Wokler, 88–111. Berkeley: University of California Press, 1995.

Smith, Samuel Stanhope. *An Essay on the Causes of the Variety of Complexion and Figure in the Human Species.* Ed. Winthrop D. Jordan. Cambridge, MA: Harvard University Press, 1965.

Smith, William. *An Attempt to Render the Pronunciation of the English Language More Easy to Foreigners.* London: C. Dilly et al.; Edinburgh: W. Creech, 1795. Menston: Scolar, 1969.

Smitherman, Geneva. *Talkin That Talk: Language, Culture, and Education in African America.* London: Routledge, 2000.

Smollett, Tobias. *The Expedition of Humphry Clinker.* 1773. Intro. Thomas R. Preston. Ed. O.M. Brack Jr. Athens: University of Georgia Press, 1990.

———. Review of Edward Lisle's *Observations in Husbandry. Critical Review* 3 (Jan. 1757): 1–20.

Somerville, Thomas, D.D. *My Own Life and Times, 1741–1814.* Edinburgh: Edmonston and Douglas, 1861.

Sorensen, Janet. *The Grammar of Empire in Eighteenth-Century British Writing.* Cambridge: Cambridge University Press, 2000.

Spallanzani, Abbé. *Dissertations Relative to the Natural History of Animals and Vegetables.* 2 vols. London: J. Murray, 1784.

———. *An Essay on Animal Reproductions.* [Trans. M. Maty.] London: T. Becket and P.A. De Hondt, 1766.

Spary, E.C. *Utopia's Garden: French Natural History from Old Regime to Revolution.* Chicago: University of Chicago Press, 2000.

Spellman, W.M. *John Locke and the Problem of Depravity.* Oxford: Clarendon, 1988.

———. "Locke and the Latitudinarian Perspective on Original Sin." *Revue Internationale de Philosophie* 42.2 (1988): 215–228.

Spenser, Edmund. *The Faerie Queene.* Ed. A.C. Hamilton. Harlow: Pearson, 2001.

Stafford, Barbara Maria. *Body Criticism: Imaging the Unseen in Enlightenment Art and Medicine.* Cambridge, MA: MIT Press, 1991.

Staves, Susan. *Married Women's Separate Property in England, 1660–1833.* Cambridge, MA: Harvard University Press, 1990.

[Steele, Richard, and Joseph Addison]. *The Tatler.* Ed. Donald F. Bond. Vol. 1. Oxford: Clarendon, 1987.

Steevens, George, and Samuel Johnson, eds. Vol. 4 of *The Plays of William Shakspeare. In ten volumes. With the corrections and illustrations of various commentators; to which are added notes by Samuel Johnson and George Steevens. The second edition, revised and augmented.* London: C. Bathurst et al., 1778.

Sterne, Laurence. *The Life and Opinions of Tristram Shandy, Gentleman.* 1759 and following. Vol. 1. Ed. Melvyn New and Joan New. [Gainesville]: University Presses of Florida, 1978.

Sterrenburg, Lee. "Mary Shelley's Monster: Politics and Psyche in *Frankenstein.*" In *The Endurance of Frankenstein: Essays on Mary Shelley's Novel,* ed. George Levine and U.C. Knoepflmacher, 143–171. Berkeley: University of California Press, 1979.

Stocking, George W., Jr. "On the Limits of 'Presentism' and 'Historicism.'" In *Race, Culture, and Evolution: Essays in the History of Anthropology,* 1–12. Rev. ed. 1968. Chicago: University of Chicago Press/Free Press, 1982.

Stone, George Winchester, Jr., and George M. Kahrl. *David Garrick: A Critical Biography.* Carbondale: Southern Illinois University Press; London: Fetter and Simons, 1979.

Strathern, Paul. *Mendeleyev's Dream: The Quest for the Elements.* New York: St. Martin's/Thomas Dunne, 2000.

Stubbe, Hans. *History of Genetics: From Prehistoric Times to the Rediscovery of Mendel's Laws.* Rev. ed. Trans. T.R.W. Waters. 1965. Cambridge: MIT Press, 1972.

Sullivan, John Jeremiah. *Blood Horses: Notes of a Sportswriter's Son.* New York: Farrar Straus Giroux, 2004.

Swift, Jonathan. *The Prose Works of Jonathan Swift.* Ed. Herbert Davis et al. 14 vols. Oxford: Blackwell/Shakespeare Head, 1939–1974.

Tate, Nahum. *The History of King Lear.* 1681. Ed. James Black. Lincoln: University of Nebraska Press, 1975.

Tayler, Edward William. *Nature and Art in Renaissance Literature.* New York: Columbia University Press, 1964.

Terrall, Mary. *The Man Who Flattened the Earth: Maupertuis and the Sciences in the Enlightenment.* Chicago: University of Chicago Press, 2002.

Thickstun, Margaret Olofson. "The Puritan Origins of Gulliver's Conversion in Houyhnhnmland." *Studies in English Literature, 1500–1900* 37.3 (1997): 517–534.

Thomas, Keith. *Man and the Natural World: Changing Attitudes in England, 1500–1800.* 1983. New York: Oxford University Press, 1996.

Thompson, Ann, and John O. Thompson. "Meaning, 'Seeing', Printing." In *Printing and Parenting in Early Modern England,* ed. Brooks, 59–86.

Tillyard, E.M. *Shakespeare's Last Plays.* London: Chatto and Windus, 1938.

Tinkler, F.C. "*The Winter's Tale.*" *Scrutiny* 5.4 (March 1937): 344–364.

Todd, Dennis. *Imagining Monsters: Miscreations of the Self in Eighteenth-Century England.* Chicago: University of Chicago Press, 1995.

[Toland, John, trans.]. *The Fables of Æsop. With the Moral Reflexions of Monsieur Baudoin.* London: Tho. Leigh and Dan. Midwinter, 1704.

Tonkin, Humphrey. "Spenser's Garden of Adonis and Britomart's Quest." *PMLA* 88.3 (1973): 408–417.

*Trésor de la langue française.* Paris: Gallimard, 1988.

Trooster, S., SJ. *Evolution and the Doctrine of Original Sin.* Trans. John A. Ter Haar. Glen Rock, NJ: Newman Press, 1968.

Trumbach, Randolph. *The Rise of the Egalitarian Family: Aristocratic Kinship and Domestic Relations in Eighteenth-Century England.* New York: Academic Press, 1978.

Tuana, Nancy. "The Weaker Seed: The Sexist Bias of Reproductive Theory." In *Feminism and Science,* ed. Tuana, 147–171. Bloomington: Indiana University Press, 1989.

[Tull, Jethro]. *The New Horse-Houghing Husbandry; or, An Essay on the Principles of Tillage and Vegetation.* London, 1731.

Tyson, Edward. *Orang-Outang, sive Homo Sylvestris; or, The Anatomy of a Pygmie Compared with that of a Monkey, an Ape, and a Man.* London: Thomas Bennet and Daniel Brown, 1699.

Ulman, H. Lewis. *Things, Thoughts, Words, and Actions: The Problem of Language in Late Eighteenth-Century British Rhetorical Theory.* Carbondale: Southern Illinois University Press, 1994.

Vandermonde. *Essai sur la manière de perfectionner l'espèce humaine.* 2 vols. Paris: Vincent, 1756.

Venette, Nicolas. "Si les enfans sont bâtards ou legitimes quand ils ressemblent à leur pere ou à leur mere." *De la generation de l'homme, ou tableau de l'amour conjugal.* 1686. 7th ed. Cologne: Claude Joly, 1696.

Vickers, Brian. "The Satiric Structure of *Gulliver's Travels* and More's *Utopia.*" In *The World of Jonathan Swift: Essays for the Tercentenary,* ed. Vickers. Oxford: Basil Blackwell, 1968.

Virgil. *Eclogues, Georgics, Aeneid I–VI.* Trans. H. Rushton Fairclough. Rev. G.P. Goold. Cambridge, MA: Harvard University Press, 1999.

Viswanathan, Gauri. *Masks of Conquest: Literary Study and British Rule in India.* 1989. New Delhi: Oxford University Press, 1998.

Voltaire. *Histoire du Docteur Akakia et du Natif de St-Malo.* 1753. Ed. Jacques Tuffet. Paris: A.G. Nizet, 1967.

W. D. *Æsop's Fables, With their Morals: In Prose and Verse.* [1650?] 16th ed. London: J. Phillips et al., 1706.

Wahrman, Dror. *The Making of the Modern Self: Identity and Culture in Eighteenth-Century England.* New Haven: Yale University Press, 2004.

Wald, Priscilla. "Future Perfect: Grammar, Genes, and Geography." *New Literary History* 31 (2000): 681–708.

Walker, Alexander. *Intermarriage; or, The Natural Laws by Which Beauty, Health and Intellect, Result from Certain Unions, and Deformity, Disease and Insanity, From Others.* 1839. 2nd ed. London: John Churchill, 1841.

Walker, John. *Elements of Elocution.* 2 vols. London: T. Cadell et al., 1781. Menston: Scolar, 1969.

Wall, Richard. *A Dissertation on Breeding of Horses, upon Philosophical and Experimental Principles; Being An attempt to promote thereby an Improvement in the present manner of Breeding Racers, And Horses in general.* London: G. Woodfall et al., [1760].

Wallace, Robert. *A Dissertation on the Numbers of Mankind, in Ancient and Modern Times.* 1753. 2nd ed. Edinburgh: Archibald Constable and Co.; London: Constable, Hunter, Park, and Hunter, 1809.

[Wallace, Robert]. *Various Prospects of Mankind, Nature, and Providence.* 1758. 2nd ed. London: A. Millar, 1761. New York: Augustus M. Kelley, 1969.

Watts, Isaac. *The Art of Reading and Writing English.* London: John Clark et al., 1721. Menston: Scolar, 1972.

Webster, John. *The Duchess of Malfi.* 1623. Ed. Brian Gibbons. 4th ed. London: Black; New York: Norton, 2001.

Webster, Noah. *A Collection of Essays and Fugitiv [sic] Writings.* Boston: I. Thomas and E. T. Andrews, 1790.

——. *Dissertations on the English Language.* Boston: Isaiah Thomas, 1789. Menston: Scolar, 1967.

——. *A Grammatical Institute, of the English Language.* 2 vols. Hartford: Hudson and Goodwin, [1783]–1784. Menston: Scolar, 1968.

Webster, Richard. *Why Freud Was Wrong: Sin Science and Psychoanalysis* (1995). http://www.richardwebster.net/gulliverstravelsandoriginalsin.html.

Weismann, August. *Essays Upon Heredity and Kindred Biological Problems.* Trans. and ed. Edward B. Poulton et al. Oxford: Clarendon, 1889.

Wesley, John. *The Doctrine of Original Sin: According to Scripture, Reason, and Experience.* Bristol: E. Farley, 1757.

Wheeler, Roxann. *The Complexion of Race: Categories of Difference in Eighteenth-Century British Culture.* Philadelphia: University of Pennsylvania Press, 2000.

Wiley, Tatha. *Original Sin: Origins, Developments, Contemporary Meanings.* New York: Paulist Press, 2002.

Williams, Raymond. *The Country and the City.* 1973. New York: Oxford University Press, 1975.

——. *Keywords: A Vocabulary of Culture and Society.* 1976. Rev. ed. New York: Oxford University Press, 1983.

Wilson, Harold. "'Nature and Art' in *Winter's Tale* IV.iv.86ff." *Shakespeare Association Bulletin* 18.3 (1943): 114–120.

Wilson, Philip K. "Eighteenth-Century Monsters and Nineteenth-Century 'Freaks': Reading the Maternally Marked Child." *Literature and Medicine* 21.1 (2002): 1–25.

Winston, Michael E. *From Perfectibility to Perversion: Meliorism in Eighteenth-Century France.* New York: Lang, 2005.

Wood, Roger J. "The Sheep Breeders' View of Heredity (1723–1843)," in *A Cultural History of Heredity II,* ed. Rheinberger and Müller-Wille, 21–46.

Wood, Roger J., and Vitezslav Orel. *Genetic Prehistory in Selective Breeding: A Prelude to Mendel.* Oxford: Oxford University Press, 2001.

Wucker, Michele. *Why the Cocks Fight: Dominicans, Haitians, and the Struggle for Hispaniola.* New York: Farrar Straus Giroux, 1999.

Young, Arthur. Vol. 2 of *Annals of Agriculture, and Other Useful Arts.* London: For the editor, 1784.

——. *The Autobiography of Arthur Young, with Selections from his Correspondence.* Ed. M. Betham-Edwards. London: Smith, Elder and Co., 1898.

Zirkle, Conway. *The Beginnings of Plant Hybridization.* Philadelphia: University of Pennsylvania Press, 1935.

——. "The Early History of the Idea of the Inheritance of Acquired Characters and of Pangenesis." *Transactions of the American Philosophical Society* 35.2 (1946): 91–151.

Žižek, Slavoj. "Bring Me My Philips Mental Jacket." *London Review of Books* 25.10, 22 May 2003, 5.

# INDEX

accent, 124–125

accessibility, 197–198. *See also* jargon

acquired characters, inheritance of, 7, 21, 85, 95, 190–91; notion refuted by August Weismann, 36–38. *See also* inheritance, resemblance

Adams, James, 147

Adams, John, 199–200

adaptations: theatrical, as cultural indicators, 15; of *The Winter's Tale*, 29–34

Addison, Joseph, 59, 70

Aesop, fable of cat turned woman, 54

Africa, 96, 161–62. *See also* Ebonics

agriculture: celebrated in georgic mode, 59–64; lambasted by Rousseau, 113–114. *See also* cultivation

"Airs, Waters, Places," 3, 132. *See also* Hippocratic writings

amateurism, ethos of, in criticism, 198. *See also* accessibility, disciplines, specialization

animals, 73, 155–158; affected differently from man by culture, 117, 165–166; domesticated by Crusoe, 65–66; natural equality of, 115; parallels between people

and, 43, 91–92, 130, 156; man considered as animal, 52, 96–97, 112

anti-French sentiment, 133, 138

anti-Scottish sentiment, 139

apple, differentiated from crab-apple, 109–110. *See also* grafting

Arbuthnot, John, 67; *An Essay Concerning the Effects of Air on Human Bodies*, 3

aristocracy, 131, 141, 172–173; idea of "natural," 154; science of, 200

Aristotle, 20–21, 32

art: art-nature debate in *The Winter's Tale* absent from later adaptations and discussions, 30; defined by Thomas Sheridan as nature improved, 128; versus nature, 60

associationism, 40, 169; congruent with climate theory, 95; compatible with theories of human difference, 42; hard-line version rejected by Godwin, 179–180; and racist language of human "varieties," 91

Augustine, 28, 48–49, 182–183

Austen, Jane: *Mansfield Park*, 66; *Persuasion*, 151; *Sense and Sensibility* and

Austen, Jane (*continued*)
  *Mansfield Park* read by Charles
  Darwin, 36

Bacon, Francis, "Of Nature in Men," 54
Bakewell, Robert, 93
Barthes, Roland, 10–11; "rib chop" removed
  from chest of, 210 n. 28
bastards, 107; "Nature's bastards" exchange
  in *Winter's Tale*, 25–27
Bate, James, 94
Baugh, John, 194–195
Beattie, James, 142
Beer, Gillian, 2
bees, generation of, from bullock's head, in
  Virgil's *Georgics*, 61
bent, 46–47, 121–123; language of, 41. *See also*
  bias, propensities
bias, 46. *See also* bent
Bickerstaff, Isaac, 3–4, 81; invoked by Malthus, 185. *See also* breeding, selective;
  eugenics
*Bildungsroman*, 36
biology, 2
birds, 130; learning habits of, invoked
  by Locke and others, 43; songs of, as
  analogy for human language, 129; songs
  of, as Boswell's illustration of why
  elements of regional accents should be
  retained, 145
Bishop, Elizabeth, 64
Blair, Hugh, 127
blank slate, human mind as, 39–48, 68, 129,
  130, 171. *See also* metaphor
blood, 1, 4, 21, 55–56, 58, 93–94, 124, 135,
  136–137, 163, 176; aristocracy based in
  difference of, 77; as keyword in *Clarissa*
  and elsewhere, 239 n. 58; kinship models
  based on consanguineal versus conjugal
  ties, 33; pitted against mechanism in
  theories of horse-breeding, 83–86; notion that "blood will out," 12
Blumenbach, Johann, 96–97
Bolingbroke, Lord (Henry St. John), 168
Bonnet, Charles, 87–88

Boswell, James, 40, 125, 127, 219 n. 66; on
  Scottish accents, 145–46
Bradley, Richard, 86–87, 94
breastfeeding, 21
breeding, 1–3, 14–15, 27, 48, 55, 65–66,
  101, 124, 229 n. 49; climate's influence upon, 93–97, 155–156, 171–172;
  elocutionists make widely accessible,
  125–126; gentlemen's, 45, 53; global
  experiments in, 99; government
  intervention in, 50–51, 52, 99 (*see also*
  eugenics); history of heredity, considered in relation to animal, 94; and
  human inequality, 200; Hume uses
  language of, 98; in *Humphry Clinker*,
  101, 109; Johnson's definition of, 1,
  207 n. 1; in *A Modest Proposal*, 81–83;
  and population control, 76–83, 97–99;
  and pregnancy, 16–17; recapitulates
  theological arguments about original
  sin, 41, 48–49; selective, applied to
  people as well as animals, 79–80,
  86–90, 92, 130, 161, 166, 176, 184–188
  (*see also* Bickerstaff, Isaac); selective,
  of horses, 79–80, 83–86; selective, illuminates nature's production of new
  species, 89; selective, as practiced by
  Houyhnhnms, 77–81; shibboleths of,
  196; as synonym for education, 1, 45;
  as synonym for training or rearing,
  130
Buchanan, James, 127–128
Buffon, Comte de (Georges-Louis
  Leclerc), 76, 91, 92; equates domestication with degeneration, 116; position on
  animals of New World refuted by Jefferson, 155–157; theorizes reproduction
  by way of *moules intérieures*, 220 n. 73
bulls, in language and husbandry, 146–147
Burgess, Anthony, identifies "Neo-Pelagianism" as great menace of the present
  time (1952), 49–50
Burke, Edmund, 17, 145; *A Vindication of
  Natural Society*, 168–169
Burney, Frances, 64; *Evelina*, 34–35, 101

Burns, Robert, 141
Bushnell, Rebecca, 28

Cabanis, Pierre-Jean-Georges, 187–188
Caliban, 27, 201
canonicity, 198
Carol, Anne, 92
caste, Monboddo attracted by notion of,
    135
cats, 66, 71, 87–88, 231 n. 72; cat turned
    woman in Aesop's fable, 54
causality: dangers of causation as explana-
    tory mode in human psychology, 204–
    205; difficulty of disentangling cause
    and effect in cultural history, 33–35
Cavalli-Sforza, Luigi, 191–192
Chesterfield, Lord (Philip Stanhope), 63,
    128
Chomsky, Noam, 39, 192–193
classification, 70
climate, 93–95, 155–157, 165, 170–171; "climate
    theory," 3, 94–96; and determinism,
    171–173; humans and plants affected
    by, 76 (*see also* animals); paradox of,
    expressed in Steele's anecdote, 147; rein-
    scribed as culture during the eighteenth
    century, 157
Cochran, Johnnie, 195
Coetzee, J.M., 64
Coles, Edward, 163
Condillac, Étienne Bonnot de, 128–129
Condorcet, Antoine-Nicolas de, *Sketch for
    a Historical Picture of the Progress of the
    Human Mind*, 4, 166–167, 183–184
consent, 142, 152, 158
constitution, 46. *See also* temper
copulation, 71, 75–76. *See also* sex
Cornwell, Patricia, 195
corruption, 159
Cottom, Daniel, 130–131
counterfactual, science-fictional mode of:
    in historical investigations, 8, 86; and
    Rousseau's *Discourse on Inequality*, 114
Crawford, Rachel, 62–63
Crawford, Robert, 100, 127

criticism, demands of, on readers, 197. *See
    also* specialization
cross-breeding, 66, 86–88
cultivation, 65, 67, 110, 113–114, 153–156; its
    effects on plants and people, 28, 63, 90;
    and suppression of reproduction, 53. *See
    also* animals, domestication, education,
    improvement
culture, 1, 2, 4, 58, 100–111, 117, 120, 147, 157,
    161–165, 197; affects man and animals,
    165–166 (*see also* climate); affects nature,
    103; becomes nature, 132; equated with
    grace, 115; exclusive to humans, 235 n. 9;
    limits of, 54, 62, 135, 153, 164; *Robinson
    Crusoe* as novel of, 64; as symptom of
    biology, 41. *See also* habit, custom
custom, 7, 43, 132, 159, 168, 173–174; and
    convention in language, 139, 142; incom-
    patible with liberty, 144; power of, to
    modify human bodies, 73. *See also* habit,
    Hippocratic writings

Danticat, Edwidge, *The Farming of Bones*,
    189–190
Darwin, Charles, 24, 36, 69; believes
    acquired characters can be inher-
    ited, 37
Defoe, Daniel: *Mere Nature Delineated*,
    67–69, 226 n. 32; *Robinson Crusoe*, 59,
    64–67, 114
deformity, 131–134, 150, 162, 187
degeneration, 59–61, 77, 91–95, 112, 114,
    116, 140, 155–156, 173; of animals and
    people, 155–157; of governments, 154; of
    language, 126, 138–139
de Grazia, Margreta, 19
Della Porta, Giambattista, 87, 132
democracy, 143–144, 158–159, 199–200
depravity, 50–51, 169
Derrida, Jacques, 115, 130, 134
determinism, 204–205; associated by
    eighteenth-century writers with
    custom, climate and habit, 6, 58, 118;
    of climate theory, antithetical to human
    freedom, 171–172

Deucalion, 55, 60
dialect, 141
Diderot, Denis, 99
difference, 101, 131, 179–181, 185–186; based
on color, among Houyhnhnms, 77–79;
cultural rather than natural, 116, 172–173,
179; elocution movement both erases
and reinscribes, 134; human, 193–194;
individual, 129, 174–182 (*see also* genius);
linguistic, 124–126, 144–146, 189–190;
and Methodist arguments against social
distinction, in *Humphry Clinker*, 108;
"natural," 42, 53–57, 67–68, 121, 136–137;
national, potentially eradicated by
elocution, 128–129; need to maintain,
164; produced by climate, 94–95; racial,
96, 156, 161–165; regional, 139; relationship between linguistic and political,
141–142; sexual, 122–123; toleration of,
146–148; visible, 135–136, 191; in writings
of Scottish Enlightenment, 246 n. 30.
*See also* inequality
Dimock, Wai-Chee, 14
disciplines: interconnected, in the humanities, 8; problem of, 197
disinheritance, of daughters, 25, 33
distinction, romance wedded to notion of,
53. *See also* difference
Dobson, Michael, 31
dogs, 94, 190–191
domestication, 65–66, 116–117, 120–121,
155–158
Dove, Rita, 189
Dryden, John, 59–62; adapts *Paradise Lost*
as *The State of Innocence, and Fall of
Man*, 60; popularity of translation of
Virgil's *Georgics*, 224 n. 5
Dubner, Stephen J., 203
dunghills, 78, 103, 108, 230 n. 59
Dunn, L. C., 37

Eagleton, Terry, 115
Ebonics, 193–194
Edgeworth, Maria, 146–148
Edgeworth, Richard Lovell. *See* Edge-
worth, Maria

education, 43–44, 154, 159, 166, 201, 205;
Godwin's commitment to, 173; its
importance for Helvétius, 170–171;
in Locke's *Some Thoughts Concerning
Education*, 45–48; as moral end, 181–182;
in Plato's *Republic*, 78–79; power of,
177–178, 180; as property, 141; as remedy
for natural inequality, 167; as remedy for
nature's imperfections, 68; in Rousseau's
*Émile*, 120–124; as supplement to nature,
115
Edwards, Jonathan, 51
eighteenth century, the: characterized by
its orientation towards culture and
cultivation, 58; field of eighteenth-century studies, 169, 197–198; sometimes
idealized by specialists in, 197
elocution, 124–134, 137–148, 196; committed
to rescuing nature by cultural means,
124; identified by Webster as tyranni-
cal, 142
Elphinston, James, 140–141
empire, 99, 125
enhancement, genetic, 201–203
Enlightenment, 11; ideas of, 108, 196–198,
199–205; as origin of present-day culture, 5–6; and self-critique, 146
environment, 3; effects of, on animals,
84–85, 155–157; limited in its effects on
man, 96, 174–175 (*see also* culture); man
as product of, 69; power of, 93–97,
121–122; question of whether it affects
moral as well as physical aspects of
man, 95–97, 171–172, 176, 187
epic, stigmatized by its association with
warlike values, 59
essentialism, 7
ethnography, 100
eugenics, 3–5, 27, 50–51, 79–80, 86, 89–90,
92–93, 97, 183, 187–188, 197; and extermination, 5, 76–77; practiced by Frederick
of Prussia, 90, 92, 187. *See also* perfectibility, genetics
experience: difficult to distinguish from
nature, 128; grounding for all knowledge, according to Locke, 43

experiments, 150–151; in human nature, 88–89, 171–172, 187

expertise, origins of, 203

extermination, 52–53, 77, 158, 160–161, 183–184, 186; dehumanizing language enables campaigns of, 71; of Haitians at order of General Trujillo, 189–190

family, 108, 127, 201–202; unjust preference for members of, 182–183; as web of dependency, 118–119

Farber, Leslie, 204–205

fathers, influence of, on form of children, 20. *See also* resemblance

Fell, John, 138

feral children, 39, 67–69, 130, 135

Fliegelman, Jay, 130

foot-binding, in China, 131

Foote, Samuel, 139

Foucault, Michel, 196–197, 204

Franklin, Benjamin, 8, 143, 157

Frederick of Prussia, eugenic efforts of, 90, 92, 187

Freud, Sigmund, 120

Galen, 20, 21; "Of the Soul," 203–204

Galton, Francis, 5, 36, 208 n. 9

gardening, 60, 130, 166

Garrick, David: adapts *The Winter's Tale*, 12–13, 31–34; as authority on pronunciation, 142; departs from Aristotelian tradition on generation, 33

Geertz, Clifford, 8–9

generation, 17–18, 24–25, 34, 36, 55, 61, 76–77, 87–88, 149–150, 156. *See also* reproduction

Genesis, Book of, 4, 22, 90, 160

genetics, 2, 89, 191–194; discontinuities in histories of, 36; invoked in language of Ebonics controversy, 193–195. *See also* breeding, selective; perfectibility

genius: differences in individual, 136; natural, 46; sources of, 177–181. *See also* bent, difference, propensities

gentleman, 62; education of, 42, 47–48, 53, 122; notion of "gentleman born," 56–57

georgic, 59–64, 152–153, 225 n. 23; and Blumenbach's vision of human perfectibility, 97; and doubts about culture, 164; versus pastoral, 102–103; as positive value in *Humphry Clinker*, 101; Rousseau's *Discourse on Inequality* as reverse, 112–113; rise of prose, 63

germ, analogy of, 93, 162, 181. *See also* cultivation, improvement, metaphor

Godwin, William, 149, 150, 165–186, 201; abandons hard-line Helvetianism, 174; *An Account of the Seminary*, 171; antiwar position taken by, 167–168; "Of Awakening the Mind," 177; borrows language of Augustan satirists, 70; considers merits of essay versus philosophical enquiry, 176–177; *Enquiry Concerning Political Justice*, 165–176; on importance of determining suitable calling for young children, 179–180; "Of the Sources of Genius," 177; *Thoughts Occasioned by the Perusal of Dr. Parr's Spital Sermon*, 186; *Thoughts on Man*, 178–182

Goffman, Erving, 46

government, 168–169, 171–173; American, as characterized by Jefferson, 158–159; and manners, 154

grace, 49, 108, 115

grafting, 16, 25–30, 53, 60, 109–110, 188; as metaphor for transmission of sin, 28. *See also* hybridity, inheritance

Gregory, John, 92–93, 130

Guillory, John, 14

habit, 45–46; as second nature, 58, 132, 135; power of, 117, 129; responsible for mother's affections for child, according to Rousseau, 118. *See also* custom

Haldane, J. B. S., 183

Harris, James, 129

Harte, Walter, 63, 105

Hartley, David, 40, 91, 95, 170, 171, 175

Heinzelman, Kurt, 59

Helvétius, Claude-Adrien, 40, 95, 167, 170–171, 174, 175, 179–180, 199 heredity, 2, 5, 88–89, 135–136, 164, 177–178, 196–197; concept of, 93; special status of dogs and horses in eighteenth-century theories of heritability, 94; theories of biparental, 34, 89

Herries, John, 129–130

Herrnstein, Richard, 194

Hilts, Victor, 50–51. *See also* perfectibility, genetic

Hippocratic writings, 7, 95, 131–133. *See also* "Airs, Waters, Places"

historicism, limits of, 12

history, and metaphor of hearing the dead speak, 8

Holbach, Baron d' (Paul-Henri Dietrich), 167

horses, 52, 66, 78–79, 83–86. *See also* Houyhnhnms

hospitality, 198

Houellebecq, Michel, 182

Houyhnhnms, 72–80. *See also* Swift, Jonathan, *Gulliver's Travels*

humanities: failure of, to respond to scientific arguments about human nature, 40–41; rediscovery of work by Mendel affects, 30

humanity, possible eradication of, 55

human nature, 1–2, 7, 155, 168, 169; in Aesop's fables, 54; birds as illuminating, 43; and blank slate, 39–48; as ecumenical value, 147–148; experiments in, 69, 192; feral children reveal underpinnings of, 67–69; horses illustrate theories of, 83–86; languages for discussing, 198; social policy dependent on theories of, 40

humans: characterized by infinite potential for improvement, 166 (*see also* Rousseau); seen as vermin by King of Brobdingnag, 71

Hume, David, 95–96, 125, 172–173; adopts essay as preferred mode of inquiry, 177; "Of National Characters," 96, 161; "Of the Populousness of Ancient Nations," 97–98; style inflected with Augustan ironies, 98

husbandry, 59, 62–64, 105–106, 152–154

Huxley, Aldous, 182

Huxley, Thomas, 36

hybridity, 87–88

hybridization, plant, 30

hybrids, 88, 91

identity: linguistic, discontinuous with racial, 194–195; national, related to language, 143; natural and cultural aspects of human, 107–108; personal, 72–73; species, and reproduction as test of kind, 75–76, 150

imagination, power of maternal, 21–23; "proofs" of inheritance of acquired characters likened by Weismann to proof of, 37–38

imitation, 75, 129, 133, 159; role of, in pronunciation, 133

immortality, 150, 182

imprint, 122; as metaphor for resemblance, 19, 46, 212 n. 12. *See also* metaphor

improvement, 51, 58, 63, 83, 93, 100–106, 162–163, 187–188; ambivalence toward, 66; of breed, 80–81; cause of, set back by French Revolution, 199–200; central for elocutionists, 127–128; characteristic of human animal, 169–170; language of agricultural, 82; interpenetration of language concerning people, plants, and animals, 130, 237 n. 29; limits of, according to Malthus, 184–185; Swift's skepticism about, 230 n. 58; synonymous with education, 68. *See also* cultivation, perfectibility

Inchbald, Elizabeth, *A Simple Story*, 35–36

Indians, American, 162

inequality, 112–120, 134–137; abolition of, called for by Condorcet, 167; natural, 78, 199–200; natural or artificial, as reason for difference between individuals, 135–137, 179; traced back, by Rousseau, to invention of property, 113. *See also* difference

287

*Index*

inferiority, of blacks, asserted by David
Hume, 96, 161; asserted by Thomas Jefferson, 161–164
inheritance, 12–13, 16; biological, 86, 187,
190–191; breakdown of, 106–111; and
deformity, 90, 134; of moral versus
physical qualities, 135–136, 156, 177–178,
200; of properties, 83–86; theories of,
revealed in garden manuals, 27–28;
and transmission of qualities from
parents to children, 4. *See also* acquired
characters
innate ideas, Locke's refutation of, 42–43
innateness, 192–193; mapping of secular
values onto theological arguments
about, 28–29
instinct, 67, 168, 190–192

Jacob, François, 89
jargon, 198
Jefferson, Thomas, 149, 150; *Notes on the
State of Virginia*, 152–165; on natural
inequality, 199–200
Jensen, Arthur, 39, 194
Johnson, Samuel, 1, 29, 140; on influence of
education, 40; linguistic and literary au-
thority of, 142, 147; on Monboddo, 134;
*Plan of a Dictionary*, 126; "Preface to the
Dictionary," 126; disparages Sheridan's
efforts as elocutionist, 146; indignant at
Sheridan's receiving pension, 145

Kames, Lord (Henry Home), 64, 90, 155,
164; subscribes to Sheridan's *Lectures on
Elocution*, 127
Keller, Evelyn Fox, 6
Kenrick, William, 139
Kevles, Daniel, 5
keywords, 11
Knight, Thomas Andrew, 190–191
Koestenbaum, Wayne, 210 n. 28

Labov, William, 194
Lamarck, Jean-Baptiste, 36–37
la Mettrie, Julien Offray de, 92

language: Black English (AAEV) and Afrocentric linguistics, 193–194; as biological or cultural phenomenon, 190–196;
figurative, 146; of *Gulliver's Travels* in
later discussions of original sin, 167–169;
of human nature, 198; of human "varieties," linked to racism, 157; nonstandard
forms of, 139, 141; power of myths about
biology and, 193–196; and race, 189–190;
Rousseau's vision of human life before
invention of, 118–119; satire inflects later
eighteenth-century styles of, 70, 98,
162, 185; written versus spoken, 137–142,
195–196. *See also* metaphor
Lawrence, William, 91, 229 n. 49
Lawson, John, 40
Leeuwenhoek, Antonie van, 24
Lehrer, Jonah, 41
Leonard, Tom, 141
Levi, Primo, 9
Levitt, Steven D., 203
liberty, 7, 117, 171–173. *See also* determinism
lineage, 16, 94
Linnaeus, Carl, 157, 163
Lisle, Edward, 63–64, 105
literary criticism, and problem of scale, 14.
*See also* methodology
Locke, John, 40–51, 53, 57, 63, 121, 130, 167,
170, 171, 200, 201; and blank slate, 40;
*Essay Concerning Human Understand-
ing*, 42–45, 197; and notions of perfect-
ibility, 49–50; on personal identity,
72–73; *Some Thoughts Concerning Educa-
tion*, 45–48, 57
Low, Anthony, 62
Luccock, John, 93
luxury, 59, 100–101, 109, 153; evils of, countered by georgic values, 104–106
Lycurgus, 80
Lysenkoism, 6

machine, animal as, 117
Malebranche, Nicolas, 23
malleability, 164
Malthus, Thomas, 183–186

manners, 100–101; effects of slavery on, 159

Marshall, John, 50

Marx, Leo, 113, 153; *The Machine in the Garden*, 14

mastery, impulse to, 202

Maupertuis, Pierre-Louis Moreau de, 88–92, 130

May, William F., and "openness to the unbidden," 202

medicine, 92–93, 164

memory, 9–10, 119

Mendel, Gregor, 3, 30

metaphor: of the blank slate, 39–48, 68, 129, 130; of the germ, 93, 162, 181; of hearing the dead speak, 8; of the imprint or stamp, 19, 46, 122, 212 n. 12; intriguing use of, by Boswell, 145; self-defeating use of, by Thomas Sheridan, 131–134. *See also* blank slate

methodology: advantages and disadvantages of drawing evidence from works written across an author's entire career, 165; of cultural anthropology, 9; historicist, 12; and keyword approach, 11; and role of little-known works in illuminating significant conversations, 124; associated with "topic," 11

Midgley, Mary, 7, 198

mind, metaphors of, 42–43, 47. *See also* blank slate

mixing, fear of, 152, 158, 161–164, 189–190. *See also* purity

mobility, dangers of social, 139

mock-heroic, tropes of, 162. *See also* metaphor, satire

modernity, blamed by Rousseau for distorting sex roles, 123–124

Monboddo, Lord (James Burnett), 132, 134–137; peculiar beliefs of, 134

monogenesis, or unity of the human species, 90–91, 96

monsters, 22, 87, 150. *See also* deformity

Montaigne, Michel de, 119

Montesquieu, Baron de La Brède et de (Charles-Louis de Secondat), 3, 95

More, Thomas, 79–80, 167. *See also* utopianism

Moretti, Franco, 14

moulds, 35. *See also* Buffon, resemblance

Mugglestone, Lynda, 138

Murray, Charles, 194

Nares, Robert, 138–139

Nash, Richard, 83

native, definition of term, 71, 73, 145, 147

natural history, 70, 92; descriptive language in, 72; of destruction, 10; and racial difference, 163–164

nature, 44, 46, 60–61, 122; and art, 26–27; and culture, in pastoral, 17; confused with culture, 159; custom subdues, 54; and distinction between natural and acquired properties, 114–115; predominates over education, 93; elocutionists vexed by contradictory aspects of, 124–134; habit as second, 58, 118; Houhynhnms as perfection of, 73; language in relation to, 128–129; reconceived by Locke as artificial, 44; and nurture, 6–7; Robinson Crusoe subordinates, 64–65; and sex roles and sexual desire, 123–124; state of, 51–53, 113, 114–115, 119–120; as telos, 164; tension between nature- and nurture-based explanations frames ongoing crisis in liberalism, 130; as term, 2. *See also* human nature

nature-nurture debates, 39–41, 192, 205; and conversation about language and its origins, 128–131; not resolvable in strictly scientific terms, 50; echoing theological debates on original sin, 49–50; worked out in arguments about feral children, 69; worked out in the genre of the novel, 36. *See also* blank slate

neutral, concept of the, defined by Roland Barthes, 10–11

nonstandard Englishes, 146, 192–196

Nourse, Timothy: *Campania Fœlix*, 51–54; *Discourse Upon the Nature and Faculties of Man*, 80

novel, genre of the, suited to working out nature-nurture arguments, 36
nuance, importance of, 11

oratory, 127, 162. *See also* elocution
original sin, 28–29, 41, 48–53, 69, 94, 169; and inheritance of acquired characters, 95; inherited through conception, 48; reimagined by Godwin as legacy of environmental deformation, 173–174; rejected by Rousseau, 120
origins, myths of, 61, 76–77. *See also* Deucalion
orthoëpy. *See* pronunciation
orthography. *See* spelling
Osmer, William, 83–86
Outram, Dorinda, "The Enlightenment Our Contemporary," 5–6
ovism. *See* preformation

Pakenham-Walsh, H., 68
Paré, Ambroise, 22
parsley, 189–190
partial, advocacy of the, 12
Passmore, John, 49–51, 200–201
Pelagian heresy, 48–50, 97
Perec, Georges, 9
perfectibility, 6, 49, 50–51, 76–80, 97, 112, 114, 165–167, 182–186, 199–205; as capacity for improvement, 170; and Helvetian theory of mind, 179–180; genetic, 50–51, 88, 90, 91, 97–99; and hostility to sexual generation, 151, 183; as responsiveness to culture, 117–118; tenacity of commitment to, 201. *See also* improvement, original sin
Perry, Ruth, 33
personal identity. *See* identity
Peter of Hanover, 67, 135. *See also* feral children
physiognomy, rejected by Godwin as system of fatalism, 181
Pinker, Steven, 121; *The Blank Slate*, 39–40; *The Language Instinct*, 191–193
Pinto-Correia, Clara, 24–25

Plato, *Republic*, 78–79, 122, 167
Plutarch, 80
politeness, 125, 128, 141, 145–146
polydactyly, 89
polygenesis, or theories of multiple human origins, 5, 90–91, 164
Pomata, Gianna, 164
Pope, Alexander, 162
population, 97–99, 152, 158–159, 160–163, 165, 182–188; control of, 77, 81–83, 79; risks of expanding by immigration, according to Jefferson, 158
preformation, 87; as anti-democratic doctrine, 25; logical shortcomings of, 25, 89; ovist versus animalculist inflections of, 24, 34
pregnancy, 16–17
presentism, 5–6, 197
Price, Richard, 167
Prichard, James Cowles, 187
Priestley, Joseph: *Course of Lectures on the Theory of Language*, 141–142; *An Essay on the First Principles of Government*, 165–166
primitivism, 112, 118
print, 143; role of, in work of elocutionists, 126; in *The Winter's Tale*, 19. *See also* imprints
progress, 112; "progress theory," 63; Rousseau's rejection of, 120
progressivism, 112
pronunciation, 125–126; effects of spelling on, 138; of letter *r*, 133; peculiar to different localities, 142–143
propagation, 52–53, 61, 110, 119, 152, 182, 186; gone awry in Smollett's *Humphry Clinker*, 100; of horses, 84–85; versus imitation in definition of original sin, 48. *See also* reproduction, sex
propensities, 46, 174. *See also* bent, bias
providence, 65
pugs, 89. *See also* dogs
purity, 140–141; idea of, related to xenophobia, 144; in elocutionist fantasies, 127, 137–145

race: definition of term, 227 n. 40; Jefferson on, 161–164; and language, 189–190
racism: charged by Johnnie Cochran in O.J. Simpson trial, 195; scientific, 90–91, 96
Ray, John, 76
realism, filthy, 103
rearing, 155, 208 n. 9. *See also* breeding
reason, 72–75, 77, 82–83, 108, 196–197, 201; as basis for American government, 158; preference for members of nuclear family incompatible with, 79, 183; sex ideally subject to control of, 182–183; Yahoo corruption of, 168
Réaumur, René-Antoine Ferchault de, 89
reproduction, 78, 88, 150, 215 n. 30, 243 n. 1; disrupted in *Humphry Clinker*, 106–107; hostility towards sexual, associated with Augustine, 49; implicated in human sinfulness, 81. *See also* generation, propagation
republicanism, 153
resemblance, 1, 16, 18–19, 20–25, 29–38, 89, 101, 150–151, 160, 177–178, 218 n. 63; fantasies of, as form of attachment to the past, 38; of Gulliver to Yahoo, 75; maternal outweighs paternal input into, 34–36, 85; paternal, 22, 61, 216 n. 40. *See also* imprint
restoration: elocutionists' fantasies of, 128; in *The Winter's Tale*, 19–20
retirement, ethos of rural, 61–62, 101–102
revolution, 143, 160; in France, 137, 169; seen by John Adams to arrest progress of human improvement, 199–200
Richardson, Samuel, *Clarissa*, 239 n. 58
Rickford, John Russell, 194–196
Rickford, Russell John, 194–196
Rittenhouse, David, 157
Roger, Jacques, 8
romance, 15–16, 53–57, 101, 109, 175; affiliated with nature over culture, 27
Rondet, Henry, 49
Rousseau, Jean-Jacques, 64, 100, 159, 164, 167, 171, 199; *Discourse on the Sciences and Arts (First Discourse)*, 112–113; *Discourse on Inequality (Second Discourse)*, 49, 112–120, 165, 197–198; *Émile*, 120–124; and figure of supplement, 130; on inequality, 135; influences Monboddo, 136; literary afterlife of, 124; parodied by Burke, 168–169
Russell, Nicholas, 94

Sandel, Michael, 201–202
satire, 167–169; and influence of Augustan stylists on later eighteenth-century writers, 70, 98, 162, 185
scale, literary criticism's neutrality with respect to, 14
Scotticisms, 125, 145–146
Sebald, W.G., 9–10; *The Rings of Saturn*, 10
secrets, books of, 87
Sedgwick, Eve Kosofky, 6–7, 59
selective breeding. *See* breeding, selective
self: claims of the, 146; self-improvement, 203–205
servants, 51, 53–54, 62, 77, 109
sex, 49, 118–119, 182–183; difference between the two sexes as natural or cultural, 123; eschewed by Victor Frankenstein, 149–151
Shakespeare, William, 147, 201; invoked as authority, 193; *King Lear*, 25, 113; popularity of, in eighteenth century, 15; *The Tempest*, 27, 201; *The Winter's Tale*, 12–13, 14–20, 21–22, 25–28, 29–36, 53–57
Sharp, Jane, 29
Shattuck, Roger, 39, 69
sheep, 93–94; story of Jacob and Laban's, 22
Shelley, Mary, *Frankenstein*, 149–152
Sheridan, Thomas, 126–134, 137–139, 142, 145, 146; influenced by Locke, 130
Sherman, Martin, *Bent*, 47
shibboleth, 148, 189–196; of "ask" as "axe," 195–196
Simpson, O.J., trial of, 195
Singh, Rev. J.A.L., 68
slavery, 97–98, 150, 153, 159–164; in ancient Rome, 162–163

Smith, Adam, 159; on custom in language, 144

Smith, Ernie, 194

Smith, Roger, 2

Smith, Stanhope, 187

Smitherman, Geneva, 193

Smollett, Tobias, 164; as author of prose georgic, 59; *Expedition of Humphry Clinker*, 100–111

Snow, C.P., and question of "two cultures," 41

sociobiology, 39, 192

Socrates, 78

soul, 4, 68, 203–204

Spallanzani, Lazzaro, 87–88; experiments with frogs in taffeta breeches, 24–25

Spary, Emma, 92

specialization, academic, its advantages and drawbacks, 198

species, 90, 145, 149–152, 182–183; defined by copulation and reproduction after same kind, 76, 229 n. 49; Gulliver's use of term, 70–71; identity of human, 62; language of, 163; and man considered as *Homo sapiens*, 69–70; problem of creation of new, 89–90

speech, antecedent to writing, 137

spelling, 137; movement to reform, 139–145

Spellman, W.M., 50

Spence, Thomas, 140

Spenser, Edmund, 218 n. 63

Steele, Richard, 147

Steevens, George, annotates *The Winter's Tale*, 29

Sterne, Laurence, *Tristram Shandy*, vii

Stocking, George W. Jr., 89

sumptuary laws, 53–54

Swammerdam, Jan, 24, 87

Swift, Jonathan, 126, 128, 162, 183, 186; *Battle of the Books*, 73; on blood, 77; as geographer of modernity, 98; *Gulliver's Travels*, 69–81, 105, 162, 197; invoked by later writers, 167–169; *A Modest Proposal*, 53, 81–83, 98; on population, 82; on propagation, 82–83; proposes regulation

of language by academy on French model, 138

talent, 203. *See also* genius

Tayler, Edward, 27

temper, 46–47

temperament, 164

Temple, Sir William, 73

Terrall, Mary, 89

Theognis, 79, 200

topic, investigative procedure of the, 11

transmission. *See* inheritance, resemblance

Trent, Council of, defines original sin, 48

Tull, Jethro, 105; *The New Horse-Houghing Husbandry*, 59, 62

Turgot, Anne-Robert-Jacques (Baron de l'Aulne), 49, 112, 165

Twiggs, Robert, 194

Union, of 1707, 125; of 1801, 146–148

utopianism, 50–51, 76–80, 98–99, 120, 165–167, 182–186, 199–201

Vandermonde, Charles-Augustin, 92, 130

varieties, 157, 163

Venturi, Robert, 8

Victor of Aveyron, 69. *See also* feral children

Virgil, 113; *Georgics*, translated by John Dryden, 59–63

virtue, fostered by georgic values, 153–154

Voltaire, 88

Wahrman, Dror, 157

Walker, Alexander, 190

Walker, John, 125–126

Wall, Richard, 83, 85–86

Wallace, Robert, 98–99

Washington, George, 157

Watt, Ian, 102

Webster, Noah, 142–145

Wedderburne, Alexander, 145

Weismann, August, 7, 37–38

Wesley, John, 51, 169

Wheatley, Phyllis, 162

Wheeler, Roxann, 244 n. 11, 250 n. 28

Wiley, Tatha, 48
Williams, Raymond, 2, 11, 100, 102; *The Country and the City*, 14
Williams, Robert L., 194
Wilson, Harold, 30
*Winter's Tale, The. See* Shakespeare
Wolf Girls of Midnapore, 68–69. *See also* feral children
Wolfram, Walt, 194
writing: as way of speaking across time

and space, 8, 198; valorized over speech, 141–142

xenophobia, 158–159. *See also* purity

Yahoos, 70–77. *See also* Swift, Jonathan
Young, Arthur, 64, 66

Zingg, Robert, 69
Žižek, Slavoj, 202